shining trumpets

shining trumpets

A HISTORY OF

BY

RUDI BLESH

O silver trumpets, be you lifted up,
And cry to the great race that is to come!
Long-throated swans upon the waves of time
Sing loudly, for beyond the wall of the world
That race may hear our music and awake.

WILLIAM BUTLER YEATS

SECOND EDITION, REVISED AND ENLARGED

A DA CAPO PAPERBACK

Library of Congress Cataloging in Publication Data

Blesh, Rudi, 1899-
  Shining trumpets.

  (A Da Capo paperback)
  Reprint of the ed. published by Knopf, New York.
  Discography: p.
  Includes indexes.
  1. Jazz, music. I. Title.
  [ML3561.J3B47 1976]   785.4'2'0973   75-31664
  ISBN 0-306-80029-2

ISBN 0-306-80029-2
First Paperback Printing 1976

This Da Capo Press paperback of *Shining Trumpets* is an unabridged
republication of the second revised and enlarged edition published in
New York in 1958. It is reprinted with the permission of the author.

Published by Da Capo Press, Inc.
A Subsidiary of Plenum Publishing Corporation
227 West 17th Street
New York, N. Y. 10011

shining trumpets

TO MY DAUGHTER HILARY

AND HER TAILGATE TROMBONE

AND TO ETHEL AND LITTLE NELL

INTRODUCTION

Jazz music is a purely American phenomenon. In its pure and authentic form it has been in existence perhaps seventy-five years and has been a part of the general American scene for the last twenty-five. Throughout this time it has been an object of wide and often bitter controversy. Its true nature and its relation to other kinds of music have been but little understood. The possibilities of revolutionary development within jazz, and in Western music through the use of its technical principles, have hardly been perceived at all.

The importance and value of jazz begin to become apparent only today. In the meantime its origins have become obscure, its essential nature and its significance lost in a fog of misunderstanding. A half-dozen kinds of music bearing no structural relation to jazz are accepted by the vast public, not only as jazz, but each as its only form.

The need of a serious book about authentic jazz is therefore imperative at this time. Such a book will explore the beginnings and trace the progress of this music, analyze and define its nature, evaluate and compare it with the kinds of music we know. This is the sort of book I have tried to write.

Fortunately, jazz in many of its phases has an invaluable sort of documentation — that of the phonograph record. More than in any other musical field the recording is vital in jazz, a spontaneous, improvised — though systematic — music, *composed in the playing*. I have found it a pleasant necessity to study hundreds of records, many old favorites of mine and some unfamiliar ones, and to cite and describe a number of these in this book. It is unfortunate that the majority of these are not, at this writing, available to the public. However, their analysis was essential. It is gratifying to know that steps are being taken to assemble large libraries of recorded jazz that will be available, and it is to be hoped that the large commercial recording companies will continue and accelerate the reissues of their priceless old discs for general sale.

This book represents a large attempt. Jazz music, itself a big and surprisingly little known subject, includes lesser ones. It is, in turn, part of several of wider implication: all Afro-American music for one thing, an influence on the "serious" composer for another.

A thorough treatment of jazz as music not only deals with the American Negro but goes all the way back to Africa. It carries both the writer and reader into questions of deep sociological import relating to the position of the Negro in this democracy and questions of our white attitude toward the art of this black minority. And thus we are led, through general considerations of our society, into equally general, equally vital ones concerning all music and all art and the relation of the everyday human being to these high manifestations of the creative urge in man.

There is no clearly defined road through this complex field. If misunderstandings cloud the history of jazz, they are symptomatic of subtler and more deep-rooted ones that befog the history of all human culture. For man does not always understand what he or his brother is compulsively impelled to do and to create.

This book, accordingly, should reflect the nature of its material: it should be complex and yet simple; it should be serious and gay at the same time; it should be both factual and poetical. It will be unavoidably technical in certain passages, but I shall try to lighten these by sections reflecting those basic human feelings, experiences, and aspirations from which all real art springs.

This is the large attempt. The scope and the importance of the subject matter have made it well worth the try. If it has succeeded I ask only an amanuensis' credit, for my material was as rich as the rich earth itself.

I am most grateful for the kinds and amount of help I have received from jazz critics, friends, scientists, and institutions of learning, and from the men who play jazz.

It was at the San Francisco Museum of Art in 1943 that I gave the jazz lectures which have led finally to the writing of this book. To recall the Museum is to think gratefully of its director, Dr. Grace L. McCann Morley, and its then curator, Mr. Douglas MacAgy, who so enthusiastically sponsored my lectures.

The anthropologists Professor Melville J. Herskovits and Dr. Richard A. Waterman have rendered great and generous assistance. The former put at my disposal the fine recorded library of African and Afro-American music at Northwestern University.

Mr. B. A. Botkin similarly assisted me through the rich mazes of recorded American folk music in the Library of Congress. And I am indebted to Dr. L. D. Reddick, curator of the Schomburg Collection of Negro Literature and History in New York, for his valuable help.

I thank Mr. Roy Carew for needed information concerning ragtime, Miss Marili Morden for certain important historical data, and both for lists of ragtime compositions and jazz tunes.

I am indebted, for varied information and for access to certain rare records, to the jazz critics and writers, Frederic Ramsey, Jr., Nesuhi Ertegun, Kenneth Lloyd Bright, and others.

Mrs. Frances Oliver and Mrs. Amedé Colas have furnished me with vital information about their brother, the late Ferdinand (Jelly Roll) Morton. For this, as well as for the loan of rare photographs of Morton, I am very grateful.

My thanks are due to Judge Nathan R. Sobel for technical help and to Helen Hall for illustrative material.

The musical scores in this book were done by the American composer Lou Harrison, who worked enthusiastically and indefatigably with difficult and virtually unscoreable material to produce the most nearly accurate scorings ever, to my knowledge, made of Afro-American music. They reflect his serious approach.

I am in the debt of the noted composer and critic, Mr. Virgil Thomson, and likewise of the writer, Mr. Herbert Weinstock, for generous and discerning critical suggestions.

Help, freely given and of great importance, came from the players of jazz. For all of this, the priceless historical data, technical information, rich anecdotes, and rare photographs, I am heavily indebted to these men. Among the many, I must mention and thank the great Negro musicians: Willie (Bunk) Johnson, Louis (Satchmo) Armstrong, Johnny St. Cyr, Alphonse Picou, Wallace Collins, Edward (Kid) Ory, Thomas (Papa Mutt) Carey, George Lewis, Louis de Lisle (Big-Eye) Nelson, Peter Bocage, Joseph Petit, Warren (Baby) Dodds, Jim Robinson, Minor (Ram) Hall, Sidney Bechet, George (Pop) Foster, Jimmy Yancey, Albert (Buster) Wilson, Ed (Montudi) Garland, Omer Simeon, Darnell Howard, Tom (Georgia Tom) Dorsey, Bertha Gonsoulin, Montana Taylor, Arthur (Bud) Scott, Charles (Cow Cow) Davenport, Sid Le Protte, and the blues singer, Bertha (Chippie) Hill. Valued help was likewise forthcoming from the noted white players: George Brunies, Melvin (Turk) Murphy, Paul Mares, and Paul Lingle.

Finally, constant assistance has come to me from Harriet Janis. Without her lucid advice and penetrating critical suggestions, freely and generously given, this book would never have seen the light.

It remains to be said that, regardless of documentation, the basic ideas I express and the conclusions I reach herein are my own.

R. B.

CONTENTS

ILLUSTRATIONS

(FOLLOW PAGE 210)

xiii

shining trumpets

BOOK ONE

SONG TO THE EARTH GOD

The need is great,
And great our need to sing,
For days of trouble are upon us.

The bullock of Abomey
Says to him of Cana,
It is the day of trouble;
The carrier of grain,
Says to the bearer of salt,
Thy load is heavy, brother,
And this the day for carrying;

The bearer of the dead
Says to the carrier of ladders,
It is the day for carrying loads,
It is the day of trouble.

TRANSLATION FROM THE DAHOMEAN
BY FRANCES S. HERSKOVITS

1.

black music

Jazz began about three quarters of a century ago. In New Orleans, soon after Emancipation, there occurred an extraordinary concatenation of circumstances that could not have occurred elsewhere and, perhaps, can never occur again, even there. From them jazz emerged. It began not merely as one more form of Negro folk music in America but as a fusion of all the Negro musics already present here. These, the worksongs, spirituals, ragtime, and blues, all stemmed back more or less completely to African spirit and technique. Negro creative power, suddenly freed as the Negroes themselves were freed from slavery, took all of this music and added elements of American white folk musics. It added, as well, the music and the distinct instrumentation of the marching (brass) band and the melodies of French dances (memories, even, from the French Opera House), the quadrille, polka, waltz, the rhythms and tunes of Spanish America and the Caribbean, and many other musical elements.

The American Negro poured these rich and varied ingredients into his own musical melting pot and added his undying memories of life on the Dark Continent and the wild and tumultuous echoes of dancing, shouting, and chanting in New Orleans' Congo Square. Under the pot he built the hot fire of creative force and imagination and then, preparatory to a miracle, stirred them all together. For jazz is no musical hybrid; it is a miracle of creative synthesis.

Jazz is the music that the whites in New Orleans saw only as "nigger" music, scarcely as important, even, as those silly, shallow, and condescending white imitations of Negro song, the minstrel melody and "coon" song. It was something to be listened to with guarded pleasure in the honky tonk or in the Negro street parades that, even today, the white children are not freely allowed to follow; something perhaps even to be danced to if the inferior black men of the orchestra sat on a platform with their faces to the wall. The guarded pleasure and the inhibited response are only explainable in part as a fear of the power of the Negro musical genius to break down the social and economic barriers set up against the race. Deeper still, perhaps, the motivation was the age-old human fear of the strange and the new, for jazz and the Afro-American music it culminates are a new and revolutionary element in our culture.

The understanding of jazz, as opposed to the mere emotional reaction to it, requires effort. This is even more true than with our own serious, or classical, music, for the latter, unlike jazz, represents a continuous development in our own native culture. Yet never was understanding more richly rewarded. Jazz has widened our artistic horizons immeasurably; subtly but unmistakably it has influenced our own musical practice. But, more important still, it is an art in itself, profoundly different in concept and practice from our own. The pure development of its own values is imperative if we are to avoid a grave cultural loss. A music, improvised freely by blacks and whites together, it sounds a summons to free, communal, creative living. A music of vital and forward motion, jazz is a symbol of that improvisational process, guided by the instinct for freedom, which all social progress essentially is.

We were and are unprepared to accept the Negro as an equal member of our democracy; we are unprepared to accept his jazz at its true value. Of what avail is it that it be accepted with intelligence and discrimination outside America, if here, where it is made, it is distorted and devitalized by social pressures exerted upon its creators? Perhaps the growing appreciation of the epochal importance of jazz as an art form will not only ensure its continued and free development and constructive white participation therein, but will bring — through an understanding of his art — an increasing awareness of the Negro's stature and integrity as a man.

Jazz, the original musical creation of the American Negro, is a synthesis of African and European [1] material so predominantly African in character and method that it might be more accurate to define it as an African art form which, arising in this country, utilized and transformed much European material. It was, and where still played it remains, a unique music, different from European music. Its uniqueness depends upon its combination of certain qualities.

Throughout the music the Negro has made in our country, we can trace with special clarity the purity or dilution of the African character that enters so decisively into jazz.

In the early rural work-songs we find much African material and some foreign material treated in a very Negroid manner. The evolution of the spiritual involves selective borrowing of European melody with a slight adoption of harmony; African technique plus the selective process, itself, preserves the cultural continuity. The spiritual is the first type that is recognizably Afro-American.

The process of selective assimilation and technical treatment resulted, about 1870, in the creation of a new *musical form* in rural areas — the blues. This form signifies that a balance has been obtained between Western material and African technique. It is the stabilization of the Afro-American quality.

At about the same time, Negro urban folk music in New Orleans resulted in an instrumental music, jazz. This music represents the borrowing of the widest variety of non-African musical material that the Negro had attempted, together with the adoption of European instruments. African technique transformed the material while evolving an African instrumental

---

[1] In this book European will be used to apply equally to all American *white* art forms, inasmuch as we are a part of the European tradition in art and music.

method. In jazz, the balance between African and non-African is delicate but firm, the over-all effect still markedly African. Its richness of content, complexity of development, and unique musical character make jazz the first fine-art form created by the American Negro. Classic jazz, from 1890 on, is the high point of Negro musical achievement in this country to date. It is an achievement only the Negro could have made, and not even the Negro elsewhere.

The dilution and deformation of jazz took place from 1920 on because of the influences of commercialism, white playing, and sophistication of the Negroes themselves. This has advanced to the point where the music frequently ceases to be predominantly a Negro form, becoming a hybridized popular music rather than a fine-art form.

The development of swing music began in the early 1920's. Swing, which is not jazz, is a type of European music with transplanted Negroid characteristics. Even when produced by Negroes, it is Negroid only in surface manner.

Simultaneously, the educated Negro devoted himself more and more to accepted European forms — opera, concert music, et cetera — in which the creative element has largely disappeared and the Negroid character is diluted to the vanishing point. It lingers only in unchangeable timbres, rhythmic characteristics, and occasionally in a notable technical proficiency.

This dilution of African character occurs on one level of Negro society, while elsewhere Afro-American music continues in certain of its pure, earlier stages. Today we find the singing of the true Afro-American spiritual widespread among the churches of at least one sect; that of the fine archaic blues undiminished in unsophisticated secular sections; and the improvised performance of early classic — and even archaic — jazz still carried on strongly by a minority.

The whole development of Afro-American music from its African technical origins is summed up in the first part of the chart on pages 18–23. The first part lists the *African survivals in Negro jazz.* The second part of the chart is a corollary, point by point, of the *deformations of Negro jazz;* it can be used as a measure of the decadence within jazz or as a guide to those deceptive elements, not numerous or decisive enough, which, borrowed from jazz, make the present-day commercial swing falsely seem another form of that music.

This listing of African cultural survivals in jazz, entirely apart from the rich variety of European material incorporated, prefigures the complex nature of the music. Its complexity, strangeness, and novelty tend to explain why, on the whole, it has not been really understood, much less adequately evaluated. Criticism of jazz from the point of view of European music must be misleading and fruitless because our modules do not fit or our criteria apply. On the other hand, the approach from the African point of view is not adequate: it cannot take into sufficient account American environment plus European art influence and too often has no critical function in an aesthetic sense. Something like a combination of these approaches into a new critical process is needed.

About half a century after its inception, when jazz had traveled out of New Orleans and over the United States, it had a reception that, if more open-armed in its enthusiasm, was still as shallow and undiscerning as it had been in New Orleans. Jazz as played by Negroes in Chicago or New York, was still "nigger" music to white listeners.

An extraordinary apparition, exciting and disquieting, in the years of World War I, jazz was accepted by the white public as no more than a pleasurable aid to dancing or as a phenomenon of war hysteria. It was as though the dislocation of feeling and purpose that war causes in other fields were operating in *our* music, a music we share in the general European tradition!

Had jazz appeared in more peaceful times would it, perhaps, have been received differently? Would it have been perceived as the new and unique music it was and is, with its own style and content, rigorously opposite, with a final polarity, to European music today? Or to any phase or possibility implied therein? It scarcely seems likely. Classic jazz began when European music, in the late nineteenth century, was about to reach the ultimate stage of harmonic chromaticism within which free melody is all but stifled. Everything in jazz is opposed to such a harmonic-chromatic process; in it harmony is allowed no such power. If jazz is similar to any European music at all, it resembles most nearly the antiphony and horizontal polyphony of medieval European music and the ultramodern polyphonal and dissonantal school of today. Nearly three hundred years before the origin of jazz, we had lost sight of or forsaken the possibility of development from such a base, just as the principle of improvisation was abandoned later in favor of that advance charting by the blueprints we call musical compositions. Only in France, the first country to accord intellectual recognition to jazz, did free-melodic music survive through Rameau, persisting to the present day through Satie, Milhaud, and others in the face of the pseudo-French school of post-Wagnerian harmonic tendency exemplified by Franck, Fauré, and Chausson. It was scarcely to be expected that jazz, a pure improvised polyphony falling on unaccustomed ears, would be immediately understood.

Neoclassicism in modern European music means a revolt against the harmonic smothering of melody, a revolt that jazz had already won. This tendency toward a polyphony free of the requirements of consonant harmony first caught the public ear forcefully in 1913 with the initial performance in Paris of Igor Stravinsky's *Le Sacre du Printemps*. The compositions of this modern school, while admitting a high degree of dissonance, are not wholly free of preoccupation with harmony, and this is most true when the use of clashes is most deliberate.

We find a true polyphony of the neoclassic sort in African choral singing, with its dissonances arising logically through the polyphonal development of the melodic lines. This polyphony, of course, combines with a complex percussion in a melodic-rhythmic counterpoint unknown in European music. And we find this Negroid polyphony, as early as the 1870's in New Orleans street band jazz, in an instrumentation and in melodic derivations more directly comparable with European music.

By the 1890's jazz was in firm existence in New Orleans, where a long-standing tradition of light and classical European music could have been expected to furnish a guide to the meaning of jazz as an art form separate from the European tradition. Instead, its thrilling and deeply moving qualities, its direct appeal to the heart, its amazing virtuosity and astounding musical complexity, its demands on spontaneous creativeness — posing then and thereafter difficulties almost insurmountable for the white player — all these qualities, even those immediately perceivable, fell on deaf ears and oblivious minds as mere "nigger" music.

More is involved in this than the position of the Negro in Southern society or in our society as a whole. There is more to it than our unconscious racial complex, our jealous guarding and fostering of a hypothetical white superiority. The conditioning of the ear by European music, and — more important — our grounding in classical European theory act as a barrier to our appreciation and understanding of this music.

Nevertheless, Negro music, if not ragtime and jazz, had early champions among white people, learned or otherwise. Early in this century, for example, the American music critic, H. E. Krehbiel, began to investigate American Negro folk music. His critical work is of lasting value because he clearly perceived the African material and spirit in this music. But a blind spot operates in peculiar ways in Krehbiel's work. He is impressed with the necessity of proving this music American after having shown its African origin and character; he cannot forget that he is the "superior" white, these the "inferior" blacks. "Why savages who have never developed a musical or any other art should be supposed to have more refined esthetic sensibilities than the peoples who have cultivated music for centuries, passes

9

my powers of understanding," [2] he says at one point. Yet in another he speaks of the Dahomeans: "The players showed the most remarkable rhythmical sense and skill that ever came under my notice. Berlioz in his supremest effort . . . produced nothing to compare in artistic interest with the harmonious drumming of these savages . . . it is impossible to convey . . . the wealth of detail achieved . . . by exchange of the rhythms . . . syncopation of both simultaneously, and dynamic devices." In another he deplores ragtime, meaning also jazz: ". . . the dance which is threatening to force grace, decorum and decency out of the ballrooms of· America and England is a survival of African savagery, which was already banished from the plantations in the days of slavery. It was in the dance that the bestiality of the African blacks found its frankest expression."

And the other early critics? Most of them were artistically blind or morally purblind. A little later a few, Ernest Ansermet and Darius Milhaud among them, saw rather clearly the newness and greatness of the music. But jazz suffered nearly as much harm from the blindness of its friends as from the hostility of its enemies, regardless of the walk of life of either.

One cannot exaggerate the protest with which jazz was met when, in the 1920's, it had spread to Chicago and New York. Composers, critics, ministers of the church, laymen, pundits, and ignoramuses had their fling. The storm was historic. An entire era was called the Jazz Age. Not only the sins of its *flappers* and gin-toting *lounge lizards* came to be blamed on this ineffably nefarious music, but also nearly all of the woes of the postwar world up to and including the 1929 crash in Wall Street. [3]

Although many knew then that jazz had been played in, among other places, whorehouses and wine shops, and judged it

---

[2] This and succeeding quotations are from Krehbiel, H. E.: *Afro-American Folksongs.* New York: 1914.

[3] Reverberations of the storm penetrated even to New Orleans, where the *Times-Picayune* rose hastily to disavow any connection of jazz with its native city.

accordingly, none knew that it was a fine art transcending its surroundings. Nevertheless, many of the people knew that it was *their* music, a music created for them by men using lack of formal musical education as a freeing factor in hot and spontaneous creation. The men wanted, needed, to create it; their fellows wanted, needed to listen, to dance, to respond to, and to be freed by it.

In our society there is a prevailing factor slower but more relentless than the war cries of all the minorities. It exists in the whip of economic pressure that assails from outside and the dry rot of commercialization that eats from within. Taken together as components of one evil force, they can spell the ruin of any art. They extend the concept of the profit motive into aesthetics, where profits can have no benign or constructive meaning at all.

The commercial era in music was well under way in America by the early 1920's. Through radio and the talking motion picture it extended its octopus hold, which today is fastened upon virtually all the sources and public outlets of professional music. Everywhere its strangling pressure is felt, in the limited symphonic repertory and the gagging of the new composer, who can scarcely achieve public hearing; in the increasing banality of popular music, and in the appearance of swing, an aural activity devoted to neurotic excitement and the cliché. Such classical music as survives in the commercial repertory fares well enough, in a sterile sort of way, protected by its unalterable score and its traditional interpretation. But true jazz, which must be improvised by inspired and devoted players, withers in such an atmosphere.

Commercialization was a cheapening and deteriorative force, a species of murder perpetrated on a wonderful music by whites and by those misguided Negroes who, for one or another reason, chose to be accomplices to the deed. The story does not make pleasant reading for those who love art or believe in progress, and it has implications far beyond art. To read it is to be forced to question to a degree some of the basic things in our society.

What happened to jazz is a little laboratory test, if you will, of democracy. "Giving the people what they want," in this case at least, consists of planning a product that can be put together by hacks, that can be profitably sold to the people, and then, amidst an advertising campaign unrelenting and continuous, can be unobtrusively substituted for what the people already wanted and had. As long as this is a diffused process arising more or less as the end result of a social-economic system, it may be accepted by the many and resented or feared by the few, and is seldom seen in its full implication. A case can be made for the nationalization of the resources of the human spirit, for the taking of buying and selling out of art, for the subsidizing of artists and the preservation of artistic values, uncontaminated and undistorted, for all the people.

Commercialization is almost always inimical to the integrity of an art in the creative stages. When we consider that real jazz is always improvised and is, as long as it exists, perpetually in the state of creative inception, we see that commercialism is a thing not only hostile, but fatal, to it.

An equally powerful force, subtler and more disarming and able to seduce sincere and seemingly intelligent people, may be called the "illusion of improvement." It springs from a dual misconception about jazz. The first part of the misconception postulates jazz as crude and imperfect because its creators were Negroes of humble origins, uninstructed in the technique and theory of European music. Unseen is the fact that, except for this fortunate circumstance, jazz could never have been created.

The second part of the misconception is that jazz is potentially a new form, not in itself, but as a part of the European tradition; that it was hit on, luckily and fortuitously by its "gifted, but ignorant" creators and, therefore, should be taken over and developed from this point by trained, "superior" musicians. In this connection it should be pointed out that primitive does not mean crude and unformed or ill-formed, tentative or barbarous. It means instead a point of view, a way of looking at the world innocently, directly, and imaginatively.

Like the primitivism of children, it sees without veils and records in its own peculiar, powerful, magical symbols. This helps
to explain the easy adaptability of the Negro to Western ways
and the ease with which he adopts elements of arts foreign to
him. This process can be seen in our American public schools,
where children of all races and nationalities tend to get along
much better than their elders.

So the attempt began twenty-five years ago, and is still going on, to "improve" jazz by making its content, method, and
execution more and more like the whole European tradition.
It was tempting to those outside, who were able to avoid the
labors of trying to understand a new art form and at the same
time to rationalize this sidestepping in an apparently laudable
attempt to work improvement. It was equally alluring — and
thrice disastrous — to the practitioners of jazz itself. Only a
few of them, through their own integrity, or because one thing
or another forced them out of the playing of jazz during its
unpolluted Golden Age, were able to stand aloof from this sudden urge of jazz players to "improve and refine" their music.
It is obvious now that if jazz can be left free to develop properly, it will certainly find, in its own forms and implications,
its own progress and proper refinement.

But while Paul Whiteman and George Gershwin and a host
of others outside jazz, began to "improve" it and try to make
of it symphony, concerto, and opera (all the things it was not,
and which, if it needed ever to become, it needed to become by
its own means), men like Louis Armstrong were at work within
the inmost core of jazz. On its outmost fringes were men like
Fletcher Henderson and Duke Ellington, Count Basie and
Jimmy Lunceford, all busy expanding the small jazz group
into the large swing band, which deserts polyphonic practice
to embrace harmonic development and the arranged playing of
instrumental sections.

The larger band might have come about properly in jazz.
But it would have come when the individual skill in playing improvised polyphonic parts had grown to the point at which

more voices could be added to the polyphony beyond the three or four then within the reach of the performers and the perceptive power of the listeners. There were moments when King Oliver's large band, or even Erskine Tate's, gave a momentary glimpse of the jazz possibilities of the large group.

Had the unchecked tendency to "improve" jazz sprung from understanding, undistorted by the white's supreme difficulty in playing and creating it, and had it not been misdirected by the Negroes' hypersensitivity to criticism, it would have been a factor powerfully favorable to the development of the music. Unfortunately, it has led to the creation of a hybrid Afro-European form of doubtful worth. It has led to a painful and superficial sophistication in its player-creators, to a deluge of the mere noise called swing, to a dozen forms of hybrid jazz, and to a spate of symphonized jazz and pseudo-jazz masterworks. Nevertheless, unspoiled jazz is a Negro art as important as it may be disturbing, as richly rewarding as it may be stimulating. It throws a many-sided challenge to the white race, a challenge we have pretended to misunderstand or have chosen to ignore, a challenge that is only a part of the unsolved problem, not forever to be ignored, of the Negro in our democracy.

The history of jazz has been a short one, a span of development and fruition remarkably compressed in time. In this music's history a year has been roughly equivalent to a decade in the history of European music. In the latter, development was slow and periods long; in the general sanction given to the art as a whole, it could comfortably wait for critical vision and popular acceptance to catch up with the progress of the art. But with jazz, the total misunderstanding of the music, the dubious position of its Negro creator in white society, as well as his pathetic and ill-founded desire to please the white, created an unstable condition in the art itself. It tended in part to vacillate and to respond to the winds of ignorant opinion. It should not be thought that jazz is, or was, therefore, an art without strength or integrity.

BLACK MUSIC

All fine arts, more divorced than the folk arts from ordinary life, have in all times and places needed support, have sought and found the sponsor, the enthusiast, and the wealthy patron, either among the individuals in society or in a paternalistic and discerning government. Yet, while jazz is a fine art, it has not been recognized as such, has found few patrons, and has been forced to attempt to subsist as a folk art. This, as a form requiring arduous and lifelong devotion, fanatic and unworldly absorption from its practitioners, it could not do. It could live in New Orleans, as it still does to a very considerable degree. Even there, as a big and growing thing, a folk academy with its adepts and novices, it could exist only as long as, to the patronage of parade, funeral, and public dance, was added the scope of employment and the handsome largess of commercial vice in the Tenderloin.

In this, too, there is involved the whole position of the Negro in a society where, after three and a quarter centuries, he represents an unassimilated and despised minority. Many a Negro found, fairly early, that his best chance of a measure of success among the whites was to canalize his vast creative power into forms of European art. Thus, he early tended to alter his spirituals, deforming them by a recasting into the European mold. This Europeanization began about 1871 at Fisk College. Today Negroes like Paul Robeson and Marian Anderson, capable of great creative work, devote their powers to the mere interpretation of European repertory and Europeanized Negro music. Jazz itself has largely yielded, except for a few incorrigible veteran players and groups of young enthusiasts, to its own Europeanization.

Meanwhile, under the surface, the ferment of creative power goes on. Most of the forces comprising the jazz spirit remain alive. Everywhere, in the city and in the country — even, unrecognized and unwittingly, in the churches — the Negroes are singing the blues. This, the hot core of jazz, seemingly cannot be extinguished. The elaborate instrumental jazz structure

15

reared upon it may fall before the winds of prejudice, hostility, or lack of understanding. Underneath, the beginnings of jazz are still nurtured as with the jealousy of a mother.

Is it possible that, from these unquenchable sources, from the efforts of the remaining players of pure jazz, from the tradition of the art at its highest point of evolution, and with the help of the white understanding that has recently been awakening, these forces can be concentrated once more into the form jazz took in its own Golden Age? Can progress resume, undistorted and unvitiated, from that point?

There are signs that this may happen. Jazz, whose fair-weather friends deserted it twenty years ago, has been finding new friends among enlightened and liberal people. At this moment everything points to a great and imminent revival, all opposing forces to the contrary. When that happens — tomorrow — we shall hear the shining trumpets again.

CHART SHOWING AFRICAN SURVIVALS IN NEGRO JAZZ AND THE DEFORMATIONS OF NEGRO JAZZ

AFRICAN SURVIVALS IN NEGRO JAZZ

THE HOT CONCEPT:

I. Tendency to use any melody or harmonic pattern as a base for free improvisation of melody.

II. Inducement of the *Trance* — Intuitive creation.
    A. By rhythmic repetition.
    B. By melodic repetition.

III. Creative participation
    A. Tendency to group improvisation.
    B. Forming a rhythmic-tonal whole by inclusion of
        1. Rhythm-pattern of dancers' feet.
        2. Dancers' singing, shouts of excitement, approval, et cetera.

IV. Avoidance of monotony by incessant variation:
    A. Rhythmic
    B. Tonal
    C. Melodic

RHYTHM:

I. African patterns in rhythm instruments, especially the drums.

II. Over-all rhythm of the band:
    A. Perpetual syncopation.
    B. Polyrhythm.
        1. Displaced accents forming a different pattern than the basic one — *inner-rhythm.*
        2. Polyrhythm in European sense, i.e. two or more meters or patterns simultaneously — *over-rhythm.*
    C. Single over-all patterns.
        1. *Stomp.* Melody is made to fit to the *Stomp* pattern.
        2. *Riff.* Perhaps derived from the *Stomp,* this repeated, simple, melodic-rhythmic figure is sparingly used in jazz.

III. The *beat* or *pulse,* evolves in meter
    A. Through *live* accenting.
    B. Through playing very slightly before or after the strict metric beat, principally after.

TEMPO:

I. Strict tempo or controlled acceleration.

II. Moderate, never too fast. Relaxed, and with room for improvised part-playing.

DEFORMATIONS OF NEGRO JAZZ

DEPARTURE FROM THE HOT CONCEPT:

I. Tendencies to
    A. Straight playing of melody.
    B. Mere embellishment or rhapsody.

II. Inability to achieve the *Trance* — Substitution of
    A. Intellectual conceptions, especially *a priori.*
    B. Uncontrolled excitement or gross sentimentality.

III. Diminution of creative participation.
    A. Loss of ability in group improvisation and substitution of arranged ensemble, while limiting improvisation to solo.
    B. Tendency to concert, not dance, music.

IV. Monotony versus variety:
    A. Use of monotonous repetition to build up neural excitement.
    B. Variety through mere effects.

RHYTHM:

I. African patterns in rhythm instruments dropped or used in stereotyped way.

II. Over-all rhythm of the band:
    A. Perpetual syncopation progressively dropped — loss of momentum.
    B. Polyrhythm:
        1. Little *inner-rhythm.*
        2. Little European polyrhythm.
    C. Single over-all patterns.
        1. *Stomping* dropped out early.
        2. Overexploitation of the *riff*, because it is facile of execution, adaptable to written or memorized arrangement, and an easy substitute for melodic invention.

III. The *beat* or *pulse.*
    A. Return to European idea of *beat*
        1. By giving even time-value to all beats — a *dull* beat.
        2. By playing on the beat or else by *pushing*, i.e. anticipating the attack.

TEMPO:

I. Unconscious tendency to *Rubato* or to uncontrolled acceleration.

II. Tendency to overfast *tempi* — unrelaxed and crowds and distorts the part-playing.

AFRICAN SURVIVALS IN NEGRO JAZZ
(continued)

INTONATION:

I. Contrary to European pitch:
   A. Intonation free of the fixed scale.
   B. Microtonal flatting, especially the third and seventh *blue notes,* as derived from pentatonic and hexatonic scale structures.

II. Fluctuations in pitch.
   A. Wide use of *glissandi.*
   B. Tone coloration by *undulation* or wavering of pitch.
   C. Use of very wide vibrato.

TONALITY:

I. Tendency to reduce the scale to pentatonic or hexatonic and to improvise within the simple tonic-dominant chord sequence.

II. Disinterest in key changes, lack of modulation, except in marches and ragtime.

MODALITY:

I. Indeterminate although predominantly major in feeling. Constant shifting in area between major and minor through microtonal flatting of third and seventh, especially in *glissandi.*

TIMBRE:

I. Vocalized instrumental tone.
   A. *Dirty* tone, growl, *wa-wa.*
   B. Great variety of unorthodox tone qualities.
   C. *Hot tone.*

MELODIC FACTORS:

I. Stress on melody developed independently of harmony.

II. Antiphony (The Call-and-Response).
   A. In the *Blues* form.
      1. In the order of vocal or lead phrases.
      2. In the relation of these to the accompaniment phrases.
   B. In alternation of solo and ensemble.
   C. In the placing of instrumental *breaks.*

DEFORMATIONS OF NEGRO JAZZ
(continued)

INTONATION:
  I. Conforming to European pitch-norms:
      A. Strictly *in-tune* playing.
      B. Semitonal flatting only (See *HARMONY*, below).

  II. Fluctuations in pitch.
      A. *Glissandi* rarer, used decoratively and sentimentally,
         not structurally.
      B. Little *undulation*.
      C. Narrower, European vibrato.

TONALITY:
  I. Tendency to preserve the full European diatonic scale.

  II. Tendency to modulation and key changes in European
      tradition.

MODALITY:
  I. Definite mode and changes from major to minor. The *Blues*
      generally distorted by playing them completely in the
      minor.

TIMBRE:
  I. Vocalized tone not characteristic of white or of much so-
      phisticated Negro playing.
      A. Tendency away from *Dirty* tone, toward pure.
      B. Limitation of tone to accepted *Pure* types.
      C. *Hot tone* rarely achieved, as this results from true
         Negroid improvisation.

MELODIC FACTORS:
  I. Melodic invention shaped by harmony.
  II. Antiphony.
      A. Preserved — with phrase mutilation — in the *Blues*
         form.
      B. Tendency toward a continuous series of solos.
      C. Breaks progressively minimized.

21

MELODIC FACTORS (*continued*):

III. Polyphony (development from antiphony).
  A. Parallelism and unison very rare.
  B. Polyphony (combination of varied melodic lines) tending away from harmonic domination.
  C. Heterophony (developing out of B), i.e. counterpoint of melodic variations that have reached status of new melodies as compared with the theme.

MELODIC CHARACTERISTICS:

I.   Direct survivals of African melody.

II. Negroid alteration of white melody
  A. In line.
  B. In compass.
  C. In rhythm.
  D. In variation.

HARMONY:

I.   Tendency to eliminate harmony.
  A. Reduction to the simplest progressions.

  B. Polyphony preferred to
    1. Melody with harmonized accompaniment.
    2. Melody *in* harmony.

  C. The approach to prevailing dissonance, by
    1. The progressive dropping of harmony in the heat of improvisation.
    2. The development of polyphony into heterophony.

II. Substitution of varied rhythmic, tonal and melodic interest for paucity of harmonic interest.

DEFORMATIONS OF NEGRO JAZZ
(continued)

MELODIC FACTORS (*continued*):

III. Polyphony.
    A. Parallelism and unison increase, become predominant in swing.
    B. Polyphony decreases and eventually, when it exists at all, is vertical (harmonic).
    C. No heterophony in white jazz except a chaotic sort in Chicago-style jazz.

MELODIC CHARACTERISTICS:

I. Alteration in line with the white tradition of surviving African melody.
II. No alteration of white melody toward an African character.
    A. When melody is played straight, it is in European manner, sometimes with faked jazz idiom.
    B. Variations are European, including much ornamentation and figuration.

HARMONY:

I. Re-establishment of harmonic predominance.
    A. By augmented instrumentation, duplication of imstruments precluding group improvisation and leading to section playing in harmony.
    B. Amplification of harmony.
        1. Through symphonic scoring, involving rich and varied harmony.
        2. Tendency of popular song toward more varied harmony.
    C. The shunning of dissonance.
        1. The brass band not a strong factor in white jazz. Furthermore the white brass band adheres to harmonized arrangements.
        2. Dissonance in the white or mixed *Jam Session* arises from rivalry rather than from polyphonic development; is wild and chaotic.
II. Varied harmonic richness and interest gradually supplants the Negroid rhythmic and melodic variation.

2.

drums to america

Musique nègre! Que de fois loin
de l'Afrique, j'ai cru t'entendre,
et subitement se recréait autour
de toi tout le Sud . . .

ANDRÉ GIDE

AFRICAN music is the key that unlocks the secrets of jazz. For jazz, regardless of the origins of its melodies, is a *manner* of playing derived directly from the music of the West African Coast. The continuity of this manner is directly traceable musically and, in part, historically, from the first importation of slaves to this country through all the different kinds of music the Negroes have made in their three and a quarter centuries here.

Great importance has been attached to the fact that much American Negro music is based upon white melodies, ballads, and Scotch hymns. Actually, this is of slight importance compared with the profound transformation of this basic material in its Negroid rendition. The Negro transforms all that he sings or plays. The hymn, for example, partly transformed, becomes the spiritual. Completely transformed, it becomes the blues, a truly new musical form. The basic material is recast in its scalar compass and its tonal intervals, revoiced in its timbres, and completely altered in its rhythmic character. (See Appendix A, p. 342.)

African, particularly West African, music has been a complex and highly developed art for centuries. Its origins are perhaps more remote in the past, its continuum of development perhaps of a longer span, than those of European music. Built

25

upon the simplest fundamentals of all music, namely rhythm and tone, it evolved into an art profoundly different from ours in shape, spirit, and meaning. Basically it emerged, as did all music, from dancing and from speech developed through chanting and declamation into song. All music probably began on the improvisational plane, as a communal rather than a specialized activity. A high degree of formalization is likely to follow, making the art the province of skilled professional performers. In Africa, however, and in really Negroid music everywhere, the communal and improvisational aspects are largely retained.

In our music, formalization forced out improvisation, led to the growing importance of the composer and the scored composition, and led, likewise, to the growth of a professional body devoted to the practice of an increasingly esoteric art. In our culture, dancing and music were separated centuries ago in the religious and serious secular pursuits of the art; folk music was split from the main musical trunk; music as a fine-art form began to develop. But the vitality of a music is to be found in its communal aspect and in constant invention in performance. Our composers inevitably have had to turn to folk music for melodic ideas and rhythmic life. As the split between the people and music has widened, this process has become increasingly eclectic and artificial.

As nature strives to close and heal a wound, society constantly is trying to take music back to itself. But the secret of singing and dancing as a natural human activity gets partly lost. Music today is packaged in radio, motion picture, and phonograph record; it is taken like pills. Amateurs in every town form little symphonies and chamber societies. Playing the scored masterpieces of our music, they have, in the feeling of communal activity, the illusion of creation, just as one toiling in the gymnasium might have that of active and creative living. Meanwhile, the composer languishes; the real seriousness of music — original creativeness — is lost and its real nobility — vital connection with life — disappears.

When jazz appeared on the American scene seventy-five

years ago, the African concept of music as a creative, participative artistic activity was presented to America by the Negro.

Music is the most highly developed and universally practiced of the arts in West African culture. On the plastic side, this culture produced the superb wood sculptures of Gabon and the bronze ones of Benin, work that, early in this century, decisively altered the course of European painting and sculpture, and provided space concepts utilized in modern architecture. The music, as it survived and developed in Afro-American music, is exerting an equal effect upon our composers and performers. Particularly in jazz, it has developed into an art of prime importance in itself, unassimilable as a whole into our music.[1]

The pure Negroid influence, freely acknowledged throughout Europe, is discounted in America because of the inferior position the Negro, originally the slave, always has occupied in our society. A false concept or stereotype of the character and the past of the Negro was formed early in this country. Emancipation, precipitating economic rivalry between black and white intensified this stereotype as a defense mechanism. Melville J. Herskovits has outlined and refuted it. His chief points follow:

1. Negroes are naturally of a childlike character, and adjust easily to the most unsatisfactory social situations, which they accept readily and even happily, in contrast to the American Indians, who preferred extinction to slavery;

2. Only the poorer stock of Africa was enslaved, the more intelligent members of the African communities raided having been clever enough to elude the slavers' nets;

3. Since the Negroes were brought from all parts of the African continent, spoke diverse languages, represented greatly differing bodies of custom, and, as a matter of policy, were distributed in the New World so as to lose tribal identity, no least

---

[1] "African and European music are constructed on entirely different principles, and therefore they cannot be fused into one, but only the one or the other can be used without compromise." Hornbostel, E. M. von: *African Negro Music.* (Reprinted from *Africa,* Vol. I, No. 1 (London?) n.d.

common denominator of understanding or behavior could have possibly been worked out by them;

4. Even granting enough Negroes of a given tribe had the opportunity to live together, and that they had the will and ability to continue their customary modes of behavior, the cultures of Africa were so savage and relatively so low in the scale of human civilization that the apparent superiority of European customs as observed in the behavior of their masters, would have caused, and actually did cause, them to give up such aboriginal traditions as they may otherwise have desired to preserve;

5. The Negro is thus a man without a past.[2]

The stereotype operates in two ways. As propaganda that, in the South, approaches a conspiracy, it is used to justify and conceal repressive and discriminatory measures and activities. It is apparent justification for the poll tax, which prevents the "ignorant" Negro from voting. It bolsters the exclusion of the Negro in many areas from many professions, particularly, perhaps, medicine. It conceals sexual rivalry in accusations of rape and the horrible continuance of lynch law. Yet the stereotype is more dangerous and more insidious as unconscious bias and prejudice in our thinking. Otherwise intelligent people base their whole approach to what is called the *Negro Question* upon the unreasoning acceptance of this myth. In literature, and from the black-face minstrels down to the motion pictures, the Negro has been portrayed either as a lazy, shiftless, childlike clown or as a devious and dangerous liar, until this portrait is etched deeply into our consciousness. Our thinking about the racial problem is thus clouded by uncensored and diffused emotionalism, by stubborn and subtle misconception.

The misunderstanding of jazz is to be seen as part of the larger problem of the Negro in our society. And, as the understanding of African music clarifies that of jazz, so knowledge of the Negro character and his past clarifies and helps to solve the problem of the Negro in our democracy. Such a clarification is needed, not only among the whites, but among the

2 Herskovits, Melville J.: *The Myth of the Negro Past.* New York: 1944.

many Negroes who have come to accept the myth. Herskovits writes:

> It is little wonder that to mention Africa to a Negro audience sets up tensions in the same manner as would have resulted from the singing of spirituals, the "mark of slavery," to similar groups a generation ago. Africa is a badge of shame; it is the reminder of a savage past not sufficiently remote, as is that of European savagery, to have become hallowed. Yet without a conviction of the worth of one's own group, this is inevitable. A people that denies its past cannot escape being a prey to doubt of its value today and of its potentialities for the future.
>
> To give the Negro an appreciation of his past is to endow him with the confidence in his own position in this country and in the world which he must have, and which he can best attain when he has available a foundation of scientific fact concerning the ancestral cultures of Africa and the survivals of Africanisms in the New World. And it must again be emphasized that when such a body of fact, solidly grounded, is established, a ferment must follow which, when this information is diffused over the population as a whole, will influence opinion in general concerning Negro abilities and potentialities, and thus contribute to a lessening of interracial tensions.[3]

Music, including drumming and singing combined with dancing, plays a very large and important part in the social, economic, and religious life of West African Negroes. It is rich in corresponding elements from tribe to tribe.[4] Of all the arts of West Africa, music — at least singing — is the most communal.

In the music of the African, and equally in that of the American Negro, it is difficult to attempt a rigorous separation into

---

[3] Ibid, p. 32.

[4] Outside the United States, particularly in Brazil and Haiti, the Negroes set up their own African religious cults parallel to or syncretized with Christianity, especially Catholicism. They have been able, also, to continue many African social customs, such as marriage and burial ceremonies. In this country, the work-song and certain social dances survived; the religious ceremonials died out. In their place, new musical forms arose. Everywhere, however, tribal differences, lingual and social, failed to impede the making of a music that, as in Africa, has a general form free of tribal limits.

rhythmic and melodic elements. The nature of the melody is rhythmic; even where a part of the rhythm is kept separate in drum battery, piano bass, or jazz-band rhythm section, the melodic voices are not only complexly rhythmic in their own right, but tend to flow over into, or absorb into themselves, the basic rhythm. They are profoundly interacting; the whole forms not only a polyrhythm, but one not set to a formal, pre-determined pattern. It is a thing alive and growing in itself, as sensitively interconnected and inter-responsive, as the branches of a tree, weaving in several directions and in several rhythms while they respond to the same wind.

Rhythm and its development are the fundamental African aims; form and formal development of melody *in* harmony are the European. Thus one has to begin with movement and mo-mentum on the one hand, the structure of forms on the other: the locomotive or the airplane, the mountain or the temple.

Rhythm, in Africa, is expressed in percussion and in melody that can be free and improvisational, antiphonal or polyphonic, but never limited by considerations of a prevailing harmony. Form, in Western practice, is expressed in melody and melodic development that, imbedded in harmony, produce form and formal arrangements.

In Africa, development, variety, and contrast come through unstemmed motion, through constant variation or mutation, often improvisational, through the combination of several rhythmic and melodic parts. In our music, rhythm is an ad-junct, not the prime consideration; the momentum is checked or altered by changes in tempo or in the basic metrical pattern itself. Essentially, the forms in Western music are different melodies or the same melody variously expressed in different keys and rhythms, in contrasting major and minor modes, in a variety of harmonizations and instrumentations, in various inversions and variations of line. These forms are juxtaposed and contrasted to secure a feeling of architectural balance and satisfying structural completeness.

In African music, one melodic or purely rhythmic voice, or

several combined, continue to flow in a basic pattern of rhythmic and melodic repetition. This never flags, but, on the contrary, is likely to build up slowly and controlledly in tempo. These repetitions, which produce a rapt and hypnotic state in players and listeners, are nevertheless infinitely varied in many musical ways and grow constantly in complexity.

Essentially, Western music is one of structure; African, one of free, continuous, creative energy. The European concept is one of building from contrasted moods; the Negroid is one of complete and exhaustive exposition of a particular mood.

Such distinctions are, of course, ultra-simplified, too broad. For European music has movement, too. Our medieval music moved in a horizontal combination of voices similar in some respects to African polyphony. There never was, however, the feeling for an inexorable rhythmic momentum or the combination of vocal polyphony with percussion that are characteristic of African music. And, for centuries, harmony became more and more important in our music. By Bach's time it was beginning to limit the melodic voices in polyphony. It ended by strangling polyphony completely until modern times.

Harmony, though produced adventitiously in any combination of voices, is not a concept basic to music in the sense that melody and rhythm are basic. Harmony, with its developing theory of consonance (or agreeable sound) opposed to disonance (clashing sound), becomes, in time, a vertical element opposed to the horizontal flow of melody and rhythm. Melodic lines are restrained by the necessity of conforming to a developing chordal pattern and (even more basically) by the limitations of the fixed pitch and the tempered scale that result from an elaborated harmony.

In all so-called primitive music, pitch is not limited to the full-tones, half-tones, and scales of our system. The pentachord, or tonic-dominant of our system, is played or sung in Africa with faultless pitch, furnishing a stable base around which the other tones are used in an infinite variety of gradations with differences as subtle as those of the sixteenth-tone.

31

Pitch, too, limits our music in its use of the glissando or sliding tone, one of the expressive features of Negro singing and playing. With us such long glissandi, sliding upward or downward are considered in bad taste and, heard in the "tailgate" or circus-style trombone of jazz, are thought vulgar or merely humorous in a crude way.

The glissando is a natural characteristic of the human voice in speaking or singing and in the playing of all *absolute* musical instruments, those in which the pitch is not fixed. A rich source of expressiveness, it is found in all Afro-American music, vocal or instrumental, and outstandingly in jazz, not only in the trombone and clarinet styles of New Orleans, but also in the wide and fantastic trumpet glissandi with which Louis Armstrong confounded symphony players who had considered the feat impossible except by use of a mechanical device.

With its freedom of pitch and linear formation, African melody does not need chromaticism, the succession of half-tone intervals. On the contrary it tends to avoid half-tone steps. Chromaticism, with us, signalized — in *Tristan und Isolde* or the *Verklärte Nacht* of Schönberg — a revolt against the limitations that harmony imposes, as well as the actual dissolution of harmony. Breaking down in the development of modern music toward a dissonant polyphony, harmony did not lose its hold on our musical thinking. For the tones fixed in pitch, which harmony had led to, remained; to seek dissonance is still to be preoccupied with the idea of consonance. A music free of harmonic rule, like the Negroid, seeks neither.

Harmony enters into African music in the main only in the chanted chains of consecutive thirds, fourths, and fifths, rising and descending. This harmonic device, one of great beauty, strengthens rather than weakens the melodic line, in no way impedes the rhythmic flow, and is not harmonic progression in our sense of the word, but a colorative enrichment of the idea of unison singing. We find these *chord-chains* in the spiritual, as severely limited as in Africa to accord with antiphonal-polyphonal practice.

Harmony, with us, limits the concept of timbre. The combination of voices or instruments in a chord requires, besides accurate pitch, a quality of tone that will blend. Thus we have the concept of pure tone, which excludes all the wide variety of timbres that are so expressive and of such essential importance in Negro music.

Negro voices have characteristic quality and variety of timbre. Expressiveness and variety of tonal qualities are sought rather than pure [5] tone. In the exploitation of vocal range the upper reaches of the falsetto are used. The qualities, in their variety, include a rough gravelly tone, known in jazz as *dirty tone,* guttural, shrill, rich, husky, hoarse tones of a flutelike and woodwind quality, and, occasionally, the *pure* timbres of European singing. There is the vigorous *recitative* type of singing that Negroes call shouting; humming also is used. The development of harmony in Europe caused many expressive timbres to be discarded. The concept of richness of tone, especially in solo work, came to be added to that of purity because this quality in the single tone produces the feeling of richness of the chord. There are many degrees of richness and purity in African and Afro-American singing and in the instrumental playing of jazz. But tone with the Negro develops, like melody, from its own natural basis of expressive significance.

The common characteristics of most African Negro tribal musics are: antiphonal and polyphonal singing combined with percussion; a tendency for rhythm — especially in the drum percussion — to reach a high degree of development in pattern formation, syncopation and polyrhythm; and the contrapuntal combination of separate rhythms. These same characteristics are carried over into all Afro-American music up to, and including, jazz.

Antiphony in Africa is the *statement* of the leader and the *answer* of the male, female, or mixed chorus. The leader chants, often improvisationally, in strong declamatory phrases. The

[5] Pure, as descriptive of tone, is different in meaning than when used to describe melody free of harmonic limitation.

chorus responds in beautiful periods that rise and fall in free melodic undulation, high, clear, and in unison or in haunting chains of thirds or fourths.

Polyphony in Africa developed from the overlapping of these calls and responses. The chorus tends to enter before the leader's phrase is finished or to continue after it has begun. This combination of leading and choral melody becomes a two or three-part polyphony.

The musical styles of various African areas are not yet fully documented or differentiated, though important work is in progress. The West Coast area, from which the slaves were taken, concerns us, particularly the related musics of Dahomey, the Ashanti, and the Yoruba. According to Herskovits, a large proportion of the slaves in New Orleans were of Dahomean provenance, brought there directly from Africa or from the Caribbean islands, particularly Haiti.

A valuable study of West African music is the unpublished manuscript, *Die Musik Westafrikas*, by M. Kolinski, in the anthropological library at Northwestern University. Much of this study is based on the 600 or more cylinder recordings, chiefly Dahomean, made in Africa in 1931 by M. J. and F. S. Herskovits. Some of the data used in the following comparison of African and Afro-American music are drawn from this source.

In Afro-American music many kinds of percussion — handclapping, foot-stomping, et cetera — may be subistituted for drums to a greater extent than in Africa. The African drum rhythms are characterized by cross-rhythms. The term *polyrhythm* has become a highly controversial one in the field of modern music, and has come to have several conflicting meanings. I shall therefore substitute my own terms, based on what happens rhythmically, for the term *polyrhythm* in either of its accepted senses. The first is the *inner-rhythm*, which creates rhythmic patterns by the shifting of accents or by the use of tacit (silent) beats. The second is the *cross-rhythm* or *over-*

rhythm, a sort of rhythmic counterpoint produced by the simultaneous playing of two or more distinct rhythmic patterns. (See Appendix B, p. 344.)

In the United States drumming and the manufacture of drums were not freely encouraged by the slave-owners. In their fear of slave revolts many did their utmost to stamp out African customs and rituals. Yet legends persist of nocturnal meetings in the woods where, as Dorothy Scarborough relates,[6] homemade drums were beaten under washtubs to muffle the sound. Nevertheless drums were made. One from Virginia, (dating from 1728), is in the British Museum. It is a matter of record that drumming went on from about 1817 until the middle 1880's in New Orleans' Circus Square (called Congo Square by the Negroes) and elsewhere in that city.

Drumming, however, was much more circumscribed in the United States than elsewhere in this hemisphere. Despite this, the tradition of percussive polyrhythms has persisted in the hand-clapping and stomping of the spiritual-singing in the churches, in the jazz band, and, in one form or another, in all Afro-American music. But while polyrhythm has persisted, its character has changed somewhat. Perhaps this is because of the clandestine character it assumed for a time and its later emergence in new social contexts in which the set and formalized character of the African originals tended to be lost. In this country it is at once simpler and more complex. The basic figures, evolved in 2/4, 4/4, or 12/8 time, and expressed in stomping and clapping in the churches and by the rhythm section in jazz, are in general far simpler than in Africa. They tend to form an *ostinato* (a continuous repeated figure) with a comparative lack of mutation. A high degree of complexity, however, enters with the factor of free and continuous voice improvisation that characterizes Afro-American music, for this introduces complex and changing overrhythms. This is clearly

[6] Scarborough, Dorothy: *On the Trail of Negro Folk-Songs.* Cambridge, Mass.: 1925.

shown in the notation of a section from a recorded spiritual, *I Am a Soldier in the Army of My Lord.*[7] (See Ex. 48, back of book.)

The same principle of free rhythmic-melodic improvisation over rhythmic *ostinato* prevails in instrumental jazz. It is much more systematized than in the church singing and demonstrates the close nexus between this music and that of West Africa. The survivals are inner. They might be considered merely symbolic were they not functioning parts of the music as well as tendencies that survived in the whole body of Afro-American music up to, and including, jazz.

There is, first, the basic rhythm in which the percussive section of the band functions like the drums in Africa. Above this, cornet, trombone, and clarinet are conceived of as *voices* and are played with the vocal tone that, significantly, the Negro imparts to the brass and reeds. Although, as in some African music, a continuous polyphony has superseded the antiphonal process of call (or statement) and answer, the roles of leader and chorus can still be determined. The cornet part is always called *lead* in New Orleans, the cornetist (or trumpeter) is almost invariably the actual *leader* of the band. Like the African leader, he sets the tempo and enunciates the commanding lead phrases. Around his part, the trombone and the characteristic clarinet play (actually *sing*) melodic parts that function almost precisely as the choral parts do in African singing when these parts have flowed out over the lead and antiphony has changed into polyphony. From the nature of the tone, as well as from the melodic character of each, it is clearly evident that a mixed chorus is represented by these two instruments. The trombone represents the male singers; the clarinet, the female.

All that is lacking, theoretically, in the imaginative reconstitution of this music of the African chorus with drum group are the all-important elements of inner-rhythms and over-rhythms. These elements, which in Africa are found mainly in the drumming, are, in fact, not lacking in jazz or any Afro-

[7] See Appendix G, p. 355, for a detailed analysis of the record.

American music. They are, however, introduced in a different way. In the rhythmic *ostinato* of the foot-stomping and hand-clapping of church singing or in the rhythm section (various combinations of drums, guitar, bass, and piano) of the jazz band, we find either a single rhythm characteristically established and maintained or rhythmic superimpositions of the simplest nature, as syncopated 2/4 over regularly accented 4/4.

Complex rhythmic counterpoint enters with the voices or the horns,[8] which provide overrhythms in either or both of two ways. The first of these is in free improvisation, which includes, besides melodic, an equally wide range of rhythmic variation. This is the secret of the complexity of Afro-American rhythms: the improvisational quality carries the African principle of rhythmic mutation to its ultimate point. The second way in which one rhythm is superimposed upon another is the *stomp pattern* of jazz, in which one or two of the horns concur in tied, syncopated rhythmic figures that produce an overrhythm with the fixed *ostinato* of the rhythm section. The sequences of poly-rhythms in African drumming give over-all repeated patterns. These arise from the unisons and divergences of the several parts. The stomp pattern in jazz is an evolved and highly learned manifestation in which the net result of rhythmic counterpoint, rather than its separate parts, is introduced into instrumental jazz.

Highly significant is the elaborate and subtle symbolism by which the horns in jazz function *both as voices and as drums.* We shall find the same functional symbolisms in barrel-house, boogie-woogie and ragtime piano music. In these, as in the Afro-American work-songs, spirituals, and jazz, there is a separation of voice from percussive rhythm and a combination of the two in rhythmic counterpoint. In the piano styles, the left hand, or bass, provides a rhythmic *ostinato* with a minimum of improvisation; the right hand presents a more or less improvised impersonation both of drums and of choral voices.

8 In jazz terms, *horns* include cornet or trumpet, trombone, and clarinet or saxophones.

Jazz is so distantly evolved from West African choral music that these correspondences — parts, really, of a continuity of cultural tradition — go unperceived. It is difficult to find anywhere a tradition deeper or more stubborn than that of African music. It has retained its essential forms and its vigor through more than three centuries of independent development on an alien continent, throughout a progressive racial dilution. It has done so despite the wholesale adoption by the exiled Negro of white musical material and social customs. The result is a transformation of such material into a music of Western melody recast and rendered in the African techniques. Thus, it is neither African, European nor a hybrid of the two. To attempt to interpret it as either, is to fail to describe its real nature. Correct analysis, which separates *material* from *manner*, indicates this real nature and furnishes the technical basis for calling Afro-American music a new phenomenon in musical history.

Multiple repetition of the same note, with or without rhythmic variations, is a tendency in Negro singing and in jazz trumpet playing. This type of *ostinato* or broken *pedal-point* [9] probably is a tendency in West African music. Kolinski's analysis shows it as a characteristic in 71 per cent of the Dahomey and 54 per cent of the Ashanti songs which he examined.

Afro-American music very seldom uses triple meters (3/4, 6/4, etc.) in its basic rhythm. The duple meter (2/4, 4/4 etc.) is characteristic as it is in much West African music. Thus, when the European dance tunes heard in New Orleans began to be taken over into the repertory of dancing jazz in about 1885 or 1890, the triple meters were converted into duple. We have a documented example of this in the transformation of a French quadrille into the famous *Tiger Rag*. (See Chapter 8.) In this process the triple-metered waltz and mazurka sections are changed to common (4/4) time.

Complexity develops, as we have shown, with the entry of

[9] An unbroken pedal-point is a single note held a long time.

inner-rhythms and overrhythms. In Afro-American music these occur most frequently in oppositions of odd-numbered to even-numbered meters. We frequently find the type of odd against, or within, even meter in the blues, jazz, and Afro-American piano music. In boogie-woogie, for example, many passages are best scored in 12/8 (or 12/16) instead of the apparent 4/4, the 12/16 falling into four groups of three notes each. For an example of this, see the score of Jimmy Yancey's *Make Me a Pallet on the Floor*, Ex. 16, back of book. The odd-numbered rhythms *within* an even-numbered one are found extensively in Dahomean music, where the 12/8 time signature is equally useful in removing the unintelligibility of a 4/4 designation.

Great flexibility obtains within the African system while, at the same time, the general formal requirements are well defined. We encounter marked independence between percussion and part singing which, however, does not exceed the limits formally set. In Afro-American music, as we shall see, such flexible formation clearly enters the form called the blues and operates in jazz with the greatest freedom and the most intelligible clarity.

Consideration of salient rhythmic characteristics from Africa can conclude with the phenomenon loosely known as *perpetual syncopation*. Technically, this extended displacement of normal accent is called an *off-beat ostinato*. In its simplest form, in African and in all Afro-American music, it consists of the displacement of the two accents of 4/4 time to the normally weak beats, the second and fourth, sometimes called *off-beats*. The example shows normally accented 4/4 and an off-beat *ostinato* in the same meter. (See Example 1.)

Actually, this is not an inner-rhythm because inner-rhythms use shifted accents, with or without tacit beats, to form a *different* pattern within the basic meter. It is, instead, a time-shift of the basic metric pattern *itself*. A psychological factor enters in the fact that, in the case of a single rhythm like that of one drum, if such a shift continues past a certain point "the placing of the measure division tends to shift, the counting is advanced and the off-beat becomes the principal beat." [10] This phenomenon is adroitly used in African music and in Afro-American forms, particularly ragtime and boogie-woogie, where the normal is restored just before the shift of attention occurs. Such manipulations show accurate, practical knowledge of the quantum of time-lag involved. Because the exciting and stimulating quality of extended syncopation is desired, we find African and American Negroes circumventing the difficulties involved by making the perpetual *syncope* one part only of a polyrhythm. Thus, the displaced beat is used as overrhythm above the basic, normally accented meter which holds the unshifted meter in the focus of attention. This device, very effective in a rhythmic way, depends upon different timbre as well as pitch range as between the two parts. Examples 2, 3, and 4 (back of book) show ways in which this is accomplished in Africa and in this country.

The remarkable strength and purity of rhythmic survival in the American Negro is shown in the following record made early in 1946.

CITATION 1. *Drum Improvisation, No. 1.*, by Baby Dodds. This solo, by the greatest drummer in jazz history, was produced in a state that definitely resembled possession. The full complement of jazz percussion, bass and snare drums, tom toms, wood blocks, cowbell and cymbals, is utilized in an amazingly complex and polyrhythmic improvisation. The drums are meticulously tuned to intervals that correspond to those of African singing and the 'performance is at times as complex as that of the three-piece African battery. It must be emphasized, moreover, that Dodds has no first-hand knowledge of African drumming and music. He thinks of himself, on the contrary, as a "modern" jazz drummer and evolves all of his effects directly from the unconscious.

10 Rudi Blesh: *This is Jazz,* Lectures at the San Francisco Museum of Art, 1943. (This is a phenomenon somewhat similar to various types of optical illusion and the seeing of complementary hues during color fatigue.)

Tempo is properly considered in connection with rhythm. Moderate tempo and fixed beat are basically characteristic of African and Afro-American music.[11] Overfast tempos did not appear in Afro-American music until very recently, and then by way of certain types of swing music. It seems obvious that the moderate tempo is desirable because of playing for long periods (often in the heat or when using the music with work or dancing) and, also, because rhythmic — as well as melodic — counterpoint is more transparent (i.e. intelligible) and therefore more effective at moderate speed.

A psychological corollary of the fixed beat, especially in rhythmically exciting music, is a tendency to gradual acceleration. We see this operating in the music of both hemispheres when it is not tied to a limiting function such as work. It is equally true of jazz used for dancing. The impulse toward a fixed beat seems as strong, or nearly as strong, as that toward acceleration. Much of the inner tension of African drumming, and of jazz, arises from this fact and is a practical example of the proverbial irresistible force and the immovable object. Later we shall see that, in jazz, the build-up of urgent tensions through the restraint of natural momentum takes the place of the climax in European music. Because of these opposing tendencies, it is almost invariably true that in Negro music everywhere, when acceleration occurs, it is gradual and controlled. It is fair to say that rhythmic variety in European music often derives largely from the use of *rubato* and tempo changes in their widest sense, while Negro music, holding a strict beat, avoids monotony by rich and complex polyrhythms and because of the principle of constant change of pattern.

Particularly in Dahomey [12] we find a complex polyphony developed from the overlapping calls-and-responses of part-singing as well as from the severe limitation of harmony which is not allowed to become predominant. We shall find this type of po-

---

[11] For a specific example Ballanta (*Music of the African Races*) describes Yoruban music as being characterized by its moderate speed.
[12] Vide Kolinski, ibid.

lyphony and limited harmonic procedure in jazz, originating from the Negroid performance of European melodic material.

The vocal vibrato is carried over from Africa into Afro-American singing. Its characteristic use in jazz in the playing of the cornet, trombone, and clarinet has been the subject of much comment. The American Negro employs the vibrato in his own way. As he uses it, controlled and extraordinarily broad, it fulfills two functions. It is a rhythmic device that often furnishes, in its timed oscillations, an inner-rhythm within the continuous tones. Beyond that, it is an intonative device used to produce regular variations in pitch. These variations, often as broad as a half-tone, produce the coloration of tone known as *blue*.

The West African languages are tonal, and much of their vocabulary is built on variations in the vowel sounds, just as in Chinese. These tonal qualities with their variations are carried — together with speech rhythms — over into drumming and singing, ultimately for their expressive qualities but primarily with the actual lingual meanings. It is difficult, if not impossible, to determine with what vestigial meanings such timbres have gone over into jazz. Nevertheless, in blues and in jazz any sensitive listener becomes aware that overtones of meaning persist in the timbre and are communicated from Negro player and singer to Negro listener.

Such verbal meanings, attenuated but actual, subsist in African drumming, persist in the foot and hand *ostinati* of the spirituals, in the plangent percussion of boogie-woogie, and in the rhythm section of the jazz band. African drums speak in two ways and in two directions: they call the gods, and the gods, responding, speak through them. These instruments, tuned with meticulous accuracy and played with sure and complex rhythm, set the air vibrating in pleading or in authority, with the tones and the sequential time-patterns of human or divine speech.

Similarly, when those *possessed* in ritual *speak with tongues*, we have a supernal language. These strange, often guttural, sounds are unforgettable when once heard. Thousands of miles

42

from Africa, one can recognize the same cryptic tones and phrases in Louis Armstrong's jazz playing and singing and in the rapt, unconscious responses of his devotees when both are *sent out of this world.* In many West African tongues the adjective *hot* refers to the mysterious trancelike state of possession, to the heated and inspired improvisation and the tonal qualities evoked at such a time, to the exciting over-all tonal-rhythmic texture of the music, and the emotional state which is superinduced. All of these meanings persist in Negro language throughout the Western Hemisphere. Their descriptive quality is too unique and their reference too varied to permit the belief of any but an African origin of the terms.

African music and the Afro-American music which preceded jazz are both, in the main, vocal. Jazz, as we shall see, refers to these antecedents in the highly vocalized tone quality with which the melody instruments are played. It has been assumed that this characteristic timbre arises from the self-taught nature of the Negroes' performance on European instruments. However, since vocal tone in a trombone is not the *natural* tone of this brass instrument but is, rather, an *artful* manipulation, such reasoning would seem to be inaccurate.

If one pictures the Negro as following his own choral tradition and as *singing* on these instruments, the behavior pattern becomes clear. The impression of vocalization is so strong, and the feeling of polyphonal choral work so pervasive in a New Orleans jazz band, that I shall frequently refer to the cornet, trombone, and clarinet as *voice instruments.*

The musical tonal African quality in the speech of both Negroes and whites is found in the American South. Here again is a point, now tenuous but one which later study may well prove to be a cultural carry-over from the African to the English speech of the Negro, which acted in time as an acculturative influence upon the white man.

When the lingual characteristics of Negro speech are separated and analyzed, and their formative entry into his music made clear, it will be obvious that this music is a language with

43

its own communicative qualities. One can then refer without mysticism to its power to convey, through an abstract and derivative phonetics — an abstruse, inner syntax — recondite meanings generally obscured in the written or spoken word.

An important element of Negro tonal production is in the attack and termination. Western practice (except, by necessity, on the piano) in order to ensure accurate pitch and pure tone, attacks or initiates the tone somewhat more softly and then swells its volume. Negro practice is precisely the opposite. Each tone is struck relatively louder and then the volume is diminished and is clipped off sharply at the end. This technique transfers percussion to the sung tone and is one of the rhythmic bases of hot tone quality. It is especially obvious in jazz trumpet tone which begins with a bell-like sound before the blowing tone emerges.

While, in Western music, we have evolved complex diatonic scales, the scalar concept scarcely enters into African music although it is constantly referred to as predominantly pentatonic and hexatonic, i.e., five and six-toned.

This arises from the question of pitch as it is based on the five-note interval or *pentachord.* We shall find the pentatonic compass a factor of great importance in the blues and the jazz of the American Negro. In most primitive musics two notes are fixed in pitch, the first and the fifth intervals in whatever scale is being used. These frequently correspond, as in Afro-American music, to the tonic and the dominant, respectively, of our scale and our harmony. We shall see how the Negro in America, adopting our music, chose hymns and other pieces built on a simple tonic-dominant harmony because this sequence and the melodies built on it lend themselves sympathetically to African Negroid treatment. We shall examine the characteristic changes wrought in our scale by pentatonic thinking with the microtonal (less than the half-tone of European music) *flatting* of certain intervals, especially the third and the seventh.

With simple scalar thinking, tonality — in the sense of different scales and the modulation from one to another — and modality, i.e., major and minor mode, are of small technical importance with regard to the music itself. Key, in Africa, is nothing more than the placing of a melody to fit the range of the voices. Modulation is unknown there. As we might expect, it is virtually unpractised in all Afro-American music except for the march and dance tunes of several themes which were incorporated in the early jazz and in ragtime.

Mode, in Africa, is an amorphous thing. The change from major to minor in our music is effected by the semitonal flatting of the third and seventh intervals of the scale. These are precisely the intervals in all Negro music which are flatted indeterminately in degrees much less than the necessary half-tone and generally approximating a quarter-tone. These, too, are frequently subjected to glissandi. The effect obtained is that of an extremely haunting and plaintive music which hovers continually between major and minor. This sliding, microtonal flatting of the third and seventh is a universal practice in all Afro-American music, and gives the quality known as *blue*. The intervals themselves are called *blue notes*.

Two records document important points of our discussion of West African music and the survival of its characteristics in the New World.[13]

Detailed study of African music emphasizes its strangeness as the product of a culture remote in spirit from our own. Yet, since it has become, through Afro-American music, a part of our culture, it remains a language which we need to learn.

No one can truthfully say that African music is crude or barbarous. Although its beauties are as strange and cryptic as those of Gabon sculpture, its beauty will nevertheless unfold to the willing ear and its complexities will become intelligible. Its inmost meanings will reach our consciousness at last, and its driving power will energize our spirits with a part, at least, of the fertile and unflagging creativeness of the African. An

---

[13] These discs, made by Professor Herskovits, are to be found at Northwestern University and copies are in the Library of Congress. For an analysis, refer to Appendix C, p. 346.

ocean's interval, the catastrophe of slavery on alien soil, three centuries of oppression and intermittent effort to stamp out every vestige of "heathen" Africanism, were not enough to prevent the Negro's construction of his own music from the materials of ours. As we study this music, from work-song through spiritual to the blues and jazz, we shall begin to perceive a musical edifice profoundly different from ours, one of a strange but meaningful beauty. Seeing it thus, we shall understand that this music, which we have been accustomed to think of as humble folk song, is already important and may well develop into one of the great musical systems of history.

3.

in southern fields
and churches

THE SLAVES in America represented a heterogeny of Negroes torn from the autonomous societies of their various tribes, cast into the ocean stream of a barbarous commerce, mixed together at random, and deposited on the shores of an alien continent.

In Africa they had had the status of free men, within the limits of tribal government, and the arts of free men: painting, sculpture and, to a very marked degree, music. In America they shared the misery and the nearly intolerable conditions of servitude. These shared conditions effaced the remnants of tribal barriers and created, in effect, a supertribe. The tradition of music as an art, intimately infused into daily life, persisted. If it ceased to be the music of freedom, it became that of freedom remembered or imagined, the expression of life in slavery and its ameliorant. The fact that American Negro music, like the African, is at the core of daily life explains the immemorial African quality of all Negro *folk* music in this country, if not of the Negro in exile everywhere.

However, another fact must be recognized to explain completely such a phenomenal survival. This is the stubbornness of the African character, not only in Africa but on alien soil, and through racial dilution even to the evolution of a new physical type.[1] This character persists in spite of the unusual adaptability of the Negro to foreign influences. It is at its purest, the most *Negro*, where the transplanted black man is kept ignorant

[1] See Herskovits, Melville J.: *The American Negro*. New York: 1930.

47

and isolated from surrounding society, as in slavery. It becomes less purely *Negro* in proportion to the degree of his assimilation. It will, perhaps, always retain a Negroid character, not only because the art of the Negro is different in character from other arts, but more basically still, because a strong case may be made out for the belief that the Negro is different physically and psychologically, from other peoples. (See Appendix D, p. 349.) Anyone who has watched the Negro in athletics or in ballet is aware of the different quality of his movements. Psychologically, too, he is different in a great many of his reactions. Where he speaks characteristically in ellipsis, for example, and with double meanings, he is not evading the issue. Instead, he is presenting it, more complexly than we, in various meanings and from various points of view, simultaneously as it were. And his power of *direct communication beyond the spoken word* is vital and unatrophied.

From the first "twenty negars" which John Smith bought at Jamestown, Virginia, in 1619, to the end of slavery (the last slave came to America in 1864), the lot of the black man in America was work. The white owner may have delayed the conferment of his religion upon the slave but the imposition of his labor was instantaneous. The slave thus found his store of work-music, remembered from Africa, useful and necessary in his new surroundings. The functional principle of this music, to heighten energy, to facilitate physical motion by making it rhythmic, and to furnish mental diversion without interrupting labor, he found applicable here. Work-music, in effect, converts labor, at least to a degree, into games or dances that furnish an excitement monotonous drudgery cannot. Excitement heightens energy that, channeled into a pattern that excludes non-useful movements, generates its own momentum and expends itself with little waste. The whole implication of game or dance diverts the worker's mind from his troubles. The hypnotic singing becomes the reality; the work becomes automatic.

Some of the African types of work-song doubtless were directly applicable to the new labor while others were usable with modification. The Negro, with his musical creativeness, made new types where needed even before he had access to our music and to our religion. The Afro-American work-songs, therefore, preceded Afro-American religious music and, in their early stages, represented purely African material. Thus the cruel labor of slavery had the accidental effect of preserving musical Africanisms. Preserved, they entered into the Negro folk musics that followed, and gave a treatment and profoundly African form to the extensive European material they included. The work-songs shaped the spiritual; without them both, the blues and jazz almost certainly would never have evolved.

The markedly eclectic character of American Negro essays in other arts, such as painting and sculpture, is partly explainable by the hiatus or time-lag which fortunately did not intervene in the Negro creation of music. The slave masters approved all music-making that aided work or diverted leisure. This approval was opportunistic without implications of aesthetic approval or understanding. There was no approval at all of Negro sculpture and painting, no desire to collect it — even the curio craze had not as yet seized the American public — nor to use it decoratively in the home. Not until 1906 were Picasso and Matisse to rescue some dust-covered pieces of African sculpture from Paris second-hand stores, their vision, sharpened by spiritual need, penetrating the strangeness as decisively as it penetrated the dust, to reach the enigmatic meaning, the cruel and powerful beauty beneath. They found this beauty and meaning, which were to exert so formative an influence on twentieth century painting and sculpture, in the junk-heap remains of the work of black men long dead on a far continent, an influence cabalistic and magical emanating darkly and secretly from artifacts.

Music had been commonly practiced among all the African tribes, danced and drummed in a daily heated improvisation in which all the members of the tribe participated. Sculpture, and painting too, may have been created spontaneously, but once a piece was created it had a permanent, unchanging form; al-

49

though used with music in magic-making or ceremonial, it was a realized object about which the whirling chemical tides of sound could crystallize. Too, sculpture and painting are solitary occupations, executed by specialists as it were; unlike music, the communal use of these art products followed their creative fashioning. In America the Negro, with no immediate need for sculpture and painting, did not create objects that, unlike the music that crossed the ocean in his memory and in the habits of his heart, he necessarily had left behind in Africa.[2]

Early comment on slave music is sparse but occasionally significant. Thomas Jefferson, in 1784, for example, wrote [3] "In music they [the Negroes] are more generally gifted than the whites, with accurate ears for a tune and time, and they have been found capable of imagining a small catch. . . . The instrument proper to them is the *banjar*, which they brought hither from Africa." Besides the great Virginian's brief but discerning observation on Negro improvisational and rhythmic skill, another eighteenth century note exists which applies to the creation of antiphonal work-songs in America. This is to be found in *Parkes' Travels*.[4]

They lightened their labour by songs, one of which was composed extempore for I was myself the subject of it. It was sung by one of the young women, the rest joining in a sort of chorus: The air was sweet and plaintive, and the words were these:

Leader: *The winds roared and the rains fell,*
            The poor white man, faint and weary,
            Came and sat under our tree.
            He has no mother to bring him milk,
            No wife to grind his corn.

[2] "During afternoons of serene weather, men, women, girls, and boys are allowed while on deck to unite in African melodies which they always enhance by an extemporaneous tom-tom on the bottom of a tub or tin kettle."
Quoted by Lydia Parrish (in *Slave Songs of the Georgia Sea Islands*. New York: 1942) from *Captain Canot, or Twenty Years of an African Slaver* (1827–1847).
[3] In *Notes on Virginia*.
[4] Quoted in *Carr's Musical Journal* (1801) Vol. 2.

Chorus: *Let us pity the white man,*
             No mother has he!
             Let us pity the white man,
             No wife has he!

Despite such contemporary comment, specific technical
knowledge of American Negro music from the seventeenth to
the middle of the nineteenth centuries is almost nonexistent.
There exist, indeed, more definite data concerning African music of the same period. Yet the process of development is clear,
even if the original form of the work-music is largely unknown
except by inferential reference to that of appropriate West
African areas. It stemmed from Africa directly and without a
time lapse. Its purity and its function combined to keep it more
free from hybridization and dilution than church music which
began by adapting Anglo-American melodic and harmonic material. Yet even church music today is remarkably African in
form and manner. This African spirit and tradition, preserved
through the work-song, and transmitted through the spiritual,
is alive today in the blues and jazz and, more generally still, as
a creative musical potentiality.

Slavery made possible the creation of American Negro folk
music and the art-form, jazz, but this fact furnishes no con-
donement of slavery or any phase of it. Any praise to be de-
duced is praise of the invincible spirit and courage of men of
any color, of the unquenchable human need to find beauty and
to produce art even in the midst of the most intolerable and inhuman conditions. It is praise not of "man's inhumanity to
man," but of his refusal to be degraded under the blows of
insensate cruelty. It is praise, not of Pharaoh, but of Moses who
goes down and sets "my people free."

One might speculate on the Afro-American music which would
surely have developed had the Negroes come here with social
and political equality. One might wish that they had been free
to develop artistically, unconditioned by social pressures, with-

51

out needing to seek social equality through the imitation of white men.[5]

The work-songs survived Emancipation because the Negroes were not freed thereby from a virtual labor conscription which still exists in parts of the South. Ironically, it was the machine which later, began to free the Negroes from the sort of communal labor that naturally gives rise to, and perpetuates, the work-song. Economic logic found the counterpart of the slave in the machine. Both can be owned, can be bought and sold; food or fuel, preservation of health or mechanical maintenance, are equally necessary protections of investment. So machinery came and the work-songs began to die out. There finally remains the double irony that the work-song has survived virtually in prison only. Prisoners, like slaves, must work but need not be paid; only the minimum requirements of life need be provided. And in the prisons of the South, with their preponderance of Negro inmates, in Mississippi, Louisiana, or Texas, are to be found most of the surviving work-songs. Elsewhere, we can hear the Afro-American work-song today only in a rare and sporadic group survival and in the singing of a few individuals, like the fabulous character, Lead Belly (Huddie Ledbetter).

Recorded work-music is recent and not extensive. John and Alan Lomax have recorded, in various penitentiaries and prison farms of the South, a number of examples for the Library of Congress Folk Archives. Among the prison recordings, the following shall be cited:

CITATION 2. *Jumpin' Judy,* sung by Kelly Pace and Group at Cumins State Farm, Gould, Arkansas, (1934). This ax-chopping song, recorded during actual work, is almost completely African in musical form, in timbre, and in spirit. Over the *ostinato* of the ax blows, which function musically like drum

[5] Not even in Africa has the Negro been left free to pursue his own arts without interference. Douglas H. Varley writes in the preface of his *African Native Music,* "While one group of well-meaning workers has attempted to impose a European cast on native singing, another group from Misionar Witte to the Rev. A. M. Jones has collected important evidence and attempted to work out a logical compromise which takes into account native tone-values, form and rhythm."

percussion, the leader calls and the chorus responds in the consecutive thirds characteristic of West Africa. The responses rise and fall on an undulant melodic line almost precisely as on the Dark Continent. With the freedom of some African singing, the chorus shouts approval and comment on the leader's improvised lines and responds to his bitter irony. *Jumpin' Judy* should be compared directly with a portion of *Manbetu Song from the Belgian Congo.* (See Ex. 5, back of book.)

The basic similarity of these surpassingly beautiful songs, one sung by convicts in Arkansas, the other by a tribal group in West Africa, is evident even in our musical score so ill-adapted to indicating African music.

CITATION 3. *Long Hot Summer Days*, sung by Clyde Hill and Group at Clemens State Farm, Brazoria, Texas, (1939). This is beyond question one of the most hauntingly beautiful of all recorded work-songs. Although the harmony is clearly European, its whole character is greatly modified in an African way by the extreme portamento of the singers and by the incessant *numes* or quavering downward figures, mainly around the diminished third and seventh intervals. *Long Hot Summer Days* is closely related to church singing and its effect is that of a solemn, devotional requiem. Through these moving, majestic choral sequences one can hear the dark depths of bitterness, frustration, and vain regret in the hearts of imprisoned men.

Another record from the Library of Congress Archives, *Long John*, is of special interest because of its similarity to Negro children's songs. (See Appendix E, p. 351.)

The records cited above typify the choral work-song that evolves in group labor. The foreman, as a rule, is the leader in this singing that, regardless of melodic derivation, so clearly exemplifies the African call-and-response antiphony.

"The holler is the work-song of solitary occupation. The cowboys 'hollered' at their cattle to keep them moving or to quiet them at night; lumberjacks, to let the world know another big tree was coming down; field hands, to relieve the loneliness of their plowing. This habit of hollering has particularly marked the American Negro at work. On the levees, in the cotton field, on the railroad, he has hollered and moaned his troubles and his observations on the ways of the world. The holler is a way of singing — free — gliding from a sustained high note down to the lowest register the singer can reach, often ending there in a grunt." [6]

The Negro hollers originally had specific musical forms to fit specific occupations, as well as names to fit each. A few of these names have survived sporadically. An example is the name, *arwhoolie*, for the cornfield holler. Among recorded examples of hollers are, *Don't Mind the Weather, Diamond Joe*, and *Joe the Grinder* (Library of Congress AAFS–16), *Arwhoolie, Quittin' Time Songs*, and *Mealtime Call* (Library of Congress AAFS–37).

Among the finest Negro work-songs recorded outside of the prisons are those sung by Lead Belly, self-styled "King of the twelve-string guitar players of the world." Huddie Ledbetter was born in 1885 in western Louisiana, near the Texas line and only thirty miles north of the large gulf coast city of Shreveport. Lead Belly never forgot the work-songs, ballads, play-party and dance songs of his people, which he learned as a country boy. Later in life, he had long hours in the penitentiary to play and sing them over and over, expanding and varying them with his own genius in the immemorial way that folk music grows. Pardoned dramatically after singing for the governor of Louisiana, Lead Belly has since become an outstanding national folk artist. He plays and sings the work-songs, ballads, dance-songs, and blues with an artistry of the highest order, his work animated with his dynamic, almost hypnotic, magnetism.

CITATION 4. *Ol' Riley*, sung by Lead Belly with accompaniment by his own twelve-string guitar.

Also known as *In dem Long Hot Summer Days*, this song is a work holler and, at the same time, a ballad of the epic or

[6] Lomax, John A. and Alan: *Negro Folk Songs as Sung by Lead Belly.* New York: 1936.

54

legendary type. It is of great beauty and its melodic line is
mobile, expressive, and of a marked African rhythm. (See Ex.
6, back of book.) Identified here with the Brazos River in
Texas, it may go back as far as slavery days with Ol' Riley,
the legendary hero, typifying in his speed and prowess the unquenchable spirit of the Negro, and in his escape foreshadow-
ing his eventual deliverance from slavery and oppression.[7] Lead
Belly sings slowly like a narrator:

> *Ol' Riley walked de water*
> *In dem long hot summer days.*

> *Ol' Riley he's gone*
> *Ol' Riley he's gone, gone, gone*
> *In dem long hot summer days.*

> *Ol' Riley left here walkin'*
> *In dem long hot summer days.*

Faster, as if descriptive of the chase, the guards call the dogs:

> *Here Rattler, here Rattler, here Rattler, here*
> *Here Rattler, here Rattler, here Rattler, here.*

> *Ol' Riley's gone like a turkey through the corn*
> *Here, Rattler, here*
> *Ol' Riley's gone like a turkey through the corn*
> *Here, Rattler, here.*

> *Rattler come when I blow my horn*
> *Here, Rattler, here*
> *Oh, the Rattler come when I blow my horn*
> *Here, Rattler, here.*

> *Too-oo-toot-too*
> *Here, Rattler, here*
> *Toot, toot, toot*
> *Here, Rattler, here.*

Slowly once more as if Riley has escaped and the guards are
returning reluctantly:

[7] Like *Run, Nigger, Run,* a slavery-time song and one of the early plantation type.

> *Ol' Riley walked de water*
> *Ol' Riley walked de water*
> *In dem long hot summer days.*

> *Ol' Riley he's gone*
> *Ol' Riley he's gone gone gone gone.*

Fast and soft and far away:

> *Here Rattler, here*
> *Here Rattler, here.*

In Lead Belly's singing, this dramatic, if sketchy, ballad has become a sort of nostalgic tone poem. The singer seems content to forget the bitterness of prison and to sing a song of summer in the South. The dramatic old song emerges from the singer's memory as a thing of soft and lyrical tenderness, a tonal evocation of a drowsy summer day. It is like a dream dreamed on the warm grass, in a cottonwood's shade at the busy field's edge, a dream of something that happened long ago. *What was it? A slave's escape? A convict's escape? I remember only a few words of the old song I sing for you, nothing of what it means.* Into the dream come distantly, secretly, the voices of workers, the barking of dogs, the call of a horn — all the sounds of summer day, multiplex and gentle, drifting down slower than rain, remote, muted, soft as the air.

In *Take This Hammer* (Asch No. 101), a steel-drilling song sung by Lead Belly, the verse formation, with its serial groups of three identical verses followed by an answering refrain, is strongly antiphonal. In this sort of song, the leader might sing the verse, the group responding with the refrain. From the functional aspect, the tempo is important in regulating the pace of the labor which would be steady and, presumably, as leisurely as the "straw boss" would permit. Lead Belly sings with strong African rhythm and timbre, and characteristic use of long sliding tones.

The unaccompanied calls and street cries constitute a distinct type of work-song, one that has remained very African in form.

Their melody, pure and free from considerations of harmony, is declaimed and chanted; it follows the distinctly African formula of developing melody from the rhythms, inflections, and timbres of spoken language. As in the native tongues, the melody of the calls and the street cries is colored by the tone qualities of language and moves with spoken rhythms; the melodic line rises and falls, or fluctuates on a single tone with the free characteristics of speech.

On the Mississippi, this sort of melodic call or chant was developed by the Negro calling the depth soundings to the river-boat pilot. The sounding call is distinctly different from the river chanty sung by a group. The following is a fine example.

Citation 5. *Heaving the Lead Line,* called by Sam Hazel, Greenville, Mississippi, (1939). The voice sounds like a horn blown far off in the fog around the river bend. The undulant melody rises and falls. We can trace the ancient history of language, of language become poetry and of poetry become song, in the simple, called numbers, poetic evocations of the great river. (See Ex. 7, back of book.)

> *Tell me there's a buoy, a buoy right on the bar*
> *The light is twisted and you can see just how.*
> *Pull a little over to the la'board side.*
> *Lawd, Lawd.*
> *Quarter less twain,*
> *Quarter less twain,*
> *Lawd, Lawd, now send me quarter less twain.*
> *Throw the lead line a little higher out.*

One remembers the origin of Samuel Clemens' pseudonym, remembers that he found his pen-name while he piloted river boats on the Mississippi. One night in moonlight or in fog, he listened to the wild, rich Negro voice blending with sounds of water, chanting the depths as the line was heaved:

> *I've gone low down, so mark twain,*
> *Mark twain.*

Perhaps the most familiar form of work-chant is the vendors' street cry, which is almost universal throughout the United

States; the cry of the scissors grinder and the wagon peddler in New York's streets, the call of the newsboy in the Middle West, and everywhere in the "rags and bottles" of the junkman. The Negro in the South has carried the development of these street cries to their highest point in our country. They are heard everywhere below the Mason-Dixon line. Those of Charleston, South Carolina, are perhaps the most famous. Some of these, fortunately, have been recorded there. (See Appendix F, p. 353.)

These calls show clearly the Negro's conversion of speech into song. This tendency seems to be changing even the conversation of the Negro into a sort of singing. They exhibit also, a typically African variety of rhythm, abounding in syncopations, displaced accents, and anticipations and retardations of the basic beat. Finally, these cries are rich in tonal qualities, in variety and in variation of timbre, and in the vocal-instrumental tone quality we find in jazz. They prophesy New Orleans jazz as clearly as they recall Africa.

Strangely enough, dancing, an activity universal among African Negroes, tended for a long time to be suppressed in this country. Undoubtedly, abandonment of the more uninhibited of the African dances was brought about by the slave-owners almost immediately. In other cases dances disappeared with the banning of the appropriate tribal activity or ceremonial. Many rituals and social diversions, inextricably connected in Africa with dancing and music, were objectionable to the slave-owners. Not only an activity as obviously dangerous as the war dance, which might be considered destructive of the servile spirit, but all dances of a communal type were naturally suspect as aiding potential self-organizing of the slaves. Organization might be expected to become, in their hands, a weapon of flaming revolt.

The Negroes, in point of historical fact, refused widely and stubbornly to accept bondage. Slave revolts were frequent and bloody, yet no more so than the abuses which caused them. Despite the stereotype of the kindly, paternalistic plantation owner (a type that did, of course, exist to a degree), appalling inhumanities, often motivated by uneasy fear and by suppressed feelings of guilt, were all too frequent. Over a period of more than two hundred years (1663–1865) there were, according to Aptheker,[8] no less than one hundred and thirty uprisings.

In the imposition of their religion, the slave-owners found a ready-made instrument for taming and diverting their human property. The Christian religion, which eschewed dancing long ago [9] and came to condemn it as an evil secularism, led the converted slaves to a self-censorship of their natural activity.[10]

Especially significant is the reference here to French and Spanish tolerance, precisely the condition to be found in New Orleans where African dancing was allowed during, and long after, slavery.

That fresh slaves were constantly being brought to this country is a fact which bears on the continued strength and purity of African influence in all Afro-American music. Each boatload poured a new infusion into the slowly diluting stream of native Negro inspiration. This largely explains not only the persistence of African form, method and spirit, but the sudden recrudescence from time to time of expressions like the dance.

Some of the earliest forms of secular slave dances have been preserved. A well-known one is *Juba*, which some writers believe to be an authentic African melody. Miss Scarborough [11] gives a version of this dance-song which is a severe, oversimplified, and non-Negroid notation. (See A in Ex. 8, back of book.) As Negroes would sing and play it in their native rhythmic manner, syncopating and displacing accents, it would vary endlessly. (See B in Ex. 8.)

[8] Aptheker, Herbert: *American Negro Slave Revolts*. New York: 1943.
[9] Havelock Ellis points out that dancing by priests or laity actually went on in European churches up to the eighteenth century (*The Dance of Life*).
[10] "This ban on dancing was set up, not by the white masters, but by the Negroes themselves, or by their religious leaders. The dances that the captured slaves brought over with them from Africa were heathen and obscene, and so they must be 'laid aside' in the new life. They were permitted, with certain restrictions, in the sections under Latin influence — French and Spanish — but not elsewhere." (Scarborough, Dorothy: *On the Trail of Negro Folksongs, op. cit.*, p. 97.)
[11] Ibid. p. 98.

Juba illustrates the simple harmony which the Negroes extracted from the Anglo-American hymns as the only harmonic base required for their complex and ceaseless melodic, tonal and rhythmic variations. The melodic character of this dance and the call-like statement followed by the last two-measure response, clearly hark back to the African call-and-response and are strongly prophetic of the later eight-bar blues form. Similarly the *Calinda* survived in New Orleans, on the Georgia Sea Islands, and elsewhere.

Lead Belly provides a number of fine examples of the rural folk dance in vocal form with guitar accompaniment. Two examples, full of a pastoral poetry, are *Green Corn* [12] (Musicraft No. 225 and Asch No. 5612) a fiddle sing for square dancing and *Corn Bread Rough* (Asch No. 101), a reel with accordion accompaniment.

Thus the Negro began to create in America, as he had done in Africa, a body of musical types intimately connected with his daily life, evolved from and used with different parts of the new pattern of living.

The Negro had religion here, although it was a new one. What remained from his African faiths we can, in the main, only guess. Yet the tendency of primitive peoples to amalgamate their own religious rites and customs with, and to conceal them within, the new dogma and ritual, is well known. Equally well known is the tendency of the missionary, or the indigenous church, to tolerate and condone these duplicities (even creating festivals to correspond with pre-existent pagan ones) in the long view that envisions over-all and gradual conversion.

So, from the African work-songs of three hundred years ago, the Negro took his next step. The spirituals, which soon began to resound in the open fields and to rock the bare, wooden country churches, were the first music definitely to transform Eu-

[12] "Lead Belly always sings this old-fashioned air tenderly and joyfully, as if softly and pleasantly drunk on green-corn whiskey just off the mash. A feeling of spring runs through the song, the sound of sappy fodder rustling in a June wind; and each repetition of 'green corn' is like a young corn sprout pushing up through the brown earth." Lomax, John A. & Alan: *Negro Folk Songs as Sung by Lead Belly.* New York: 1936.)

ropean melody by African rendition, the first music, in short, clearly Afro-American. The spiritual which, with its offspring, the blues, was the first Negro music to elicit general white praise, is the fountainhead of racial inspiration from which jazz was to flow. So, in the New World, a body of religious Negro music was created. It was made — at certain times and in certain sects — to include (as it still does to a considerable degree) dancing, which also continued to be carried on as an activity separate from the church.

Hurry Angel hurry! Hurry down to the pool.
I want you to trouble the water this mornin'
To bathe my weary soul.
Angel got two wings to veil my face,
Two wings to fly away.

Early in the mornin', 'bout the break of day
Two angels came from heaven and rolled the stone away.
Angel got two wings to veil my face
Angel got two wings to fly away.

I would not be a hypocrite
I tell you the reason why
'Cause death might overtake me
And I wouldn't be ready to die.
Angel got two wings to veil my face
Angel got two wings to fly away.[13]

The slavery church did not bring the bright angel of deliverance the Negro sought. The dark angel came often, descending by night and day, for, to natural death and that of exposure and ill-tended disease, was added the appalling rate of suicide and infanticide among the rebellious slaves. Nor did Emancipation bring immediately, or ever wholly, the freedom of political and social equality. But art, to a creative race, is a kind of deliverance; the opportunity to practice and create it, a kind of freedom. Music was to be this fairer angel, an angel with two wings. One, dark, was African music; the other,

[13] An old spiritual.

bright, was the melody of the white man; shielding wings that would veil the black face, bitter symbol and inescapable cause of shame; wings of deliverance on which to fly away home. This fusion of two musics, as remote as black is from white, came with the spiritual and was to find its greatest expression in jazz.

Afro-American music falls into the broad categories, *religious* and *secular*, or as church Negroes will have the latter, *sinful*, or *worldly*. The religious category included, in the beginning, congregational preaching, singing, and dancing, first carried on in the open fields or in the hut villages. This followed a marked African pattern still to be heard in rural, and even in urban, churches where too much sophistication has not crept in. From this congregational singing came the hymn, or spiritual.[14]

The secular music included, originally, work-songs, dances, children's games and play-songs. A later development, partly derived from white sources, was the ballad, although, to be sure, there is African precedent for the chanted narrative and the animal myth. The final development in secular form was the blues, a form of great importance.

As the number of his occupations increased, particularly after slavery, the varieties of Afro-American music grew. With Emancipation, the Negro moved about more, thus spreading the music about. Also, seizing the opportunity for independent employment in music, he became a wandering entertainer, singing and playing the guitar; he became the itinerant "professor," playing ragtime or barrel-house piano music in drinking places, boarding houses, and bordellos; he became the street evangelist, often blind, preaching and singing on the corners while he played a battered guitar. Along the dusty roads, along the railroad tracks, in the crowded, dirty streets, and on the river boat, the Negro moved, singing and spreading his music as he went. Where, for a third of a century, it had been dis-

[14] Also called a *mellow*, a word derived from melody, and, in the Georgia Sea Islands, an *ant'em* from anthem.

seminated in the form of grotesque and inept parody, in a spirit half sympathetic and half contemptuous, by the white minstrel with cork-blackened face, the black man now had the chance himself to circulate and sow his songs, even to form his own minstrel shows and blacken his dusky face to the traditional inhuman ebony. And thus he could laugh — although with a deeper humanity — at those who had laughed at him.

The spirituals, like all Afro-American vocal music, are a part of Negro double-entendre and are full of hidden meanings. If God is presented to the converts as a just God, the Negro, faced with injustice, is appealing to justice when singing of his woes to Him. Singing of Egypt, he sings of slavery; appealing to Moses, he invokes the genius of his own race. The River is a symbol of many references: the many great streams of Africa and liberation as well as death, so that Beulah Land means freedom as often perhaps as it signifies Heaven. In a very real, if indirect, sense the Negro churches were stations on the underground railroad which was being surveyed and built long before it began to carry runaway slaves in the days before the Civil War.

Until Emancipation, the spiritual enforced and strengthened tendencies which, even in Africa, are ingrained in the race. These are to use music as language and to employ speech in a circuitous and double-edged way. Negro speech everywhere is indirect and implicative as well as direct; its reference is many-faceted; it is universal as well as specific and, in these dualities, it is essentially poetic. "Many elements of the Uncle Remus stories are encountered in the [African] sacred myths, and these elements, even where the animal personnel has been retained, are handled in a subtle . . . manner. They often exhibit a *double-entendre* that permits them to be employed as moralizing tales for children or as stories enjoyed by adults for their obscenity." [15]

Slave speech aimed in two directions; disarmingly simple, it was also code. Language, like drums, could conceal messages

[15] Herskovits, Melville J.: *The Myth of the Negro Past, op. cit.*

while conveying them. The visitor to New Orleans' Congo Square could watch the African dancing and ceremonial, hear the music. How could the Negro prevent this? But if he asked for a translation of African words or an interpretation of symbolism, he met a blank wall. These Negroes, many just arrived from Africa or Haiti, entering so vividly and knowingly into the proceedings, professed a transparent but impenetrable ignorance as though their activity were only the improvised, idle play of grown-up children, or else an outworn ritual which had ceased to signify anything.

From the Negro tendency to mytho-poetic creation come the *sayings*. "In addition to the tales are numerous proverbs and riddles, the former in particular being used at every possible opportunity to make a point in an argument, or to document an assertion, or to drive home an admonition." [16] Making a promise, under duress perhaps, with a secret determination not to keep it, the Louisiana Negro would say, "*Lalangue napas lezos*," which is to say, "the tongue has no bones." "A large majority of negro sayings . . . possess a chameleon power of changing hue according to the manner in which they are placed . . . the art of applying one proverb to many different situations is one in which the negro has no rival." [17]

That strange language or patois which takes its name from the Indian flavoring of ground sassafras leaves, the *gombo* of Louisiana, a mixture of French, Indian and African words, is supposed to have died out. (The original Indian word, *gombo*, meant the brown earth of the Mississippi prairies.) Yet I have heard — and very recently — New Orleans jazz players converse in fragments of this tongue. This was done partly for secrecy, and it was for this reason that neither English nor French was employed.

The Negro everywhere, while poetic, is primarily musical. "Poetry is likewise not lacking [in West Africa] though poetic

[16] Lafcadio Hearn: *Gombo Zhebes,* 1885.
[17] Ibid.

64

quality derives principally from a rich imagery; the association of poetry with song, moreover, is so intimate that it is not found as an independent form." [18] It is not surprising, therefore, to find the first Negro poetry in America in the work-songs and spirituals and then in the blues, with literary poetic creation, independent of music, not emerging as a strong Negro activity until a full 300 years after the first slaves came here.

The number of spirituals evolved during slavery was immense. Their creation was continuous. Any gathering of the devout in a small church, in open air services, or by a riverside for baptism, might see new ones arise in the spontaneous chanting of texts. Most were forgotten as soon as sung; others, remembered, became standard, although the variants of any one spiritual throughout the South would be almost as numerous as the churches.

Only a small proportion actually came directly from white hymns; many were influenced by them; the vast majority sprang from the native Negro creativeness. There is not, for example, only one *Swing Low, Sweet Chariot*. That sung today is a chance survival. The early version adopted by the Hampton Student Singers, as shown in the 1874 collection of their songs, is entirely different. A title by no means indicates a certain piece of music but is merely a text to which a spiritual has been improvised.

J. B. Towe writes of the creation of a spiritual, *En Dat Great Gittin'-up Mornin'*.

The student who brought it to us . . . has furnished all that he can remember of the almost interminable succession of verses, which he has heard sung for half an hour at a time, by the slaves in their midnight meetings in the woods. He gives the following interesting account of its origin:

"It was made by an old slave who knew nothing about letters or figures. He could not count the number of rails that he would split when he was tasked by his master to split 150 a day. But

[18] Herskovits, Melville J.: *The Myth of the Negro Past. op. cit.*

he tried to lead a Christian life, and he dreamed of the General Judgment . . . and then made a tune to it, and sang it in his cabin meetings." [19]

In the early creation of Afro-American music, a tune might perform both secular and religious duty. Many spirituals were used as work-songs. *Bright Sparkles in de Churchyard* was thus used by hands in the tobacco factories of Danville, Virginia; another, *I Hope my Mother Will be There*, came to be called "The Mayo Boys' Song" in Richmond from its habitual use in the Mayo Tobacco Factory.

Before beginning an analysis of the spiritual, we can make a partial list of Negro folk music in America prior to the blues and jazz:

Religious: A. Congregational.
      1. Preaching with responses.
      2. Congregational singing, the spirituals.
      3. Singing the spirituals, solo.
      4. "Holy" dancing.
      5. Ring shouts.

      B. Street singing, the revivalist.

Secular: A. Work-songs, (partial listing).
      1. Plantation and rural (choral).
         cotton picking
         hoeing, cotton chopping
         water songs
         plowing
         mule and ox driving
         chopping sugar cane
         quitting-time songs
      2. Various occupations, (choral).
         ax chopping (lumbering, etc.)
         sea chanties
         river-boat chants
         levee chanties
         railroad songs
         steel work

[19] Quoted in *Cabin and Plantation Songs, as sung by the Hampton Students,* 1874.

3. Various solitary occupations.
   hollers for many occupations
   street cries, vendor's chants and songs
   river-sounding calls

B. Dances.
   square dances, reels
   fiddle songs
   cake walks
   jigs and ragtime struts

C. Play-songs, especially children's.
   kissing games
   hiding games
   ring games
   dancing games
   lullabies

D. Ballads.
   narrative
   epic or legendary

Fortunately, there exists a considerable body of recorded material from which a study of these Negro folk-music forms may be made. It is very important to hear this music in actual performance or on records, not only because of the great variety in the improvisation but because the music is, from many aspects, unscoreable.

The following records, from the Library of Congress Archives and various commercial recording sources, illustrate various phases of congregational singing and services.

CITATION 6. *The Gambling Man,* by Rev. W. M. Mosely and Congregation.

This is Negro preaching with spontaneous congregational responses, shouted and chanted, bearing a direct relation to African antiphony. It is a typical example of the participative, spontaneous creation of a complex tonal-rhythmic piece. The preaching flows naturally into singing and, with the responses, is itself music, an improvised and chanted recitative. The preacher's phrases, like "Oh, I wonder where [is] the gamblin' man? " combine with a woman's chorus of high, clear,

Negroid timbre, that sings, part antiphonally, part polyphonally, in undulating lines of chain-fourths. Although rhythmic and improvisational, the music is not wildly excited but has an eerie, timeless detachment like that in African performance of an established ritual, centuries old. Only the drums are missing.

Negro services are notably unostentatious and strongly democratic, furnishing a free and joyous good time for all. They remind the thoughtful observer of what the earliest Christian services in Rome may have been like when the Christians needed then, as the Negroes have needed in America, to cling almost tribally together, a despised and ostracized minority.

The preaching and the prayers are informal and impassioned, chanted melodically and rhythmically rather than spoken prosaically. An inspiring section of the service is that given over to testimonials which, whether long and detailed or only a short "Praise the Lord," are followed by the testifier's leading off with a spiritual in which the congregation quickly joins with handclapping and singing. It is executed with remarkable effects of rhythm and polyphony, and the familiar moaned or shouted responses, "Amen," "Yes, Lord!" and the like. Sometimes the power is so strongly generated and so magnetically communicated that dancing begins quite spontaneously.

Frequently, one sees in the churches the mysterious phenomenon of possession which is a frequent concomitant of West African religious rites. With one worshipper, the possessed state comes on gradually; with another, the seizure may be instantaneous. In one case, it resembles a motionless and rigid catalepsy; in another, the person is vitalized into inspired action, dancing, singing, or uttering the sounds of spiritual possession. In such an activity the Negro follows the pattern which has enabled him to avoid the romantic and the sentimental in his artistic creations, the pattern that leads him to express deep emotion in a catharsis of rhythmic action comprised in sound and movement.

It would seem to the close observer that the subject's consciousness focuses upon a different field or plane of experience than the one we are accustomed to call normal. In cases of active possession (with dancing, etc.) this new focusing occurs while the subject simultaneously keeps in contact with his surroundings. The state of possession might be compared roughly with the print of a photographic double exposure or, more accurately, with the projection of a double-exposed cinema film.

During possession, something may occur similar to an involuntary suspension of the inner-psychological conflicts of the subject, thus producing a harmonization. This could explain, at least roughly, the refreshed state of the subject when he returns from the most active possession to fully resumed use of his normal faculties. Possession, in any event, would seem definitely not to be identified, as it tentatively has been, either with hysteria or mild epilepsy. When active, it leaves intact — even seems to heighten — physical and mental power and accuracy; the after-effects are generally observed to be beneficial rather than harmful.

I recall vividly an evening service in a San Francisco Negro church where the singing began with hand-clapping and the percussive tinkle of tambourines throughout the congregation. The small and nondescript orchestra [20] participated, and soon numbers of the communicants, adults and children, were dancing in the pews and in the aisles. After perhaps ten minutes, the pastor and, one by one, the elders, began to dance on the platform. The last, a white-haired man, reached under his chair, pulled a fiddle from its case, and began to play while swaying, totteringly but rhythmically. For about twenty minutes the music, like a tidal wave, rose in intensity and fervor. As spontaneously as it began, the singing stopped, and, joyous and refreshed, the congregation took up the service again. The total impression was that of a vast and vital creativity, rich, august, and powerful, solemn and joyous, wildly reverent and

[20] Drums, piano, trumpet, saxophone, guitar, and ukulele

69

infinitely tender. Only a complex and deeply serious music could produce such an effect.

The following records illustrate this phenomenal sort of community worship and thanksgiving in song. Although recent, they are similar to the singing that went on prior to jazz and may, therefore, be used to trace its origins. Some of them are compared here directly with African records.

CITATION 7. *I'm Gonna Lift up a Standard for my King*, sung and played by the Congregation of the Church of God and Christ at Moorhead Plantation near Lulu, Mississippi, (1941). (Voices, hand-clapping and guitar, foot-stomping in latter stages.)

This truly remarkable record in the store of recorded folk music is typical of the Negro church singing unrecorded throughout America. Its noteworthy qualities are in a norm or average which anyone may hear, on any Wednesday or Sunday evening, in a thousand humble Negro churches. The respectful and interested white spectator is almost always welcome at these services. This record illustrates *holy dancing* as well as congregational spiritual singing.

A rhythmic, hand-clapped pattern or ostinato on the offbeat is set in the first measure and immediately the surging momentum of perpetual syncopation is released. The singing is free and varied, wild but controlled; it is chanted chorally, with much unison and octaval coincidence, combined with the freest polyphony into which voices enter at will on varying notes and with sporadic, variant melodic phrases. Notable is the almost complete lack of harmony. There is a sense of unfolding form evolved unconsciously in a logical and implicit pattern. Episodes develop; by mutual consent, the momentarily inspired individual is accorded the opportunity for a solo; mutually, the group closes about his last notes with a new communal outburst. The steady building up of urgency is characteristic.

The dancing is clearly portrayed in the episodic arrangement. The hymn, probably 16 bars in length, is chanted in full polyphony by the whole congregation, evidently to incite and encourage the dancer. Alternating with each of these full chants, the dancer herself sings in a *dirty-toned* voice, hoarse, expressive, exciting, very *hot* in feeling, and amazingly like a man's voice or the hottest trumpet possible. Her song, wild, urgent, possessed, soaring over the inexorable, beating rhythm, seems to collide in midair with calls, shouts, and exhortations. After a number of these repetitions, building even more urgently in excitement, the singing largely ceases and the dancing goes on to calls and shouts entering irregularly over the rhythm.

There is the most gradual and imperceptible acceleration throughout. The amount of control exercised in all this apparently wild excitement, is best shown by saying that the music which begins at $\downharpoonleft = 176$, ends [21] five minutes later, after a very gradual accelerando, at $\downharpoonleft = 194$. The atmosphere is surcharged with feeling; it is at once dark and magic, ominous and exultant.

The variety of timbres through all the gamut of expressiveness — clear, piercing, strident, pure, dirty — is utterly and remarkably African. As part of the development, the rhythmic pattern grows more complex: the stomping of feet on the floor accents the strong beats (1 and 3) while the hand-clapping (each clap is a quick triplet) becomes duple, striking all beats while accenting the weak ones (2 and 4). This record can be profitably compared with:

CITATION 8. *Bahutu Songs and Dances,* a record made in the Belgian Congo by the Denis-Roosevelt Expedition which produced the memorable film, *Dark Rapture.*

In Section 2 of this record, just as in *I'm Gonna Lift up a Standard,* a hand-clapped, rhythmic ostinato is immediately set up. The ostinato patterns are essentially the same although, in the Moorhead record, they undergo a number of mutations.

There is great similarity, too, in the vocal timbres, although, in the African example, the voices chant in unison and in a set rhythmic pattern with little or no rhythmic interweaving of polyphonic voices. Nevertheless, the Moorhead record derives

---

[21] More accurate: the recording ends. These performances often last fifteen to twenty minutes, then stop suddenly with disregard for formal ending.

its polyphony from African sources and not from European music which has had no comparable polyphony for centuries. *I'm Gonna Lift up a Standard* should be compared with another African record:

CITATION 9. *Circumcision Ritual of the Babira,* another Denis-Roosevelt record from the Belgian Congo.

The mutations of rhythm within a definite meter, so notable in the singing of the Moorhead Congregation, have a striking counterpart in the first part of the Babira record. Here the meter is established immediately by the drums and a series of variations develops in the same spirit as in *I'm Gonna Lift up a Standard.* Despite different basic meters, both records show the tendency to constant mutation. This tendency is ingrained in the race — is, indeed, a principle — and, basic in all Negro musical art, is of prime importance in jazz. Although it follows a variation scheme, *A, A', A'',* et cetera, that in Western music is considered a simple one, in Negro usage it often takes on a high degree of complexity. Improvisation, the basis of Afro-American music, is set forth in a constant series of variations on a theme. These are fourfold in nature, involving melody, tone, rhythm and instrumentation, the latter including varying combinations of human voices as well as instruments. In vocal improvisation, variations occur in verbal phrases, and the changes in word or syllable length and emphasis alter the idea or imagery. This produces a fifth type of mutation that may be termed poetic variation.

Other congregational records, illustrating important points of cultural survival from Africa or anticipations of jazz, are listed and discussed in Appendix G, p. 355.

A fine example of the religious dance called the ring-shout is found in the following record:

CITATION 10. *Run, Old Jeremiah,* sung by Joe Washington Brown and Austin Coleman, alternate leaders, at Jennings, Louisiana, (1934). This record is a very important one.

The ring-shout, earliest Afro-American religious dance, still survives in isolated Southern communities. As in Africa, the dancers, never crossing their legs (this, to the religious, would constitute dancing), move in a counterclockwise circle which presents only the right shoulders to the Deity. The feet, hands, and voices set up formidable polyrhythms. It is interesting to note that the forbidding of musical instruments in many churches, as in this case, virtually restores the African drum and chorus form.

The African quality of a performance like this would have been surprising in this country at almost any time. In 1934 it is amazing, especially from the point of view of the theory that there are no Africanisms left in American Negro culture. One can argue that this sort of phenomenal survival may be found only in isolated rural communities; that it is no longer possible among sophisticated Negroes. Such a view appears to be supported by the Negroes' obvious adaptability to non-Negroid customs. And yet in the heart of the New York Harlem, the largest and most sophisticated Negro community in the world, one can hear church services of a surprisingly African stamp.

Run, Old Jeremiah is on-the-spot creation of a rhythmic-musical form achieved by pouring the ingredients of deep feeling and strong communal enthusiasm and excitement into the ever-existing and ready mold of the call-and-response form. This antiphony has a deep social significance. It is the archetypal expression of the way in which the Negro tends to live. Its inclusion of all in the participation is profoundly democratic; its acceptance of the necessity of a leader is realistically so. Both the possibility of changes in leaders (as we see it happen in this record, when the first becomes possessed) and the free, individual way in which the group is allowed to respond to, and comment upon, his exhortations, are deep expressions of democratic functioning. Most significant is the consciousness of a commonly felt concept of pre-existent form which operates to ensure the participation of all, while at the same time it limits the contribution of each only by its ultimate consideration as a just part of the whole.

In *Run, Old Jeremiah* the leader improvises lines in a sort of free poetic style, often repeating one a number of times for emphasis or while thinking of a line to follow.

> *I've got a rock.*
> *You got a rock.*
> *Rock is death.*
>
> . . . . .
>
> *O my Lord.*
>
> . . . . .
>
> *Run here, Jeremiah.*
> *I must go*
> *On my way.*
> *Who's that ridin' the chariot?*
>
> . . . . .
>
> *One mornin'*
> *Before the evening*
> *Sun was goin' down*
> *Behind them western hills*
> *Old number 12*
> *Comin' down the track.*
> *See that black smoke!*
> *See that engineer!*
> *Tol' that old engineer*
> *Ring his ol' bell*
> *With his hand.*
>
> . . . . .
>
> *Ol' fireman told,*
> *Told that engineer,*
> *Ring your black bell,*
> *Ding, ding, ding,*
> *Ding, ding, ding, ding.*
>
> . . . . .
>
> *I was travelin'.*
> *I was ridin'*
> *Over there.*
> *Ol' engineer*
> *This is the chariot*
> *This is the chariot.*

Each line is picked up by the congregation and tossed back in free, urgent antiphony; the calls of the leader are echoed or responded to with wails that fall downward, like bodies to the earth. The development of antiphony, from ordered call-and-response to free overlapping phrases, that is, into polyphony, is wonderfully illustrated here.

The evocation of the Dark Continent is profound and nocturnal. It is as if these people were lifted bodily from a poor country church in Louisiana and deposited on an African plain or in an African forest, where, long ago and in just this way, their ancestors had danced and chanted, not to Jesus, but to Ogun or to Shango.

Melody and harmony are things unheard of, things unneeded. Pure sound, spurting up out of unconscious life, capriciously consonant or fortuitously dissonant, seems to form a primordial, moving music enacted as mysteriously as the beginnings of man.

The dance moves like a tide gathering momentum and speed in a constant acceleration, the recording beginning at $\downharpoonright = 126$ and ending at $\downharpoonright = 166$. The African tendency to gradual acceleration contrasts with the equally African predilection for a fixed tempo. The latter is almost unfailingly characteristic of jazz where the beat is tied to the requirements of group social dancing. In both cases, there occurs a build-up of urgency.[22]

In all cases rhythmic complexity tends to increase progressively, polyrhythms enter, and rhythmic enunciation clarifies into patterns more clipped and incisive. The last half-inch of this record is in overrhythms so complex that the mind gropes for the basic concept or combination which will make order out of the seeming confusion.[23]

Inner-rhythms and overrhythms are to be heard in profusion in *Run, Old Jeremiah*, the former throughout in the amazing

----

[22] There is a phase in African music as well as in some American Negro music, including jazz, that is in a lyric and relaxed mood, as in the *slow blues.*

[23] Early notators of native African music faced this problem, conditioned by the absence of such polyrhythms in Western music and without any a priori knowledge of the rhythmic principles involved. Their attempts to render African polyrhythm in one basic meter instead of the concurrent two or more meters, led them astray into a notation hopelessly complex and confusing, involving the needless use of symbols to indicate rests and displaced accents.

and unpredictable shifting of accents, the latter in a form related directly to the African drum polyrhythms. Notably, these polyrhythms are accomplished by the same people, each of whom stomps, claps, and shouts in three separate rhythms. This voluntary action is relaxed and unstrained and sounds as natural as the involuntary polyrhythms of a man who walks in one rhythm while he talks in another and his heart beats in still another.

Spiritual singing by the small group is well illustrated by the following:

CITATION 11. *Jesus Goin' To Make Up My Dying Bed*, sung by Mitchell's Christian Singers, a quartet of male Negro singers from Kinston, North Carolina. This group barnstorms through the South and the men [24] frequently sing Negro spirituals in the Negro manner, not in the concert-hall manner of Robeson or Marian Anderson, or in the equally Europeanized manner of the Fisk Jubilee Singers. If their singing seems somewhat polished, this effect derives from the classic precision of all good Negro music for the singing is truly African in feeling and method.

Jesus Goin' To Make Up My Dying Bed is sung with great syncopation and shifting of the accent to unexpected beats and abounds in inner-rhythms and overrhythms. The melody is rephrased in a manner distinctly African as well as characteristic of jazz.

The words of this spiritual are in the simple, earthy poetry of the Negro, full of graphic images drawn from his world. The idea centers around the railroad train, the omnipresent train that haunts his dreams, the fiery chariot that will carry him to better times, to greener fields, and even, on a phantom trestle, over the River to Heaven. His dying bed is a Pullman berth, which Jesus, the porter, makes up for him. Friendly God, in the humble black man's own shape, comes to perform this final act

---

[24] Wilder Hobson writes in *American Jazz Music* (New York: 1939): "Brown has recently been a truckdriver, and Davis a tobacco-factory worker; David runs an ice and coal business and Bryant is a mason."

of mercy, as touching and as tragic as the Biblical washing of feet. He does this to erase the Negro's servitude and shame!

> *Oh, let the train run easy*
> *Hallelujah.*
> *I'm goin' to heaven in the morning*
> *Jesus is comin';*
> *God knows*
> *He's goin' to make up my dyin' bed.*

A scoring of the first two choruses will be found in Ex. 9, back of book.

Music of this character is so resistant to notation that this score must be considered no more than an approximation, a sort of good shorthand, of the actual performance. It is fairly accurate in rendering the rhythm, but the magnificent timbres and the smooth glissandi cannot be shown at all, nor can the microtonal variations of pitch which abound in all real Negro music. The Negro characteristically flats certain tones in the quarter, eighth and even sixteenth degree and perhaps less, while varying this flatting by portamenti or by undulations. The constant shifting of accents, with the resulting inner-rhythms, are likewise nearly impossible to render. It is to be doubted whether any readable notation can be devised to render such characteristic subtlety and variation. This emphasizes the necessity for hearing records or actual performances.

Solo singing of the spiritual in the Negro church may be by any member of the congregation, by the minister or an elder, or by a visiting pastor. Accompaniment may be by piano, a small reed organ, guitar, or any instrumental combination available. There is no great difference in style between the singing of the church soloist and that of the wandering street evangelist with his guitar. Both have the same fervor, tend to the same expressive roughness; both are highly syncopated and rhythmic; finally, they both tend to improvise variations on the melody. As a rule, they simplify the melody to a final starkness which frequently, like that of the blues, derives from the pentachord and shows a deep disinterest in harmony.

A magnificent example of this sort of singing is to be found on a Library of Congress twelve-inch record (AAFS–47), *Ain't No Grave Can Hold My Body Down*. Bozie Sturdivant sings with the Congregation of Silent Grove Baptist Church at Clarksdale, Mississippi. The singer's improvisations, quite evidently produced in a state of possession, are darkly African, phrased in remarkable gliding portamenti and abrupt changes of register. Covering three full octaves, the voice varies from clear to dirty timbres, from open voice to strident falsetto. A notable feature is the lack of antiphony. The congregation moans continually in low chords and, the implacable stomping of feet is a veritable recrudescence of the African drum battery.

Solo singing of the spirituals with the singer's own instrumental accompaniment is illustrated on another Library of Congress Record (AAFS–50), *Meet Me In Jerusalem*, *When I Lay My Burden Down*, *In New Jerusalem*, and *Steal Away*. The singer, Turner Junior Johnson, renders the hymns in a voice of indescribably beautiful, rough texture. His harmonica answers each phrase antiphonally, its mournful, reedy tones duplicating almost exactly the timbres and vibrato of the voice. The tempo, of an almost dirge-like slowness, projects a sad fatefulness that is heightened by the muffled foot-stomping. There is a close connection between this solo hymn singing and the sung blues.

Another record (Circle R–3012), *I Couldn't Hear Nobody Pray*, is a fine example of the authentic early "Jubilee" hymn singing. It is sung by Sister Berenice Phillips with instrumental and hand-clapped background.

The following record is an outstanding example of street singing:

CITATION 12. *Jesus Make up My Dyin' Bed*. The singer, Blind Willie Johnson, was a guitar-playing, singing evangelist, a ragged, blind character of the New Orleans streets. The version he sings, a very different one from that of the Mitchell's Christian Singers cited before, is even more profoundly African. The singer's voice is rough and husky and, though repellent to ears accustomed to *pure* tone, is deeply expressive of a whole area and range of human feeling inexpressible in any other way.

Blind Willie animates his guitar and, with life breathed into it, it is his companion. The guitar, consecrated like drums in the age-old magic of primitive people, and Blind Willie are really two singers. In the record grooves are frustrated lone-liness, hungry poverty, fanatical devotion to heaven, and the ascetic waiting for it. The singing, strongly rhythmic, is the call-and-response, bare and clear, in which the singer is both leader and responding choir. He enunciates cruel and peremp-tory phrases in a voice harsh and burred; in one that is thickly rough and crooning, he answers with pathetic downward me-lodic turns that are like appeasements, conciliations, solaces, and pardons. Throughout, the guitar, sweet and ringing, weaves a polyphony with the singer. These are, by implication, the voices of many people.

So supremely natural are the Negro's gifts of rhythmic and melodic expression, that he is either largely unaware of them or ascribes them to his own sphere of activity. So, though the music of the church singer is like the blues, and that of the con-gregation is one of the sources of jazz, nevertheless, to the religious Negro such kindred music is *sinful* or *worldly*. Yet all are essentially the same music, African in form, evolving in this country with the inclusion of European material.

If the religionist does not perceive his own fervor and rever-ence in jazz and the blues, if the jazz player does not find the hot qualities of his music in church singing, it is because of the functional character of Negro music. Relating intimately to the uses and acts of daily life, it may seem remarkably alike in all its forms to observers from a different culture. But within the culture these forms are explicit and differentiated. Each is colored with the overtones of its particular activity. Gravity, ominousness, or gaiety comes to reside in the music as actually as sadness resides in our minor mode or sanguineness in the major.

We have traced the development of Afro-American music along the lines of its continuity from Africa down through two hundred and fifty years of slave work-songs and spirituals. To arrive at jazz, we must first complete our outline with the remaining elements of the Negro ballads and the songs the little dark children sing at play.

4.

along the roads

THE NEGRO is a natural maker of ballads, that folk minstrelsy whose poet-composers are almost always unknown, whose songs, composed bit by bit by scores of humble bards, spread and grow like vines. The ballad sprouts from the soil, its tendrils spread in the sun, its seeds travel on the wind. Long after the end of the ballad-making period in England, the old English songs were preserved in the mountains and on the plantations of our own South, by the white descendants of the Scotch and the Cavaliers who settled there and by the Negro slaves who took over their masters' songs. In one place the old ballads remain pure. In another they have been altered, particularly by Negro singers, in that process of change which marks the ballad so long as it is a living thing.

"In the early days on the plantations in the South, when books and newspapers were less plentiful than now, songs formed a larger part of the social life than they do at present. At the 'great house' the loved old ballads would be sung over and over, till the house servants, being quick of memory and of apt musical ear, would learn them, then pass them on in turn to their brethren of the fields. This process would be altogether oral, since the slaves were not taught to read or write,[1] save in exceptional cases. . . .

"By cabin firesides . . . the old songs would be learned . . . as part of their natural heritage to be handed down to their children and their children's children. Such a survival among the Negroes was remarkable, far more so than song-preserva-

[1] This was a deliberate withholding of education to prevent dissatisfaction and revolt. (Author's note.)

81

tion among the whites, who in many instances kept old ballads by writing them down in notebooks, and learning them from old broadsides or keepsake volumes; while the Negroes had none of these aids, but had to sing each song as they learned it from hearing others sing it, and must remember it of themselves. And yet they cherished the old songs and had their own versions of them." [2]

We find Negro versions of many old-world ballads. Among these are the famous and beautiful *Barbara Allen, The Maid Freed From the Gallows,* (called the *Hangman's Tree* in American versions), *Frog Went A-Courtin',*[3] the horse-racing ballad, *Skew Ball,* and many others. Among contemporary white American ballads which the Negro has adapted into his own versions, is the well-known epic of the brave engineer, *Casey Jones.*

With his love of dramatic action, his aptitude for mimicry, and his tendency toward many-meaninged symbolism, the Negro invented many ballads of his own. Some of these seem incomplete and fragmentary as narrative poems, but Negro renditions must be actually heard. In them the impersonality of the traditional ballad is forsaken; they are acting-pieces set to music; every device of facial expression and bodily gesture is used; there are nuances of meaning, shades of suggestion, and a great amount of direct communication which tacitly relies upon a store of common knowledge.

Examples of original Negro ballads are *Ole Mars'r Had a Yaller Gal* (from slavery days), *Cotton-Eyed Joe,* the famous *Frankie and Albert,*[4] *Stagolee, The Grey Goose,* and *Mr. Boll Weevil.*

Frankie and Albert, the narrative of a Negro woman and her trifling, unfaithful husband, is widely known. It is the prototype of Petunia and her troubles with Little Joe in the light opera, *Cabin in the Sky.* But the ballad's denouement is not the opera's nick-of-time repentance. The ends of simple justice,

---

[2] Scarborough, Dorothy: *On the Trail of Negro Folk Songs. op. cit.*

[3] Registered November 21, 1580 in the Register of the London Company of Stationers.

[4] Also, variously, *Frankie and Johnny, Pauly, Lilly, Franky Baker,* etc.

or vengeance at least, are effected by Frankie's smoking six-shooter. The dying Albert, his luck played out, is left to the higher and final justice of St. Peter.

> *Rubber-tired carriage,*
> *Kansas City hack,*
> *Took poor Albert to the cemetery*
> *But forgot to bring him back.*
> *Oh, he was my man,*
> *But he done me wrong!*

Stagolee, the ballad of the legendary bravo, shows the Negro's revolt and his blind attempt at revenge by becoming a "bad-man." In this ballad, probably based on the life of an actual person, his lurid adventures are melodramatically recounted to their end in his death from another's bullets. Stagolee, although an outlaw, is the legendary hero of the earlier slave revolts, leading forlorn hope blindly and singlehandedly.[5]

Comparable with *Stagolee,* is the ballad by the great jazz pianist, Jelly Roll Morton, about the New Orleans bad man, Aaron Harris. The only recorded version of this ballad is in the Library of Congress Archives, as played and sung by Morton.

Mr. Boll Weevil, a narrative about the cottongrowers' enemy, the weevil, is, in a wider sense, an epic in which the Negro personifies, in the elusive and unyielding antagonist, his own indomitable racial spirit and his age-old search for a home. This is magic animation of the beetle with human life or even with the divine life of a tribal deliverer god; it is transference of the Negro's tribulation to an invincible foe imagined as the Negro himself. The ballad is rife with pathos but implicit with hope.

> *'Member one time I taken a boll weevil. Put him in a bottle an' stopped it wid a cork. In a week I looked at it an' it was still lively. I don' believe nobody can kill a boll weevil. An' de farmer was doin' ev'ything in de worl' he could to him . . .*[6]

[5] Parts of the *Stagolee* ballad later became *Stack O'Lee Blues.* A fine recorded version is sung by the great blues singer, Ma Rainey, on Paramount No. 12357, recently reissued on the Signature label.

[6] Lomax, John A. and Alan: *Negro Folk Songs as Sung by Lead Belly, op. cit.*

The psychological transference is clearly expressed in this version from Texas: [7]

> *Fahmah say to de weevil,*
> *"Whut makes yore head so red,"*
> *Weevil say to de fahmah,*
> *"It's a wondah ah ain't dead,*
> *   Lookin' foh a home, lookin' foh a home!"*
>
> *Nigger say to de weevil,*
> *"Ah'll throw you in de hot sand."*
> *Weevil say to de nigger,*
> *"Ah'll stand it like a man.*
> *   Ah'll have a home, ah'll have a home!"*
>
> *Says de Captain to de Mistis,*
> *"What do you think ob dat?*
> *Dis Boll Weevil done make a nes'*
> *Inside my Sunday hat;*
> *   He'll have a home, he'll have a home!"*

By the time the weevil begins to prey on the Captain (the white master), he has become the victorious black man himself or his supernatural champion. Later, in *Bo-Weavil Blues*, the weevil is the living symbol of deliverance, taken for granted, to whom the singer can address her own personal woes.[8]

Another famous ballad, perhaps of Negro origin and often used as a work-song, is *John Henry*. This legendary character [9] appears in dozens of ballad versions from West Virginia to Florida and to Mississippi, dying from the blows of a "nine-pound hammer" or on the gallows with a rope around his neck. An even earlier hammer-song is the spiritual *Norah*, quoted by Dorothy Scarborough and concerning which she writes: [10]

[7] Scarborough, Dorothy: *On the Trail of Negro Folk Songs, op. cit.*

[8] *Bo-Weavil Blues,* by Ma Rainey, on Paramount records Nos. 12080 and 12603.

[9] There was a John Harvey, a West Virginian known as the strongest steel-driller ever to work there. He was murdered in the way depicted in the ballad and this event is supposedly the origin of the song. A good version of the *John Henry* song is to be found on a Library of Congress record, AAFS–15, 10-inch.

[10] Scarborough, Dorothy: *On the Trail of Negro Folk Songs, op. cit.*

"Here is a hammer-song that has to do with a more ancient event that John Henry's untimely taking-off. It is a spiritual adapted to use as a work-song, for the antiphonal questions and responses mark the rhythmic strokes of the hammer — which tool here is given power of thought and speech."

> *Norah was a hundred and twenty years buildin' de ark of God,*
> *And ev'ry time his hammer ring, Norah cried, "Amen!"*
> *Well, who build de ark*
> *Norah build it.*
> *Hammer keep a-ringin', said, "Norah build it!"*
> *Well, who build de ark?*
> *Norah build it.*
> *Who build de ark?*
> *Norah build it.*
> *Who build de ark?*
> *Norah build it,*
>   *Cut his timber down.*

As in the work-songs, Lead Belly furnishes many of the best recorded versions of Negro ballads. These are to be found both in the Library of Congress and on commercial records. His singing and style are almost invariably authentic.

A version of *The Noble Skewball* is available under a variant title:

CITATION 13. *Stewball,* sung by Lead Belly with the Golden Gate Quartet.

This version alternates verse and chorus. Each verse is sung by Lead Belly with chanted responses by the male quartet; all the singers join in the choruses. Where Lead Belly elsewhere has presented the straight version of this ballad, here he shows it, not only in its normal course of folk transformation, but also as a white ballad being transformed into African antiphony. Lead Belly becomes the leader; the quartet furnishes the choral responses which at the same time imitate guitar chords.

The singing is Negroid and the melody is fitted into the type of inner-rhythmic pattern which occurs with frequency in jazz and is called the stomp. In this instance, the pattern is formed in a rhythm of three-over-two. This, like other stomp patterns, is directly derived from guitar and banjo playing. (See Ex. 10, back of book.)

The *Grey Goose* is a fine example of the Negro's epic ballad, one used on occasion as a work-song. A good and full version is the following:

CITATION 14. *Grey Goose*, sung by Lead Belly with the Golden Gate Quartet.

> *It was one Sunday mornin'*
>   *Lawd, lawd, lawd!* [11]
> *The preacher went a-huntin'!*
> *He carried 'long his shotgun.*
> *Well, 'long come a grey goose.*
> *The gun went off boo-loo [zulu?]*
> *And down come a grey goose.*
> *He was six weeks a-fallin'!*
> *And my wife and yo' wife,*
> *They give him feather-pickin'.*
> *They was six weeks a-pickin',*
> *And they put him on to parboil.*
> *He was six weeks a-boilin',*
> *And they put him on the table,*
> *And the knife wouldn't cut him,*
> *Aw, the fork wouldn't stick him.*
> *And they throwed him in the hog-pen,*
> *And the hog couldn't eat him,*
> *Aw, he broke the hog's teeth out.*
> *They tak'n him to the saw mill,*
> *And the saw wouldn't cut him.*
> *Aw, he broke the saw's teeth out.*
> *An' the last time I seed him,*
> *He was flyin' cross de ocean*
> *With a long string o' goslin's.*
> *An' they all goin', "Quack, quack."*

Here is the triumph of the man with dark skin: it is clearly not vengeance, for a *grey* goose is shot, not a *white* one.

The development of African Negro music through antiphony into polyphony is clearly discernible in the singing of *Grey Goose*. We encounter here, in a single song, the sequence of

[11] This response by the quartet follows each line by Lead Belly.

development that characterizes the whole history of African music.

The Golden Gate singers start by responding to Lead Belly's lines with harmonized antiphonal responses, "Lawd, lawd, lawd!" which are distinctly separate from his lines. Very soon they begin to hold the responses past the beginning of the leader's lines and African polyphony, in its most rudimentary form, has begun. With the line, "The knife wouldn't cut him," the responses begin to come in before the end of Lead Belly's lines, and overlapping occurs from both ends of the line, as rising water climbs up both sides of a dry sandbar. With the line, "Aw, he broke the saw's teeth out," complete overlapping begins: the water has closed over the top of the sandy mound. Simultaneously, the response lines begin to lose their strictly harmonic division into set chords and separate into independent melodic lines woven together polyphonically. With the line, "An' the last time I seed him," leader's voice and chorus sing continually together in a free Negroid polyphony with the leading line tossed along like a piece of flotsam on the swirling current. With this — so close to jazz form — the development of Negro singing into band music is clear.

The wild and compelling quality of Lead Belly's singing, an almost hypnotic power which he projects even in his most tranquil moments, acts like a reagent on the sophisticated veneer of the Negroes who sing with him, dissolving it and exposing the true racial character. Prophetic of jazz, this singing is also a strong reversion to the African spirit. These singers are literally *sent* into an unconscious projection of their racial music which forms anew from a growing excitement that verges on the trance. In three minutes' time, from first note to last, the reversion is surprisingly complete. In Africa, Lead Belly in all probability would have been a priest using his powers in sanctioned ritual, dealing openly and directly with dark magic.

In this same way, a perfunctory or studied performance in the later and decadent period of jazz is sometimes galvanized by a hot and imperious trumpet, suddenly inspired, which sweeps the other players out of set arrangement into unrehearsed, hot, weaving polyphony. To the uninitiated observer, particularly one deeply versed in the ways of our Western music, this occurrence is apt to seem a wild and unaccountable departure from order and sanity, as though the players were suddenly seized by hysteria. To believe this, is to misunderstand jazz and the spirit and processes of African improvisational art. What actually happens is not a descent into chaos. It is progress from an order that is artificial to the Negro to one basic and truly creative. It is a sudden movement, like a shudder of relief when one is done with a lie, at once a liberation and a reaffirmation of integrity recaptured.

A section of wholly delightful and diverting Negro folk music is to be found in the children's songs. These have the naïve charm of all children's songs, which everywhere preserve primitive elements of culture. They stress dancing, and have a syncopated, rhythmic piquancy and a racial warmth peculiarly their own. They reward study by revealing a wealth of surviving Africanisms.

The most remarkable feature of the singing and dancing of Negro children, one never missing from their music, is rhythmic ability. Young Negroes are rhythmically accurate and imaginative; they are able, without aberration, to maintain a beat that may speed up but does so by a smooth and almost imperceptible gradation. They are able to maintain this beat in the midst of the most varied and baffling of displaced accents. They can add other beats at will in a rhythmic counterpoint difficult even to analyze. They have the ability, finally, to wander into independent rhythms during which the basic beat disappears only to reappear suddenly, showing that it has been remembered all the time.

In countless Negro churches, I have seen mere infants clap their hands or stand in the pews dancing in rhythms that are simple but amazingly sharp and elastic. I have seen a Negro piano teacher instructing a child who responded with an instantaneous grasp of the necessity of accuracy and the inner, pulsating life of rhythm. The marked contrast of this phenomenal rhythmic ability of the Negro child with its comparative lack among white children, poses again the scientific problem discussed in Appendix D. Is not the Negroid rhythmic skill a racial attribute?

How can all of these wide discrepancies develop out of the common environment of black and white children? For is environment only in the home? The sounds of machinery, the rushing locomotive, the purring automobile engine, as well as the host of rhythmic patterns in nature — rain, wind, the repeated calls of bird songs — are in the common environment of all Americans.

It is obvious that rhythmic ability can be *learned* by many whites. Yet even so, when observing a dancing class of white children or listening to young white violinists or pianists, one is impressed by the weak rhythmic sense generally displayed. Even when listening to Gene Krupa's drumming in his best period, to Frank Melrose' Negroid piano playing, to Fred Astaire's tap dancing, one comes to the reluctant conclusion that the learned rhythmic skill is just that, a learned thing falling into repeated patterns, lacking to a marked degree the relaxation, the unpredictable nuance, and the expressive, improvisational inspiration of the Negro.

The current scientific theory, as we have noted, is to discount inherited instincts and abilities, to credit environment with such musical characteristics repeated in generations of one family or found repeatedly in one race. How does it stand up in the face of strong contrary evidence?

To believe that one race has a particular set of aptitudes, another race a different set, that these aptitudes are inborn, only affected in degree by environment, is to clarify the way that the arts of each race begin with, and, over a long period of time, come to express fully in an aesthetic form, these native aptitudes.

A Library of Congress record offers no less than twelve examples of Negro children's songs. Descriptions of several follow.

CITATION 15. *American Negro Children's Songs.*

a. *All Hid?*, sung by Hettie Godfrey at Livingston, Alabama, (1940).

b. *Little Girl, Little Girl,* led by Ora Dell Graham, with children, at Drew, Mississippi, (1940).

c. *Pullin' the Skiff,* led by Ora Dell Graham, with children, at Drew, Mississippi, (1940).

d. *Old Uncle Rabbit,* sung by Katherine and Christine Shipp at Byhalia, Mississippi, (1939).

e. *Sea Lion Woman,* sung by Katherine and Christine Shipp at Byhalia, Mississippi, (1939).

f. *Shortenin' Bread,* led by Ora Dell Graham, with children, at Drew, Mississippi, (1940).

g. *Poor Little Johnny,* sung by Harriet McClintock, at Livingston, Alabama, (1940).

h. *Gon' Knock John Booker to the Low Ground,* sung by Harriet McClintock, at Livingston, Alabama, (1940).

All Hid? is a rhyme used for counting in hide-and-go-seek. Its chanted, rhythmic, undulant line is very much like the street cries which in turn resemble the improvisation of the African leader, and it is similarly free from even implied harmony. A characteristic Africanism is found in the partial flatting (not a full semitone) of certain notes of the scale. The words printed in capital letters in the following verse indicate notes flatted in this way:

> *All HID?*
> *All hid?*
> *Five, ten, fifteen, twenty,*
> *'S ALL hid?*
>
> *Way down yonder by the devil's town,*
> *Devil knocked MY daddy DOWN.*
> *Is ALL hid?*

"*Little Girl, Little Girl* stems from a very old chasing game known as *Old Witch.* This game is part of the same tradition as *The Hawk and Chickens,* variants of which have been recorded in many European languages. Yet in the present version a steam locomotive appears, furnishing a syncopated refrain for a little fancy stepping by the players." [12] The omnipresent image of the locomotive that haunts the Negro, asleep and awake! This record, chanted like the street cries, is a perfect example of the African call-and-response antiphony in an American Negro song. The leader improvises and the chorus responds in a set phrase.

Leader: *Little girl, little girl?*
Chorus: *Yes, ma'am.*
             Did you go downtown?
               Yes, ma'am.
             Did you see my brown?
               Yes, ma'am.
             Did he buy me any shoes?
               Yes, ma'am.
             Stockin's too?
               Yes, ma'am.
             Put him on the train?
               Yes, ma'am.
             The bell ring?
               Yes, ma'am.
             Whichaway did he go?
   All: *Choo-choo!*
             All night long
             Choo-choo!
             All night long.

Pullin' the Skiff is chanted or declaimed in very syncopated *raggy* style, with the lines falling into four-quarter bars, accompanied by the stomping of the children's feet on the offbeats

                        I went downstairs
                        To milk my cow;
                        I made a mistake
                        And I milked that sow,
                        Just a-pullin' the skiff.

[12] Alan Lomax in the descriptive leaflet that accompanies the record.

91

> *Tomorrow, tomorrow,*
> *Tomorrow never come;*
> *Tomorrow, tomorrow,*
> *Tomorrow's in the barn.*

> *An-a humph-unh, an-a humph-unh,*
> *an-a humph-unh, humph-unh, humph-unh.*

The children break out in a little silvery storm of laughter
like the song of swamp frogs through a cabin door just opened.

Old Uncle Rabbit is a form of call-and-response similar to
Little Girl, Little Girl. This type of song relates clearly to the
West African animal myths around which much musical and
narrative lore has gathered.

> Leader: *Ol' Uncle Rabbit*
> Chorus: *Chool-dy, chool-dy*
> *Got a habit,*
> *Chool-dy, chool-dy*
> *In my garden*
> *Chool-dy, chool-dy*
> *Eatin' all my cabbage*
> *Chool-dy, chool-dy,*
>
> *An' if I live,*
> *Chool-dy, chool-dy,*
> *To see nex' fall,*
> *Chool-dy, chool-dy,*
> *I ain' gon' raise*
> *Chool-dy, chool-dy,*
> *No cabbage at all.*
> *Chool-dy, chool-dy.*

The rhythmic quality of the responses and the regularity of
their spacing suggest a work-song, perhaps used while hoeing
the cabbage patch. If so, the promise to plant no cabbage next
fall would be a pleasant prospect to the working children.

Sea Lion Woman is a song very African in form and feeling.
The musical quality and the haunting sadness of the voices cannot be described. The words are cryptic, seem to hide a riddle;
the short song is an enigmatic rune, full of a forgotten sorcery.

It disposes the listener to believe in racial memory, a memory that half remembers, half forgets.

The metrical division is extraordinary and similar in intent to the Dahomean drum mutations which we examined in an earlier chapter. The mutations of *Sea Lion Woman* involve three different meters, 9/8, 10/8, and 7/8, divided inwardly as follows: [13]

9/8 into 2–2–3–2
10/8 into 2–2–3–3
7/8 into 2–3–2

(See Ex. 11, back of book.)

Shortenin' Bread. This song exists in a number of versions. The one recorded here is remarkably simple and primitive, the refrain especially so, using the five notes of a pentachord which extends from the third to the seventh intervals, inclusive, of our scale. The song begins and ends on the blues third, leaving the melody suspended, in midair as it were, on that plaintive note so near the minor. (See Ex. 12.)

The two songs which follow were sung by an aged Negro woman. Alan Lomax wrote of her in 1940, "Aunt Harriet Mc-Clintock (McClention?) is now well over eighty years old. She was born a slave on an Alabama plantation, and on this record she gives us . . . songs that she sang as a young girl on the plantation. All . . . undoubtedly date from the period of the Civil War and earlier." [14]

Poor Little Johnny is apparently a version of a work-song. "Aunt Harriet said that *Poor Little Johnny* was sung as a cotton-picking song. . . . Little Johnny is picking in the wet river bottom field where the cotton has been rotted by exposure to damp. Therefore he won't be able to pick a hundred pounds of cotton in a day. One hundred and fifty to one hundred and seventy pounds a day is considered good picking for a strong woman, two hundred up to five hundred for a man." [15]

---

[13] The same process as the successive polyrhythms of modern music.
[14] Alan Lomax in the descriptive folder accompanying the record.
[15] *Ibid.*

> *Way down in de bottom*
> *Wha' de cotton so rotten*
> *You won't get yo' hundred here today.*
>
> *Po' little Johnny*
> *He's a po' little fellow,*
> *He won't get his hundred here today.*

Aunt Harriet's voice is mellow and quavery and she sings the simple melody with a continuous gliding portamento along which the syllables curve and undulate with a serpentine motion. This singing treats English as though it were an African language. Although Aunt Harriet recorded in 1940, we can safely take her singing as that of her youth. It prefigures amazingly the way in which the New Orleans Negroes, in the 1870's, taught themselves to play the European instruments of the jazz band. Here is the characteristic vibrato they employed in the horns. Here are the tone quality, the controlled waverings of pitch of the New Orleans clarinet. Here is much of the message, although not the form, of the blues.

Of great importance is the rhythmic treatment in the metric division of the song. The four-quarter measures are maintained, but the way the poetic lines are fitted into the measures might surprise those unacquainted with the Negro's resourcefulness at creating inner-rhythms. The first line has six syllables, the second, seven; the fourth has four, the fifth has seven. This is contrary to the traditional English poetic practice of composing lines of equal syllabic length. It may not be well known that in Greek and Latin prosody the quantity of syllables, rather than stress pattern, constitutes the metric unit. The African and the Afro-American system is something like a combination of the English and Graeco-Roman prosodies. The basic measure is maintained or implied but stresses may be displaced or syncopated; the time duration is the consideration, not the number of syllables. In the spirituals and the work-songs, as well as in the blues, each line occupies a certain space in time; the line itself may have few or many syllables. The quantity variation, in fact, gives variety and forms various polyrhythms. In jazz, the musical phrase corresponds to the sung poetic line and, whether of few or many notes, it is similarly confined to a given metric space. This is the essential secret of the jazz phrase which derives from Afro-American singing.

Gon' Knock John Booker to the Low Ground. A play-song sung with youthful spirit and great rhythmic energy by aged Aunt Harriet. The melody, apparently of Anglo-American extraction, is rendered at an exciting tempo over a stomped and hand-clapped rhythmic base. As already mentioned, the singer exhibits freedom with the poetic lines. Here she spreads a line out beyond its proper musical phrase and then hurries the next one to catch up; she compresses another line into less than its normal duration and then brings the next line in early, creating an effect of poetry anticipating music. Later on we shall hear Bunk Johnson and Louis Armstrong playing cornet phrases in much this manner in the New Orleans jazz band.

Aunt Harriet seems to carry us back to the primal, formative stages of African musical art. Although she shows great spontaneous creativeness she functions as more than just an isolated creative individual: she reminds us that the character of Negro folk music in America is more than a handful of African traits and mannerisms in an adopted music. It is the survival, rather, of an informing spirit, a racial consciousness, if you wish, with the power to borrow at will and to form and transform alien material into a style and shape unmistakably African. This one old woman, singing a song of her childhood derived, perhaps, from an old English tune, is many things in one. She is the leader calling and the tribal chorus responding; her hands and feet are the urgent, ominous, speaking drums. She is at once the slave and the free, uncaptured Negro living still in West Africa. She is the living symbol of the tribe and a manifestation of the unfathomable creative force which has created in America a half-dozen profoundly racial sorts of folk music and the complex art form called jazz. Aunt Harriet is only one among the countless thousands who, compulsively and unconsciously, externalize the genius of their race throughout America.

The songs *Old Uncle Rabbit* and *Poor Little Johnny* showed the work-songs as used by children. To the extent of their ability, children worked along with their elders. Not for them was the seeming affliction of white children — school — but the very real one of hard labor. Even so, the children, like their parents, were able to lighten the dark burden with gleams of happiness, part remembered, part imagined, greatly hoped for.

The origin of the children's play-songs and work-songs is an interesting speculation. Most of them, no doubt, are the songs of their elders, sung literally or in simple imitations by the children. Some of the adult work-songs probably were used by the children as play-songs and dances in the way in which children imitate their parents' work, making a game of it. When Negro children do this, they tend to convert the motions of a task which they have observed daily, or participated in, into a pantomimic form of dance done to music.

These little Negroes, like all children, often invent tunes and dances transmuting the sounds and movements of the outer world into simple but richly expressive art forms, with a way of striking directly to the human heart.

One can still see this happen. I remember sitting at the window of a train a few years ago, Chicago-bound from New Orleans, gliding slowly through the lovely Mississippi evening. The patches of woodland seemed to be releasing the shadows which they had guarded all through the sunny late spring day to let them flow outward over the open fields and pastures, and over the humble, scattered, Negro cabins. These are all of a pattern, small square wooden cubicles, set up on stilts to be clear of the spring rains that fall and converge into a shallow flood over the fallow dark bottom land. On each hut, the low, pyramidal, shingled roof continues its slope to cover an open pillared porch extending across the front.

On this May evening in Mississippi, from the slow train, through the shadowed green light, I saw three small figures on one of these porches, silhouetted against the open doorway's rectangle of yellow lamplight. Hand in hand, three little Negro girls, gingham-clad, were singing while they skipped and clogged a simple dance, backward and forward, pigtails flying. They danced their carefree steps to the time of the wheels clicking on the rails, to this rhythm and to all the other sounds of spring twilight. What flowed into this simple music? An obbligato of frogs, perhaps, in the drying puddles; the sweet, rasping drone of cicadas in the cottonwoods; the plaintive evening song of birds flying homeward; the orchestra of fields and groves; sounding drums of the moving train, that friend and deliverer, that tribal god almost, of the exiled black man far from home. The dance of childish happiness, it was that, as well, of unremembered worships, long-forgotten rites, somewhere long ago on West African plains.

I saw this little improvised dancing-song clearly as a part of the art of the people, perennial and strong. I saw clearly that music which comes directly from the people need never thread its way from Elysian fields, down Olympic slopes to the Thessalonian plains. It begins on the plains, stays on the plains, and high above the rural revelry the high sounds float, to settle like dew on the parched heavenly groves, on the thirsty amaranth.

5.

the blues:

one

COMPLETE and complex art forms like the blues do not happen by the caprice of chance; they are neither arbitrarily created, nor discovered ready-made; they originate and develop spontaneously yet inevitably out of the creative urge in man.

Through the long years from Jamestown to Emancipation, the Negro searched for a spiritual home; his deep need to create, as gentle and obstinate as water, as hot as white lightning or lava, sought and found forms, discarding, retaining. He had the work-songs, the spiritual, the ring-dance. But life, even the Negro's, is not confined to labor or to prayer. He carries play over into work, religious force into everyday life. The Negro needed a secular musical form, universal in expressive scope.

In artistic creation the search for forms is endless; the variety of tentative ones formed and abandoned is almost as numberless as those biological shapes left fossilized and inert in the strata of terrestrial history. From the endless, seemingly aimless movement and mutation of cells, from the ceaseless counterpoint of natural forces, there sometimes emerges a form that endures, a generic form. In nature the tree, the crystal, the vertebrate, the ape, man; in the creative biology of man's spiritual history, the wheel and the column, the sonnet, the sonata, and the blues.

When the spiritual need is permanence, man leaves gigantic pyramids on the face of the earth. When the need is ideas dis-

tilled into truth, he writes a *Phædrus;* when it is momentary
perfection of shape or movement to be made timeless, he builds
a Parthenon, carves a Winged Victory. If his need is practical
yet visionary, he plots the paths of uncountable stars, com-
poses symphonies, builds cathedrals and skyscrapers like tower-
ing ladders into the sky. These spiritual needs are born from
the obsession with causes and meanings ; their result is all architecture — philosophy, symphony, building, even machinery,
which is the architecture of predetermined and limited movement and of utile force.

But if his need is movement unhampered, unlimited, a free
intuitional flow, a spiritual flight as unconcerned with galaxies
as it is with the counting of coins, he builds no architecture. On
the ground, under the open sky, he sings and dances. He spins
endless, inspired, improvised variations in rhythmic sound,
yields joyously to that creative stream which is the only ultimate, definitive symbol and solvent of time, space, and matter.
They are the externalization — these moving variations — of
pure flight.

He is the Negro come from Africa to America, and this form
which directs movement in space, spins out sequential time and
gives to tone a soaring pattern, like the processional of the
stars, is the humble and profound music we call the blues.

Creation of the work-songs, the spirituals, and the children's
play- and dance-songs, none of which is a generic musical form,
showed the need of the hyperactive creative impulse to find such
a form, of its ceaseless, experimental search for it. A generic
art form is essentially an abstraction, a flexible framework built
up of directives and limitations, within which the creative impulse can pour its molten, metaphysical substance, to be shaped
— but not so rigidly — as by a mold. Such a form compounds
and emphasizes meanings, making more communicative the
inner meaning of the fiery flux which cools and congeals within
it, and adding the significance implicit in the shape the mold
itself imposes.

The blues are such a form, simple but profound and, therefore, infinitely complex and surcharged with meaning. The blues, developed, could provide a nucleus for New Orleans jazz with its distinctive repertory, instrumentation, theory, practice, and style. In this same way, European music of the latter half of the eighteenth century developed from the earlier dance suite and, thence, on through the nineteenth poured into, and shaped itself in, the elastic mold called the sonata form.

We shall look at many aspects of the blues which explain this music in outward detail. But this is what it is within itself: a little song yet an epochal expression of the human spirit; something simple as a sphere yet complex as a tree or as a moth wing under the microscope. It is that almost incomprehensible thing, a form comprised in movement as flexible and as ceaselessly stirring as the invisible wind. This is not a flight of birds, but that ethereal tide, itself flight, which sustains the feathered body, holds up and enfolds the thrashing wings.

To hear the blues as barbarous, cruel, or lascivious song, as the music of poverty, degradation, and despairing vice, or as a vital and compelling form of folk song, is to listen with the ears only and to judge with the shallow mind. It does have all these things in it. Drunken snores in the barrel-house, the snarl of the hop-head, prostitutes' shrill laughter, shivering, ragged poverty singing for pennies on a cold and windy corner. But there is much more in it than these. Steamboat horn and locomotive's whistle; the spiritual ringing and rocking in a bare, small church; children laughing at play; the racking sobs of bereaved slave mothers; gay bright tinkle of ragtime; a calliope outside the circus tent; chant that rises with the steam from the hot rice field; the delicious, yellow, brassy blare of the parade band — *in all of this, a lost race is searching for home.*

The blues have an extraordinary effect — out of all proportion to the bare starkness of their form and their seemingly simple content — both on singer and listener. These qualities of simplicity and starkness seem to lend an elemental naturalness and grandeur to the performance. The constant repetition of the form, far from palling and producing monotony, unites performer and audience in a common spell from which they awaken only when the music has ceased. It is a possessive spell, seemingly autohypnotic upon the singer, which is projected to the listeners and in which they are enmeshed. While the blues are sounding, this spell holds all in a sort of spiritual telepathy. There is a direct communication of intangibles, of the most impalpable meanings, of references to human feelings, impulses and knowledge deeply hidden below the conscious, references oblique as a figure with unseen face disappearing around a corner of the mind. These meanings and messages, these responses, have no necessary connection with the words nor with melodic meanings on the conscious level; they are surreal communication ultimately direct, more direct than wireless or word; they are the meanings we sense and grasp when we listen to the tones and overtones, but not the words, of human speech. These emanate from the music with the purity and freedom of music's independence of words, emanate and course on unknown wave lengths through an uncharted dimension. They reach an area of consciousness which precedes thought, which forms thought. With a sensitivity recondite, more precise and exquisite than that of radio, the listeners receive and sort the waves, receive them with a living, not mechanical, automatism, yet one constant as that of the heart and infinitely more sentient.

This is the large simplicity, the pregnant grandeur, of the blues, like that of the eight-note "Fate" motive of the *Fifth Symphony* of Beethoven. Nor are the simplicity and grandeur of the blues less majestic, less noble, or of less intrinsic worth from the standpoint of vital communication. Beethoven uses a formal development into which repetition enters only in part. The blues are embodied in a ceaseless repetition like the human pulse; like jazz, they neither have nor require formal beginning and ending. We seem to come within and depart from the range of hearing while the blues go on without end. One singer stops and another begins with naturalness and fatality. The blues, in their repetition day and night by thousands of dark

101

singers in America, seem to express, not the questionable permanence of stone or even of any form evolved by man, but the invincible permanence of the life force itself.

Although the immediate origin of the blues is unrecorded, either in writing or in phonograph records, we know that its precursory forms came into being around the time of the Civil War. They were the result of the carrying over into secular music of the Negro tendencies to syncopation and polyrhythm, to antiphony and polyphony, and to a habit of simplified harmonic progression upon which rests the whole essential structure of the blues and jazz. By the middle of the last century, short secular forms were arising which, like the earlier *Juba*, embodied the tonic-dominant harmony derived from the hymns. The constant use of the antiphonal calls-and-responses in the earlier music was the projection of ineradicable memory of Africa, the overpowering impulse itself, but not the settled development it had achieved on the home continent. The structure of metric division (number of bars) and harmonic progression to encompass and direct the improvised call-and-response, came with the blues in an eight-, then twelve-bar [1] antiphonal form. Antiphony was henceforth no longer haphazard and capricious as memory, but formulated in a cogent and fateful repetition, in a ceaseless but controlled variation. Apparently primitive, deceptively simple, this was the form to express the complexity of Negro character.

The harmonic sequence of the blues is scarcely a consideration of the blues' development, for the progression has hardly changed in its whole history, not even today when the Negroes are showing, in various highly Europeanized musical trends like swing, considerable aptitude in harmonic development and enrichment. There are variant harmonic formulas to the blues, to be sure, but the progressions are appropriate and the limits narrow. The Negro knows the proper function of harmony in the blues, as in New Orleans jazz. This is to direct the melody horizontally and its unimportance *qua* harmony is evidenced

[1] Sometimes sixteen or twenty.

by its own lack of development, by the extent to which it can be disregarded in pitch changes, and by the degree of dissonance permissible. The basic blues harmonic pattern and several variants are shown in Ex. 13, back of book.)

The base pattern, A, is called the standard blues. B is a frequent variant in which the G-seventh and C-seventh chords give variety and permit interesting melodic changes. The frequently used harmony, C, to be found in *St. Louis Blues*, differs from the standard form only in its use of the F-seventh introduction. Such slight changes, however, produce important variations in the line of the melody improvised over the blues base. Progression D is one of the typical New Orleans forms.

From these, or similar harmonic bases, the melodic pattern is derived. This is superimposed upon, and integrated with, the chord progression. Part E shows a blues melody of markedly archaic character over the standard harmonic base.[2]

All blues melody is antiphonal. In the twelve-bar form it consists of two vocal statements, each of two measures' duration, and a two-bar vocal response. The first statement occupies bars 1 and 2, the second statement, bars 5 and 6, the response, 9 and 10. These are accompanied by guitar, piano, or any of a great variety of instrumental combinations, playing in the base harmony. It is not accurate to call the instrumental portion an accompaniment or obbligato, although in rare instances it is only this. It is more frequently an antiphonal-contrapuntal element, which, in the case of a single instrument like the guitar or piano, poses one or more melodic voices against that of a singer while furnishing at the same time a rhythmic ostinato. Where there is a larger instrumental group concerned, the singer's voice sets forth a melody in antiphonal phrases against a full, weaving, instrumental polyphony.

The complex possibilities inherent in the basic blues form now begin to emerge. The guitar, piano, or instrumental combination which combines with the singer's voice polyphonally

[2] From *State of Tennessee Blues* (Memphis Jug Band) sung by Jennie Clayton on Victor No. 21185–B.

during the vocal phrases, plays without the voice in six measures and sets up its own antiphony: first statement, measures 3 and 4; second statement, measures 7 and 8; response, measures 11 and 12. Furthermore, these instrumental measures function as antiphonal answers to the voice. For example, the first vocal statement in measures 1 and 2 is immediately answered instrumentally in measures 3 and 4. The instrumental tendency is to play softly with the voice and to emerge more loudly in the measures during which the singer is silent. Thus if one disregards the vocal part, the instrumental portion presents dynamically a still additional antiphonal series: three statements *piano* alternating with three answers *forte*.

Possibilities of development extend into the process of improvisation and variation characteristic of all Negro music. The complex possibilities of the blues, as a form to channel creative activity, begin to be seen clearly in the thoroughly Negroid improvisations in tone, melody, rhythm, and poetry.

Tonal variety, for one possibility, is not limited even to the wide range of possible instrumental combinations from single guitar and piano to full jazz band. Exotic instruments may be utilized as well, such as harmonica, kazoo, jug, washboard, wood blocks and musical saw. In Negro hands, they become highly expressive instruments.

Additional tonal variety is achieved in two ways. The first is by variations of tonal timbre through tone coloration and by lines sung without words, either by humming, or by the method known as *scat* singing, which consists of explosive rhythmic sounds, verbally meaningless, musically abstract, and highly instrumental in feeling. The second is to be found in the wide range of tonal possibilities the Negro has discovered and exploits in European instruments. The trumpet, for instance, is played with a wide variety of vibratos (tremolos) which alter not only the timbre but frequently the pitch as well; it is played *open,* or with different mutes including the hand, with qualities varying endlessly from pure *hot* tone, to growl, *wa-wa,* and *dirty* tones of every description. These tonal variations are not mere eccentricities or novelties. Even when used humorously, as they sometimes are, they are essentially expressive.

The American Negro has vastly extended musical expression through tone. Not only has he based his phrasing on the rhythms of human speech, as Moussorgsky did, or as the opera of any country — if it is successful — does with its vocal line, but he makes an intelligible, highly articulate and communicative language of his music by introducing the infinite variety and nuance of the speaking voice into musical tone. The meaning of his music, which is difficult to listen to analytically and perceptively, becomes clear when it is heard as a conversation. Thus the distinction between polyphony and harmony, including unison, becomes apparent to the untrained ear. Listen to the blues and real jazz not for the familiar harmonized music, but for a conversation of people, all talking about the same thing, with statements and answers, questions, comments, exclamations, interjections, and even asides, humorous or tragic, but all pertinent and to the point. This has its inner logic when we understand the language and know what is being talked about. It is participative and creative, as true conversation — nowadays almost a lost art — always is.

Melodically, too, the improvisational range is wide. The singer is free to create melody within the harmonic framework. Her first phrase is constructed from the notes of the tonic major chord and this can be repeated, gaining new coloration from the subdominant which follows, while at the same time it introduces the element of *polytonality*, which is the simultaneous playing in two or more keys. Her third phrase builds from the dominant, or the seventh, chords which tend to be formed. Several considerations regulate the character of the improvised melody. First the requirements of the statement-answer concept make it advisable that the first two phrases have a certain similarity in line, but the different harmonic derivation of each gives a different coloration and emotional feel. The response has in its melodic line, the quality of an answer and thus expresses musically what the words convey.

The blues harmony, like that of its source, the spiritual, combines well with melodies of a pentatonic character. These melodies do not extend beyond the five-tone span of the tetrachord and in their formation clearly refer to West African melody.

The type of pentatonic scale found with great frequency in Afro-American music is shown in A of Ex. 14, back of book.) In this scale the fourth (subdominant) is omitted. A very large number of work-songs, spirituals and blues melodies can be completely written in this scale transposed to the proper key. So, likewise, can a great many West African melodies.

Adding the perfect fourth gives the six-tone or hexatonic scalar type which is shown in B, Ex. 14.

Taking these, as well as African scales, a very large part of all truly Afro-American melody can be approximately notated.

Both of these scales are definitely major in feeling, and so is the bulk of African and Afro-American music. Yet these scales approach the minor, as we observed previously, through the flatting of the third interval by less than a full half-tone. The partly flatted third is the more important of the two *blue notes,* the other being the seventh similarly flatted. Since the seventh interval does not appear in either of the two scales shown, this brings us to the full or extended *blues scale.* Such a scale is the composite of many of those shorter ones used in a large number of blues melodies.

The microtonally flatted fifth also occurs, although with far less frequency than the *blue notes.* A good example is to be heard in the second clarinet solo in the beautiful *Deep Creek Blues* by Jelly Roll Morton and his Red Hot Peppers (Victor V–38055, reissue Victor 40–0119). This solo puts the semitonally flatted third and fifth in phrasal conjunction and then rises to include the seventh and the blue third and fifth an octave above.

The American composer, Lou Harrison, has extracted a composite scale from a number of blues performances. It is shown in C, Ex. 14. In this the added intervals of the fourth and sixth are shown flatted. By the use of this scale an approximate notation of much blues singing can be made. But of course there still remain the basic difficulties, from the tonal angle, of notating all African and Afro-American music. These are the subtle gradations in degree of *off-pitchness*, the portamento, the undulation, the downward *nume* around the blue intervals, and the highly important range of timbre.

The blues scale, or more accurately, African intonation, enters into and colors all singing and playing by American Negroes. It is an important part in the *language quality* of all this music. Vocalism and instrumentalism are strongly shaped by it. Fifty or more years ago Negro piano playing began to use the *tone-clusters* which are known as blue. Simultaneously sounding the flat and natural keys of the third and seventh, these clusters are an attempt to render microtonal pitch on the piano.

The instrumental part of the blues is free to improvise melodic variations in the same way, with the same latitudes, and within the same limits as the singer. The sort of polyphony that is set up revolves around the vocal part as the key voice, just as it does around the leader in Africa and the trumpet in jazz. This procedure is similar to the choral prelude polyphony of baroque European music, where each instrument (voice) pursues its invention of melodic line with quasi-independence. The imitation characteristic of fugal counterpoint rarely enters in, but the various voices often enter in canon style and refer to the leader obliquely, furnishing significant embellishment, agreement, and even clashes of disagreement.

In the rhythm of the blues, the Negro reserves the same rights to constant mutation and variation which he applies in all his other music. Syncopations, retardations, rhythmic suspensions, inner-rhythms, and overrhythms are all abundantly present.

Besides the variation within the twelve-bar chorus of the blues, the sequence of choruses functions as a set of variations. Further, the occasional use of an instrumental episode without voice for twelve or twenty-four measures, besides giving the rendition an over-all sense of form beyond that of variational repetition, makes of these episodes a variation as related to the sung portions.

In addition to the straight and steady variational stream there is a revolving, cyclical quality. The harmonic changes, simple, rugged, and Beethovenesque, leaving the tonic, traveling through the dominant, through the subdominant and back again to the tonic, a simple and repeated cycle, have an effect primordial as the sequential, cyclical changes in nature. They are like the arc of daylight — from "Kin to Kan't" [3] by which the Negro measures his labor from dawn to dusk — like the cycle of the seasons or the orbicular voyaging of the planets. In these ceaseless cycles unfolding like a spiral, the music seems like a phenomenon of nature itself. And who is to say that it is not so, in the nature of which all human beings are a part?

The blues had undoubtedly appeared in their established form by 1870, although even an approximate date must remain conjectural. It is certain, however, that the blues were established, in some of their variant forms, quite early and more or less simultaneously throughout the South. That these regional variations in form persisted is indicated by the story which old barrel-house piano players relate. They claim that they could tell where a visiting player hailed from by the sort of blues he played. The blues in any of their shapes are not indigenous to the northern states, or to the East and West coasts.

In their authentic form, the blues are often called primitive, a term which unfortunately has come to be associated with the crude and barbarous. The form is neither, but its stark and simple completeness requires a simple and heartfelt style of singing, a lack of self-consciousness and a naturalness almost naïve. Early blues are archaic in the aesthetic sense, which means prior to the fullest development of the form. They seem ages old; there is an unquenchable power in them, a power direct and unornamented, completely unmixed with cloying sweetness, languor or sentimentality. They are dry on the ear as some wine may be on the tongue. They may be squeezed, acrid, and bitter,

[3] From dawn (can see) to nightfall (can't see).

but they are never disillusioned; the acceptance of despair does not preclude the existence of hope; the tragedy-ridden singer does not publicly disavow — and then secretly or unconsciously find — happiness either in lamentation or in a romantic posturing which reduces catastrophe to a buskined and bathetic strutting. Tragedy is so real, so bare, so fatal that simple statement attains the eloquence of a reality succinctly stated to understanding ears. And always present are the double-edged speech and the humor of the Negro, the deadpan, ironic, unpredictable wit, the salt with which he tempers his good native sweetness and sweetens his far saltier tears.

The blues are a naturally evolved form and sophistication acts like a blight upon them. Besides their development within jazz, which we shall examine later, they have gone through a number of phases in half a century. Yet concurrent with this, like seedlings sprouting between rows of ripening corn, new singers perennially appear, singing the blues as they were sung in the beginning. Thus the blues, the generic form, show vigor and ever-renewing vitality.

The blues are essentially a song form, but they always have been extensively played in jazz and on various solo instruments. These instruments, piano, guitar, et cetera, have functioned as accompaniment for the blues singer. The vocal blues fall into several categories. One of these is the rhythmic style of singing which we shall call *shouting,* a style clearly derived from, or related to, the declamatory sermons of the rural preacher. Like these, this type of blues melody falls almost invariably within the close compass of the tetrachord or five-tone interval. Contrasting with the shouted blues is the opposite type, the *melodic,* which is less strongly rhythmic and emphasizes the linear beauty of the melody whether it be one of wide or narrow compass.

The other pair of categories, into one or the other of which any blues can be fitted, are *dramatic* and *lyric.* While we find each archaic singer falling fairly definitely into one or the other of each of these sets of qualities, we find the great classic singers able to sing either rhythmically or melodically. So basic in the human character are the dramatic or lyric qualities, that even the great classic blues artists tend to remain firmly one or the other.

The first phase of the blues as an established form is the *archaic*, or preclassic blues. These must be regarded in their various forms as authentic blues in every sense. They are sung in the country throughout the South, in the hamlets and towns, and are carried along the dirt roads by the wandering singers who pack their troubles and their hopes with their battered guitars.

The next phase came in the cities, with the blues as they were sung in Birmingham, Atlanta, and New Orleans, in the cities connected with the Crescent City by the Mississippi River — St. Louis, Memphis — and in Chicago and Kansas City. The distinction between preclassic blues and the city blues is partly arbitrary. While the archaic blues were, and are, widely sung in these cities by obscure singers, still the exceptionally gifted and powerful singers tended naturally to gravitate to the urban centers. It is their singing that constitutes the *classic* blues, blues that still have spiritual simplicity, greatness, and natural poetry, to which are added the clarity and power with which greater singers infuse the form. The classic blues, as compared with the preclassic, show a growth in expressive means and in communicated power. The polyphony tends to assume more importance and the piano or guitar may occasionally reach the equality of importance with the voice that the piano attains in Beethoven's violin sonatas. The cornet of Louis Armstrong, loftily inspired, may sing with moving, human accents, weaving with Ma Rainey's voice, or Maggie Jones's, or Bertha Hill's, an inexpressibly moving antiphony of two voices. The performances tend, also, to include more instruments up to the full five- or seven-piece instrumentation of the jazz band. Into such a context the singer's voice, while the leading one, is still but one of the voices of the polyphony. In all of these cases, the term *accompaniment* becomes meaningless because we have an ingrated musical whole.

THE BLUES: ONE

The classic blues appear on records before the archaic. Because of the urban location of these singers, their work came first to the attention of the recording companies.

The classic period is comprised in the work of a handful of singers, the greatest, Ma Rainey, followed by Bessie Smith, Bertha "Chippie" Hill, Sippie Wallace, Hociel Thomas, and a very few others, most of whom are dead or have disappeared. Their ample but not voluminous recorded output was imprinted on wax during little more than a decade from the middle 1920's to the middle 1930's. The period ends approximately with its recording, but began much earlier. Ma Rainey was singing publicly by 1902; Bessie Smith, nine years younger, was reputedly launched on her professional career a scant three to five years later when she was ten or twelve years old. So telescoped is the history of the blues, like that of jazz, that even during the classic period the preclassic period was continuing and, not only was the postclassic period well underway but an eclectic revival of the blues had begun.

From the records of these now silent singers, can be judged the depth and scope of their great art, the debt that New Orleans jazz owes to the form which they set forth in perhaps its ultimate perfection, and the contribution which jazz made, on the other hand, to some of their greatest performances. These records are a yardstick, as well, by which to measure other periods of the blues. That the blues could conceivably exist without jazz is not only their glory, but the result of their earlier position in the history of Afro-American music. That jazz, for its integrity, needs the blues at its core is, on the other hand, but a phase of the complex integrity of its nature, a fusion of many and varied elements.

To hear the classic blues singers of today one must mainly go to the churches. We find many spirituals cast in forms that are all but identical, harmonically and melodically, with the blues. For example, *Nobody's Fault But Mine* relates to the eight-bar blues, while *Precious Lord Hold My Hand* shows close resemblance to the sixteen-bar type. While the blues in their complete form are not sung there, the great singers today are in the churches, their work deeply but unconsciously influenced and formed by Ma and Bessie. They sing the spirituals. The very name of the blues is anathema to them but they sing with the spirit and much of the form of the blues in the plain congregational halls from which the blues first came. There one can hear throbbing tones like Ma Rainey's deep contralto, and sad, unhurried, implacable and strangely triumphant phrases like those of Bessie Smith. In the churches is revealed that deepest quality of the blues which often eludes us, but which we can sense in their starkness and in their reconciliation of hope with despair. That revealed quality is religious devotion. For when the blues sing the cruelty and injustice of life or of love — with a simple recognition of infidelity, murderous jealousy, heartbreak or the natural and unashamed hunger of the human body — faith, passionate devotion, and the courage of dark pilgrims are to be found underneath.

The obscure city blues singers felt the influence of Ma Rainey, Bessie Smith and "Chippie" Hill. By their records and through frequent personal tours, this influence penetrated even into rural areas, coloring and changing the work of lesser singers. From this and through the natural development of the blues, arose the first of the two types of postclassic blues, the *contemporary* blues. These are of considerable smoothness and expressive means, but without sophistication, even that of artful simplicity. Of course the development of expressive means without the great natural inspiration of singers like Gertrude Rainey and Bessie Smith, leads to occasional clichés and set patterns. These, apart from the lack of deep, communicated feeling, are the chief faults of the contemporary blues. They have been extensively recorded for the last fifteen years in race lists of records produced by major recording companies for Negro consumption. Typical singers of contemporary blues are Roosevelt Sykes, Lonnie Johnson, and Tommy McClennan.

The classic blues in the city led to another type of postclassic. Some good singers of natural blues, corrupted by city ways, fell into cheap or sophisticated singing. Their blues, whether vulgarizations by emphasis on pornography, or on a slick and trivial sophistication, represent a decadent type of the form. These blues, the second postclassic type, are the *decadent* or *sophisticated* blues. The pornographic element has become prevalent among certain blues singers probably because a market has been built up for it, a market only partly consisting of Negroes. Many Negroes, and many whites as well, buy the race issues to satisfy personal tendencies or to use them for the "smart" entertainment of sophisticated groups. When white groups go slumming in various Negro purlieus in quest of such prurient stimulation, the singers are encouraged in a kind of singing that elicits white approval. No matter how dubious, this seems to them the only white praise they are likely to receive. So prevalent has this form of inferential pandering become in certain circles of the Negro blues singers, that in the commercial musical jargon of today, smut in song lyrics or comedy patter is called *blue*. The reference to sex in many good blues is of an unselfconscious naturalness tempered by native Negro humor.[4]

This slick and shallow singing is the degeneration of the highly expressive blues form into mere entertainment. Sex is not necessarily overemphasized, nor, for that matter — though the poetic lines are intact — are any of the meanings given any depth of expression. The performance, where not perfunctory, is shallow, slurred, and unimaginative. It is like an empty recital of dead history, a ritualistic service that fails to unloose the power or to evoke the glory; it is the callow schoolboy mouthing Cicero by rote.

The final development in the blues comes from singers who, in the main, are city bred, and whose singing may have an almost completely convincing air of sincerity and creativity. Their work, like that of the fashionable *diseuse* of the blues, Billie Holiday, is, nevertheless, artful and eclectic, and even

---

4 The pornographic tendency, exemplified in the 1920's by singers like Lizzie Miles, is typified today by ones like Jazz Gillum.

when it is not done for easy success, it is no more than a sophisticated revival. This type is the *electic* blues.

A number of recorded examples will now be analyzed to illustrate the various types of blues. Two great archaic singers, Memphis Minnie and the late Leroy Carr, should be mentioned although none of their records is cited.

Archaic Blues

CITATION 16. *Cat Man Blues*, sung by Blind Lemon Jefferson, with guitar accompaniment.

Faithlessness in love or in marriage is a recurrent theme in the folk documents called the blues.

> *Cat man, cat man, stay away from my house at night;*
> *I said, cat man, cat man, stay away from my house at night;*
> *Prowling 'round my back door when I'm gone —*
> *You know that ain't right.*

Cat Man shows the preclassic blues in a very early stage, far earlier than the middle 1920's when Jefferson made this record. Blind Lemon was a familiar character in Dallas and Fort Worth for years, and his records were at one time best-sellers among the Negroes. For a while, Lead Belly sang and played with him in the saloons and brothels of the Texas cities. Huddie still sings a blues that he calls *Blind Lemon Blues*.

Blind Lemon's voice is clear and high; his melodic singing is almost without vibrato and abounds in wavering inflections and the downward wailing figures around the third and seventh notes of the scale which are a characteristic of the blues scale and of Negro church singing. His guitar playing, deceptively simple like his singing, is full of startling dynamic changes. The whole style is archaic in the extreme.

CITATION 17. *Raidin' Squad Blues*, sung by Charley Jordan with guitar.[5] Almost in ballad fashion, Jordan sings of sudden arrest and imprisonment. Made during Prohibition, this record probably refers to bootlegging rather than gambling. Jordan, who was a blues singer in and around Kansas City, has a voice

---

[5] This is a version of the older *TB Blues*.

114

that is clear, expressive, and of an unusual tenor quality. The lines are sung with marked but light rhythms, gently and patiently, with no effort at pathetic accent. Pathos resides in the words.

> *When I was on my feet I couldn't walk down the street*
> *For the police lookin' at me, from my head to my feet*
> *But oh-oh these raids is killing me*
> *See I want nobody buried, lawdy, down in Tennessee.*

In the chorus quoted variations occur in the poetic line. The first line is expanded into two rhyming lines completely filling the first four measures of the chorus. The harmony shows interesting variations from the standard blues. Strong polytonality occurs in the second vocal phrase, measures 5 and 6. (See Ex. 15, back of book.)

The guitar plays these elemental dry sequences in light and beautifully patterned broken rhythms, a single string often imitating the wavering downward cadences of the singer's voice. The connection between early blues guitar and barrel-house piano playing is obvious, the guitar sounding at times startlingly like a tinkly, battered, upright piano. The guitar furnishes chordal accompaniment, almost drumlike in its rhythm. Concurrently the upper strings sing in polyphony or in answer to the voice. The guitar often furnishes uncannily accurate imitations of the voice.[6]

Another fine archaic singer is Jesse James. His records, of great rarity, are discussed in Appendix H, p. 357.

Jimmy Yancey is one of the great creative figures of American Negro music. His shy and introspective nature, that prevents him from public playing and singing, belies his true power and fervor while at the same time it has limited his reputation to an inner circle of jazz lovers. The creator of a school of boogie-woogie blues playing whose pupils, Clarence "Pinetop" Smith, Meade Lux Lewis, and Albert Ammons went on to a

---

[6] Two good examples of imitation are *Mamie,* by Blind Boy Fuller, Melotone No. 7–05–56, and *Travelin' Blues,* by Blind Sammy, Columbia No. 14484–D.

public acclaim that he himself did not covet, his piano work is discussed in a following chapter.

He is an archaic blues singer of the most touching accents but he has recorded only two vocal solos,[7] and can be induced to sing only after much persuasion. Yancey is a sensitive, serious, and thoughtful man, with remarkable creative integration. With relatively simple technical means, he erects, on the bare blues form, organic structures of sound that, in their range of expressiveness and their imaginative and exhaustive development of idea, are great — if unpretentious — works of art.

The recognition that came late to Jimmy Yancey, was even later in coming to his wife, one of the very greatest of archaic singers. Her first two records, made in Chicago in 1943, are cited here.

CITATION 18. *Pallet on the Floor*, sung by Mama Yancey, piano by Jimmy Yancey.

Pallet on the Floor, a traditional blues in the sixteen-bar form and one of the most beautiful of all blues melodies, is widely sung in New Orleans and throughout the South. The words are those of a poor prostitute asking shelter for the night.

1.
Make me a pallet on your floor
Make me a pallet on your floor
Make me a pallet, Baby, a pallet on your floor
So when your good gal comes, she will never know.

2.
Make it very soft and low
Make it, Babe, very soft and low
Make it, Baby, near your kitchen door
So when your good gal comes she will never know.

3.
I'll get up in the morning and cook you a red hot meal
I'll get up in the morning and cook you a red hot meal
To show you I 'preciate, Baby, what you done for me
When you made me a pallet on your floor.

[7] One, *Death Letter Blues,* is discussed in Appendix H, p. 357.

4.

Make it soft and low
Make it, Baby, soft and low
If you feel like laying down, Babe, with me on the floor
When your good gal comes home, she will never know.

As a human document, this poetry refers not to one race, or one time, but contains a deep universality. Mama Yancey sings as church singers do, with simplicity and a devotional feeling, in a pure, unadorned, and beautiful tone, and with a poignancy derived from her frequent flatted tones. The deep rapport between the singer and her husband is clearly felt in the spiritual and organic interweaving of the voice with the piano.

The freedom of poetical metrics, and the rhythmic variation introduced by changes in the footage of the lines, are well illustrated in the poem. The prosodic variation is not a sign of primitivism, because a singer who can divide music into measures accurately, can divide language into syllabic feet just as accurately. It is, rather, one of the flexibilities of the blues form in permitting rhythmic and poetic variation. It relates to the fact that poetic lines are frequently improvised and, even more fundamentally, relates to a feeling for the expressive qualities of changes of pace in speech. It constitutes a vital element of blues singing, namely phrasing, and has shaped the musical enunciation of the instruments of jazz. Negro phrasing is a potent means of expression through rhythm and rhythmic variation. Identical lines are phrased differently each time and the words are seldom directly on the beat: they hesitate, come slowly, then rush together, constantly syncopating against the fixed pulse of the accompaniment, whether sounded or only felt. The phrasing varies endlessly — no matter how complex it may be — with a plastic, dimensional feeling. Of all the technical peculiarities of Negro music, this seems the most difficult for white players and singers. (For the score of the last vocal chorus and the closing piano chorus of *Pallet on the Floor*, see Ex. 16, back of book.) The rhythms, which cannot be notated accurately

117

in 4/4 time, show clearly in 12/16 as they follow the Dahomean pattern of inner-rhythms in a twelve-beat measure.

The other available record by Mama Yancey should be briefly mentioned. *How Long Blues*, with organ accompaniment by Jimmy Yancey, is a traditional blues of the very early and archaic eight-bar form. Its harmonic structure is shown in Ex. 17, back of book. The poetic lines are extremely simple, consisting of one call line and one response line to each chorus. This number is deeply devotional in feeling, in the manner in which it is sung, in the lines which reiterate the question of right and wrong, and in the reverence of the reed organ accompaniment. The performance, authentic in every way, shows clear evidence of derivation from the spiritual. A partial score is given in Ex. 18.

CITATION 19. *Down In Boogie Alley*, by Bessie Jackson, with piano. This singer, who also recorded under her real name, Lucille Bogan, was an archaic singer who nearly attained classic stature.

Way down in Boogie Alley — ain't nothin' but skulls and bones [8]
And when I get drunk, blues gon'ta take me home.

I'm gonna stop my man from runnin' 'roun'
'Cause down in Boogie Alley is where he can be found.

He goes down in Boogie Alley — house number two
And when he get down there, the women won't let him come to
  see me.

I went down in Boogie Alley with my razor in my han'
And the blues druv me — I brought back my man.

The very archaic singing has turns of line like the spirituals and street cries. The Negroid timbre and African intonation are plain, but have great beauty and expressiveness. The simple piano part, with its strange harmonic changes and the constant repetition of the name, *Boogie Alley*, create a feeling of ominous foreboding.

[8] Each first line repeated.

In the still continuing archaic stages, the blues are far from a solidified state. There is endless creative flux producing new, variant forms. The possibilities seem infinite for gifted players and singers to invent original melodies or to construct new harmonic progressions. If these are made in the authentic blues spirit, richness is added to the form and new fields are opened up for invention. Several good examples of variant blues follow.

CITATION 20. *I Can't Sleep*, sung by Montana Taylor with piano.

Taylor, one of the teeming school of Midwestern blues pianists of the 1920's, made a few rare sides for Vocalion in 1928. A self-taught but fantastically accomplished and imaginative player, he then disappeared during the financial depression. The circumstances of my finding him again, eighteen years later, are recounted in a subsequent chapter.

While recording his piano work in 1946, I urged him to sing and he did so, reluctantly, never having sung in public before. The naturalness of the blues as a folk expression was never better illustrated than by the resulting records, which established him instantly as one of the greatest archaic singers so far discovered.

I Can't Sleep is a masterpiece of despair, conveyed in song. The accents of Montana's rough, low voice are haunting beyond description. Technically, this blues is an extraordinarily personal twelve-bar variant of the standard blues. Beginning in C minor, it modulates to E flat major, a device that greatly extends the tonal coloration without violating the just harmonic blues form. The scheme of poetic lines is also remarkably personal and original. Instead of the usual two call lines and one response a much more complex arrangement is offered:

1

I can't sleep
I count sheep
Get up in the mornin', Baby, and I can't eat;

119

I just worry, Babe,
Worry the whole day through

Don't know how I'll make it,
Baby, if I don't have you.

2

I'm dead broke
All my clothes in soak
I can't find a frien' and I'm all in;

I just worry, Babe,
Worry the whole day through

Don't know how I'll make it, Baby,
If I don't have you.

Montana is a between-the-beat singer and his singing sets up polyrhythms with his piano playing. The first group of three lines, for example, enters just before the third beat of the first measure and ends in a similar position in the fourth measure. Poetically, this first group of lines forms the first call; the second group (of two lines) forms the second call; and the final group (of two lines) forms the response. It is important to note that the lines total seven, which, poised within the twelve measures of each chorus, represent an odd-within-even figure corresponding exactly to the Dahomean rhythms discussed earlier. (See Ex. 42, back of book.)

CITATION 21. *Dyin' Rider Blues,* sung by Romeo Nelson with piano.

Nelson, who plays his own accompaniment, was one of the obscure but prodigious barrel-house and boogie-woogie players with whom Chicago once abounded. About 1929 he made two record sides of boogie-woogie and two of the blues. These have established his fame as a pianist of complex, dynamic energy and a singer of markedly personal style. Then, like Montana and many another player of his day, he lapsed into oblivion.

The innovations in *Dyin' Rider* are harmonic and melodic. We are presented in the opening bar with an unorthodox chord in which the fifth is sharped. The vocal line, built upon a most unusual scale, causes constantly recurring clashes or dissonances and the effect, sorrowfully grotesque, is of great beauty. (See Ex. 19, back of book. The notation shows the chordal characteristic, the basic scale, and the nature of the dissonances.)

Nelson's typically Negro timbre combines harshness and gentleness in one clear tonal quality. He sings dryly and rhythmically and, like all good blues singers, with a completely unsentimental simplicity. His melodic innovation appears in two choruses where he omits words and simulates weeping with the rhythmic punctuations of sobs. This simple, almost naïve onomatopœia is vivid and convincing precisely because it is presented factually and unromantically.

CITATION 22. *Hell Hound on My Trail,* sung by Robert Johnson, with guitar accompaniment.

With all its strangeness, *Hell Hound* is not only an authentic blues, but a remarkable variation in which the standard harmony is altered in a personal and creative way to permit the expression of uncanny and weird feelings.

Johnson's strident voice sounds possessed like that of a man cast in a spell and his articulation, like speech in possession, is difficult to understand. (See Ex. 20. This score shows introduction and one chorus and, separately, the peculiar harmonic sequence.)

I got to keep moving, umm — I got to keep moving
Blues falling down like hail; blues falling down like hail;
Umm — blues falling down like hail; blues falling down like hail.
And I can't keep no money, for a hell hound on my trail;
Hell hound on my trail; hell hound on my trail.

I can tell the wind is runnin' [by] the leaves shakin' on the tree,
Shakin' on the tree;
I can tell the wind is runnin' [by] the leaves shakin' on the tree;
Huh-uh-uh-ummm;
All I need's my little sweet woman-uh- to keep my company.
Huh-uh-uh-ummm
My company.

The voice sings and then — on fateful, descending notes — echoes its own phrases or imitates the wind, mournfully and far away, in *huh-uh-uh-ummm*, subsiding like a moan on the same ominous, downward cadence. The high, sighing guitar notes vanish suddenly into silence as if swept away by cold, autumn wind. Plangent, iron chords intermittently walk, like heavy footsteps, on the same descending minor series. The images — the wanderer's voice and its echoes, the mocking wind running through the guitar strings, and the implacable, slow, pursuing footsteps — are full of evil, surcharged with the terror of one alone among the moving, unseen shapes of the night. Wildly and terribly, the notes paint a dark wasteland, starless, ululant with bitter wind, swept by the chill rain. Over a hilltop trudges a lonely, ragged, bedeviled figure, bent to the wind, with his *easy rider* held by one arm as it swings from its cord around his neck.

6.

the blues:

two

With Gertrude "Ma" Rainey, greatest of all blues singers, come the classic blues. Born April 26, 1886, in Columbus, Georgia, Ma Rainey was the daughter of Negro troupers who toured in the country in Negro minstrel shows. Her first public appearance, around 1898 to 1900, was in a local talent show and shortly thereafter, when scarcely fifteen, she met and married Will (Pa) Rainey and traveled with him in a road show. It was while in this troupe, the *Rabbit Foot Minstrels*, that Ma Rainey discovered the child, Bessie Smith, in Tennessee, taught and assisted her toward recognition.

During the following years, spent in minstrels, levee camps, cabarets, tent shows, and on the old T. O. B. A.[1] Negro vaudeville circuit, Ma's fame gradually spread, particularly through the South and the Midwest, until her name became a household word among Negroes. Hearing her records, one can glean an idea of the hypnotic spell with which she captured her audiences. No singer has ever had a greater measure of sheer, vital power than this short, black, heavy woman of whom most of Europe and white America have not heard even now.

Ma Rainey also owned two theatres in Rome, Georgia, *The Lyric* and the *Airdrome*. In 1933, after perhaps more than 35 years on the stage, she retired to her native city where she lived with Thomas Pridgett, Jr., her brother, until she died on December 22, 1939 at the age of fifty-three years.

[1] Theatre Owners' Booking Association.

Many of the players whom Ma Rainey met on her southern tours — pianists, guitarists and jazz musicians — were used during her recording career in the latter half of the 1920's. Her records, of which nearly one hundred sides are known and some no doubt remain still undiscovered, were made in New York and Chicago and were done for a rather obscure and now defunct recording company, the New York Recording Laboratories of Port Washington, Wisconsin. This concern recorded, mainly for the Negro trade, on the Paramount label. Even in the worn-out condition in which they are usually found, its records are collector's items.

Much of Ma Rainey's work was recorded by the obsolete acoustic process which was played and sung into a horn without benefit of electrical engineering or microphone. Even her later Paramount electric recordings are not comparable in fidelity to those of Bessie Smith. According to the legend, Paramount Company labeled its discs *Electrically Recorded* when a lone electric light was installed in its studio, making it easier for the singer to find the horn than in the previous kerosene-lamp gloom.

One cannot state with certainty to what degree Gertrude Rainey was an innovator. She began to sing the blues a bare twenty to twenty-five years after the probable time of their origin, finding them, no doubt, in a fairly early stage of development. At the height of her career she left a recorded legacy of the blues in their perfect, definitive and classic form, clearly imprinted with her strong personality. More than anyone else, she is responsible for the growth in variety and complexity of the accompaniments from simple guitar and piano to the full instrumental jazz combinations which help to give some of her records their timeless depth, breadth, and richness.

Ma Rainey's singing, monumental and simple, is by no means primitive. It is extremely conscious in its use of her full expressive means, definitely classic in purity of line and its rigid avoidance of the decorative. Such art as this must, of necessity, transcend the level of the spontaneous and purely instinctive. Thus her effects are carefully calculated and full of meaning; they are neither naïve nor spurious, sentimental nor falsely sophisticated.

Rainey's voice is somber but never harsh, and its sad and mellow richness strikes to the heart. Her vibrato, slow, controlled and broad, is one of the important and characteristic elements in her tone production, and her tones are projected by sheer power with an organlike fullness and ease. The deepest and most genuine feeling fills her every note and phrase with gusty humor or with an elegiac and sometimes almost gentle sadness.

One must go even deeper to gain an inkling of Ma Rainey's secrets. Her voice has a throbbing quality which comes from the profundity, the gentleness, the gravity, and the warm humanity of the person herself, which no technical terms, even if they existed, would suffice to describe. She has a slow majesty phrased almost incredibly in the most rocking rhythm. This phrasing is the very definition of the term, at its purest and most classic, both in the blues and in jazz. It is this phrasing, infinitely rhythmic, varied, unpredictable, sinuous and elastic in line, which delineates and sets forth musically the deepest meanings of her thought with every shade of feeling throughout the vast gamut which was hers. Gertrude Rainey was a great person, a deeply human and completely articulate one, and the song she made is great art.

No picture of Ma Rainey is complete if it omits her humor. This side of her nature is well illustrated in an anecdote told by many older New Orleans players. Early in this century, Ma's tent show was appearing in a vacant lot in the uptown part of the city. One evening Ma was singing to an audience that packed the tent until the canvas walls bulged. Standing on the wooden stage, the short, heavy, black woman, with her magnetic eyes and flashing teeth, had her hearers rocking and swaying to her blues.

If you don't believe I'm sinking,

125

she sang, and suddenly the platform began to collapse. Imperturbably she continued

> *Look at the hole I'm in!*

The timbers gave way with a crash but Ma, standing on the ground with only her twinkling eyes visible above the wreckage, calmly finished the old song

> *If you don't think I love you, Baby,*
> *Look what a fool I've been!*

CITATION 23. *Shave 'Em Dry*, sung by Ma Rainey with guitar duet accompaniment.

Here is an archaic eight-bar blues but, unlike the *How Long Blues* which resembled the standard twelve-bar blues with its first line omitted, this is complete, harmonically and poetically. *Shave 'Em Dry* may very well be the type from which the twelve-bar form developed by expansion. It is difficult to imagine the rich possibilities of development within this short form. In its clipped harmonic sequence are latent the most varied and expressive melodies and counter melodies ever created in the blues and, from the blues, in jazz.

These are the blues in embryo as it were, with Ma Rainey showing the rich expressive power of the form in itself without elaboration or formal development. No matter how late in blues history it was recorded, this record is of great importance, since it indicates a very early stage of development. (The vocal line of one chorus of *Shave 'Em Dry* over the harmonic base is shown in Ex. 21, back of book.)

Ma was accompanied on many of her records by a jazz band called Lovie Austin and Her Blues Serenaders. The New Orleans cornetist and trumpeter, Tommy Ladnier, led this group, which included Lovie at the piano. Ladnier, who died several years ago, was one of the *bluest* of all cornetists and his phrasing was a model of driving simplicity. The Austin group provided accompaniments that are the instrumental equivalent of the archaic vocal blues.

Among Ma Rainey's great records, which include *Levee Camp Moan, Bo-Weavil Blues, Moonshine Blues, Stack O' Lee Blues,* and *Slow Driving Moan,* with its wonderful brass accompaniment and its memorable combination of the blues with popular music in the real folk meaning rather than in the Tin Pan Alley sense, there are three records made about 1925 with an instrumental group which included Louis Armstrong. These, *Jelly Bean Blues, Counting the Blues,* and *See See Rider,* are monuments of the most classic stage of the blues. Accompaniment is by cornet, trombone, clarinet or soprano saxophone, piano, drums, and banjo. This is the basic instrumentation (except when the saxophone substitutes for the clarinet) of the New Orleans jazz band. Louis Armstrong's cornet work of this period, which immediately preceded his great Hot Five records, is of the purest, bluest and simplest line, authentically New Orleans in character, clearly deriving from the styles of earlier masters. Although strongly influenced by King Oliver, it bears the deep imprint — which it has never wholly lost — of Bunk Johnson's original and definitive style. Buster Bailey's work, especially on clarinet, is in his simple early manner, based on the classic New Orleans pattern. The trombone playing of Charlie (Long) Green, who is said to have frozen to death later during depression days on a Harlem doorstep, is hot and plain, very blue and vocal in tone.

CITATION 24. *Jelly Bean Blues,* illustrating one side of Ma Rainey's genius, shows the melodic phase of the blues. The choruses, over their rich brass ensembles and plucked guitar cadenzas, present different melodies which develop one out of the other, expand in range, and progress in complexity and intensity to the final one which soars and swells in rich diapason tones. (It is shown in Ex. 22, back of book.)

These choruses which, considered together as of one piece, branch and grow like a living organism, are all developed upon and out of a harmonic base substantially as simple as that of *Shave 'Em Dry.*

CITATION 25. *Counting the Blues,* illustrating another facet of Ma Rainey's art, shows the rhythmic shouting phase of the blues. These long rhythmic phrases, that swell with strong feeling, show that shouting is clearly derived from the preaching and spiritual singing in the churches.

The poetic lines are answered by solo responses which follow this pattern throughout: first response an acrid, wailing, muted cornet; second response, plaintive downward phrases by the soprano saxophone; third response, hoarse, shouting, muted trombone. At intervals heavy off-beat drum blows occur precisely as hand-clapping occurs in Negro churches.

CITATION 26. *See See Rider*. Ma Rainey never surpassed the unadorned tragedy she achieves here. Nor can a more perfect fusion of voice and instruments be found anywhere else in recorded blues literature.

See See Rider [2] shows prepared aspects which indicate that this favorite of Ma Rainey had achieved a compositional form which is more typical of her concert pieces than the standard blues. It opens with a four-measure instrumental introduction. A twelve-measure verse, reminiscent of the popular song formula, follows. After a two-beat pause, Ma Rainey sings three complete twelve-bar blues choruses and the record ends with a four-bar instrumental coda.

VERSE

I'm so unhappy,
I feel so blue,
I will feel so sad:
I made a mistake
Right from the start —
Oh, it seems so hard to part.
Oh, 'bout this letter
That I will write
I hope he will remember
When he sees it:

[2] In rural Negro parlance, *see see,* or *easy, rider* meant the guitar (or "box") carried suspended by its cord. In the double meaning of Negro imagery, the femininely formed guitar, solace of loneliness, typifies also a woman companion. In Negro "city talk," the term *easy rider* has come to mean either a sexually satisfying woman or a male lover who lives off a woman's earnings.

THE BLUES

1.

See See Rider, see what you done done!
Lawd, Lawd, Lawd.
You made me love you, now your gal's done come.
You made me love you, now your gal's done come.

2.

I'm goin' away, Baby, won't be back 'till Fall.
Lawd, Lawd, Lawd.
Goin' away, Baby, won't be back 'till Fall.
If I find me a good man, I won't be back at all.

3.

I'm gonna buy me a pistol just as long as I am tall.
Lawd, Lawd, Lawd!
Gonna kill my man and catch the Cannon Ball,[3]
If he don't have me, he won't have no gal at all.

After the slow, grave introduction in deep brassy tones, the voice begins while the band continues in a slow moving polyphony which weaves together the voices of cornet, trombone, and clarinet in the classic New Orleans way. Following the verse, this polyphony swells out almost explosively between the sung lines. Rainey's deep voice is full of tears and Louis' cornet sings continuously with her, responding to her phrases and her inflections in a tone veiled and dark and so startlingly human that the two parts sound like a vocal duet. Finally, in the coda, the cornet responds like the voice of Rainey herself, singing phrases of overpowering, regretful sadness that rise unexpectedly to a moment of deceptive triumph on the high tonic only to sink slowly back to the blue third interval as if overcome by despair.

The name of Bessie Smith must unquestionably be put next to that of Ma Rainey. She alone combines, as Ma did, glorious voice and natural power with the richness, range, and versatility of a great personality. Bessie, called *Empress of the Blues,* followed her great contemporary's path, touring the South with

[3] An express train on the L. and N. Line, from Cincinnati to New Orleans.

129

minstrel and tent shows. Her Columbia records, made in New York, began to appear perhaps a year or two earlier than Ma Rainey's first records. In little more than twelve years, she saw the $2.50 a week originally paid her with a traveling show climb to nearly $1000. Before the depression of the 1930's, Negroes throughout the country stood in long lines at the record shops to buy her new recordings. Slimmer days came later, but Bessie was saved from dire poverty by an honest white manager, Frank Walker, who during her heyday had put $20,000 away for her.

In her later years, Bessie was the victim of mismanagement and, faced with diminishing returns, succumbed at times to the temptations of commercialization and pornography and even belittled herself and her race singing *coon* songs. But the years of her decline cannot dim the memory of Bessie in her great days, a tall, ample, bronze woman, vitally, richly, earthily beautiful with the dusky bloom of dark fruit, striding onto the stage, pushing the microphone contemptuously aside, to fill the theater with the glistening beauty, the commanding magic, the triumph of her voice.

Bessie died in Clarksdale, Mississippi, September 26, 1937. Hurt in an automobile accident, she was taken, it is said, with some injured whites to a hospital. While waiting her turn as the others were treated first, she bled to death. If this be true, she died tragically, the victim of the racial injustice from which sprang the richest vein of the blues she sang so gloriously.

It is difficult to choose from the more than 150 issued sides which Bessie left us. The list abounds in masterpieces: *Baby Doll;* the exuberant popular songs, *Cake Walking Babies* and *Jazzbo Brown;* the immortal, traditional *Careless Love; You've Been a Good Ole Wagon* and *Put It Right Here,* with their humorously ironic comment on the man's failure to provide money or love and their relation to the African *songs of derision;* the healthy, frank sex imagery of *Empty Bed Blues;* the eerie *Spider Man's Blues;* the bitter but magnificent *Nobody Knows You When You're Down and Out;* the socially significant *Poor Man's Blues;* the bitterly despairing *Hard Drivin' Papa;* the

melancholy description of Mississippi floods, *Back Water Blues.*
The list is rich and long beyond these.

CITATION 27. *Careless Love,* sung by Bessie Smith with Louis
Armstrong, cornet; Charlie Green, trombone; Fletcher Henderson, piano.

The Negroes have taken this dark and passionate song of the
Kentucky mountains and made it into one of the most beautiful
of all blues, a song that strikes deep and straight to the heart.
Blues, if you will, ballad, if you will; it is an expression of the
utmost sadness, a bitter song and a sweet song. In its unavailing, bitter regret there lingers unforgotten love, faintly and
warmly sweet.

> *Love, O love, O careless love,*
> *You flood into my head like wine;*
> *You wrecked the life of many a poor gal*
> *And you left me fault this life of mine.*
>
> *Love, O love, O careless love,*
> *In your clutches of desire*
> *You make me break many a true vow,*
> *And you set my very soul on fire.*
>
> . . . . .
>
> *Love, O love, O careless love,*
> *Night and day I weep and moan;*
> *You brought the wrong man into this life of mine;*
> *For my sin 'til judgment I will 'tone.*

Bessie's singing of *Careless Love* is a completely realized
dramatic-narrative form in which voice and instruments play
their appropriate parts. Bessie's narration is inexpressibly bitter and tragic, while alternately the cornet and then the trombone sing behind her. Louis' tone at one moment is sober and
sad; at another it utters imploring downward phrases; in his
cornet we hear the singer's conscience. "Long" Green's muted
trombone utters mocking periods: it is the very antagonist,
careless love.

A subtlety in *Careless Love* is Bessie's rhythmic variation of
the first line of each stanza. Following the African tendency

of permutation, as in the drum rhythms, this device in her hands gives a constantly changing dramatic emphasis. (The five variants are shown in Ex. 23, back of book.)

CITATION 28. *Put It Right Here* (*or Keep It Out There*), sung by Bessie Smith with Charlie Green, trombone; Fletcher Henderson, piano.

The light side of Bessie's genius is shown in this song. She shows a rich and earthy humor in this imaginary upbraiding of a nonproviding husband. Not a blues, this popular song with verse and chorus is sung, as Bessie always sang, with blue intonation.

> *I've had a man for fifteen year;*
> *Give him his room and board;*
> *Once he was like a Cadillac,*
> *Now he's like a old worn-out Ford;*
> *He never brought me a lousy dime*
> *And put it in my hand;*
> *So there'll be some changes from now on*
> *Accordin' to my plan:*
> *He's got to get it, bring it, put it right here*
> *O' else he's gonna keep it out there;*
> *If he must steal it, beg it, or borr' it somewhere,*
> *'Long as he gets it, child, I don't care.*
>
> *The bee gets the honey and brings it to the comb*
> *Else he's kicked out of his Home Sweet Home;*
> *To show you that they brings it, watch the dog and the cat,*
> *Everything even brings it from the mule to the gnat;*
> *The rooster gets the worm and brings it to the hen:*
> *That ought to be a tip to all you no-good men;*
> *The groundhog even brings it and puts it in his hole:*
> *So my man is got to bring it, doggone his soul!*

Bessie sings *Put It Right Here* in a rocking, triumphant, shouted style. The phrases syncopate, fall off the beat, and introduce a wide range of inner-rhythm. The tone is *hot* at times, at other times thickly burred with the quality called *dirty*. The trombone plays brazenly and derisively throughout in phrases that sound like contemptuous laughter.

THE BLUES: TWO

The description of the good-providing habits in the animal kingdom is sung and played like a *stop-time* in jazz, which is a free solo over a punctured bass on one or two beats only of each measure. Bessie's singing in this section, which stays within the pentachord and most of which is on two notes with heavy reiteration of the blue third, is scolding in the grand manner.

This type of humor is often found in the blues and it relates closely to the African *songs of derision* which are used to intimidate and enforce social conformity. *Put It Right Here* also has definite affinities with the animal fables of West Africa, many of which survive in the Uncle Remus stories and in many Afro-American songs. So strong is the continuity from Africa that in 1925, or equally today, a popular tune written by an American Negro may not only refer to Africa in its melodic form and in its whole technique of presentation, but even in its subject matter.

Both Ma Rainey and Bessie Smith transcended even the blues to which they gave the final definitive shaping and development. Both singers made dramatic works of art of the folksong which they inherited, gave real depth to popular forms. Apart from the blues, both could take trivial material, ennoble it, and transmute it, through their own creative magic, into great art. Ma Rainey combined tragedy with humor, Bessie triumph with despair. From the just degree with which each quality tempered the other, came the simple nobility of their art.

Ma held her audiences mesmerically in a bond of common experience and sympathy: she sang *their* songs for them. Bessie gripped her listeners dynamically and, while hinting at the falseness of triumph, showed them to themselves as liberated and in full possession of their own potential powers.

Ma, the tragic, died peacefully, prosperous and triumphant, and thus, in the end, involuntarily gave the lie to the tragic expression of her art. When Bessie died, her catastrophe, through an inexorable logic was illuminated with the inward meanings of victory.

Both singers left the dramatic blues completed with the first strokes of a new masterpiece brushed in. Their early guitar and piano accompaniments grew, as their dramatic sensibility grew, into more and more complex forms. Their greatest work, sung with great creative players in a full New Orleans jazz band, is more than the blues with great accompaniment, more than even jazz. It fuses the two into a greater single form. The blues of the classic period — despite the fine male singers — are pre-eminently the music of Negro women as jazz is the lusty music of Negro men. The one seems to embody healing, maternal sympathy, which gestates and conserves life; the other externalizes the vitality and power of male procreativeness.

In the lifework of these two singers is to be found the first stages of a new and integrated dramatic art form, encompassing the feminine blues and masculine jazz but transcending both, a continuous sung and spoken monologue or colloquy interfused with great improvised instrumental polyphony. It cannot be confined to the short minutes of a ten-inch phonograph record but demands and needs the space it often has received in actual performance. It is chamber music with some of the potential attributes of opera and the drama, with unexplored possibilities of its own, which include choreography and pantomime. It is one answer to the supposed need of jazz for larger form, a need to which the ridiculous and pretentious hybridizing of a Duke Ellington and other so-called "jazz modernists" is a trivial answer and a travesty on the creative genius of the American Negro.[4]

The late Ferdinand Morton heard the rich, pure, archaic blues as a child in the New Orleans of the 1890's. Yet his blues singing is in no sense archaic. From his earliest playing in the bawdy houses of the New Orleans "district" [5] to his great bands twenty years later, Jelly Roll, more than any other individual, represented the fusion of cultural influences in jazz. So Mor-

[4] Such a development is clearly forecast in *Blues the World Forgot* by Ma Rainey, Paramount No. 12647; reissue, Paramount No. 1.

[5] "One may assume he made himself at home with the unrighteous women of his environment, for he became known as 'Jelly Roll,' a folk expression with strong connotations in this realm." Bontemps and Conroy: *They Seek a City.* New York: 1945.

ton's blues are more than the pure form which arose from the soil of the South; in his hands they appear on the highest classic plane plus a transformation peculiarly his own. Jelly Roll poured into the form his own lyricism and some of the French elegance and melodiousness of ragtime, while greatly extending the harmonic and melodic possibilities. Where Bessie and Ma carried the blues to dramatic heights, he developed the lyric possibilities to a high degree. He is at one time (*Mamie's Blues* and *Winin' Boy*) tender, plaintive, and nostalgically melancholy; at another (*Michigan Water Blues* and *Doctor Jazz*) he shouts with a robust and ebullient vitality. Thus Morton's blues — colored by many artistic overtones — achieve the definite status of art songs, yet art songs in which the African improvisational elements of rhythm, tone, and phrasing are largely retained.

Jelly Roll Morton was a complex personality. He had the assimilated knowledge and breadth — if not the educational background — of the truly cultured person. That he combined these attributes with traces of naïveté, underlined his lifelong integrity and accounted for a large measure of his charm. He had sophistication of the true kind: imagination and skill tempered by sincerity and a personal, artistic awareness. He was beyond doubt the most creative figure in jazz, performer, leader and inventor of melodies, a crotchety egoistic genius whose passionate devotion to his art disarms all criticism.

Mamie's Blues, Buddy Bolden's Blues (*I Thought I Heard Buddy Bolden Say*) with its evocation of the atmosphere of New Orleans at the turn of the century, *Michigan Water Blues*, and *Winin' Boy Blues* are all bona fide masterpieces of American Negro music. Morton's piano accompaniment, in lieu of more complicated instrumentation, shows the utmost possibilities of piano and voice combined in a lyric expression of the blues.

CITATION 29. *Winin' Boy*, played and sung by Jelly Roll Morton.

No more haunting music, white or black, has ever been recorded than *Winin' Boy*. The name, a Negro term of uncertain origin and meaning, was originally Jelly Roll's nickname. As in the work of Ma Rainey and Bessie Smith, we find here the full ripeness and expressive power of mature, definitive art. Jelly's tenor voice is clear and mellow in *Winin' Boy*. Rapid vibrato alternates with steady tone and the phrasing is spaced and varied endlessly, on the highest creative plane. No listener will fail to be enthralled, few will ever forget the thrilling tones, the subtle, incomparable nuances, of this singing, the rich restrained piano, or the deeply affecting hummed tones of the last chorus.

CITATION 30. *Mamie's Blues*, played and sung by Jelly Roll Morton.

Unforgettable are the simple, opening broken chords of *Mamie's Blues*, intimating the degree to which Jelly Roll develops the basic blues harmony. Equally unforgettable is his soft, rhythmically spoken prologue. The first piano chords state a theme and then the voice joins in like another instrument. The introduction is in the later and more complex sixteen-bar form, while the vocal choruses are in the original twelve bars. (See Ex. 24, back of book, for a partial score: A, introduction; B, first vocal chorus; C, final piano chorus or coda.)

The classic blues period rounds out with a handful of names: Hociel Thomas, Bertha "Chippie" Hill, and Sippie Wallace. Each of these has individual and classic style without combining all the attributes — richness, power, breadth, and creative versatility — which characterized the work of Ma Rainey, Bessie Smith, and Jelly Roll Morton.

Hociel Thomas had a voice of fruity richness, a little less powerful than that of Ma and Bessie. She sang with solemnity and majesty in a manner closely related to church singing. Her phrasing had a good plainness, but was often solidly on the beat thus sacrificing the swing and the provocative, unpredictable, imaginative quality derived from inner-rhythms. It is her expressive power, transcending any technical lack, which makes Hociel a classic blues singer.

CITATION 31. *Gambler's Dream*, by Hociel Thomas.

Louis' sparse, driving open horn has a compelling, authentic New Orleans quality. Johnny Dodds's slow, slashing clarinet breaks are very effective, and in one chorus, he supplies an ecstatically melancholy obbligato for Hociel's spoken words. Hersal Thomas' solid piano chords alternate with player-piano tremolandi of great beauty. Nevertheless a little is lacking in the accompaniment. The banjo is practically inaudible and, with the drums and trombone of the classic New Orleans band absent, there is a certain lack of rhythmic drive.

Gambler's Dream has a strange effect which derives from the singer's invention. It is found in the scalar construction and line of the melody and the peculiar relation of melody to basic harmony. The six-tone scale avoids the third in a manner strange to the blues and the melody begins on the tonic or keynote around which the two call lines hover insistently to end, after a downward curve, on the fifth. The effect is not blue in the usual sense but, through a peculiar reversal of melodic direction, a sort of dull despair is expressed. This melody is the African and Afro-American type which starts around the fifth and ends on the keynote, *turned backward*, suggesting, in a very subtle way, introspection or unhappy memory.

This strange quality, like a reflection in a mirror, is enforced by Hociel's way of avoiding the beat. Her attack never *follows* the beat in the usual strong Negroid tendency but, whenever it is off the regular pulse, moves it forward by very slight anticipations. To the ear accustomed to the rhythmic swing of delayed off-beat timing, the effect is that of swinging *backward*. *Gambler's Dream* exemplifies the tendency of even the classic blues to develop through change.

Bertha "Chippie" Hill appeared momentarily at this period and then disappeared, leaving a few Okeh records which are indisputably classic. From her recordings of this period her expressive, deep and beautiful voice, full of haunting inflections, would seem to lack a little of Ma Rainey's power and richness, particularly in low register, and her rhythmic emphasis would seem less forceful.

Twenty years later, in 1946, I found "Chippie" living obscurely in Chicago and immediately recorded her. The inconclusiveness of comparisons on the basis of scanty recording is well shown by these later records. In these she reveals the greatest range and power, a rhythmic shouting more forceful than will be found on any of the known records of Ma and Bessie, and a clipped, hot phrasing that barely appears in her earlier work.

Certain numbers she recorded in 1946 are unquestionably masterpieces. *How Long Blues*, for example, a blues derived originally from a spiritual, is filled, as she sings it, with a somber, tragic power. Her *Careless Love*, melodically simpler, more archaic and more Negroid than Bessie's, even, is a work of controlled power and epic simplicity that surely ranks with the great Bessie's version.

CITATION 32. a. *Trouble In Mind* (1926), by Bertha "Chippie" Hill, accompanied by Louis Armstrong, trumpet, and Richard M. Jones, piano.

b. *Trouble In Mind* (1946), by Bertha "Chippie" Hill, accompanied by Lee Collins, trumpet; Lovie Austin, piano; John Lindsay, bass; and Baby Dodds, drums.

Trouble In Mind is perhaps "Chippie" Hill's greatest recorded achievement in both periods. Poetically and musically it is of a rare order. The voice sings in high register except for the downward cadences which end the phrases; the taut, muted trumpet is very blue in tone; underneath, the piano is simple and rich. Bertha's singing is fervent and Armstrong's varied antiphonal responses are of a high creative order in the early version. Lee Collins' expressive trumpet and Austin's powerful ballad-style piano dominate the background of the rocking later disc in which "Chippie's" singing, full of *dirty* inflections, alternates with humming of an indescribable beauty.

> *Trouble in mind; I'm blue but I won't be always.*
> *The sun gonna shine in my back door someday.*
>
> *I'm all alone at midnight and the lamps are burning low;*
> *Never had so much trouble in my life before.*

Trouble in love comes with me, and it sho' do grieve my mind.
Some days I feel like livin', sometimes I feel like dyin'.

I'm gonna lay my head on some lonesome railroad iron
And let the 2:19 train satisfy my mind.

Trouble in mind, I'm blue, but I won't be always.
The sun gonna shine in my back door someday.

In her early records, Sippie Wallace has a voice of beautiful quality but its power is chiefly in the upper register, the lower range lacking the full richness and force which Ma and Bessie possessed. She sings rhythmically, with sensitive changes from syncopation to attack on the beat. Her phrasing is varied and full of the feeling of the spirituals and the church; it has a shouting quality and abounds in the downward quavering phrases which we hear in the congregations, those numes, centering around the third and seventh intervals, which are so characteristically African. Sippie's ending of the shouted phrase with a nume recalls and symbolizes both the preacher and the responding congregation.

CITATION 33. *Trouble Everywhere I Roam,* by Sippie Wallace and Clarence Williams' Blue Five.

We find this fine twelve-bar blues to be, to all intents and purposes, a spiritual; its words

There is trouble here, trouble everywhere
There's trouble here, trouble everywhere
Lawd, I would go home but there's trouble over there.

. . . . .

Ever since my dear old mother have been dead,
Ever since my dear old mother have been dead,
The rocks have been my pillow and the streets have been my bed,

recall vividly such spiritual poetry as *Nobody Knows the Trouble I've Seen* and *Rocks Cried Out, "There's No Hidin' Place."*

This record and its reverse side, *Baby I Can't Use You No More,* another fine blues, suffer from inadequate accompaniment. Nevertheless, *Trouble Everywhere* has a severe and beautiful melody which shines through the muddy ensemble.

The work of Sippie Wallace, of the early period, was of great importance; its varied nature is interesting and sometimes significant. *Section Hand Blues,* for example, is not a blues at all, but a very interesting semi–ballad, semi–blues variant of the traditional *John Henry.* Portions are sung like a work-song:

> *If my captain ask for me*
> *Tell him Abe Lincoln done set us free;*
> *Ain' no hammer on this road*
> *Gonna kill poor me.*

> *This ol' hammer*
> *Killed John Henry,*
> *But this hammer*
> *Ain' gone kill me.*

> *I'm headin' for my shack*
> *With my shovel on my back,*
> *Altho' money what I lack*
> *I'm goin' home.*

Parlor Social de Luxe besides being a gusty rendering of a good tune of real jazz character, has social references of some import. It refers to the well-known rent parties, given in Negro homes to defray the overdue rent. These *socials* offered, besides food like the famous chittlin's and pigs' feet, and drink like the contraband moonshine whisky and gin, the musical entertainment of blues piano playing (boogie-woogie and barrel-house) and the semi-ragtime party piano style. The likely prospect of fights and police raids was presented as well, a prospect which did not seem to reduce attendance.

> *Down at that house rent party*
> *Each and everybody*
> *Got full of gin and corn,*
> *And, folks, they had their habits on!*
> *Big business for some bootlegger*
> *And bigger business for the undertaker.*

Thus Sippie sings, and the second-rate jazz-band background gives much of the gay, devil-may-care, disorderly atmosphere of a *Saturday Night Function*.

Sippie Wallace, like "Chippie" Hill, was rediscovered and recorded in 1946. Unfortunately she seems not to have grown in stature like "Chippie," but to have deteriorated into mere sophistication and cliché.

Postclassic Blues

The first of this type, the contemporary blues, represents a falling off in power but not in sincerity. Good recorded examples are plentiful and two of them will be mentioned here.

CITATION 34. *Skeet and Garrett* [6] by Roosevelt Sykes, recorded on Okeh about 1929, a blues of great beauty, is sung in a taut, strident voice, almost falsetto. The melody dips and soars over a rich piano which exploits strange harmonies and swells out during the responses in disquieting tremolandi which are like shudders.

CITATION 35. *When You Feel Lowdown*, sung by Lonnie Johnson with guitar, string-bass and piano.

Johnson is one of the finest of the blues guitarists as well as a good singer. Occasionally he has recorded pornographic songs of a disarmingly humorous nature, but he has remained immune to false sophistication.

Lonnie sings in his clear, high voice:

You can stay in a town so long: you feel yo'self sinkin' down
You can stay in a town so long: you feel yo'self sinkin' down
You jest change your way of living and don't forget to change
    your town.

The next chorus is an instrumental response in which departure from the town is symbolized in a train imitation highly evolved and sublimated, with a steady rhythm and the sound of train bells converted into a musical guitar figure.

We find, in the decadent or sophisticated blues of the post-

[6] A southern brand of snuff.

classic period, a far different thing than mere cliché or dilution. The sophisticated blues are not a continuation of the classic in a sincere but enfeebled or dilute manner, but show a real decadence with their spurious elements of insincerity and their grasping for easy success in the pornographic, the theatrical, or the merely clever.

The pornographic is well typified by Jazz Gillum's *Deep Water Blues* (Bluebird 34–0709) which sets forth an over-elaborate as well as much too obvious sexual symbolism.

A best-seller on today's records, the singer Lil Green typifies the faults of sophisticated blues. In such a record as her *Just Rockin'*, we find stilted and coy phrasing in an affectedly harsh voice, pruriently suggestive phrases by which the most un-Victorian listener would not be amused, and the effete, so-called modern, piano that interlards its meaningless runs with unconvincing boogie-woogie eclecticisms.

Another popular recording artist, Josh White, exhibits sophistication of a different sort. His approach is the intellectual one and he uses the blues for their social significance. There is a measure of artificiality in this, although the singer's sincerity is not to be questioned. Such singing may be, in some degree, effective as propaganda, but it remains to be seen whether it is more so than the stark power of the pure folk blues, the grim drama of Ma Rainey, Bessie Smith, or "Chippie" Hill. There is a certain lack of conviction in White's singing. It seems that he is quoting — not speaking first-hand. This lack of a deep conviction is especially evident when he essays a great traditional blues like the following:

CITATION 36. *Milk Cow Blues*, as recorded earlier under White's pseudonym of Pinewood Tom.[7] His style then — a little less than ten years ago — was, as it is now, pleasant and melodious but scarcely deep and vital. More recently, White has recorded the same number, *Milk Cow Blues*, with the New Orleans clarinetist Sidney Bechet under rather less commercial

[7] In this period he also recorded spirituals under the pseudonym of The Singing Christian.

conditions on the Blue Note label, but the same faults are to be found. White's singing, indeed, could and perhaps should be classified as a revival of the blues.

Another present-day singer, Bea Booze, shows how sophisticated tricks can spoil the work of a sincere singer. In her record, *See See Rider Blues*, her singing holds genuine feeling but the sophisticated mannerisms, the crooner's grace note and turn of phrase have entered in and the power has gone out. Ma Rainey's *See See Rider* is a great dramatic expression; this record is mere fourth-rate entertainment.

Chief among those who offer smart revivals of the blues is the well-known singer, Billie Holiday. Misguided critics have compared this beautiful *diseuse* of popular ballads to Bessie Smith and have praised her agreeable but enervated voice, at the same time calling Bessie's superb and vital vocal organ harsh. Her sophisticated phrases, uncreatively repeated mannerisms, and her thorough exploitation of ennui soon pall on any informed listener.

Billie Holiday is not a real blues singer but merely a smart entertainer. That is why her popular songs, trivial material at best, recorded with effete Negroes like the pianist, Teddy Wilson, or technically flashy but strictly non-jazz players, like the white clarinetist, Benny Goodman, are her most characteristic work. Nevertheless, she attempts the blues (for which she is not qualified), presenting them in an eclectic form to the special pleasure-seeking audiences of New York night clubs.

CITATION 37. *Fine and Mellow*, by Billie Holiday and her orchestra.

The small band, overloaded with two lethargic saxophones, shows in its meaningless riff style [8] that it never heard of jazz beyond the mention of the name. The trumpet responses are thin and unconvincing and evoke no memories of the answers, curt or eloquent, of an Armstrong or a Ladnier. Holiday's singing, which follows adequately the blues formula of flatted notes,

[8] A riff is a repeated rhythmic phrase incorporating an unrelated melodic fragment.

seems to have, at first hearing, a dispirited and rather poignant melancholy, but beneath the surface are only artifice and insincerity. The performance is devitalized, languishing, and sentimental. The reverse of this record,

CITATION 38. *Strange Fruit*, is a commentary on lynching. With its artificial jungle effects, as hollow and stagy as Ellington's, and its unconvincing singing of artificial lyrics, it is neither a blues, a pop tune, nor a ballad, but is a mood piece, an atmospheric bit of musical stuff too gauzy to hold a tragic content.

The blues abound in social significance, but the real significance of *Strange Fruit* is that of the Negro adapting himself to our smart society while he sells out the birthright of his own great and original art. In his minority fight for an equal place in our society, he too frequently deprecates his own achievements because they represent a past and a present he wishes to forget while adopting uncritically the customs and arts of the white majority.

We find in the blues, therefore, as we shall in swing, an artificial sophistication arising either in an entertainer's glibness, or, on the higher level, in the desertion of the blues for our concert hall repertory. It is significant that the Negro takes more to singing than to classic instruments. He is a natural singer but the vocal tone he imparts to our brass and reeds seems unsuitable in our music. The opera remains closed to him except, of course, for *Otello* and such rarities as the *Four Saints in Three Acts* of Gertrude Stein and Virgil Thomson.

Some white players and singers have shown a fair mastery of the blues idiom, and some very young high school students whom I have heard have shown considerable aptitude under Negro tutelage. When the white musician approaches the blues casually or without understanding, however, the results are worse than the poorest Negro efforts. An example in point is:

CITATION 39. *That's a Serious Thing* by Eddie's Hot Shots. This record, made about 1929, is an attempt to play and sing the blues. It was considered authentic enough for the uncritical

Victor Company to issue in its race catalog. It has been accepted as the real thing by many critics and a large section of the jazz following.

The instrumentation and personnel are as follows: trumpet, Charlie Davis; trombone and vocal, Jack Teagarden; alto saxophone, Milton Mezzrow; tenor saxophone, Happy Cauldwell; piano, Joe Sullivan; banjo, Eddie Condon; drums, George Stafford. *That's a Serious Thing* is played in the white jazz manner which has been called Chicago Style; since this is to be discussed fully later on, only one or two salient points will be pointed out. The instrumentation is faulty, omitting clarinet and including two saxophones; because of this, and because of an obvious lack of jazz ability on the part of most of the players, no real jazz polyphony is produced. Davis plays an acceptable blues trumpet; the saxophone solos are meaningless; the trombone in solo is fumbling and its phrases are overloaded. In ensemble, that instrument's fine, and necessary, New Orleans role of harmonic fill-in and propulsive rhythmic phrase is completely missing.

Teagarden's singing of the blues words:

If your house catch on fire, Lawd, there ain't no water 'round
If your house catch on fire, Lawd, there ain't no water 'round
(Now everybody knows that's an awful serious thing)
Throw your trunk out the window, Lawd, let the shack burn down.

is pleasant and nonchalant but essentially trivial; the melody has certain turns characteristic of European melody and foreign to the blues. The wide gulf which separates this performance from real blues is shown by a comparison with *Southern Blues* [9] in which Ma Rainey sings a version of the same lines. Significantly, however, the spoken, un-Negroid line shown in parentheses, does not appear in her record and the singing has a power and feeling beside which Teagarden's efforts are ridiculous. To paraphrase his own comment, the blues *are not* a serious thing to Teagarden.

[9] Paramount 12083.

145

Besides white imitations, various pseudo-blues have arisen. One kind originated in New York's Harlem around 1915–20. In harmony and phrasing it is not a true blues. Vocal examples can be heard in the work of singers like Sara Martin and instrumental ones in the piano records and player-rolls of that period by James P. Johnson. In the early 1920's, when the blues began to receive general attention, popular songs, erroneously called blues, began to appear. *Mobile Blues, Washboard Blues* and *Wang Wang Blues* are of this sort.

There also developed a rural type of song that the white singers call blues and which certain writers designate as white blues. This, again, is not blues, nor is it even an established form. It preserves faint echoes of the real Negro blues, but in mountain districts it is a hill-billy song and in the Southwest it is a cowboy tune.

As we have seen, the real blues grew spontaneously into a form; the pretensions of any individual to its invention are preposterous. Even to claim, or accept, the title of "Father of the Blues," as W. C. Handy has done, is as absurd as it is presumptuous. Although a Negro, Handy is, and in sympathy always has been, rather remote from the racial wellsprings from which the blues and jazz emerged. He seems, from the time of his youth, to have been in the un-Negroid tradition that goes back to the Fisk Jubilee Singers or farther, a tradition that always has aimed to "disinfect" Afro-American music by Europeanizing it.

The blues were being sung long before Handy wrote down and copyrighted a few he had heard. *Yellow Dog Blues*, for example, has enriched Handy but not those obscure troubadours who have sung it for perhaps sixty years. Even the *St. Louis Blues* adds only a tango section to the regular twelve-bar blues of an earlier number, *Jogo Blues*, which Handy apparently did not compose. Fatherhood of the blues is out of the question; Handy's sponsorship, although it helped to awaken interest in the blues, has retarded accurate knowledge of them and certainly was of no influence in their development.

146

There is a story that Jelly Roll Morton, once in Memphis with a redoubtable blues-playing New Orleans band, challenged Handy and his painfully "legitimate" orchestra with its full complement of violins, to make good Handy's claims to jazz. The challenge was not accepted. Jelly Roll retained for Handy and his pretenses, the contempt a great creative personality might be forgiven for feeling. In later years, Ripley ill-advisedly introduced Handy, on the *Believe It or Not* radio program, as the originator of the blues and jazz as well! Jelly answered this misrepresentation promptly and, it may be said, with some authority. In a published article, the great New Orleans Negro wrote:

> Mr. Handy cannot prove that he has created any music. He has possibly taken advantage of some unprotected material that sometimes floats around. I would like to know how a person could be an originator of anything without being able to do at least some of what they created.[10]

Since Handy's efforts on violin and trumpet are completely out of the jazz tradition, the point of this polemic is conclusive, for jazz is not composed music but one improvised in actual performance.

The real blues singers have never claimed the invention of what they sing. In true folk style they have freely borrowed lines and melodies from others; when their names appear as composers on the record labels this is only a necessary legal step in issuing records and clearing them for radio. There is a significant anonymity about the blues; they have an existence, almost a personality, of their own. Perhaps they stand as a personalized, heroic, and martyred symbol of the sufferings of the Negroes in America, as the *Grey Goose*, a ballad, stands for the black man's ultimate victory. We find the blues, indeed, often personalized, as in the lines,

> *The blues jumped a rabbit and run him a solid mile;*
> *Yes, the po' fellow lied down and cried like a natural child.*

[10] *Down Beat Magazine*, 1938.

147

Like fate, they are often a cruel and catastrophic force, but one palpable to the senses, as when the singer relates:

When I got up this mornin': blues walkin' 'round my bed;
I went to breakfast: the blues was all in my bread.

Some believe that the blues originated with, and celebrate, Emancipation. No doubt they began then. Perhaps earlier versions, now lost, are in this vein. But there is no doubt that the blues for the last sixty years have sung of a continuing slavery against which the Thirteenth and Fourteenth Amendments stand as empty and mocking gestures.

The blues are the music of a race, a music beloved by us all because none of us is wholly free. They furnish a compressed and perfect expression of the mixed goodness and evil of life as we find it in the world. The anonymity, worn like an actor's mask, is a part of the universality of this music and not even the greatest of the blues singers has claimed its creation. Ma Rainey sings in *Last Minute Blues:*

If anybody ask you who wrote this lonesome song
Tell 'em you don't know the writer, but Ma Rainey put it on.

BOOK TWO

7.

new orleans and the
beginnings of jazz

THE MISSISSIPPI DELTA rests like a foot poised on the brink of the Gulf of Mexico, the great river's four outlets defining its five toes. A flat mysterious region, this, where water seems, in an indefinite flux, to become land, and land water, as if this were all happening in an earlier age when even the elements were not yet firmly fixed. Miles of winding bayou, haunt of alligator and mocassin; shallow lakes brimful of the snowy heaped cumulus clouds that float above; watery forests of cypress with trist, trailing mossy veils, sassafras, and dwarf palmetto; endless forests gray and brown and green, home of the fur trapper and the animals he seeks; and brown mud, bottomless mud, fertile mud, the richest soil of America carried down 4,000 miles of river current. A lonely and mysterious region, the Delta has changed but little in the two and a half centuries since Iberville anchored in the Bay of Biloxi and Louisiana came under the first of the five flags that have floated over her territories.

Up from the Gulf, are, first, the four passes of the River and then the Head of the Passes. One hundred and ten miles upstream, the river swings around in a broad shining crescent, within which lies New Orleans. Here in the fever-ridden swamp, a bare twenty years after they landed, the French laid out the city, eleven squares riverwise and six squares deep. In this area — the original Nouvelle Orléans, now called the French Quarter or Vieux Carrè — arose the first rude wooden shacks.

For time untold the River had carried mud down, most of it

swept out into the sea, a small part rescued in the land's final clutch. And now, the city founded, the ocean currents began to bring inland deposits of a different sort, human flotsam, hardy adventurers, priests, thieves, cutthroats, pimps, and girls of easy virtue recruited in France to assuage loneliness. Men of many kinds and conditions from widespread parts of the world, in two hundred years the living deposits came to include French, Spanish, Italians, the exiled Acadians, Americans, and, of course, the Negroes, first from West Africa, later by way of Haiti and other Caribbean islands: white sediment and black sediment settling out in strata on the wet brown mud.

Just as its site through years of periodic floods could not decide whether to be land or water, so through its long youth the city could not decide whether it was to be French, Spanish, or American.

Never were contrasts so violent in degree to be seen in one community. Silk-garbed wealth and abject destitution; holy Masses said by brocaded priests in a boarded warehouse church while profligate sin prospered outside; fruitful labor and reckless gambling; beautiful, flaming life and the hideous death of yellow fever; and forever the white and the black. New Orleans grew like a swamp lily in its noisome mud, now and for long a beautiful city, almost always an evil one. Desolated time and again by yellow fever and cholera, consumed by fire, swept by hurricane, buried by flood, the city rose again and again like a lily's new blooming from the old, mud-buried corm.

There was indecision in the attitude of white master to Negro. Here a class of free Negroes, almost an anomaly in the South, arose early. Some even came to own slaves of a skin darker than their own. In many an eddy the black and white soil settled down and mixed into a damp creamy brown loam, fertile, secret, and rich. These *creoles of color* can be accounted for in part by human passions, in part by Gallic tolerance, in part by the perennial *laissez-faire*, child of the indecision and indolence of the Crescent City.

Tolerance, too, allowed the colored Creoles to become, in the nineteenth century, an elegant society that educated its young in France and supported a large symphony orchestra and chorus. Not a few of its members "passed" into white society. This same tolerance — or indolent indecision — permitted the blacker slave Negroes to carry on their African music and dancing in Congo Square.

Although she faces the River, New Orleans is a seaport. Once one of the world's greatest, she is still the natural outlet of the great Mississippi basin. Cotton and sugar made her rich — at least they made her wealthy Creoles wealthier — before some of her greatness passed with the coming of the railroads, which, unlike the great river, traverse our continent laterally, from east to west.

The nineteenth century was a great century for speculation and sudden wealth, riotous living, daily bloody duels beneath *The Oaks*. Creole society, haughtiest in the South, lived side by side with the abject blacks and tolerated, if not condoned, the countless *mesamours* of white gentlemen with ripely beautiful quadroons. A great century, when the Americans came and their boats moved up and down the river like a continuous fleet — rafts, arks, mackinaws, broadhorns, keelboats, and the majestic steam packets: the *Enterprise*, the *Sultana*, the *Belle of the West*, and the *Robert E. Lee*. Ships that made history once — names that make magic still! These ships were once much more than means of transportation, more than floating investments. They were parts of the very spiritual life of every Orleanian, parts that went out to the unknown outer world, a world in which New Orleans never has had any great interest, to return betimes to the home quay. Quay and wharves of a city where even the streets bespeak indecision or tolerance: where *Desire Street* follows *Piety Street*, or *Piety* follows *Desire*, depending on how you approach the matter!

This was the great century of the Mardi Gras, the carnival that began late in the eighteenth century to grow into a long revelry lasting a month and a half. On the Thursday before Shrove Tuesday the parades begin. For a hundred years they have been symbolic processional tableaux, almost unbelievably elaborate. By day and night, the processions pass through the gay, reveling crowds. On Monday afternoon Algiers, across the river, holds its aquatic parade, a beautiful procession of decorated water-floats moving slowly upstream in a discordant fanfare of steam whistles. On Mardi Gras morning, Zulu, King of the Africans, arrives from his yacht in New Basin Canal and his parade of Negroes marches along to the fine street-band jazz with which these streets, Canal and North Rampart, Royal and Orleans, have intermittently echoed for seventy-five years. An hour more, and Rex, scion of old King Cole and Terpsichore, King of Carnival and Misrule, appears unmasked, genial and grandiose, at the head of his procession. He receives the keys to the city and proceeds to his waiting Queen and her court. The streets swarm with revelers in masks which must be removed at sunset. And with evening, the eve of Ash Wednesday, the last and greatest parade, that of Comus, god of Mirth and Joy, winds through the shadowed and narrow streets of the Old Quarter.

Most of these parades have twenty floats and fourteen complete bands. And such bands! Like yellow sunlight the sweetly blatant, brassy sounds float through the streets, echo by day and by night from the old, balconied houses, resound in the dim courtyards, carrying the thrilling sounds of the old marches: *High Society, Gettysburg, Panama, If I Ever Cease to Love.* If you turn from the white bands with their military precision to the Negroes playing the same march with their incomparable elastic, skipping, syncopated rhythm, you are hard upon the very source of Negro jazz.

Throughout most of the nineteenth century, and to this day, the brass band and the parade have been an integral part of New Orleans life to a greater degree than anywhere else. Almost anything furnishes a pretext for a parade — politics, lodge celebrations, weddings, and funerals.

In 1870 New Orleans was vastly different from any other American city. Into its air, loud with steamboat whistles and the work-chants of stevedores busy with cotton bales, sounded the first high notes of the shining trumpets. Then the swift notes poured out, a black, calithumpian music, and the first jazz had fallen on human ears. It was black music because it came, at first, from the black ex-slaves and not from their lighter and more elegant cousins in the Old Quarter. In its first sounding it seemed only an imitation of the trained white bands. And so it was; but in the Negroid character, which transforms whatever it imitates, it became, as the spiritual had become, an Afro-American music. Its potentialities were greater than those of the spiritual. It was the Negro's first essay with our instruments. He was to find at hand a wide variety of cultural ingredients the spiritual never had. He was to find a large number of secular uses that encouraged his playing while they formed his manner.

The Negroes had their own street bands in New Orleans much earlier than is commonly supposed. In 1881, in the funeral ceremonies for President Garfield, there was a huge procession replete with bands as usual. In this procession, some thirteen or more permanently organized Negro bands took part. They represented fraternal and benevolent organizations, labor unions of longshoremen, teamsters, and cotton yardmen. These organizations antedated the procession, one, at least, having been founded as early as 1871.[1] It is reasonable to suppose that the bands were organized earlier than this procession: so salient a part of local life and one so congenial to Negro temperament must have been adopted as early as possible.

An aged Orleanian told Nesuhi Ertegun that numerous Confederate brass bands disbanded in New Orleans immediately after the war. Their instruments, finding their way into the pawn shops, were plentiful and cheap.

Other direct testimony is available. A New Orleans player, Wallace Collins, familiarly called "Colley," tells of these early developments. Colley, born in 1858, says that in his early child-

---

[1] The Perseverance Benevolent Society was founded even earlier, in 1853. Its building, now a café, stands on North Villères Street near Annette.

hood, around Emancipation, he and a schoolmate, Louis Ned,[2] frequently "played hookey" from school to imitate band music. They blew on old pieces of water pipe, punched with holes, and with paper tied around the ends to give a "dirty" tone. They could simulate cornet, tuba, and trombone on these homemade instruments. The intense musicality of these little black boys![3]

This Louis Ned went on in music and soon had a band of his own. If, as seems likely, this was in his teens, the band was functioning by 1874 or 1875, perhaps earlier. Collins himself learned tuba and played with Bolden's Brass Band, which preceded his famed Ragtime Band.

Given the bands, how would they have played? Certainly not in trained European style. It can be taken for granted that these early groups played the standard march tunes in a self-taught and highly Negroid style, that here were the archaic first stages of jazz fifteen to twenty years before jazz is supposed to have begun despite the early marches that are still played today.

Buddy Bolden's Ragtime Band of 1893, generally considered the first jazz band, undoubtedly represents the transition from the archaic street jazz to a more developed, classic stage. Bolden's Band was well developed technically and had a much wider repertory than march tunes; it is not in the nature of a process as pragmatic and experimental as that of Afro-American music, for such a sudden emergence to occur.

Here again, Collins' simple but factual testimony is valuable. Playing in Bolden's Ragtime Band — which he says played "classical," meaning march, music — he saw the change. Bolden, he says, was the first to bring out the rags in band form, and the blues as well. These were two revolutionary advances from archaic jazz.

To "rag" a tune, Collins says, "He'd take one note and put two or three to it. He began to teach them — not by the music

---

2 Spelling uncertain.

3 *"En lui-même, le nègre est déjà un instrument de musique, autant par le rhythme qui le hante que par l'habilité de ses membres et par les resources de sa voix."* (André Cœuroy and André Schaeffner: Le Jazz, Paris 1926).

— just by the head. After he'd get it down right, he'd teach the others their part.

"They had lots of band fellows who could play like that after Bolden gave 'em the idea.

"*Any Rags?*, that was one of the tunes.[4] You know they had an old blind man who came around with a wagon to pick up junk. He'd go around singing — he wasn't singing, he was talking but he was really singing:

> *Any rags*
> *Any rags*
> *Any rags*
> *Ain't you got anything today?*

Bolden picked it up and made a rag out of it.

"He had the town by storm and when the people heard Bolden then you couldn't get in the place without you go early. Bolden would play, 'Don't Go 'Way Nobody — stay here and have a good time!' "

Logically, we must place the beginnings of jazz very shortly after Emancipation. Later richnesses of the music are to be accounted for by its development in the rich cultural milieu of its birthplace. The Negroid character it has never lost, is accounted for by the earlier date. Not only was Africa nearer in point of time, but in 1870 freshly landed slaves were at hand, the strongly African work-songs were current, and African dancing and ceremonial music were still continued in Congo Square.[5] Much has been made of the fact that Buddy Bolden was a boy when the Congo Square activity reached its last stages of decline in the 1880's. What, then, must have been the effect of this African survival at its height, on the children and youths who, in future years, formed the first street bands? May

4 Bunk Johnson refers to a tune played by Bolden, as *Junk Man Rag*. This rag was composed by the great New York Harlem pianist, Lucky Roberts, and published in 1912. With Bolden already permanently in an asylum by 1907, this statement is obviously in error.

5 Baby Dodds, the great jazz drummer, says that his maternal great-grandfather played "African drums" in New Orleans. This would have been in the mid-nineteenth century. "He talked on them," Baby says, and then demonstrates the drum code as it was traditionally preserved in his family.

not some of them have danced and sung, drummed or blown wooden trumpets in the historic square?

The earliest jazz was almost completely unchronicled. Even the earlier Afro-American music, being more widespread and covering a longer period, though it attracted more notice, was mainly a field for descriptive "tourist" writing or moralistic "sermons" set forth in such adjectives as "quaint and amusing" or "barbarous and lascivious."

Serious interest in jazz began only about 1920, perhaps as much as fifty years after the music originated. For some time it concerned itself with the stage of development then in progress. It was not until about 1932–35 that any real effort was made to trace its history. A few of the older practitioners of the art were then interviewed, but none of these was of the scant number whose memories could accurately extend back to 1870. By 1935 this would have required questioning men of 80 years and more.

The testimony seemed to place the origin of jazz as about 1893–95, the approximate time when those interviewed had begun to play. These players were, at least in the main, unquestionably sincere. But they may have had little knowledge and less interest in what preceded them. Or they may not have considered the earlier archaic jazz the same music as theirs. Unconscious motivation could have colored their testimony. Having suffered, as many of them had, from neglect and misunderstanding, they may well have had the psychological need to consider themselves creators, not of a stage, but of jazz itself. Deeper still is the general social need of the Negro to justify himself and to escape from the false stereotype that white "superiority" has cast upon him.

In general, too, the "views" of the practitioner of an art must be weighed carefully even where his "facts" may be accepted. Disregarding personal motivation, the painter or the musician may have no great *theoretical* knowledge of his own art. His practice of it often makes a broad, impersonal, critical, and theoretical point of view difficult to achieve. There is no need to go back to Poe's pronouncements on poetry to enforce this point. A great jazz guitarist, a veteran of New Orleans, only recently has prepared a long account purporting to prove that jazz has no African character because it derives — supposedly — solely from the spiritual! This is like saying, "I am related to my father but not to my grandfather." The intent, perhaps unconscious, is obviously to elevate the Negro by discounting his African origin, to sanction jazz by tying it to the irreproachable music of the Church.

With the proved existence of at least a baker's dozen of Negro bands in New Orleans by 1880 or earlier, we must examine the possibility of some of them having played in a trained, white manner. This hinges, in the main, on educational facilities for the Negroes in New Orleans. The first such institution of higher education was New Orleans University, founded in 1869. While it is true that carpet-bagging days laid a temporary stress on Negro education, its immediate effect in New Orleans upon the music of this race is open to doubt. These years, 1870 to 1880, were, beyond question, crucial ones for Afro-American music: in this Reconstruction period the two main tendencies of the music were established. These were the continuance of Afro-American music, of which jazz was to become the most important component, and the contrary tendency toward the Europeanization of this music, which would logically need to end with its complete abandonment. While this second tendency began at least as early as 1871 with the Fisk Jubilee Singers and the Hampton Student Singers, it almost certainly came later in New Orleans, which has never boasted an institution of the influence of Fisk College or Hampton Institute.[6] Even if the Negro academic institutions in New Orleans did begin to affect Negro music early, it is highly doubtful

[6] "At present . . . the freedmen have an unfortunate inclination to despise [the spiritual] as a vestige of slavery; those who learned it in the old time, when it was the natural outpouring of their sorrows and longings, are dying off, and if efforts are not made for its preservation, the country will soon have lost this wonderful music of bondage." Thomas P. Fenner, of Hampton Institute, in 1874.

that much attention would have been paid to the lowly street band.

Too, the mainly proletarian nature of the organizations that produced the first bands militates against such a possibility. And even considerably later, when Negro education was firmly established, the cornetist, Bunk Johnson, who had legitimate conservatory training, voluntarily chose jazz as his field. The safest statement, perhaps, is that there *may* have been, even in the beginning, a band or two playing in trained style. But this, a notably small percentage, has been maintained down to today. Even later development of downtown [7] "society" bands was of little influence on jazz music.

The archaic jazz band transferred the rhythmic and tonal characteristics of the earlier Afro-American music to band instruments. This revolutionary step took Negro music away from the choral-percussive form to which it had been limited previously. While opening up new lines for development, the African characteristics of the earlier music were retained, the tendencies to polyrhythm, to antiphony and polyphony, and toward the free development of melody unhampered by harmonic development. From these antecedents come the distinguishing features of all jazz, including the distinctive vocal timbre imparted to the wind instruments. With no formal training, the Negroes imparted vocal tone to the cornet, trombone, and even the clarinet, though it is an achieved, not a natural, tone with these instruments. Extreme musicality gave the Negroes quick mastery of even the difficult instruments and helped them to surmount difficulties they did not even know existed. Unable to read music, they promptly transformed the marches into Negro jazz just as their forerunners had transformed the hymns into spirituals. Over the bass, snare drums, and cymbal beaten like African drums, they made the cornet, trombone, clarinet, piccolo, alto horn, and tuba sing like the polyphony of the African chorus. Thus jazz is not a music separate and

[7] New Orleans' downtown is the old quarter north of Canal Street. Uptown is the district around the nucleus of the American Quarter, south of that street.

shining trumpets

distinct from the blues and the songs of the fields and churches.
It is rather a special flowering of the Negro musical genius in
which, to the existing values, are added new, rich materials and
the technical possibilities of instrumentation. It is the epochal
development to which all earlier Afro-American music had
pointed.

That this should have happened in New Orleans is inevitable.
Only there, were the brass bands on every street, the instruments cheap and plentiful for the Negroes. Only there, too, were
all the rich ingredients that, flowing into the wild, rough, archaic jazz, transformed it into a developed, classic form before
1900.

Before 1895, archaic jazz had assimilated various elements
besides the marches. These were, first, an unknown amount of
original African material direct from Congo Square and, second, through Voodoo from Haiti; and the earlier Afro-American music, the work-songs, spirituals, ballads, children's songs,
and blues. In addition, there were ragtime, minstrel music, and
early popular songs. Before discussing these, let us examine
the archaic rendering of a typical march tune.

It is significant that the early style can be shown by present-
day recordings. Just as the archaic blues have continued
through the classic period down to the present, so the corresponding period of jazz remains, even today, surprisingly vital
and singularly pure considering all the elements which might
have diluted and changed it. To some extent, the alto horns and
the piccolos dropped out of the march band during this period;
but throughout the dancing jazz or classic period that was to
follow, the older function of street parades has survived and
with it the street style. Today, of course, there is an unfortunate
tendency to include saxophones. While we may hear the march
tunes of the 1870's but seldom, march music has changed little
in the three-quarters of a century since then. Jazz musicians,
too, have alternated between dance and street jazz according to
the necessities of employment; organized bands have, with appropriate changes in set-up, alternated likewise. The requisite

changes in dynamics, tempo, instrumentation, and repertory have kept archaic and classic separate to an extent, and have kept the earlier form, at least, relatively pure.

In 1940 a jazz enthusiast, Heywood Hale Broun, in the first recording junket of modern times to the birthplace of jazz, made the first records of march-style jazz. Eight sides resulted, despite inadequate facilities and difficulties in assembling personnel. They dropped with a resounding splash into the stream of commercial recorded music and aroused a storm of controversy.

To ears accustomed to the fixed pitch and the harmonic texture of white music, classical and popular, and the ruined music of the favorite Negro bands of the day, this music sounded crude, out-of-pitch, and almost barbarous. But out of the strangeness there emerged a message new to our generation. Some ears were ready.

Together with the 1939 album, called *New Orleans Memories*, of piano solos and blues by Jelly Roll Morton, the Broun Delta records represent a milestone in the history of jazz music appreciation.

Since polyphonic ensemble is of the essence in authentic jazz of any period, the solo is a comparative rarity except when employed in certain ways. But it unquestionably was a part of the original march-style jazz and its inclusion derives from a practical reason. The street bands play in full uniform on the hottest days and the tunes are continued for a considerable time. It is thus customary to see the leader motion with his head toward some one player who then plays a solo while the other members, except the drummers, get their breath. The others march along resting, some removing and lighting cigars from the music racks of their horns, racks in which, for a number of reasons, music sheets seldom repose. After a while, there is another signal and the whole band joins in again.

Even in classic jazz the solo is used functionally, not to display individual virtuosity. Virtuosity is a necessary quality in the good ensemble and one impressively evident even if largely taken for granted. So deeply ingrained is the idea of collective creation that, in the street band, the ensemble inevitably and eagerly succeeds the solo; in classic jazz the solo often is set forth without the polyphony stopping. Frequently the other voice instruments play on softly, and the solo is really one melodic part of the polyphony, projected forte. There is no lack of showmanship in the players of classic jazz but personal display never interferes with the rigorous formal requirements of this cooperative music.

In the marching jazz ensemble, we find the developed polyphonic elements of all true jazz. The tonal power, compass, pitch, and degree of mobility of the different voice instruments led, through experiment, to the assignment to each of its proper part. The jazz ensemble can be described either as a polyphony *over* rhythm, or a counterpoint of melodic polyphony *and* rhythm.

The percussive instruments, the snare and bass drums, and tuba, are called the *rhythm section*.[8] These instruments lay a solid foundation on the four beats of the measure, or sometimes a tied four-beat rhythm, most of them — and the drums always — solidly *on* the basic figure with syncopation decidedly at a minimum. The wind instruments play over this solid rhythmic foundation. During the archaic period the larger instrumentation was gradually simplified to a triumvirate of cornet (or trumpet), clarinet, and trombone. This combination proved the most workable in producing the Negroid improvised polyphony. So, over the rhythm, the "horns" function like the African chorus.

The lead role falls to the cornet or trumpet with its dramatic, commanding tone of great carrying power and its naturally simple, forceful expression. Intricate lines of many notes are not a part of the natural lead part; they are a development of the present-day, solo-playing virtuoso. The lead, which consists

---

[8] The tuba really functions both as a voice and a rhythm instrument. The rhythm section of the later classic jazz band includes guitar or banjo, drums, string-bass or tuba, and piano.

of the original melody, or simple variations thereon, must be emphatic and rhythmic; in its simplest form it tends to stay on the beat. But the gifted player tends to place his notes a little away from the actual beat; he anticipates or lags behind while the real beat tries, like a magnet, to draw the brass note back to its own center of force. The first element of polyrhythm enters; energy and momentum are created.

Both the clarinet and the trombone, in their respective parts, so conceive their melodies that they seldom coincide with the cornet or with one another on the same note.

The tone of the clarinet is lyric, liquid, and piquantly sweet; it has a quality, especially in high register, which makes it strike clearly through the tone mass of the brass and rhythm. Fluent and highly mobile, it fills in its own phrases between the lead notes, utilizing rapid runs, protracted piercing single notes, and short, staccato, repeated ones. The marvelous New Orleans technique, based on French reed practice, makes the rapid notes seem parts of a continuous legato stream, although each must be attacked separately.

Melodies counter to the cornet are conceived which utilize fully the range of this reed instrument and the contrasting beauties of its registers; these melodies are so improvised that some of the most beautiful portions, as those in the low and weaker *chalumeau* register, are projected antiphonally after the lead phrases. Intricate or ravishingly beautiful as the clarinet line may become, it is never just an embellishment or merely fanciful, but, as it adds an indispensable part to the melodic, harmonic, tonal and rhythmic texture, it is truly functional.

New Orleans clarinet players achieve fantastic glissandi, like those of African singing, from register to register. Their tone is customarily of the greatest purity and beauty. The growl (flutter-tongue) effect and other dirty tones are seldom used. Since the Negro achieved a wide variety of timbres in the brass, this strictness in the clarinet may be questioned. But the reason is functional. Only the pure tone of the clarinet will pierce through the powerful tone of the other instruments.

The baritone and alto horns in the archaic band contributed both polyphonic and melodic elements as well as polyrhythmic variety. When these instruments dropped out in the formation of the classic jazz band, their composite functions devolved upon the trombone and this led directly to the remarkably virtuoso development of trombone style known as *tailgate.*

The carrying power of the cornet or trumpet can be relied upon in any register; against its lead the trombone sets up a brass counterpoint. The trombone is technically formidable and its part is the freest and most inventive of the three voices. This instrument, in consequence, is the most difficult of the jazz instruments. The trombonist must fill in bass or harmony when needed, add pungent, rhythmic, expressive phrases, strike sharp stentorian tones and alternate them with the sheer upward thrusting force of the glissando or "smear," that characteristic continuous gliding tone made possible by the trombone slide. And doing all this, he must be rhythmically so self-possessed that he can stay off the beat much of the time. The chief possibility of syncopation is in his hands; if he is an *on the beat* trombonist, unable to fit notes *between* the beats and to displace his accents when *on* them, the rhythmic quality which is completely essential to the jazz band never comes to life. The really great jazz trombonist performs his rhythmic and harmonic functions while actually creating, chorus after chorus, his own complete and independent melodies. If we examine these melodies we find they are either variations on the basic melody or completely new melodies which harmonize with the whole polyphony. In the first case, we have variational polyphony from the band; in the second, a true heterophony.

In 1946 I went to New Orleans, assembled a typical street band, and made a series of recordings. The personnel was an interesting one, combining older players with younger ones who still can play in the archaic street manner. The trumpeters were Kid Howard and Peter Bocage, the latter a veteran Creole who played for years with Armand Piron's Orchestra. Jim Robinson, one of the greatest living tailgate players, was trombonist, and George Lewis, finest living exponent of the New Orleans clarinet style, was included. The brass section was rounded out by Isidore Barbarin on mellophone (alto horn); Harrison Barnes, baritone horn; and Joe Howard, tuba. Howard, seventy-four, was oldest of the group. Originally a trumpeter, he worked on the riverboats around 1916–19 and taught sight reading to Louis Armstrong when he joined the band on the s/s *Sidney*. The incomparable Baby Dodds performed on snares, and Lawrence Marrero, also a fine banjo and guitar player, beat the small parade drum.

Several fine records resulted, as this group fell naturally and easily into the traditional way of playing. The music "marched" as brassily and boldly in the studio as it might have done in the street. *Salutation March*, a previously unrecorded evergreen, showed an archaic, but relatively straight, way of playing. The reverse side of the disc, as issued, is unquestionably the best document to date of the raggy early brass band jazz. The citation follows:

CITATION 20. *If I Ever Cease to Love* (introducing *Little Brown Jug*), by the Original Zenith Brass Band. *If I Ever Cease to Love* is the very old traditional Mardi Gras March. The New Orleans Negro popular song of the 1890's, *Isn't It Hard to Love*, was probably a variant of this sprightly, single-theme number. The medley on this record is full of spirited and complex cross-rhythm and the spontaneous part playing is inventive and clearly articulated. The whole creative spirit of Negro jazz seems revealed the moment when Lewis's masterful clarinet leaps out in solo stop-time. Stop-timing consists in a series of breaks, like improvised cadenzas, invented at the moment, over a broken, pulsating rhythmic figure supplied by the band. Lewis's electrifying breaks run like chain lightning over the basic rhythmic barriers.

In this record, played substantially in the archaic march style, we find the unique instrumental polyphony of jazz already developed. This polyphony naturally tends to a degree of dissonance but it is one logically arrived at and is highly agreeable to the accustomed ear. Thus, in jazz, the principle of euphony is divorced from harmony and is greatly extended.

Archaic jazz, with its polyphony derived from the spiritual and work-song and transferred to instruments, began to transform music other than the marches.

Work-songs became popular songs like *Drop That Sack.* Spirituals, like *When the Saints Go Marching In* and *Down by the River (Ain't Gonna Study War No More)* became march tunes. Every veteran jazz player confirms the statement of the clarinetist, Louis de Lisle Nelson ("Big-Eye"), "The blues were here when I came." Certainly, during this period, the Afro-American flatted *blue notes* colored all jazz playing. Perhaps the blues form was relegated then to the disreputable alley dens but it was a known part of jazz by Bolden's time.

Minstrel tunes, and ragtime which derived from them, came plentifully into the early jazz. The music of the minstrels, as performed since 1843 by white performers, represents mainly Scotch, Irish, and English melodies with a Negroid rhythmic twist. (See Appendix I, p. 359.)

Outside New Orleans, the Negro entered minstrelsy after Emancipation, took the white repertory of "coon" songs like *Jump Jim Crow, Ole Zip Coon,* and *Hamfoot Man,* and promptly Africanized them. As the blues developed he added these to the repertory, something the white performers never did. Many of these converted songs came into archaic jazz, but the blues entered considerably later.

It is significant that the minstrel band never seems to have developed, in Negro hands, into jazz, although the sliding trombone style used in jazz was played both in the minstrel and the circus bands. That jazz did not develop through minstrel and circus bands, emphasizes the fact that all the necessary factors for its origin existed only in New Orleans.

Vestiges of the minstrels remain in jazz, rhythms of the dances of the last quarter of the nineteenth century, like the *Tack Annie* and the *Cake Walk* with its Caribbean origin and African ancestry. But their accompanying tunes for nearly half a century have all but vanished from jazz music. Yet minstrel music undoubtedly leavened the stream of archaic jazz; minstrel dancing was a factor in the sudden popularity of social dancing among the Negroes in New Orleans which was to begin about 1890.

A very rare and early record was found recently. It gives an authentic, of-the-period rendition of a Cake Walk in minstrel band style. This fragile, seven-inch disc bears Emil Berliner's Gramophone stamping and dates between 1895–1897. Berliner's records, first *discs* to be made, date from 1887 and were etched in small numbers rather than stamped in quantity.

CITATION 41. *Cotton Blossoms*. Besides this title, the record bears the word, *Orchestra*, the composer's name (Hall), written with stylus by hand in the original wax, the master number 398, and the issue number 1482. It is surprisingly well recorded, although the tempo — and with it the pitch — fluctuates occasionally since the recording turntable was not even spring-driven but was turned by hand.

The tune is gay and sprightly and, in the one and three-quarter minute's playing time, no less than four separate themes are presented. The record is a remarkably condensed version of the standard song form of many dances, marches, and ragtime pieces. In its syncopated and lively rendering, this selection really shows the Cake Walk as it emerged as ragtime. About this time compositions which had been published earlier were reappearing, rescored in syncopation and labeled "ragtime."

The orchestral instrumentation cannot be determined with complete accuracy, but cornet, two flutes (or, just possibly, clarinets), trombone, and piano can be clearly heard. The greatest surprise is the trombone, playing the most sliding, unfettered tail-gate or parade style imaginable.

The first known published ragtime [9] piece dates from 1897 but

[9] The origin of the name *rag* — like that of jazz — is obscure. However, in at least one Southern area, the Georgia Sea Islands, *rags* have always meant *sinful*, i.e., secular, songs. (cf. Parrish, Lydia: *Slave Songs of the Georgia Sea Islands, op. cit.*)

shining trumpets

ragtime was played long before. Scott Joplin's *Maple Leaf Rag*, Kerry Mills's *Georgia Camp Meeting* and many others in their complete multi-theme form were in the repertory of every New Orleans jazz band earlier than 1900, just as later ones like the *Black and White Rag* of George Botsford were played in their day. Not all were called rags in the earliest days. Early Cake-Walk tunes are really rags: many, like Mills's *Whistling Rufus* (1899), were called marches; this may refer not only to the grand march of the ballroom but to the street march as well. Many, like the latter tune, are labeled *A Characteristic March, which can be used as a Two Step, Polka or Cake Walk*, such was the adaptability of this music. The chief influence of ragtime on jazz was in the repertory of tunes it supplied. The piano style itself continued as a separate style well into the 1920's. Ragtime playing, which became with the whites a quasi-European display style with set and rigid syncopations, always had, under Negro hands, the hotness and blueness, the African beat, and free rhythms of jazz. The qualitative and functional relation of ragtime and jazz are clear and important; this became evident when, after 1900, the piano began to enter the jazz band.

The popular music that came into jazz, from its beginnings to as late as 1915, was not the Tin Pan Alley product of the New York tune factories but was a song peculiar to New Orleans. The popular tunes of this Southern city were, in the main, invented by the Negroes, cousins of the Virginia slaves whom Thomas Jefferson, a century before, had found "capable of imagining a small catch." Testimony to the authorship of some of these songs of common currency, is available. Jelly Roll Morton wrote [10] it was common knowledge that Buddy Bolden composed the blues named after him. George Brunies has said that all of the "good tunes were by the colored boys." [11]

The New Orleans popular tune has certain characteristics distinguishing it from all other American popular music. It

[10] In the magazine *Down Beat*, 1938.
[11] In an interview with the author in 1944.

is completely unsentimental, for one thing, gay and sometimes slyly suggestive for another; most of all, it has a simple harmonic basis and characteristic turns of melodic line which make it completely suitable for jazz treatment.

A tune like *I Wish I Could Shimmy Like My Sister Kate*, by the violinist, Armand Piron and the cornetist, Peter Bocage, is a typical favorite:

> *I wish I could shimmy like my sister Kate:*
> *How she shakes it, like jelly on the plate;*
> *My mama wanted to know last night*
> *Why all the boys treat Kate so nice.*
>
> *Now every boy in our neighborhood*
> *Knows she can shimmy and shimmy good;*
> *I may be late, but I'll be up-to-date*
> *When I can shimmy like my sister Kate,*
> *I'm shoutin': Shimmy like my sister Kate.*

Other tunes, like Bolden's *Don't Go 'Way Nobody*, are of known authorship, but there were a host of these tunes like *Get It Right, Isn't It Hard to Love?*,[12] *Alice Fields, Won't You Please Come Home, Bill Bailey?* and *Short Dress Gal* which seemed to spring up like weeds. Once a tune became current, each band assigned its own title to it. One song, for example, was known as *To-Wa-Bac-A-Wa, Keep On Knockin': But You Can't Come In*, and *There's a Hole in the Bucket*, as well as by many other names. A considerable number of these melodies are traditional today, perhaps half a century since they first appeared. Some melodies appear under a dozen titles on as many different record labels; many more remain unrecorded. Others, like *Make Me a Pallet on the Floor*, by Bolden, and *Joe Turner Blues*, while popular songs, are really blues.

During the archaic period jazz was used mainly in the streets for the parade and the funeral. The cortege, winding its way to one or another of the weird cemeteries, miniature and veritable cities of the dead where interment is above ground in the

---

12 Probably a variant of *If I Ever Cease to Love*.

small stone or brick houses spaced on the narrow cypress and magnolia planted streets is still one of the most characteristic and picturesque features of Negro life in New Orleans. In the 'nineties the incomparable Negro marching bands, Buddy Bolden's Band, the Olympia, the Eagle, and the others, played the slow mournful dirges all the way to the cemetery while the horse carriages, and the mourners on foot, followed. As Jelly Roll Morton said, "When the funeral left with the body they would play *Flee as a Bird to the Mountain*," or, perhaps, *When the Saints Go Marching In*. The actual interment would take place decently and ceremoniously enough; but once started home, the ebullient Negro temperament was not to be long suppressed. So, as the procession filed away from the cemetery gates, the snare drums would roll, a cornet would sound its short, high, imperious, signal notes, and before the band was three blocks away, it would be tearing into a syncopated jazz rendering of *Oh, Didn't He Ramble*. And from there on home the erstwhile mourners strutted and jigged.

Much of the atmosphere of the funeral is preserved in a record by Jelly Roll Morton.

CITATION 42. *Oh, Didn't He Ramble*. This is one of a group of records issued in 1939, two years before Jelly Roll's death. This record of the famous old "leaving the cemetery" tune was made with an inferior pick-up band he called his New Orleans Jazzmen, but it succeeds in reproducing the whole proceedings from the dead march, the services and wailing, to the high-stepping return from the cemetery.

Always following the parades and funeral processions was the *second line*. This motley collection of children, mainly Negro, for many white children were forbidden to enjoy the fun, filled the sidewalks and the street. The older ones skipping and dancing, the smaller tots running to keep up, they joined in the music as best they could, singing, whistling, and playing on a variety of instruments: harmonica, flageolet, kazoo, and homemade contraptions of all sorts from cigar box guitars to any objects with percussive possibilities. This was more than infantile imitation; it was the primary class in the folk-academy of a people's music.

If few of the white spectators recognized the wild, free, joyous strains of these bands as a wonderful, new music in the making, did the children themselves? Undoubtedly they did not, but it was the music of their people in their city and they were consciously a part of its growing tradition. In a few years, many of them were to beg, borrow, or even steal, battered cornets, clarinets, or trombones and begin to learn the difficult art of improvised jazz. Among them were boys who were to become great jazz artists of the twentieth century. The older players gladly taught them all they knew or all the youngsters could absorb. On warm summer evenings, Bunk Johnson would assemble his small band at Buddy Bottler's Place in the tenderloin district and, when the music was going hot, summon from behind the piano the urchin he knew was hidden there. And Louis Armstrong, in long pants donned for the occasion, would crawl forth, his eyes wide and idolizing. He would take the cornet for the lessons he had slipped away from home to receive. The teacher rapped the pupil's knuckles at each wrong note just as, years before, Bunk's own teacher had "smacked the cornet right out of his mouth." Many a night young Louis went home with his fingers sore. In just this way, in West Africa, the novice boy receives a stinging drumstick blow on the fingers that err.

8.

classic jazz

SOME time around 1890, jazz began to have growing pains. In the long parades the Negro had schooled and cajoled his beloved new-found instruments until they began to sing the dancing rhythms he had known in Africa and would not forsake here. Suddenly the obvious, revolutionary idea occurred to him to use these dancing strains for what they were best suited, for dancing itself. Almost before anyone knew it, there was a new jazz, richer, more organized, and more developed than that of the marching bands. The leisure and the amenities, such as they were (perhaps not inconsiderable), of social dancing demanded not only variety but pieces more generally appropriate to the activity and the mood of the occasion.

Before this happened, the typical small string-bands had always played for Negro dancing in New Orleans in the period before 1890–1895. These groups, various combinations of violin, guitar, mandolin, string-bass, and occasionally piano, were to be found in many Southern cities. Here they played the French quadrilles, the waltzes, Creole and popular song arrangements, and even light classic and operatic potpourri and overtures. Their style was sweet and more or less "legitimate," with the reservation that their numbers were rendered with a certain rhythmic impetus and syncopation from which the academies had, at that time, been unable to "purify" any Negro music. During those years the function and repertory of the street brass band and the indoor string-band had been kept separate.

Perhaps this new use of jazz first occurred in street dancing during the Carnival, perhaps at some large outdoor dance or in a large hall rented for the purpose or, as is most probable, in spontaneous dancing at a Sunday band concert in one of the parks like the uptown Lincoln Park, where Bolden often played. In any event, once the powerful and rhythmic brass band was used its fitness was perceived and the idea caught on. Social dancing became the rage. Halls sprung up downtown and uptown; outdoor summer pavilions were built in New Orleans and at the resorts on Lake Ponchartrain.

The need of the gay and noisy large dancing affairs for a strong and rhythmic music led, not only to the expansion of jazz in terms of employment, but to changes, through instrumentation, in the structure of the music itself. Its repertory was enriched by the inclusion and transformation of French and Italian music of several sorts, as well as by the Creole and popular songs. Given a new creative bent, archaic jazz began to develop into its classic period.

Meanwhile the string-bands lapsed in popularity although they still played in the dives and at small social functions. Still later, 1897 to 1917, they had employment in the better class bawdy-houses where the loud brass band was taboo.

With this more or less sudden development of the street band, the genealogy of the classic New Orleans jazz, as we know it, is complete. See opposite page.

Tracing the origin and progress of archaic jazz, we find that New Orleans offered a special combination of musical ingredients not to be found elsewhere. The Negro had access to these and to musical instruments he might not have had — at least to the same degree — elsewhere. And it is by no means certain that, given all of these things in any other city in this country, jazz music would have resulted. Cities have their individual atmosphere, which, for lack of a better word, we call personality. That of New Orleans is a magical one which even today, after untold commercialization and change, is felt by the most insensitive visitor. He responds to it with a greater degree of reckless insouciance, of a devil-may-care freedom, than he is apt to exhibit in Des Moines, Buffalo, or Fort Worth. This

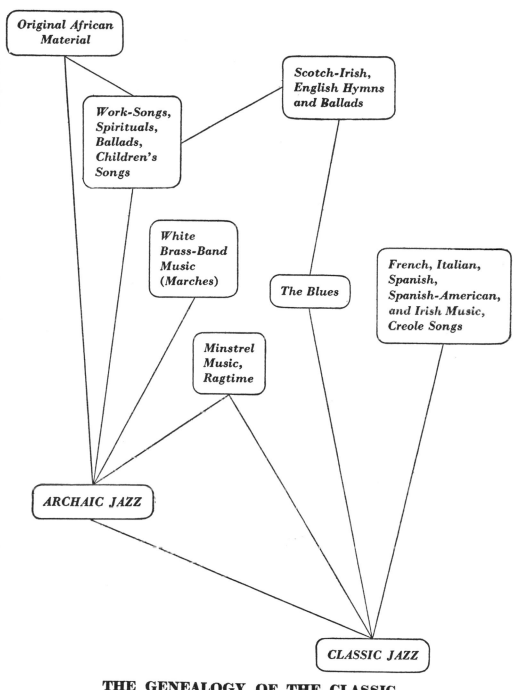

THE GENEALOGY OF THE CLASSIC NEW ORLEANS JAZZ.

175

special magic, eluding every pen, interpenetrates jazz, vitally and indefinably, like an inward, precious quality to be heard, felt, and sensed. Whenever other cities have adopted jazz, whether in white or Negro playing, they have basically altered and mutilated its construction and style. They have progressively changed it to accord with the European tradition within which it does not belong, and the incomparable accent and informing spirit have been lost completely. To this day, with rare exceptions, only New Orleans Negroes can play real jazz.

Certain musical elements flowed over from the string-band repertory into the march-style music that gives the melodic variety, richness and line which shape the classic style. These elements are the blues, French classical music (mainly operatic), and the French dance music of the quadrille and polka; Italian operatic music and street-songs; Spanish and Latin-American music of a popular vein; the Creole songs, indigenous but with strong French characteristics; and, to a minor degree, Scotch and Irish folk music.

The degree of influence of classical French and Italian music upon jazz is not commonly recognized. Although there was choral and orchestral activity in New Orleans during the nineteenth century, the chief tradition is that of French and Italian opera. Light opera began in New Orleans as early as 1810, grand opera in 1837; the French Opera House, built in the mid-century and destroyed by fire in 1919, was the focal point of the city's musical — and social — activity. Operatic arias once were sung and whistled in the streets just like today's popular songs, and some of the feeling, if not the actual melody, of these arias remains in jazz, reappearing fifty years later in an Armstrong trumpet phrase built on an air from Rigoletto.

Lorenzo Tio, Sr., first of the great Negro clarinetists, played in a classical manner and a line which still persists in the New Orleans clarinet style. His pupil, Alphonse Picou, says that he as well as Tio played clarinet, on occasion, in French opera. In a city where many light-skinned Creoles passed as white, this could easily be so. At all events, the classic line of the clarinet in New Orleans jazz, with its alternation of rapid passages and drawn-out notes which supply a varied and continuous nexus between the strong rhythms and powerful voices of the brasses, is all the inner evidence which is needed. If it were not, one would need only cite the piano playing of Jelly Roll Morton in which the Negroid characteristics of ragtime syncopations, powerful stomping, and improvisational melodic variation are all set forth in a spirit, and with a precision, classically Gallic.

The second French element in classic jazz is found in the dances which were popular in the last part of the nineteenth century: polkas, mazurkas, schottisches, waltzes, and others, many of them comprised in the five-figured dance group of the quadrille. Many of these already had been converted into ragtime. Now jazz took them over and transformed them completely. Such a transformation is actually shown in a record made by Jelly Roll Morton. This important document, made by the great pianist for the Library of Congress, shows his transformation of a complete French quadrille of unknown name into a jazz piano piece, the well-known *Tiger Rag*. Morton's playing is more than ragtime; it is conceived orchestrally and it is obvious that the process applied to the quadrille is the same as the band metamorphosis of all non-African material into jazz. This important record will be analyzed a little later.

Although much French music is transformed into jazz, its important effect is stylistic. As material it is far overshadowed by the marches and other sources. The French factor is strongly decisive in instrumentation and certain phases of instrumental style, particularly in the clarinet; it endures most of all, through colored Creole influence, in a Gallic precision and finish which informs the work of the best and the hottest of the New Orleans players.

A certain amount of popular Italian music entered jazz in the street-songs, for the Italians have been for many years the predominant part of the foreign element in New Orleans. While it is true that no one has yet uncovered a specific instance, such as the French quadrille and *Tiger Rag*, the presence of Italian and pure Spanish elements in jazz must logically be taken for granted. The intense musicality of Italians, complemented by the Negroid tendency to assimilate foreign influence, is strong presumptive evidence. Not only is the history as well as the population of New Orleans Spanish in part, but Spanish music itself, influenced long ago by Negro music through the North African Moors, is suitable to Negroid treatment.

Foreign names abound among the New Orleans Negroes. The jazz roster is full of French, Spanish, and Italian surnames: St. Cyr, Bechet, Dutrey, Santiago, Picou, Tio, Petit, de Lisle, Marrero. In the quondam Scotch and Hibernian settlement called the Irish Channel — from which Scotch and Irish melody flowed directly into jazz — came the great Negro player, Bunk Johnson. Witness the Negro jazz names, Carey, Bolden, and Noone, even though the latter may once have been Nuñez.

Latin-American music came plentifully into the seaport, New Orleans, bringing the characteristic guitar. The *tango* and *hàbanera* rhythms entered into classic jazz and these, like the *Samba* and *Conga*, are rhythms of at least secondary African origin, found variously in Brazil, Cuba, and the Caribbeans.

It may be argued that mixed blood accounts for jazz, that the presence of white blood, in other words, gives jazz its strength and character. Such a contention might be valid if the musicians of mixed blood had taken African music and transformed it into a European one; but when jazz transforms our music into a thing strongly African, it is precisely the opposite thing. It is the Negroid, not the white, character which persists. Racial mixture was, of course, widespread in New Orleans until very recently. The mixed issue was for long unrecorded, but the illegitimate children assumed the white parental name (most frequently on the staff side) with the tacit consent of the community.

The persistence of Negroid character — directed by cultural contacts — thus is seen as the explanation of all Afro-American music. In New Orleans, access to the various white cultural elements was greatly facilitated by the peculiar pattern of segregation in that city. This consisted of scattering the Negro population. Originally established partly through indolence, partly to prevent revolt, it persists today.

The downtown Creole tradition — meaning, of course, the Creoles of color — is not the tradition of early jazz. By the 1880's the "Frenchmen" had their own society bands beginning probably with those of Claiborne Williams and John Robechaux and later including the Imperial Band of the fine, legitimate cornetist Emanuel Perez and the orchestra led by the violinist Armand Piron. These bands played in a smoothly harmonized arranged style foreign to the whole jazz concept. Nevertheless, from the Creole section came elements of French style and the beautiful and melodious songs that classic jazz absorbed.

These Creole folk songs are a delightful and distinctive music that flowed into jazz amply enough to flavor it. *C'est l'Autre Can-can* is a song of this sort, one, perhaps, of actual French origin. Jelly Roll Morton has played and sung it on a record in the Library of Congress archives. A very recent record presents it in full jazz band form:

CITATION 43. *Creole Song* (*C'est l'Autre Can-can*), by Kid Ory's Creole Jazz Band: Mutt Carey, trumpet; Kid Ory, trombone; Omer Simeon, clarinet; Buster Wilson, piano; Bud Scott, guitar; Ed Garland, string-bass; Alton Redd, drums.

Much of the catchy, easy-going, pleasant melody in New Orleans jazz came from such local tunes as *C'est l'Autre Can-can.*

> As told (sung) by Ory, it's the story of a gossiping beldame named Madame Pedau (or Pedaux) who goes from door to door wagging her busy tongue. . . The response from the band is "Paix, donc!" a play on the sound-resemblance to Madame's name. In French, "Paix, donc!" is a sort of quizzical "Peace, then!" which a contemporary hepcat would probably transmute to: "Cut the jive, man, you're killing me!" [1]

By 1895 the haughty *creoles of color*, who earlier had sent their children to France for education and had boasted their

[1] Frederic Ramsey, Jr., in the magazine, *The Jazz Record*, February, 1945.

own chorus and symphony orchestra, were losing their proud position. Their cultural traditions had all but disappeared. The cultivated, charming, light-skinned men began to enter jazz and they were a personal force which, added to the cultural ones, helped to shape the classic form. While Robechaux, in his sweet band, continued to exemplify the low estate to which the colored creole classical music had fallen, these men, Lorenzo Tio, Sr., Alphonse Picou, George and Achille Baquet, and Sidney Bechet, Edward "Kid" Ory, Honoré Dutrey, Emanuel Perez, Buddy and Joseph Petit, Ferdinand "Jelly Roll" Morton, and others joined with their blacker brothers to carry this music, jazz, to undreamed of heights.

The great bands of the 1890's, Bolden's, the Indian Band, the Excelsior, Columbus, the Diamond Stone, and others were black, uptown bands. Greatest of them was the Bolden Ragtime Band and its leader, born shortly after the Civil War, was the remarkable sort of a man about whom a new style can form. It is boldly creative, versatile, dominant men like Bolden who shape prevailing tendencies into forms of a new period. Men like he become, as Bolden has become, legends after their death. Born about the time of Emancipation, Buddy typifies the Negro's expression of the political and social freedom which he still hoped for, in the creation of one of the freest, most vital and creative musics ever made. A barber with his own shop, as well as editor and publisher of a scandal sheet, *The Cricket*, (in a town where the supply of scandal could have kept all the presses running day and night), Buddy Bolden found time to play the cornet as few men have ever played it and to form, in the early 1890's, a band which was to initiate a period and to typify, actually or potentially, nearly all that jazz has meant even until today.

Bolden's band, although powerful, was a small one, varying from five to seven pieces: cornet, one or two clarinets, valve trombone alternating with slide trombone,[2] guitar, bass, and

---

[2] The former was used for staccato work, the latter for glissandi.

drums. In the Ragtime Band at the beginning, according to Wallace Collins, were Bolden, cornet; Frank Lewis, clarinet (second clarinet added later) ; Willy Cornish, trombone; Tom Adams, violin; Brock Humphrey, guitar; Tab Cato, bass viol; Louis Ray, traps. That some of the players could not read does not point to musical ineptitude on their part. On the contrary, they were exceptional men with the gift of skilled creative improvisation, and the assimilative Bolden "learned his notes" in three weeks!

Collins relates that the violin played the melody straight while Bolden ragged it except that in loud passages — "The introduction they bust out as loud as they can," Bolden led straight.

Bolden was a shrewd organizer, a dynamic and magnetic leader. Before the Spanish-American War he was a public figure of immense popularity, well known even to white New Orleans. Parades, picnics, funerals, Mardi Gras, lawn parties, dances — he and his band were in demand everywhere. By this time there were a score or more of Negro dance halls in New Orleans and Bolden was welcome in them all, from rough places like the *Tintype, Masonic,* and *Globe* halls, to the nicer ones like *Jackson Hall,* downtown halls like *Economy* and *Hopes,* uptown places like *Love and Charity, Come Clean, Providence,* and *Big Easy.*

So Bolden grew from plain Buddy, to the titles of grandeur which New Orleans Negroes began to bestow on their musical hero, the cornetist. He became "Kid," finally "King" Bolden. And the title "Kid" was not misplaced, for the popularity with women which the term also signifies, came easily to Buddy and finally, with drink, led to insanity.[3]

---

[3] Many tell this story. "Colley," however, says, "That fellow studied too hard — always trying to think up something to bring out. He could hear you play something and keep it in his head." Then he would go home where, according to Collins, Buddy lived as a bachelor with his mother, and "think up the parts." Hard work might, of course, explain his mental breakdown. His first attack was in 1902.

Bolden and his compeers established the classic repertory, expanded the archaic technical style, and formulated the chief classic instrumentations, the main change in which has been the addition of piano. When Willie "Bunk" Johnson, a leggy youth of sixteen, according to his story, joined the band in 1895, the two-cornet style, later associated with King Oliver, was established.

About 1907, Bolden's wild living caught up with him and, as some accounts have it, he ran amuck in the midst of a parade, and was committed, soon after, to an asylum where he died in 1931. But Buddy's work was done. Jazz was established as a living music and his memory lives in every note of it. His legend lives, too. Stand in the Old Quarter on a summer evening and, with little imagination, you can seem to hear the notes of his horn, coming wild and high and clear again, as they were once supposed to do, through the warm, dusky air all the miles from Gretna across the River or from Milneburg on the Ponchartrain shore. Or, in a crowded dance hall where the rhythmic shuffle of feet that is so fine a part of jazz is loud on the beat, you can seem to hear him, delighting in the sound, call to his men

> *'Way down, 'way down low*
> *So I can hear those whores*
> *Drag their feet across the floor.*[4]

We shall probably never know the names of those men in the earliest street bands whose intuitions, discoveries, and experiments first defined jazz. But with the classical period names begin to emerge. In jazz of any period, the men playing it are important almost to the exclusion of everything else because, besides the technical and musical advances which individuals have made and continue to make, jazz is, to a very large degree, composed in the playing. It is as great, therefore, and only as great, as the men playing it. A Beethoven symphony exists as a formulated musical structure, in directive and by impli-

[4] Ramsey, Frederic, Jr., and Smith, Charles Edward: *Jazzmen.* New York: 1939.

cation, in its score; and this would be true if, still in manuscript, it never yet had been played. But a jazz improvisation unplayed is uncreated; if it is played but unrecorded, it is lost forever except to the impermanent memory. Herein lies the importance, in a cultural and historical sense, of the phonograph record to jazz, more vital than the printed score to Western music. Without the records which survived from the 1920's, it is highly doubtful that the present great and widespread interest in this music would ever have begun.

Bolden is the key figure in the formation of classic jazz and his personal cornet style, one of a shouting, incredible power, established one of the two main jazz trumpet styles. It was carried on by Freddie Keppard and can be heard today in New Orleans in the powerful but more primitive playing of the veteran "Wooden" Joe Nicholas.

Willie Geary "Bunk" Johnson founded the second trumpet style, one of a lighter touch. Bunk's work is impeccably phrased. Anticipating the beat, delaying behind it and then hurrying to catch up, its swinging, yet driving, momentum is almost the essence, in each single tone, of what the whole band does. His tone is clear and dark, his downward phrases, so like African ones, are lucidly thoughtful and compressed with feeling. Bunk's gift of ceaseless, fresh variational invention seems to derive from a perpetually youthful inspiration. No one has ever excelled him in all of these qualities.

King Oliver had a personal style as delicate in some of its phases as that of Bunk. He used more variety of tone, however, supplementing open horn with the use of mutes and he was a very early exponent of the "wa-wa," produced by the cupped hand moved in front of the cornet or trumpet bell.

Bunk's imprint appeared in the work of Tommy Ladnier, Louis Dumaine and others and is, indeed, a shaping force in the work of every trumpeter today, black or white, who deserves to be called a jazz player.

The great characteristics of classic trumpet are combined in the work of Louis Armstrong. Old enough to have heard

Bolden, he fuses Buddy's fiery power with the delicate imaginativeness of Bunk and, in addition, has assimilated valuable elements from Oliver. Through the tremendous influence of Armstrong, Bunk's phrasing even appears in much clarinet, trombone, and piano work. Thus a personal style becomes definitive in a whole music. It may safely be said that Bunk Johnson's style has changed in no important detail in forty years, except perhaps to grow richer and more assured. It is now part of a general language and it is modern today because jazz, in the New Orleans sense, is still far in advance of the times.

Willie "Bunk" Johnson was born in New Orleans about 1879. By his own account, he began music lessons at the age of seven and began to study the cornet one year later. At fifteen he was ready to join the band of Adam Olivier (often called O'Levy by New Orleans Negroes) and at sixteen, while still in short trousers, he joined the Bolden Band as second cornetist. After several years in this band, Bunk went on a road tour with a minstrel company, Holecamp's Georgia Smart Set, with which he appeared in New York in 1903. For a while he played in a theater band in Dallas, Texas, and a later minstrel tour took him to San Francisco in 1905. Returning to New Orleans, he played with a number of organizations and his greatest local fame and influence came during the period, 1911–1914, when he played with the Eagle Band.[5] This was the Bolden Band which, after the King's forced retirement, was taken over by the trombonist, Frankie Dusen. Up to this time Bunk had played with at least fourteen bands and had found time for two years of travel with a circus as well as tours through Texas.

After 1914 Bunk toured almost constantly but did not visit Chicago where, from 1913 on, jazz began to reach a new audience. In about 1931 his cornet was destroyed. Shortly thereafter, losing his teeth, he lived in the western Louisiana town

[5] Most of the other older players, including Louis Nelson, "Mutt" Carey, Bob Lyons, Joe Howard, Wallace Collins, and "Pop" Foster, maintain, however, that Bunk never played regularly with Bolden and that his first steady job was with the Eagle Band after Bolden's retirement. This may well mean that Bunk is not so old as he claims to be.

of New Iberia, working in the rice fields, hauling sugar cane and teaching music when the opportunity offered.

Late in the 1930's a group of jazz critics and enthusiasts, led by Frederic Ramsey, Jr., and William Russell, began to search for him. After a tip from Louis Armstrong, a letter, sent in 1939 in care of the New Iberia postmaster, reached him. His rehabilitation followed. Fitted with his new teeth and supplied with a new trumpet, he promptly amazed all who heard him by the vigor, freshness, and creative power of his playing. In the compressed history of jazz this event was as important and revealing as, in European music, it might be to hear Chopin or Beethoven play today. Events followed rapidly. He was recorded, with the best New Orleans band which could be assembled, in June, 1942, by David Stuart on the Jazzman record label.

In the spring of 1943, during a series of lectures on jazz which I was giving at the San Francisco Museum of Art, money was raised to bring Bunk to the Pacific Coast, and he appeared as guest, playing and talking, on the last lecture. Several weeks later, the museum sponsored a historic concert at the Geary Theatre in San Francisco where Bunk appeared with Mutt Carey, Kid Ory, the clarinetist Wade Whaley, and other great New Orleans players. Part of this concert was broadcast on a network and recorded by the Office of War Information and rebroadcast by short wave to American soldiers all over the world. By this time Bunk, one of the greatest figures of the classic New Orleans jazz, was launched as a national figure and he has remained comparatively active in music ever since.

Bunk today, at perhaps sixty-five or sixty-six years of age, should be a venerable figure. But the years — too many of them spent in the hard, underpaid, and virtually conscripted labor of the rice-fields — have dealt lightly with him. His tightly-curled, silver hair crowns a perpetually boyish face; the movements of his slender body are the quick, graceful movements of youth; and youth has not departed from his music while the long years have poured a thoughtful richness into it. In the creative varia-

185

tions that ennoble a cheap popular song, reiterate the immemorial blues, or raise a classic jazz melody to an even higher plane, are the accents of a true genius, singing the song of his people and the song of his time.

Bunk's own playing is clear and melodic yet his recorded band work exemplifies the dissonant tendency of the classic style. His personal style certainly would fit in a fully harmonic band polyphony and the dissonantal element arises in the playing of the three voice instruments, from the characteristics of those playing with him. Dissonant polyphony, which constantly approaches and often reaches a true heterophony, is an original tendency of the Negro marching band in New Orleans. It seems to take place only in bands of which all or the majority of the members are at least part-time street men. It was undoubtedly the distinguishing feature of the Bolden Band. The following record illustrates this tendency in classic jazz.

CITATION 44. *Panama* (W. H. Tyers), played by Bunk Johnson's Original Superior Band: Bunk Johnson, trumpet; George Lewis, clarinet; Jim Robinson, trombone; Laurence Marrero, banjo; Austin Young, contre-bass; Walter Decou, piano; Ernest Rogers, drums. This is one of the 1942 Jazzman records, on which the band is named to commemorate Bunk's Superior Band of about 1905–10. With studio facilities in New Orleans virtually closed to Negroes at this time, the barely adequate recording was done by portable equipment.

The traditional march, *Panama,* has a number of distinctive and beautiful strains. The tempo is buoyant, the beat is alive, and the rhythm is very *raggedy.* The trumpet leads with that contradictory combination of easy relaxation and driving force characteristic of good Negro jazz, and with it the trombone and clarinet weave a continuous polyphony. When the trumpet drops out for a few measures the clarinet continues as lead over a broken organ point of repeated trombone notes, suddenly rising with a booming high tone then resolving into a series of rhythmic downward figures.

Lewis' clarinet tone is rich, his style a personal variant of the New Orleans clarinet. Ceaselessly inventive, he is never at a loss; with his playing there are never any thin spots, much less holes, in the contrapuntal fabric. His are no mere obbligati or figurations around the lead, but independent melodies developing throughout the performance, and combining in polyphonic perfection with the other voices.

Jim Robinson plays a "shouting" trombone of markedly vocal tone, with less stress on the glissando than most tail-gate trombones. He plays an active part in which repeated notes in different registers alternate with rapid, staccato, vigorous figures.

The three voices together create a polyphony, fervent, eloquent, and logical, in which the harmony, while felt, is never in the focus of consciousness; this polyphony veers continuously into heterophony. The final double period of thirty-two bars offers a superb and beautiful example of dissonance. Bunk creates a figure of single and repeated high notes, one-half tone above the tonic; while he builds this from a single-note figure, to double, triple, quadruple, and then a series of rapid syncopated notes, Robinson matches him note for note on the tonic in a thrilling and beautiful dissonance. (The three voices in a portion of these final thirty-two bars are shown in Ex. 25, back of book.)

Harmony, to a degree unknown in archaic jazz, enters the classic with the guitar or banjo, and the piano. These instruments play percussive chords that constantly indicate the harmonic progression of the number being played. The string-bass, replacing the tuba, is practically never played double-stop (on two strings) and is generally plucked pizzicato and slapped. When bowed, it frequently sounds like the tuba and at such times may resemble closely the forceful exhalation of breath during African religious possession.

With the reversions typical of Afro-American music, one phase of classic jazz tends to disregard this harmony and to seek a dissonance through the voice instruments which may reach the point of a complete heterophony of independent melodies. This is the most important technical development of classic jazz, one shown on later records of the Bunk Johnson Band. Another phase carries harmony in the voice instruments to the extreme point at which it can remain consistent with Afro-American principles. Such a phase is shown by the New Orleans Wanderers' 1927 records on Columbia and the 1944–1945 ones of Kid Ory.

In jazz the Western *ingredients* are in a higher proportion than in earlier Afro-American music but, as in the others, the determining *character* is the African. This is why the Negro in his essential nature tends to place emphasis toward the African; this process can go much farther, without destroying the real nature of the music, than can the tendency of sophisticated Negro and white men to cause harmony to supplant polyphony entirely.

Rhythmically, two tendencies develop within jazz; both belong to the African side of the scales. One is that of perpetual syncopation and polyrhythm, the other that of stomping or of the stomp pattern. The former, with all its variety of syncopated figures, displaced stresses, suspensions and anticipatory-retardatory activity, is the original form of most church singing and of the marching band. It is the African impulse toward a music of the freest horizontal movement; however, temporal and dynamic control are more evident in the march, for obvious reasons, than in church music, especially in such an example as the ring dance, *Run, Old Jeremiah.* The stomp pattern, which forces the melody into a rhythmic design, derives indirectly from the polyrhythmic drum patterns of West Africa; these were transmitted through the functional figures of the work-songs and the play patterns of the children's songs, then revived in guitar and banjo strumming. It also derives from (or is associated with), the characteristic rhythmic patterns of certain dance forms, the *Cake Walk*, the *Black Bottom*, and others, and was used specifically for the dances called *The Stomp* and the *Georgia Breakdown*.

In stomping, the regular beat or pulse is maintained by the full rhythm section. The lead, one or two cornets or trumpets, plays the melody fitted into the stomp pattern. The clarinet plays a free melody of many notes around the lead, placing the accents to correspond with the stomp pattern. The trombone is left free to play at will. The stomp produces the strongest rhythmic momentum, yet preserves polyphony. The stop-time, also a set pattern, eliminates polyphony by excluding two voices.

The real meaning of these patterns is that they treat the musical flow as a language. It is the African tendency for prosody to enter the realm of pure, abstract, unsyllabled sound. The stomp is a poetical application of meter in the way that speech is fitted into the poetic line. The stop-time is a mode of lingual emphasis like the vigorously repeated spoken phrase. When the pattern is of one period, i.e., continuous, as in all stop-time and much stomping, its characteristic is prosal or continuously poetic in a formal sense. When the stomp is two-period, consisting of a first rhythmic figure stated, repeated, and then answered by a second figure, the pattern, while still lingual, is a call-and-response of African antiphony. Thus we may have in stomped jazz, antiphony and polyphony existing together; one is in rhythm, the other in melody. It cannot be doubted that stomp pattern and stop-time both stem from the talking drums of Africa. We should not lose sight of this sort of communicative quality in all truly Negro music, rhythm and dancing. Bill Robinson, the famous "Bojangles," will pause in his tap dancing and inform his audience, "Now I'm going to tell it." Then he taps out a sequence as cryptic as code, yet a sequence falling into phrase or sentence groupings.

The stomp pattern is well exemplified in the following record:

CITATION 45. *Bogalousa Strut,* played by Sam Morgan's Jazz Band. The personnel includes Sam Morgan and Isaiah Morgan, trumpets; Jim Robinson, trombone; Andrew Morgan, tenor saxophone; Earl Fouchet, alto saxophone; Johnny Dave, banjo; Roy Evans, drums; Sidney Brown (Jim Little), string-bass.

This record is an example of the fine playing of the average Negro band in New Orleans during the classic period. Made in 1928, it also shows the deteriorative effect when the saxophone, first introduced into the jazz band in Chicago probably around 1917–1919, replaces the clarinet. The tone quality of the band suffers, becoming heavy and overmellow with the reed's sharp, piquant clarity gone; the polyphony becomes unclear. The saxophone, used in jazz polyphony, can never satisfactorily assume the clarinet part. To be heard it must squeal, wail, pop obscenely, or distort the melodic part into a meaningless series of ascending or descending scales. Bunk Johnson, who knows the requirements of jazz polyphony, said, "It just runs up and down stairs with no place to go."

Bogalousa Strut is a typical New Orleans popular tune. It has two strains. The first has a highly rhythmic stomp character in the cornet lead. The second strain, which was evidently intended to have a two-bar break but is played through without it, is stomped vigorously (except for two saxophone solos) in a number of different patterns. (These are shown in Ex. 26, back of book.) The formation of the stomp into periods is clearly shown in this example. A–A are obviously related to the call lines of the blues, B to the response line and the antiphonal derivation of the stomp is readily discernible. The above series is related to the mutations of African drum figures as in the Dahomean series shown in Ex. 42.

Some listeners cannot differentiate between the stomp pattern and the *riff* of the present-day swing groups. But there is a vital difference. In stomping a *complete* melody is fitted into a rhythmic pattern. This melody goes through its full course in polyphonic treatment, and furnishes both melodic and rhythmic variation. Thus are met the jazz requirements of polyphony and rhythm open to variational development. The riff is a single — or sometimes composite — rhythmic figure which embodies only a snatch of melody. Repeated endlessly as it is nowadays by full band or complete sections, its whole aim is the hysterical excitement aroused by reiteration. No melodic development occurs within it; polyphony is completely out of its scope. The riff — which is a millstone around the neck of contemporary big-band music — is perhaps a degeneration of the stomp pattern.

In all Negro music the rhythmic characteristic most difficult to define is "the beat." This is much more than the mere basic meter. It is a live and flowing pulse, percussive yet springy and supple, and at moments when strong polyrhythm or successive suspended (i.e. silent) beats enter, the beat is felt while it exists unheard. The beat is accurate but not heavy. White players who maintain an unvarying beat almost always produce a heavy one that, as the Negroes say, drags. The dragging beat is one retarded behind the actual — but merely sensed — one, often by a time interval infinitesimally small like a one-hundred-and-twenty-eighth note. Nevertheless, it is felt as a brake on the momentum. It is the live beat in Negro music that all listeners feel and respond to, a thing often loosely described as "syncopation" or "that wonderful Negro rhythm."

We have seen that classic jazz developed out of the archaic with the widening of economic opportunity in the early 1890's. Here, suddenly, was an exciting and lucrative new field for the players. The existing small string trio used for dancing, typically consisting of violin, contre-bass, and guitar or mandolin, was expanded by the addition of brasses and reed, as well as drums. Over came the technique of the street band; no mere violins and mandolins could stand up against it; it began to work over the dance material in a way not polite, perhaps, but everlastingly effective.

The definitive demonstration of this working-over process is, as we have mentioned, the Morton record of the derivation of *Tiger Rag*. An analysis follows.

CITATION 45. *Tiger Rag*, piano solo by Jelly Roll Morton. This record is wonderfully played but poorly recorded. The first part gives an exposition of the five strains, or dance themes, of the original quadrille, played in their authentic form, but with a phrasing and a rhythmic buoyancy from which any European music could profit.

Morton speaks:

> *Jazz started in New Orleans and this Tiger Rag happened to be transformed from an old quadrille that was in many different tempos* [6] *and I'll no doubt give you an idea how it went. This was the introduction, meaning that everyone was supposed to get their partners.*

Morton plays the eight bar introduction. (See Ex. 27, back of book.)

> "Get your partners, everybody get your partners." *And people would be rushing around the hall getting their partners. Maybe five minutes lapse between that time, and of course they'd start it over again and that was the first part of it. And the next strain would be a waltz strain, I believe.*

(See Ex. 28.)

The waltz is deliciously Gallic, graceful, elegant and Chopinesque.

> *That would be the waltz strain. Also they had another strain that comes right beside it. Mazooka time.*

(See Ex. 29.)

The mazurka is remarkably evocative. Listening to the piquant rhythms, one can almost see the dancers.

> *That was the third strain and of course they had another strain and that was in a different tempo.*

(See Ex. 30.)

> *Of course they had another one.*

(See Ex. 31.)

> *I will show you how it was transformed. It happened to be transformed by your performer at this particular time. Tiger Rag for your approval — I also named it, it came from the way*

[6] Jelly means meters or rhythms as well as tempos.

CLASSIC JAZZ

*I played it by making the tiger on my elbow. I also named it —
a person said once, "It sounds like a tiger hollerin'." I said,
"Fine." To myself I said, "Fine, that's the name." So I'll play
it for you.*

A complete new composition emerges, the famous *Tiger Rag.*
The performance is masterly and, in the manner typical of Morton, is not only orchestral in sound but in concept. The moderate
beginning tempo, so unlike the unmusical present-day tempos,
accelerates very gradually, like African music, ending at a high
point of excitement.

All of the different meters are converted into 4/4, although
throughout, in a maze of rhythmical suspensions, the beat is
often felt more than heard. Salient is the introduction of two-
bar breaks of great rhythmic variety. Breaks, of which Morton
was supreme master, consist of solo phrases in which the beat
is suspended and replaced by rhythmic aberrations which temporarily alter the basic pulse. The effect is tantalizing, disturbing, and exciting. The break is a basic device of jazz and
has no structural relation to the European cadenza to which
it is sometimes compared.

All the elements of Morton's rich and highly individual piano
style are here: among them the impeccable, varied, and forceful
left hand laying the beat firmly and furnishing transitional passages of downward octaves which hesitate then accelerate dizzily
in harmonic, melodic, or thematic transitions; the right hand
chording solidly off and on the beat. Then there are the runs,
like swift coruscations through the sky, never mere ornamental
display but integral themal variations. Here is the classic precision; here the incredible technique, so assured that it is frequently unobserved; here the beautiful, unveiled tone that on
other occasions could transmit a blueness difficult to imagine.
Here is the triumphant, imaginative placing of tone groupings
in time-space in a manner that defies prediction and almost
eludes metronomic analysis.

Tiger Rag opens with sixteen bars of rollicking introduction.
(See Ex. 32, back of book.)

The music proceeds without transition into the gay, care-free mood of the transformed waltz strain. The first exposition is a variation played in *stop-time*, which is a sequence of treble breaks over a spacing of sounded and silent beats. The stop-time is used freely here over a pulse on the first and fourth beats and interspersed with straight playing. (See Ex. 33, back of book.)

A straight statement of the transformed waltz motive follows, full of rhythmic complexity. (See Ex. 34.) The whole waltz section of 48 bars is succeeded by the next theme in 32 bars worked out in rhythmic variations based on treble trills. Throughout occur two-bar breaks, each different, some complex, while one is a mere single octave on the second beat held, suspending all rhythm, until midway in the following measure.

Next is the famous Tiger section, where the roars appear as downward tone clusters executed by the left forearm. Excited, Morton calls out in the traditional way, "*Hold* that Tiger!" The tone clusters are much more impressive than the customary roars of the trombone. This piano device seems to have been used by Morton several years before its earliest employment by the American composers, Charles Ives and Henry Cowell. (See Ex. 35.)

The Tiger section is in fantastic and impulsive broken rhythms from which Morton emerges like a rabbit running for cover, as he plays with fleet treble figures over a fine ragtime bass. This thirty-two-bar section is one of ragtime development of the next theme of the original quadrille.

In the last section, the music, which has been mounting steadily in tension, undergoes a series of rapid developments. In the first fourteen bars Morton shows the proper use of the riff. Consisting of high forte treble chords, this riff is not re-peated aimlessly but states the melody reduced to its beautiful harmonic progression. Just as the tension of the riff sequence has reached the unbearable, the music plunges into ten bars of ostinato of different but greater tension, where a repeated high note is subjected to fantastic inner-rhythmic treatment; in between these high notes the left hand, close up in the treble, fills in with bell-like chords. This ostinato development, which shows the most subtle artistic judgment, momentarily seems to lessen the tension, but actually increases it. Just as the music seems ready to explode, it rides out lightly and gaily through eight measures of ragtime — a coda in effect — to the staccato closing chord. (See Ex. 36.)

The musical derivation from the original quadrille, subtle but unmistakable throughout, is a glimpse into the process by which jazz was made, a transformation into so completely new a music that the term *creation* is really merited.

It points up the fact that jazz is not a mere "jazzy" rendering, say, of a Beethoven minuet. For this is only a manner of playing with no real transformation of the material. Even less jazz, is the Gershwin *Rhapsody in Blue* that treats quasi-blues harmonies and certain jazz instrumental traits in a symphonic manner. And the music of Whiteman and the various "jazz symphonists" misses the mark by employing jazz material in a completely non-jazz manner.

In the jazz sense, a melody is no more than the theme with which the European begins to compose. In jazz it need not be written down — as like as not, the players could not read it. One player can hum, whistle or play it and then development begins in actual performance. No player even thinks of such performance as a composition for the very concept is foreign to hot music. The playing is thought of as *making* music, not re-creating or interpreting it.

This was the sort of transformation that was taking place in the golden days of Buddy, the King. And golden they were in a literal sense, for Bolden and his contemporaries had almost more work than they could handle. The parades, funerals, and holiday band concerts, sole supports of the archaic bands, were only one phase of classic activity. A parade had been one thing; the march tunes sufficed. To make a funeral a complete success only a dead march needed to be added with a spiritual or a popular tune "served up to the chillun," hot and synco-pated, on the way home.

Advertising by hand-wagons came in during this period; the bands, seated in the huge percheron-drawn drays, "rambled all around" town. In their tight "box-back" coats, the players blasted away, the trombonist relegated to the lowered tail-gate where his plunging slide could not bruise another player. The term tail-gate trombone still used to denote the New Orleans style derived, of course, from this. Inadvertently, or by design, the wagons of rival bands met on street corners and, to the de-light of the populace, the "battles of music" to which Jelly Roll often referred, ensued. From the issue of such conflicts the "Kings" were crowned, and their bands took the cream of the jobs.

Of course, the dances, indoors and out, "in and out of town," were preferred employment in which the new classic group, an amalgamation of the brass band and the string-band, could play all the variety of new music, the rags, transformed qua-drilles, Creole songs, and the rest. Social clubs sprang up like the *Buzzards* and the *Mysterious Babies* for whom Bolden played.

The Negro in New Orleans had come a long way since Eman-cipation. Even at the very start, he could plunge there into an activity which, eventually, was to place him prominently in competition with the whites who not long since had been his legal masters. The city's peculiar tolerance allowed this; it offered him a cultural mélange rich beyond estimate; it gave him the classical instruments cheaply and plentifully. Time was when, in pawn shop or second-hand store, fifty cents to a dollar bought a battered but serviceable cornet! No wonder, even in the brief freedom of the carpetbag period when the Negro en-tered politics, business, education, and the professions generally throughout the South, that in the Crescent City he leaped forth-with into his natural and beloved music.

At the turn of the century, just before the Rough Riders stormed San Juan Hill, everyone was singing, "There'll be a hot time in the old town tonight." For New Orleans Negroes, the dark men from uptown and the creamy-skinned ones from north of Canal Street, the words were prophetic of good fortune beyond their dreams. Boom days were just ahead for the black music of their drums and their horns.

9.

black and white rag

In the year 1897, New Orleans was finally compelled to face the problem of its vice. More widespread and, perhaps, proportionately greater than in any other American city, vice had been, of course, a part of the Crescent City from its founding. It had now reached proportions that were alarming to those local citizens not devoted to it professionally or by avocation. Also — and this hurt more — it was beginning to attract national, unfavorable attention. The local churches began to make an outcry. The hitherto complaisant daily press was intimidated.

Action came that was thoroughly and delightfully characteristic of New Orleans. An alderman, Sidney Story, initiated an ordinance to prohibit prostitution outside of two areas in which, while not authorized, it was nevertheless not prohibited. One of these sections was to be uptown, bounded by Perdido and Gravier Streets, and by Franklin and Locust. The other, downtown in the French Quarter, was marked off by Customhouse and St. Louis, and by North Basin and Robertson. For unknown reasons, prostitution was not actually allowed in practice in the uptown district but was confined to the downtown one, which, greatly to the Alderman's humiliation, came soon to be called Storyville. Thus came into being that area of thirty-eight lurid and lively blocks about which so much has been written and told.

So far as the New Orleans Negro was concerned, the ordinance opened up wide new employment, though not, of course

BLACK AND WHITE RAG

for the pretty quadroons in Lulu White's *Mahogany Hall*, in Josie Arlington's, or other Basin Street "mansions," or for the girls who sat naked in the sordid tiny cribs waiting for customers — girls like these had been similarly employed before, long before Storyville, long before Emancipation. But the brothels, lavish and not so lavish, the saloons and cabarets, clamored for music and entertainment. Jazz was ready, the Negro was ready; the boom was on.

Many a musician played in parades and funerals by day and in a bordello or café at night, snatching what sleep he could in between; the salary and the largess were large. Jelly Roll Morton, who went into the district as pianist at thirteen years of age, spoke of this in the last years of his life. With a poignancy perhaps unconscious he said, "When I made one hundred dollars a day I thought I had a small day and now today if I make ten dollars I think I have a great day. That is how that was. . . . I would really like to see those days back again. I'm telling you the truth. They were wonderful days."

Much has been made, at various times and for various reasons, of the intimate connection which came to exist between jazz and the Storyville of sporting-house, crib, gambling den, saloon, and house of assignation. When jazz moved to Chicago to be associated once more with an underworld (that of the speakeasy and the gangster in the midst of the loose and hectic post-World War I era), the music came to stand first as a symbol, finally as one cause, at least, of the general social upheaval. It even gave its new name (although hardly voluntarily) to the whole period. Ministers and reformers, unable or loathe to probe to the real social-economic causes — shortly to be revealed by the 1929 crash and the ensuing depression — seized on jazz as the culprit. Its origins were subjected to scrutiny — but only as far back as its entrance as a developed and classic art into the Basin Street purlieus.

The finger of scorn was pointed at jazz, glib and fiery denunciation was heaped upon it. The music was seriously considered to be destructive of morals. That the "niggers" had created jazz and were its best players only increased the storm of disapproval.

Jazz is a lean and athletic music, unobsessed with romantic or commercial love. It shuns sentimentality and the languors of romantic desire. It demands monastic and arduous devotion from its practitioners, and when it deals with sex, does so frankly, without shame or furtiveness. While avoiding invidious comparisons, it is scarcely necessary to point out the erotic basis and quality of much revered Romantic music. There are examples like the *Tristan und Isolde Liebestod*, the *Verklärte Nacht* of Schönberg, and many a church Mass, in which the amorous content, enfolded in sensuous textures, even if unrecognized, is none the less gratefully and luxuriously yielded to by most listeners.

To see, besides the great beauty of the *Tristan* music, for instance, the tortured, thwarted impulse that restrains the endless cadential flow from its resolution in the tonic that the spirit demands, is only to approach this art from a wisely human point of view. The value of *Tristan* is as undiminished by this psychological observation as is a Shakespearean tragedy by its vein of ribald comedy. To think otherwise is to miss much of the goodness and richness of life by adopting an unworldly and unrealistic point of view.

Like Lady Macbeth's spot, the false stigma attaches still to jazz, a stigma that, for nearly twenty years, has barred the way to real understanding. Even today, various writers can magnify the theme of vice, drink, and dope (largely marijuana) among the ranks of jazz and swing players, as if this manifestation were a prevailing condition among them (when, as a matter of fact, it is a very minor one) and as if — wherever it exists in Negro or White player — it were not a symptom of personal or class maladjustment to our society.

Storyville, at all events, went its merry way, purveying to the pleasure of its patrons, contributing to the convenience and profit of a considerable part of New Orleans, while bothering that city's conscience scarcely at all. And the golden harvest of gilded sin, which has sometimes helped to endow colleges and libraries and even to found homes for wayward girls, here endowed, with an oblivious hand, a growing music. Before the Negro's eyes loomed financial rewards hitherto denied to his race. This fact, at least equally with the strong lure of the music, led Negro youth in large numbers into this field, often with parental consent.

New bands sprung up overnight and the folk academy of the second line and the children's groups called "spasm bands," with their toy and homemade instruments, blossomed. Fine bands and great players emerged. We have referred to Bolden's Band and its successor, the Eagle. There was also the Olympia (1900–15) with a succession of great players: Freddie Keppard and King Oliver on cornet; Picou, "Big-Eye" Nelson, Lorenzo Tio, Jr. and Sidney Bechet on clarinets; Zue Robertson and Eddie Atkins on trombone. Up to 1912 there were Bunk Johnson's Superior Band and the Imperial with Emanuel Perez, cornet, and George Baquet, clarinet. There was the famous Creole Band led by Keppard which was later to spread jazz northward and Kid Ory's Brownskin Band that, besides its great trombonist-leader, included Bechet and King Oliver and, later, Louis Armstrong who, in succeeding Oliver, found his first important job.

Cabarets like Frank Early's had, in 1915 and 1916, the Noone-Petit Orchestra (Buddy Petit, cornet and Jimmy Noone, clarinet). George Fewclothes (sic), a little earlier, had presented the Richard M. Jones Band in which the piano leader joined forces with Keppard, Roy Palmer, trombonist, and, successively, Lawrence Duhé (Dewey), Bechet, and Noone, clarinets. Many of these instrumentalists, and others, played at the "25" in 1916, Peter Lala's cafe in 1915, and numerous other places. There were numbers of small jazz combinations of three to six pieces like the Magnolia Sweets, the Primrose Orchestra, and Jack Carey's Band.

The bordellos used pianists, singers, and the smaller combinations, including the old string trio. Hillma Burt's house next door to Tom Anderson's famous — or notorious — saloon at Customhouse and Basin, was one which employed pianists. Jelly Roll Morton expounded on the "classiness" of her place. "Beer was one dollar a bottle. And lots of wine. I don't mean sauterne or anything like that, I mean *champagne*." There were great pianists among these "professors," ragtime players like Sammy Davis or Tony Jackson, and Jelly himself who was to develop, with jazz, into one of its greatest figures. Among them were masters of the blues and barrel-house piano (or, as Morton calls it "Honky Tonk music" [1]), men like the "Game Kid" and Buddy Carter.

These men and these bands left their mark, not, it must be admitted, on Storyville, which was oblivious to all of the arts except those of riotous living, and, perhaps, that delightful sort of genre painting known as the "saloon" picture or the "whorehouse nude," not on this miniature city of gilded palace and dirty, wooden crib, but on jazz music. This is a music whose purity and classic line, surveyed today, are amazing when posed against this, its erstwhile background, and lead us to wonder whether environment in this case had its usual, ascribed potency or whether the music moved into Storyville "too old to change its ways."

But, if New Orleans accepted with equanimity the existence and nature of this city within a city, the time was approaching when the U. S. Government was not to accept it, although it took a war to provoke and to justify legally the bit of paternalistic tyranny that was to come.

Early in August (1917), Secretary of War Newton D. Baker issued an order forbidding open prostitution within five miles of an Army cantonment, and a similar ruling was made by Josephus Daniels, Secretary of the Navy, respecting naval establishments. Later in the same month Bascom Johnson, representing the War and Navy Departments, visited New Orleans, inspected Storyville, and informed Mayor Martin Behrman that the orders must be obeyed. Mayor Behrman went to Wash-

[1] Refer to Morton's piano record, *Honky Tonk Music,* Jazzman Record # 11.

BLACK AND WHITE RAG

ington and protested, but without success, and on September 24, and again on October 1, he was notified by Secretary Daniels that unless the red-light district was closed by the city it would be closed by the Army and the Navy. On October 2, 1917, Mayor Behrman introduced an ordinance in the City Council abolishing Storyville . . . the Mayor said, "Our city government has believed that the situation could be administered more easily and satisfactorily by confining it within a prescribed area. Our experience has taught us that the reasons for this are unanswerable, but the Navy Department of the Federal government has decided otherwise."

The ordinance was adopted on October 9, and provided that after midnight of November 12, 1917, it would be unlawful to operate a brothel or assignation house anywhere in New Orleans.

The exodus from Storyville had begun two weeks before November 12, but most of the prostitutes had awaited the result of Gertrude Dix's [2] application for a restraining order. When the news of her failure spread, wagons and vans began entering the district and hauling away whatever furniture had not been sold to the swarm of second-hand dealers. As late as midnight of the 12th, there was a stream of harlots and their servants, laden with property, leaving the segregated area.

On November 14, 1917, two days after the closing of the red-light district, the *Item* announced that the police planned to round up the male parasites of Storyville and send them into the country to help the farmers. Nothing, however, came of this extraordinary idea. The next day many leading church-women, and members of the Louisiana Federation of Women's Clubs, held a meeting and appointed a committee to help the prostitutes. But none applied for succor. Few, in fact, needed it. They had simply moved from Storyville into various business and residential sections of New Orleans and were doing very well.[3]

So, twenty years after its founding, Storyville closed down. In its open-handed, oblivious way, it had been good to jazz, where the deaf critics and the fatuous public had passed it by. When the ravishingly beautiful quadroons with their suit-cases and the outrageous strumpets with their mattresses on

[2] A resident "Madame."
[3] Asbury, Herbert: *The French Quarter.* New York: 1936.

their backs filed out, the players of jazz filed out with them to face, as most of the women did not, leaner days. But even before this day, when the classic period of jazz seemed to be ending, an opening had been made for it far north of New Orleans, in Chicago.

> A thoughtful government, however, which took away with one hand, gave providentially with the other. As unwittingly as Josephus Daniels had struck, the late Andrew Volstead came to the rescue. National prohibition came in; Chicago, home of the beer hustlers and the booze barons, became the capitol of the nation's thirsty. Chicago with its easy money beckoned to the jazzmen; pioneers had already marked out the trail.[4]

Social changes would likely have doomed Storyville to a slow death anyway. Before the closing of the District, that paragon of its Madames, "Countess" Willie V. Piazza, foreseeing this, uttered the historic valedictory to her period: "The country club girls are ruining my business!" [5]

Now with Negro jazz beginning to emigrate from New Orleans, let us examine the white jazz of that city. This music, which is called Dixieland, is an interesting cultural phenomenon. It is the first instance of a sincere adoption by the white man of an Afro-American art and, so far as I am able to estimate, it remains the sole instance. The efforts of the minstrels were directed toward parody and burlesque. Their imitation of Negro dancing was frequently sincere; this may seem to contradict my previous statement. But not only is the Negro's dancing, compared with his music, a relatively minor artistic expression, but it must actually be considered as a part of his whole musical activity as he retained it from the native African culture. Thus a good exposition of his dancing, combined with a music which scarcely pretended to be more than a grotesque parody, is no more than a shallow caricature.

To come to the present, Gershwin's *Porgy and Bess* is not Negro opera despite a Negro cast, a liberal use of artificial

---

[4] Rudi Blesh, in the article *Jazz Begins* in the yearbook *Jazzways*, 1946.
[5] Asbury, Herbert: *The French Quarter. op. cit.*

coloration, and the inclusion of some street cries. It is *Neg. esque*, and the earlier travesty of ministrelsy is continued in a form more subtle and therefore more invidious. This work and more recent ones, like the operetta *Cabin in the Sky*, betray a more deplorable tendency than mere superficiality and lack of understanding. By enlisting actual Negroes for the public performance of these Tin Pan Alley potpourri, a new stereotype — this time a cultural one — is being fitted to the Negro in which he is set forth as an able entertainer singing a music that the white public finds to be just like *its own*. In these works, as in virtually all of the movie output which pretends to present Negro music, the public never hears fine, real Negro music; its delight with what it actually hears is like that of the Saratoga audience which saw the real Negro minstrels with cork-blackened faces. (See Appendix I, p. 359.) And that, at basis, is the comforting feeling that the Negro is comforming, is "staying in his place." And comforting it is, too, to the pandering composer and the mercenary producer who count the fat box-office receipts.

So the white Dixieland jazz of New Orleans stands out in startling relief as an adoption of Negro music which originally, at least, embodied genuine respect for a fine music not of the white man's origination.

The first outstanding figure of Dixieland was Jack "Papa" Laine, born in New Orleans in 1873; as the father of white jazz, he deserves his sobriquet. His first organization, dating from about 1892–93, was a street outfit called the Reliance Brass Band; its original personnel included Johnny Lala and Manuel Marlow (Mello?), cornets; Jules Casoff, trombone; Alcide Nuñez, clarinet; Mike Stevens, snares; Jack Laine, bass drum. It is unlikely that this band, at least at first, played in jazz style. Such a development would almost certainly follow the slightly later success of Bolden. Nor are the memories of the white players themselves completely trustworthy no matter how honest the men are. For the change into jazz playing was, in all probability, not a sudden and planned one but rather a more gradual evolution; memory is most accurate when it deals with a decisive event rather than with a slow change.

It must be noted that there are a small group of die-hard "Dixielanders" and their adherents who staunchly claim that *all* jazz was invented by New Orleans white men. It is scarcely necessary to point out the basis of racial prejudice in such untenable claims. Many veteran Dixieland players say otherwise, in fact. Although justly proud of their own music, they do not claim to have originated jazz. The New Orleans trumpeter, Paul Mares, even said, "They had no white bands which could really play. Everybody followed the colored bands." [6]

An ironic twist comes to light when we inquire into the backgrounds of some of the leading early Dixieland players. It is known that two, Dave Perkins, trombone, and Achille Baquet, clarinet, were exceptionally light-skinned Negroes who succeeded in *passing*.

Whenever Laine and his men may have begun to play Dixieland jazz, by 1900 he had several bands; by 1905, he owned a minstrel show or circus. For a long time he had the white field to himself and his bands were in great demand. His white competition was to come eventually, in fact, only from men who had played with him.

In time there were two schools of Dixieland playing. The difference centers not around the instrumentations which, in all true Dixieland, are substantially those of the Negro's classic jazz, but around the rhythmic character of the music. One school is exemplified by the Original Dixieland Jazz Band, their rhythm fast, staccato and rather jerky; the other, by the New Orleans Rhythm Kings, their rhythm one which, while syncopated, is much smoother. Both have the rhythmic characteristic which so much white jazz has, that of forming syncopation and polyrhythm into one- or two-measure phrases which tend to be repeated. This is not used as the stomp pattern is used by the Negroes, to emphasize the melody which is fitted into it. It seems to me to point to a very basic white aversion to suspen-

[6] From an interview with the author in 1944.

sions and distortions of the basic beat. These syncopations, suspensions and polyrhythms, undeniably native to the Negro, are stimulating but also disturbing to most whites. They seem to affect the inner equilibrium as dizziness does the physical, and in prolonged syncopation the feeling of control which comes from the basic beat is lost. Thus these rhythmic developments, so truly Negroid, emerge in white playing either in the limited phrases of Dixieland and the later Chicago white style or, occasionally, in a continuous syncopation that is hectic compared with the variety, ease, and assurance of Negro jazz. Much of the relaxation of Negro playing is conveyed by retarded entry, the delayed attack which conveys the feeling that the beat is an exterior force — almost a natural one — which *pulls* the music after it. Nearly all white playing *pushes* the beat, tending to anticipate it; this practice may indicate either overeagerness or the anxiety that comes from playing a strange music. It is thus that much white playing, and that of Negroes under white influence, has come to express sheer excitement felt physically and neurally, whereas jazz, which certainly does not lack exciting qualities, conveys chiefly a gay and natural ebullience or the moody, grave thoughtfulness and fateful beat of the blues.

Such observations are not a carping criticism of anything and everything done by white players but are based on an examination of the qualities of the two musics. The basis for this is factual data on record for anyone to hear; the pointing out of essential differences cannot be imagined as detracting from the achievements of the white Orleanians or from the distinct stylistic qualities which their music possesses. That any white players, working in necessarily improvisational emulation of a Negroid music, would show divergences from the model is probably inevitable. It is nevertheless to the credit of "Papa" Laine and his followers that their work, while a serious attempt to play jazz as the Negroes had formulated it, was neither unimaginatively slavish on the one hand, or a gratuitous and ruinous "improvement" on the other.

It has been rather generally assumed that the first white band to play jazz — whether it was Laine's Reliance, or his later Ragtime Band — played in the rhythmic manner of the Original Dixieland Jazz Band. Such an assumption is apparently based on the fact that many members of the Original Dixielanders, men like La Rocca and Alcide "Yellow" Nuñez played with Laine originally and on the further fact that they were the first to carry white jazz, or Dixieland, North. That Dixieland originated with this style may very well be true: certainly it is a fact that the Original Dixieland Jazz Band manner, which has been called "ragtime," has striking rhythmic similarities to white ragtime playing. This, like all printed ragtime, but unlike most actual Negro playing, has no very extended inner-rhythmic figures. The earliest ragtime sheet music seldom carries inner-rhythm beyond one measure. Yet early Negro playing did so, extending its polyrhythms over many measures with great ease. Indeed, there is little distinction to be made, rhythmically, between the Negro's *played* ragtime and his jazz. But as white ragtime differs rhythmically from the Negro, so early white jazz would differ from its model. The white band was called a "ragtime" band simply because all jazz and hot piano music were originally called ragtime in New Orleans.

The style of the New Orleans Rhythm Kings, a band which went North only five years after the Original Dixieland, is more relaxed and rhythmically more akin to Negro playing. That, while smoother, it becomes sweeter is, on the whole, a white tendency. Among white players, smooth tends to mean sweet; fast, wild, and rather uncontrolled means hot. At all events, the question of the original qualities of the Dixieland style is far less important than the fact that this early work is an attempt to play jazz that bases sincerity and enthusiasm on something approaching a real understanding.

The recording of white jazz antedates that of Negro jazz by several years and presents us with examples of both white styles as performed by the second generation of players. Recording of the Original Dixieland Jazz Band began in 1917, and of the Rhythm Kings in 1921. The first important Negro recording came in 1922, with the first couplings of King Oliver's Creole Jazz Band.

Dixie Jass Band One-Step, first record of the Original Dixieland Jazz Band to be issued, gives a thorough presentation of the style of their playing. The tune has come to be a jazz standard and, like many of the fine numbers introduced in the North by this band, has the feeling of march music with its form, complete with trio section. These tunes also seem — and this is consistent with probable Negro origins — to show melodic affinities to French dance music, as *Tiger Rag* does. Such pieces as the *Dixie Jass Band One-Step* (originally called *Mutt and Jeff*) and *Clarinet Marmalade* are the inspiration, in part perhaps, of Larry Shields, the gifted clarinetist of this group. Concerning certain other standard numbers of this group, pieces like *Livery Stable Blues* (or *Barnyard Blues*), the Dixieland trombonist, George Brunies, specifically says, "They were tunes originated by the Negro boys of New Orleans."

All the records of the *Original Dixieland* group during its first period of organization (ending about 1924) were acoustically recorded. Considering the limitations of this method, the results are exceptional and a tribute to the recording engineer who supervised the "take." The clarity and balance are better than on many records made later, including some which were electrically recorded. Today, with the electrical process universal, engineers have developed certain ideas of placement that are supposedly based on advanced acoustical knowledge; they delight in unnatural groupings of the players around a multitude of microphones of many sizes and types. As a result, the recorded sound is unnatural and muddy. On the rare occasions when the jazz band members, playing a music which results from intuitive taste and experimental common-sense, are allowed to form their normal grouping with the microphones placed and controlled properly, the result, without exception, is realistically transparent and of a true three-dimensional quality. This grouping developed in actual performance with two functions in mind: one was the projection of sound of proper volume and balance to the audience: the other was the necessity for the musicians to see one another during improvisation.

Jazz players think of a microphone simply and sensibly as an ear; they stand at a distance from which their music will be loud but not overloud. If any part — clarinet, cornet, trombone, guitar — needs to stand out momentarily, the player simply turns his instrument more directly at the microphone or approaches it a step or two. No process could be less esoteric. It would, no doubt, have delighted that man of common sense, Edison, who invented sound recording. The same procedure improves broadcasting.[7]

Despite the exceptional quality of the Original Dixieland discs all acoustical records need to be *studied,* that is to say, listened to carefully and imaginatively. Heard for an appreciable period, especially without alternation with the electrical records, their form and meaning will emerge. The "modern" point of view in jazz is largely found among those who have heard only swing music and whose listening days, as far as records are concerned, date from within the electrical period. To their ears, an acoustical record sounds old-fashioned; if the music from it is different from that heard on newer records, they jump to the conclusion that it, too, is old-fashioned. Already prejudiced, they generally refuse to listen to modern recordings of good jazz. The word they, and the commercial critics who cater to them, delight in, is "corny." It is an epithet which has a shattering effect on all the fearful conformists, unsure of their judgment, who flock to the facile and the easily understood and would rather be caught dead than out of step with the current fad. When the real jazz on old records is, as it always is, complex and strange to unaccustomed ears, the combination becomes too difficult for the casual approach.

Yet even those who are prejudiced against it respond to fine

[7] It does not, however, remove the commercial announcements or improve the prevalent bad quality of radio music.

Speaking Drums (Ewing Galloway photo)

Modern Instruments (New York Public Library photo)

Left: Page from the Paramount Record Catalog about 1925 (From files of the Decca Record Company). Right: Ma Rainey, a professional picture (Photo from Thomas Dorsey)

Ma Rainey's Wildcat Jazz Band, about 1924–5. Left to right: "Gabriel," drums; Albert Wynn, trombone; Dave Nelson, trumpet; Ma; Ed Pollack, alto saxophone; Tom Dorsey, piano (Photo from Thomas Dorsey)

MEMORABILIA OF MA

BERTHA "CHIPPIE" HILL

Bessie Smith (from the 1929 sound film St. Louis Blues)

Mahalia Jackson

SACRED AND PROFANE—TWO GREAT VOICES

THE SUPERIOR BAND OF NEW ORLEANS

Left to right: Buddie Johnson, Bunk Johnson, Big Eye Louis Nelson, Billy Marrero. Seated: Walter Brundy, Peter Bocage, Richard Payne (Photo from Louis Nelson)

The Battle of Covadonga

The Caliph of Spain at Cordova (From the Mardi Gras Supplement in color, 1883.
From collection of Helen Hall)

MARDI GRAS FLOATS: KREWE OF MOMUS, 1883

A Funeral at Gretna (Photo by Philip Guarisco)

Street parade. Note "second line" on sidewalk (Photo by William Russell)

NEW ORLEANS: MARCHING JAZZ

At Mentes' Bag Factory, New Orleans, about 1912. Baby Dodds, third from the left, worked here to buy his first drums (Photo from Baby Dodds)

The Jaz-E-Saz Band, on the S/S St. Paul, 1919. Left to right, standing: Baby Dodds, Joe Howard, Pop Foster, Johnny St. Cyr, David Jones, Sam Dutrey. Seated: George (?) Cooper, Fate Marable, Louis Armstrong (Photo from Baby Dodds)

DODDSIANA

Jelly Roll Morton in Storyville, about 1903 (Photo from Mrs. Amède Colas)

Big Eye Louis Nelson, clarinetist, and Freddie Keppard, trumpeter, about 1915–16. Instruments in photo used only for novelty pose (Photo from Louis Nelson)

S/S Sidney, 1918. Left to right: Baby Dodds, William Ridgely, Joe Howard, Louis Armstrong, Fate Marable, David Jones, Johnny Dodds, Johnny St. Cyr, Pop Foster. Unknown bystander in rear (Photo from Johnny St. Cyr)

S/S Capitol, 1919. Left to right: Hy Kimball, Boyd Atkins, Fate Marable (at piano), Johnny St. Cyr, David Jones, Norman Mason, Louis Armstrong, James Brecheur, Baby Dodds (Photo from Johnny St. Cyr)

RIVERBOAT DAYS

Masonic Hall

Hopes Hall

Economy Hall

Providence Hall (Jeunes Amis)

NEW ORLEANS: OLD DOWNTOWN DANCE HALLS

(Photos by Philip Guarisco)

JOSEPH "KING" OLIVER

during his days in Storyville, about 1915 (Photo from Johnny St. Cyr)

RHYTHM KINGS

At the Arabella Car Barn, New Orleans, 1910. Boys left to right: Emmet (Scarf Pin), Abbie Brunies, George Brunies (Photo from George Brunies)

The New Orleans Rhythm Kings, at Friars Inn, Chicago, 1921. Left to right: George Brunies, Frank Snyder, Paul Mares, Elmer Schoebel, Jack Pettis, Leon Rappolo, Arnold Loyocano, with string bass (Photo from George Brunies)

*At the De Luxe Café, South State Street near 35th, about 1917. Left to right: Well-
man Braud, Lillian Hardin (defaced), Lawrence Duhé, Sugar Johnny, Roy Palmer,
Minor "Ram" Hall (Photo from Frederic Ramsey, Jr.)*

*King Oliver's Creole Jazz Band at Comiskey Park, 1919 (year of the Black Sox
scandal). Left to right: "Ram" Hall, Honoré Dutrey, King Oliver, Lawrence Duhé,
Lorenzo Tio, Jr., unidentified player, Wellman Braud (Photo from Frederic Ramsey, Jr.)*

NEW ORLEANS IN CHICAGO

JELLY ROLL MORTON IN CHICAGO, 1921–2
(*Photo from Mrs. Amède Colas*)

KING OLIVER'S CREOLE JAZZ BAND, 1923

while playing at Lincoln Gardens in Chicago. Left to right: Baby Dodds, Honoré Dutrey, Bill Johnson, Louis Armstrong, Johnny Dodds, Lillian Hardin, King Oliver, seated (Photo from Baby Dodds)

PART A

Directions: For each question in Part A, you will hear a short sentence. Each be spoken just one time. The sentences you hear will not be written out for you must listen carefully to understand what the speaker says.

After you hear a sentence, read the four choices in your test book, marked (and (D), and decide which one is closest in meaning to the sentence you hear your answer sheet, find the number of the question and fill in the space that to the letter of the answer you have chosen. Fill in the space so that the letter in cannot be seen.

Example I

You will hear: Mary swam out to the island with her friends.

You will read: (A) Mary outswam the others.

(B) Mary ought to swim with them.

(C) Mary and her friends swam to the island.

(D) Mary's friends owned the island.

The speaker said, "Mary swam out to the island with her friends." Sentence (C) her friends swam to the island," is closest in meaning to the sentence you heard you should choose answer (C).

1917: Looking Forward. Left to right: Henry Ragas, Larry Shields, Eddie Edwards, Nick La Rocca, Tony Sbarbaro (*Photo from Eddie Edwards*)

1937: Looking Backward. Recording in the 1917 acoustical equipment for the March of Time. Left to right: La Rocca, Edwards, Sbarbaro, J. Russell Robinson, Shields, hidden behind La Rocca (*Still photo from the March of Time*)

THE ORIGINAL DIXIELAND JAZZ BAND

LOUIS ARMSTRONG IN CHICAGO, 1923

(Photo from Baby Dodds)

THE HOT FIVE ABOUT 1926

Left to right: Johnny St. Cyr, Kid Ory, Louis Armstrong, Johnny Dodds, Lillian Armstrong (Photo from Johnny St. Cyr)

EDWARD "KID" ORY, 1945

(*Harold Trudeau photo from Marili Morden*)

New Orleans, 1944. Left to right: Jim Robinson, Bunk, George Lewis, Baby dds, Alcide (Slow Drag) Pavageau, Laurence Marrero (Photo by William ssell)

New York, 1945. Left to right: Jim Robinson, Bunk, Baby Dodds, Laurence arrero, George Lewis, Alton Purnell. Slow Drag (Photo by Warren Rothschild, cca)

BUNK JOHNSON'S BAND RECORDING

HEAT WAVE MEETS COOL WAVE

Art Hodes's boogie-woogie and Lester Young's tenor saxophone (Photo from Metronome Magazine)

THE "BIRD"—CHARLIE PARKER (1920–1955)

. . unforgettable intensity—naked communication . . ." (Photo by Leonard)

GOOD–WILL AMBASSADORS WITH WORLDWIDE PORTFOLIO

Satchmo—No. 1 plenipotentiary: "Dig this, folks: the trumpet ain't no cannon" (Photo from Columbia Records)

Dizzy Gillespie in Pakistan: "For the snake I played a fine old Arabian blue (Photo from Metronome Magazine)

jazz in actual performance. A good sign today is the tendency of high schools and colleges to offer courses in jazz appreciation which include the playing of records. If, in too many cases, the approach is shallow and the right records are not played and analyzed, this is a condition which time and the dissemination of accurate knowledge will overcome. It will become increasingly and more widely recognized that the fine old records are invaluable historical documents. Just as a written document is studied and deciphered, not thrown into the wastebasket, so the old record will, in time, receive adequate attention. That such attention will reveal a still current music, incalculably more revolutionary and modern than any other contemporary music, is a revelation which awaits every student with a serious and reasonably patient approach.

CITATION 47. *Dixie Jass Band One-Step,* played by the Original Dixieland Jazz Band: Dominique "Nick" La Rocca, cornet; Larry Shields, clarinet; Eddie Edwards, trombone; Henry Ragas, piano; Tony Sbarbaro, drums.

Dixie Jass Band One-Step (later called *Original Dixieland One-Step*) has three main sixteen-bar themes. The first, of an introductory character, alternates four bars of incisive chords with four of rapid syncopation and then repeats this arrangement. The second theme, in the same key, is more melodic in character, with slashing clarinet breaks placed in most unusual positions, the first and second, and the ninth and tenth measures. Theme one is then repeated and the second theme follows, its last four bars modulating to a different key. The third theme, a trio in character, entering in this new key, is played three times, with some variation, to conclude the record. The tempo is considerably faster than most Negro playing, a fact that contributes in no small measure to the jerkiness of the syncopation. The playing throughout is ensemble, fitting generally into the Negro tradition. It is full of momentary dissonances that pass like clouds over the clearly expressed basic harmony. The tone quality is considerably more pure — more of a "white" tone — than vocal in the Negroid way.

211

Edwards's trombone is very active, quite tailgate in feeling, and very rhythmic, abounding in long slides, with many emphatic downward runs ending in these glissandi, as well as runs constructed of a series of them. At one point Edwards uses a forceful, high, broken organ-point consisting of a rapid series of hammer-like blows punched out on the same note.

Shields's clarinet part is more an obbligato to the cornet than an independent voice. It revolves in little runs around lead notes (this is called "noodling") and emerges in occasional wailing, sliding tones which are markedly dissonant and grotesquely effective. These wails sometimes slide rapidly downward and are accented at the end by a cymbal crash. At other times they slide up and then down in a manner surprisingly prophetic of a trumpet effect developed by Louis Armstrong about ten years later. La Rocca, who once played in Laine's Reliance Band, plays a simple but not very rhythmic or forceful lead cornet.

While the playing of the Original Dixieland Jazz Band does not equal the fine Negro playing of classic jazz, or even that of the more average bands, like Sam Morgan's Jazz Band, or Louis Dumaine's Jazzola Eight, it must be considered a form of jazz. With all its faults of rhythm, tone, and polyphony, it is fairly well integrated and had much more variety in actual performance than it shows on its records. Only one of these men, Larry Shields, was an oustanding musician. Edwards was a good, but by no means a great player. La Rocca was merely adequate as were the others, although Ragas may have been a good ragtime player. (The piano suffered most in acoustical recording and is very much in the background.) But these men worked seriously and showed results which do them credit and point to what could be accomplished today by a more musicianly white band, were it equally determined to play jazz.

Not that all white New Orleans musicians showed such determination. The Dixieland vein, if deep, was not wide. The vast majority of the players attempted only a mere parody of jazz although nowadays many would have you believe that they were a part — if not actually founders — of the movement. Their music was in a state of suspension between sweet and hot, arranged to death, full of "cute" effects and endless solos. If once in a while it begins to hit a beat and, for a moment, things are happening — after all there was wonderful music in the air in those days, and these men had ears. This music can be heard on any of the Half-Way House Orchestra records on Columbia, or those of Anthony Parenti's Famous Melody Boys bearing the old Okeh red label.

Records made by the Original Dixieland Jazz Band in 1937, twenty years after their first session, give an opportunity to hear this music in modern recording. After their disbandment in 1925, most of the members retired from music. They reassembled, as mature men, to play at the Texas Centennial Exposition in 1936, at Dallas, Texas. The line-up was as in 1917, except that Ragas, who had died in 1919, was replaced on this occasion, as originally, by J. Russel Robinson. One year later, Victor recorded them and a number of sides were made. Some, with the original five pieces from which so much power had come, were new versions of the old standard numbers. These were issued over the name Original Dixieland Five. Certain other lamentable sides presented pop tunes by a large swing band into whose uncongenial surroundings the original band was inserted.

CITATION 48. *Original Dixieland One-Step*, by the Original Dixieland Five (1937). This record starts out at a slower tempo than the 1917 version but quickly speeds up to a tempo identical with the old. Inactivity in music did not seem to impair the style or playing of these men. Shields, a prematurely white-haired man by the time of this recording date, had matured stylistically and seemingly justified the frequent statement that he founded New Orleans white clarinet style. Edwards' playing, too, is riper and, while it could not be more assured that his 1917 manner, is musically more logical. The others seem to be just about where they were in 1917. The chief concession to "modernism" is the inclusion of several solos. That of Shields is inventive, free, and flexible. The last ensemble shows the band, back in stride once more, "giving out" in an ensemble — arch-typical of all ragtime Dixieland from "Papa" Laine on down.

A record by the New Orleans Rhythm Kings illustrates the smoother phase of Dixieland.

CITATION 49. *Panama,* by the Friars Society orchestra (the recording name first used by the Rhythm Kings). This 1921 Gennett record offers recording much inferior to the Victors. Personnel: Paul Mares, trumpet; Leon Rappolo, clarinet; George Brunies, trombone; Jack Pettis, saxophone; Louis Black, banjo; Steve Brown, bass; Elmer Schoebel, piano; Frank Snyder, drums. The line-up is not strictly New Orleans either in personnel or in instrumentation. Pettis, the saxophone player, was found by the band in Davenport, Iowa. The Rhythm Kings thoughtlessly added this instrument because of its popularity and many of the ensembles are nearly ruined by its doodling around the trumpet lead. The remainder of the personnel, excepting Schoebel and Snyder, are from New Orleans. Mares was a more capable player than La Rocca and this may well be because in Chicago he seized every opportunity to hear King Oliver; his style, which featured much muted and "wa-wa" work, is patterned directly after this fine model. Brunies has always been at least as rhythmic as Edwards, sounder in harmony, more vociferous, and he has, while Edwards has not, a husky Negroid tone, very vocal in quality. Rappolo's clarinet style has been characterized as "fugitive." It was restrained, certainly, but he had melodic ideas. His melancholy playing, much of it in low register, was in marked contrast to Shields's dramatic style. It was not, however, *blue* as it is commonly believed to have been, but rather a true minor style closely related to Sicilian and Neapolitan song. Finally, he provided, on the whole, more of an integrated and independent polyphonal part than the Original Dixieland man.

Panama is taken at a moderate tempo, precisely that of Bunk Johnson's record cited in the previous chapter. The playing moves smoothly and rhythmically; there is a real polyphony here and many other elements of classic jazz and yet, compared with Bunk's record, there is a wide difference. What is mainly lacking, of course, (and comparison elucidates it) is the fire, élan, and the unstoppable drive of Negro playing. The Rhythm Kings' style is pleasant — too pleasant; it is sweetened jazz; it is manners supplanting vigor. Part for part: Mares' capable trumpet against Bunk's inspired, driving one; Rappolo's introspective clarinet compared with the sheer, vibrant, fluent energy of Lewis'; and so on.

The tendency of the Original Dixieland Jazz Band was healthier; it was one that held the greater promise of producing a fine white jazz. Technical failings are more easily rectified than a lack of spirit. Jazz is a music for vital and assured men and it requires all the energy and drive that Shields and his men had — and more. And then, in the fullness of time, must be added the wisdom, ingenuity, and sheer inspiration of the Negro at his best.

The Original Dixieland Jazz Band proved in 1937 that the torch could be picked up again, twenty long years after it had been held burning at its brightest. One can believe that it has not gone out. Somewhere, in Chicago, in San Francisco, in New Orleans, in New York, are the white boys to seize it. Beginning where the Original Dixieland left off, they could make the jazz of the white man live again. But if they are to succeed they will not set out to improve a music they cannot even play at first, nor conceal their inability in easy, flashy tricks; they will not encourage the Negro to play his own music incorrectly; they will turn their own backs on easy monetary success.

The objection, of course, can be offered (and it is a perfectly understandable one) that there is no reason for white men to play Negro music at all. Then what is the merit of converting a revolutionary musical development of the American Negro into a hybridization of only the slightest value when considered as Western music — of no value at all considered as jazz? What is the value, in any large cultural sense, of encouraging the

Negroes, at the same time, to ruin their own music? Are there not, on the other hand, the strongest reasons for examining jazz from a musical and nonracial angle to determine its purely musical qualities? Among these are certain nonracial ones which can be made the basis of an important white music. When we consider the low state of popular music today, such a development seems as logical as it is desirable.

10.

chicago

Jazz first moved outward from New Orleans at the very end of the last century, when the surviving riverboats — the great packet days over — were converted into excursion steamers, the famous show boats. In the early days of the Twentieth Century the *Capitol*, the *Sidney*, the *St. Paul*, and others made their passenger-carrying voyages up the river to Memphis, St. Louis, Cairo, Davenport, and even St. Paul; they plied, as well, the major tributaries of the great Mississippi system, following the Ohio eastward to Pittsburgh, and the Missouri northwest to Kansas City and Omaha. These boats furnished entertainment for the passengers and, docking at piers or alongside the levees — or taking them aboard for short excursions — for the local populace. So, even today, the *President*, its decks thronging with carefree passengers, glides, on summer evenings, past Algiers Point around the crescent of the Mississippi, curved and glistening like a great silver sickle in the moonlight.

In the entertainment, which varied from the large orchestra down to the original and typical steam calliope, there was much jazz. Even in the larger boat bands or, more properly, orchestras like those which the pianist Fate Marable organized a little later in St. Louis, there was often a preponderance of New Orleans jazz players, men like Louis Armstrong, the drummer Baby Dodds, "Pop" Foster on tuba or string bass, and Johnny St. Cyr, perhaps the greatest of the jazz guitar and banjo players. These men were not completely restrained by a music as severely arranged and as sweet as that of Fate's bands, the real forerunner of sweet swing. St. Cyr says that they were allowed some improvising at all times and were given two numbers, out of the twelve played each three hours, to play in the freest jazz manner. Marable even had two trumpeters; one played sweet or at least legitimately, and one played hot.

So jazz went out early on the show boats. It was played in the 1890's by men now unknown and, only a little later, by players like the cornetist "Sugar Johnny" who, with Roy Palmer, the trombonist, and Lawrence Duhé, clarinetist, had an early hot band on the excursion steamers. This band later toured the country in vaudeville, playing Chicago in 1915. A year or two later "Sugar Johnny," Palmer, and Duhé were playing at the old De Luxe Café in the Chicago South Side, in a band which included Lillian Hardin, piano; Wellman Braud (Breaux) bass; and "Ram" Hall, drums.

Urge for variety and travel, more than for high pay, filled the band rosters of the boats. Jazz paid well in the New Orleans of that day and immediate fame was to be had there from a Negro public acquainted with the music. The boats seldom stayed long in any of the cities they touched, nor did the bands penetrate them to any great extent. The music was too migrant, its stay too fleeting, for its effect to be either deep or lasting in these northward cities where it fell for the first time, a strange language on unaccustomed ears. Nor did the early vaudeville tours of the fine Original Creole Band, spanning the continent from California to New York from about 1912 to 1917, leave a deep imprint on the public consciousness. Jazz was accepted, in its first brief hearings by pleasure-bent listeners, as only another "novelty" music of the Negro, confounded, like all Negro music in those days, with the white minstrel imitations and confused by all sorts of Uncle Remus or Uncle Tom ideas.

Not theater appearances but dancing opened the ears of the public and led to wide acceptance, if not critical appreciation. This is fitting in a music in which the functional aspect is so important. Intelligent appreciation of jazz as an art can, however, follow the enjoyment of its use in dancing, in which the listener participates in the music's rhythmic framework. Listening while dancing is quite as reasonable a way to grasp music which has a rhythmic and flowing form, as sitting quietly is for one of a more architectural form.

There is a dynamism in a growing art, as in a growing people, that bursts frontiers. Jazz, not taken seriously in the casual appearance outside New Orleans of the show boat or the vaudeville act, sounded differently to visitors who heard it in its native setting. Such hearings, coupled with the magnetism which the city itself exerts, left permanent impressions on many.

So when Frisco, the cigar-chewing vaudevillian of that day, heard the Dixieland players of the Tom Brown Band at a club in New Orleans where he and McDermott, his partner, were appearing, he was profoundly impressed, at least by the entertainment possibilities he perceived. This was in 1914, and Frisco carried word of this new music to Chicago. Offers soon came and finally, in June, 1915, the white band accepted a job at the Lambs' Café in the Illinois metropolis following the Negro pioneers who were already playing obscurely in the south side Negro district. Tom Brown's Band included Ray Lopez on cornet; Brown, trombone; Gus Mueller, clarinet; Arnold Loyocano, bass and piano; William Lambert, drums. Thus, even before the closing of Storyville, the spread of jazz began.

Never without its sensational aspects in New Orleans, jazz was not to lose them in Chicago. After an inauspicious opening, sensation and with it success was soon to come in a manner told in a legend concerning the origin of the name, jazz. As this story goes, the band came in without clearance from the union which, in reprisal and contempt, promptly spread the word around that this was "Jass." Greater clarity and emphasis could not have been secured with the longer but virtually synonymous title, "whorehouse music." Intrigued rather than dismayed, the public flocked to hear it; delighted rather than abashed, the band took the epithet as a title. "Presently the new sign out front read 'Added Attraction — Brown's Dixieland Jass Band, Direct from New Orleans, Best Dance Music in Chicago.' " [1]

A little later, Larry Shields came to Chicago and took Mueller's place in the Brown band. Soon thereafter, the Chicago promoter Harry James,[2] went to New Orleans in search of a similar band for another local spot. His search took him to the 102 Ranch in Storyville which some years previously had been known as the 101 Ranch.

James heard there, in 1916, a three-piece Dixieland combination which included "Yellow" Nuñez on clarinet, Henry Ragas at piano, and Johnny Stein on drums. He offered Nuñez a contract for a larger band. The one that came north a little later included, besides Nuñez and Ragas, Eddie Edwards on trombone, Dominique "Nick" La Rocca on cornet, and Tony Sbarbaro who replaced the drummer, Stein. Profiting by Tom Brown's experience, this group departed to play at Schiller's Café in the northern city under the title which later attained worldwide fame, the Dixieland Jass Band. Late in that same year, Brown and the Dixieland group effected a trade in players; from this emerged a different Tom Brown Band, later renamed the Louisiana Five, and another called the Original Dixieland Jass Band that went to New York the following year. In the meantime, having added Tony Sbarbaro at drums, the new group had played in Chicago at the De Labbe Café and the Duquesne Gardens. How it made jass (later jazz) the talk of the American metropolis and reaped, besides, the first real fame and important financial profit from the music the Negro had originated, is ironical history.

By a quirk of fate, Dixieland, which had followed Negro jazz to the two largest American cities, was the first to attract widespread attention. This reversal of historic order, as if by predesign, even extended into recording. There, as we have seen, the first hot records were played by the Original Dixieland; they sold by the millions and, in those preradio days, dissem-

---

[1] Charles Edward Smith in the book *Jazzmen. op. cit.*
[2] Not the present-day sweet trumpet player.

inated jazz more rapidly and widely than a score of traveling bands might have done. This Victor contract was first offered to the superb Original Creole Band only to be turned down by Freddie Keppard, the leader. His rejection, forced through over the objections of most of his players, was prompted by his fear that his band's tunes would be pirated and its style of playing copied from the records! On such details do historical misconceptions arise. White playing, several degrees from Negro jazz and several degrees toward nonjazz — Dixieland in short — came, almost overnight, to mean jazz to the whole country. To some extent it still does today.

Negro jazz did not come in force to Chicago until two years after the Brown Band arrived, although the Imperial Band, with Perez, George Field (Filhe), trombone, and Louis Nelson is said to have appeared there for a short period in 1914. Likewise, as we have seen, Keppard's Original Creole group had appeared there, and "Sugar Johnny" and his band were at the De Luxe about this time. And, of course, much Negro jazz had been played for some years in the South Side where segregation operated against its white hearing. But King Oliver came to Chicago in 1917 or 1918 and thenceforth, at least until 1924, Negro jazz there was spelled by his name. For that name meant more than one of the greatest New Orleans cornetists; the band he built in Chicago stood for classic jazz in one of its purest manifestations, as, in memory and on phonograph records, it still does.

Joseph "King" Oliver was born about 1885, on Dryades Street in New Orleans. He does not seem to have begun playing music, as so many New Orleans Negroes did, in early childhood. His first opportunity came as a youth of thirteen or so, when he joined a children's brass band. By all accounts he learned slowly but thoroughly. Before long, young Joe had worked into professional company, although for a time he had to work as a butler while pursuing music as an avocation. Finally he was able to play upon occasion with the fine Eagle Band and soon thereafter, at Rice's Hall in Storyville with the Onward Brass Band, led by the cornetist Emanuel Perez, who played in a style classic but hot.

Jazz was an activity of friendly but relentless competition between creative men, a rivalry only in small part economic; it spurred on the musicians, made good men great and great ones greater. This rivalry helps to explain the phenomenally rapid development of the music itself. No usurpers became "King" or even "Kid" in New Orleans in those days. The crown or the title had to be won in the rough but fair jousting of a perpetual tournament. Numerous legends explain how Joe Oliver became a recognized leader. Regardless of these, with the abdication of King Bolden, the title was divided and soon there were two Kings, Oliver and Freddie Keppard, in addition to the great — if uncrowned — Bunk Johnson.

When Oliver went to Chicago a few years later, he carried his crown packed, unseen, with his cornet. With these and his simple personal belongings, were packed, invisible, the fine old jazz tunes, most of them not committed to paper, *Canal Street Blues, High Society,* his own *Dippermouth Blues* and the others.

For the few years that intervened before the closing of Storyville, Oliver played in many bands and places; he was in demand in all. He was with Kid Ory's band in 1915 and played dances at the Tulane University gymnasium; he had his own bands, in 1916, at the "25," and later at Pete Lala's Café. He was at Lala's when the blow fell on Storyville.

For all his local fame, scuffling for a good job now faced Oliver in New Orleans. Chicago, soon to be a mecca for the masters of jazz, gave an immediate opportunity to the King. How he landed in Chicago in 1918 with two jobs already his, is a story or legend which has been told many times. At all events, for nearly two years, Oliver played cornet at the Royal Gardens with remnants of the Original Creole Band and at the Dreamland with Duhé.

During these years, while Joe doubled in brass, Chicago was learning about jazz, accepting it with an enthusiasm wholehearted if not discerning. Prohibition was in its first stages with the rackets being rapidly set up; speak-easies flourished; the post war boom was on; money flowed as freely as the bathtub gin and the phony Scotch whiskey.

In 1920 the Dreamland offered Oliver a steady and exclusive job. So, in the same year that the New Orleans Rhythm Kings came to Chicago, King Oliver's Creole Jazz Band came into existence. The personnel at first included Honoré Dutrey on trombone; Ed Garland, string-bass; Lillian Hardin, piano, and Minor "Ram" Hall, drums. The clarinetist, Jimmy Noone, left the band soon afterward and was replaced by a new arrival from New Orleans, quiet, serious, Johnny Dodds, perhaps the greatest clarinetist in the long line of New Orleans masters. A book will be written about the Creole Jazz Band some day. Its influence has been incalculable; its playing, dimly preserved on old, acoustical records, looms more modern today than it did in 1920.

For a year the Creole Band played the Dreamland every night until 1 a.m., then proceeded to the near-by Pekin Café, a cabaret with a rich and numerous — if not orderly — gangster following. In 1921 the band embarked on a not-too-fortunate expedition to California. For six months, from June to December, they played "jitney dances" at the Pergola Dancing Pavilion on San Francisco's lower Market Street. Then "Ram" Hall left, to be replaced by "Baby," Johnny Dodds's brother; about the same time, Lil Hardin, in ill health, took a leave of absence.

During this time, Oliver and his band were invited to visit Purcell's famous dive on the Barbary Coast, by the ragtime pianist, Sid Le Protte, who had a very respectable orchestra there, replete with violins and cello. Le Protte welcomed the Creole gang with some surprise, for they had brought their instruments, and was constrained to ask them to play. The Barbary Coast, no inferior imitation of Storyville itself, had never heard such music and the results were electrifying. "When the noise stopped," Sid says, "I looked around for my boys. One or two crawled out from under the tables with their violins under their arms and I said, 'Throw those cigar boxes away and get some horns!' "

The band broke up for a while and the players "gigged around" which means they held temporary jobs, "one nighters." Baby Dodds drummed for a little while with Kid Ory's Brownskin Band which was playing at the Iroquois Café across the bay in Oakland. But, before this, Baby discovered a local girl, Bertha Gonsoulin, who is said to have learned her piano playing from Jelly Roll Morton, a few years previously, in Mary's Place on Townsend Street. Bertha took Lil's place.

Soon the band re-formed and went on to Los Angeles where it played at least once with Morton in the old open-air pavilion at Leek's Lake Resort. Returning to Chicago, it opened in the redecorated Royal Gardens now called the Lincoln Gardens Café. Oliver decided to place his band above any possible local competition by adding a second cornet. He thought of young Louis Armstrong, then twenty-two, who had taken the King's place at Lala's and was becoming a sensation in New Orleans. A wire was sent and Louis was quick to accept. The band was playing when his train was due to arrive. Bertha Gonsoulin was chosen to meet him because in a real New Orleans band the pianist could have dropped dead with the mishap unnoticed. So "Minnie Mouse," as the musicians called her, met Louis and brought him back to the crowded noisy hall.

He was an awkward boy dressed in clothes that looked rustic in Chicago. Threading their way through the dancing couples, they took their places on the stand. Louis put the straw suitcase, that held all of his belongings, on the floor and took out his cornet. Oliver called the name of the tune to him and Louis came right in on the note with his beautiful and imaginative second part to the King's lead. Not a soul in the audience grasped the miracle that was happening!

In this same year Oliver began to record, first for Paramount, then for Gennett whose records appeared first. In two years the Creole Jazz band recorded for four companies, Okeh and Columbia following the two above in order. Thirty-five, perhaps thirty-seven [3] sides in all, they were, despite the defects of acoustic recording, the first definitive records of the Negro's classic jazz and they have not been surpassed since in style. Their popular appeal was fairly wide but it is more important to note that they exerted a deep and formative influence on other players, particularly the young white musicians of Chicago. We shall later examine this influence but at this point we should discuss some of the records.

CITATION 50. *Mabel's Dream,* played by King Oliver's Creole Jazz Band, is a composition of three main themes, each sixteen measures long. The treatment throughout is ensemble without solos in the present-day sense. The first theme is introductory in character. The second is full of the feeling of popular song. The principle theme is the third which is hymnlike, serious, almost grave. The anthem-like effect of the melody is heightened by the instrumentation which produces an organ-like tone above which Oliver's cornet floats high, clear, and silvery, while Dodds's clarinet, limpid and pure, weaves an independent melody. The parts of Negro church singing can be distinguished here, exemplified by the various instruments.

The ensembles are solid and forceful but relaxed. Dutrey plays a continuous part, related to the harmonic role of the violoncello in a string orchestra. Not always sufficiently rhythmic, in this record at least, it is a highly vocal part, effective and fitting. Oliver's cornet lead is in a beautiful clear open tone; his phrasing is the very epitome of the jazz phrase; one moment it drives the ensemble, the next it is wayward, lingering and then catching up in imaginative figures. This phrasing was the rhythmic gift of Bunk Johnson to New Orleans jazz. Armstrong inherited it, too.

Near the end, high and muted, Oliver's tone jets out like a blue flame, a moment that focuses all the meaning of the music. Pleading, urgent is the voice of the "key'd cornet" while the clarinet climbs upward in a poignant, close counterpoint. There are penultimate phrases of high, white cornet tone, that subside

[3] One probable Gennett disc remains undiscovered to date.

into repeated suspirations, short, plaintive downward cadences from the blues third to the tonic, and the music ends.

The first selection Oliver brought to wax for Gennett was the classic New Orleans jazz with the blues at its core:

CITATION 51. *Canal Street Blues.*

Although the developments of Oliver's life were to be ultimately tragic, and many vicissitudes were to assail jazz, this record is that of a triumphant moment. *Canal Street* is built on the twelve-bar blues in authentic New Orleans form, its tempo the proper one of the "fast" blues. The first two choruses are fine ensemble, rhythmically free with a light framing of stomp; the third and fourth are strongly harmonic with the clarinet improvising blues melodies in counterpoint to the long phrases of the cornets; the fifth is strong ensemble stomping. (See Ex. 37, back of book.)

The sixth and seventh choruses are of clarinet, solo, over a full rhythm in which the banjo, very prominent, plays beautiful counterpoint, in descending tuba-like phrases. In his solo, young Johnny Dodds demonstrates the greatness that, besides establishing at its most classic the role of the clarinet in New Orleans jazz, achieved its intrinsic richness and development within the limits of cooperative polyphony. Thus this is not a solo in the present "modern" sense, the rhapsodic show piece that, unorganically related to its context, has in the last analysis so little musical value.

Who can describe the hot inspiration, the resistless flow, the fervent lyricism, the rapt ecstasy, the victorious exaltation, the overwhelming melancholy, of this playing? One long melody that lingers on the pale thirds and sevenths, this is altogether the essence of the blues.

Mandy Lee Blues, from the first Gennett session, is a popular song rather than a blues. The breaks in this record fall in the seventh-eighth and eleventh-twelfth measures and show the correspondence of the break to the instrumental responses in the vocal blues. This device, carried over into the jazz playing of popular tunes, is really African antiphonal practice transforming alien material while the vocal-toned instruments alter the melody. Johnny Dodds plays two remarkable clarinet breaks in *Mandy Lee*. The first is a downward run of many notes divided into rhythmic patterns. In the second, a single note on the fifth interval is held for five and a half beats while the tension mounts and then the sound suddenly cascades downward.

The slow speed turntable, revolving at 33 ⅓ r.p.m., (standard speed is 78 r.p.m.) used to study these breaks, shows Dodds's tone as fluctuating with absolute regularity like an accented duple pulse in a vibrato that encompasses almost a full half-tone of pitch. Slow-speed analysis of Dodds's blue tones, on the other hand, reveals a different sort of pitch fluctuation in notes played without vibrato. Attacked accurately about a quarter-tone below the normal major third, they undulate slowly in pitch, resulting in an unusual tonal coloration.

Oliver's great period was that of his Creole Jazz Band, 1920–1924. His later and larger bands, which brought him brief fame, at the same time epitomize what was happening to jazz in alien cities. A quick degeneration occurred when this extraordinarily pure and vital music was transplanted, killing a part, deforming some of the growth, yet not striking quite to the roots.

The second important contingent of Dixieland, the New Orleans Rhythm Kings, arrived at this time. The invasion of Chicago was, to all intents and purposes, complete. In 1920 when the Rhythm Kings came to establish themselves, first at the Cascades Ballroom and later at Friars' Inn, white local imitation already had begun. Even the New Orleans boys still went to the source to learn. They were steady patrons of King Oliver, as, in those days, but to far less effect, were Paul Whiteman and Guy Lombardo. Mares' trumpet style is based directly on the King's, Rappolo's clarinet was strongly influenced by Dodds, but the Rhythm Kings were themselves to be a strong influence upon the Chicago style then just beginning.

The chief early Chicago group was the Wolverine Orchestra organized in 1923 with the famous Bix Beiderbecke as leader. Leon Bismarck Beiderbecke was born in Davenport, Iowa, in

1903. His was a well-to-do and musical family and his piano training began early. His cornet playing was self-taught; his earliest efforts were with phonograph records of the Original Dixieland Jazz Band. Thus the first influence on Bix was the Dixieland style. Later on, it is said, the early records of King Oliver came into Bix's possession. He joined his first band in 1921 at Lake Forest Academy where he was a student, but his scholarship suffered from his musical preoccupation and he was forced out of school during his first year.

In 1923 or 1924, the Wolverines made their first recordings. In all, thirteen numbers were recorded by Gennett with Beiderbecke participating. Since these records were of rather great influence, it is necessary to examine a typical one.

CITATION 52. *Jazz Me Blues*, by the Wolverine Orchestra: Bix Beiderbecke, cornet; Al Gande, trombone; George Johnson, tenor saxophone; Jimmy Hartwell, clarinet; Dick Voynow, piano; Bob Gillette, banjo; Min Leibrook, bass; Vic Moore, drums.

Jazz simply isn't in these grooves. There is no basic beat. The attack is fuzzy and uncertain despite the fast tempo used in trying to obtain the lift and vitality that jazz has at any tempo. Everything is highly arranged with hardly a pretense at real group improvisation, none at true polyphony. The clarinet plays no independent part here, only "noodling" around the lead. The trombone, providing no off-beat rhythmic thrust, provides only the most obvious "barber shop" harmony.

Much has been written about Beiderbecke's beautiful tone. Beautiful, it was not hot; nor were the attack and rhythm incisive. Bix has been praised for virtues which he really had; clear beautiful tone, a romantic accent, and a sort of nostalgic plaintiveness, but these are far from virtues in the jazz music by which Bix must be judged.

The Wolverines' spirit is that of the sweet band and of the popular sentimental balladists, and their rhythm is deformed by the peculiar, jumpy pattern often called *vo-de-o-do*. Say *do-do-vo-de-o-do* aloud and you have the pattern as it was derived, probably from attempts of white singers of popular tunes to imitate the rhythmic Negro scat song and the stomp rhythms of the band. The *vo-de-o-do*, however, has a finicky and nervous character which obsessively permeates the whole music. It is entirely unlike the Negro stomp which, limited to certain instruments, is used for rocking emphasis, not to replace a lacking rhythm. The Wolverines could not escape the *vo-de-o-do*: cornet phrases are mutilated by it and tied together with meaningless short notes that accentuate the banal pattern; droning saxophone and Rappolesque clarinet cleave to the stencil; throughout the Wolverines' records, and the whole progressive series which stem from them — Red Nichols, the Memphis Five, and the Cotton Pickers — runs the same rune: *vo-de-o-do*. Nor is there in this whole school a trace of hot tone, of the Negro speech inflections and timbres, of jazz phrasing, or of the incalculable effect of the blues upon our scale.

Romantic nineteenth-century European music, particularly German, entered with the Wolverines. The cloying, sentimental sweetness — though it may stem more directly from the "schmaltzy" little "oompah" band than from Wagner — comes from this source. The classic line of French melody, entering jazz from the quadrille and Creole song, could accord perfectly with the unromantic, unsentimental, pure classicism of Afro-American polyphony. The harmonic wanderings and musings, the adolescent, self-conscious romanticism and phony philosophy of the late German school, on the other hand, smother jazz under a blanket soggy with tears.

The Romantic tendency shows clearly in later records by Bix, such as his *Wringing and Twisting* and, particularly, in his piano solo, *In a Mist*, a rambling piece in unresolved Debussyesque harmonies. This music does not develop out of jazz and has no real relation to it, but it does prefigure the orchestral efforts of Duke Ellington which are frequently but erroneously considered to be jazz manifestations.

Beiderbecke was and is a pervasive influence. A whole school of white playing, which pretends to be jazz, stems from him;

but real jazz is a strong music. Objectively considered, Beiderbecke's playing is weak and weakness characterized his life. It permitted him to play in the commercial orchestras of Paul Whiteman and Jean Goldkette; it led him to ruin his life with drink. All of these happenings are a part of his romantic legend. Volitional acts are mistakenly considered parts of his tragic fate. Bix was neither a tragic nor a heroic character; he was a figure of pathos.

What is now known as Chicago-style jazz is not that of Beiderbecke, but was based upon classic New Orleans and Dixieland. The dark Negroid stream came in from Oliver's Creole Jazz Band, the light stream from the Rhythm Kings. The earliest playing by Chicagoans shows the predominance of the one influence or the other before the two converged for a while in the phases of this style from about 1927 to 1930. Simultaneous with the Dixieland style, made even whiter by the Wolverines, the more Negroid jazz appears with the cornetist Francis "Muggsy" Spanier. One of his groups, The Bucktown Five, recorded for Gennett immediately after the first Wolverine records. The excessively rare and obscure Autograph label of Chicago appears on another series of records made by a similar group as early as 1924. These records have faults but they are not of sweetness, rigid arrangement, or the *vo-de-o-do* spirit.

The early Spanier groups were properly instrumented. In the *Mobile Blues*, one of the Gennetts, there are cornet, clarinet, trombone, piano, and banjo; in the Autograph, *Everybody Loves My Baby*, tuba is added and guitar replaces banjo.

Mobile Blues, a popular song, is chiefly ensemble played with breaks; the arrangement consists mainly of stop-time type chords and is not the full ensemble arrangement of the Wolverines. If the tempo is overfast, there is a certain feeling of rhythmic beat. The Bucktown Five had a considerable degree of poise, relaxation, and Negroid feeling; their music is a degree of jazz while that of the Wolverines is another thing altogether.

In *Everybody Loves My Baby* the group is called the Stomp Six. Spanier emulates Oliver carefully although he occasionally falls into the *vo-de-o-do*. At this stage he had not quite attained his simple, driving, later style. The active trombone shows the study of Negro players like Dutrey and Roy Palmer. The clarinet work is a hybrid of black and white, deriving from Dodds and from Leon Rappolo of the Rhythm Kings.

The Stomp Six shows a good beat which scarcely equals, however, that of the Bucktown Five. Both groups show an emotional control in the midst of improvisation which was soon to disappear, almost permanently, from Chicago-style playing. The Spanier records, as well as such examples as the Arcadian Serenaders' records made about 1926 in St. Louis for Okeh, prove that northern white players were achieving a measure of success in mastering Negro jazz. The Chicagoans were shortly, however, to spoil the quality of their jazz by tampering with instrumentation.

As a whole the jazz situation in Chicago, from 1925 to 1930, was confused. Armstrong left Oliver's band and the King formed a larger group, the Savannah Syncopators, in which jazz was largely lost among the instrumental sections. Louis meanwhile, playing in larger bands, was recording with small New Orleans pick-up groups which, about 1927, began to expand to reach large-band proportions by 1929–30. The New Orleans Rhythm Kings disbanded early in this period and the last vestige of pure Dixieland influence disappeared from the Chicago scene. Meanwhile, the Chicago style proper received a fresh influx of players and, consolidating its errors as it consolidated its forces, went on, hobbled by instrumental anomalies, inadequate technique, and cursory knowledge, obstinately and faithfully continuing the hot, improvisational tradition. Recorded classic jazz, at the same time, went on with the Armstrong Hot Fives and the few precious sides of the New Orleans Wanderers and the New Orleans Bootblacks, to culminate in the unequalled masterpieces of Jelly Roll Morton's great period, recorded from 1926 to 1928 with his Red Hot Peppers. Thereafter, in the main stream, only Morton and the Chicagoans remained faithful to the principles of jazz, the latter within the narrow limits of their understanding and capability, the former in spirit through a downward curve of lessening opportunity. Oliver and Louis, with large bands, retained in large measure the personal virtues of their New Orleans cornet playing; but the cornet — or the trumpet — is not jazz.

About 1922 five boys from Chicago's Austin High School got up a band. Its instruments — piano, cornet, banjo or guitar, piano and two saxophones — are essentially those of the later Chicago-style band. A traditional account tells that a phonograph record started a new phase of Chicago style through these boys, Jim Lannigan, Jimmy and Dick McPartland, Bud Freeman, and Frank Teschmaker. A New Orleans Rhythm Kings' disc, playing in a soda fountain, gave these schoolboys the incentive for which they had been groping. Unlike New Orleans, it was possible in that day to be living in Chicago and yet never to have actually heard jazz. Through hard practice, and despite infrequent opportunities to play publicly, they clung together, going to hear the Rhythm Kings in person, encountering the Wolverines' records and then King Oliver's. Late in 1924, McPartland replaced Bix with the Wolverines and eventually the Austin boys made up the Wolverine line-up. By 1927 the style was fixed and recording was to come, but only two of the original group are on the Paramounts of this first session. Not until a year later did all of the group (except Dick McPartland) get on records in the first Okeh session devoted to Chicago style.

The first four Paramount sides bear the name of Charles Pierce and his Orchestra. Pierce was a Chicago jazz fan and amateur saxophonist who secured the recording date and perhaps financed it. These records give a clear picture of Chicago jazz of this period and show the players' musical background and the instrumental changes leading toward the arranged harmony of the larger swing band.

China Boy, Bull Frog Blues, and *Nobody's Sweetheart,* from this group of records, omit the trombone (except for a moment

in the last record) of the seven-piece classic New Orleans band
and add two saxophones.

At this stage, Chicago style has lost even its trace of the
rhythmic jazz pulse; the beat, wooden and heavy, is pushed;
relaxation is lost and the inner tensions of jazz are supplanted
by a hysterical mood. The rhythm section, in a way thenceforth
characteristic of Chicago style, breaks the beat up into successive patterns. The function of this section, as developed in New
Orleans practice, is forsaken; percussion pre-empts the polyrhythmic province of the horns; a basic element of order and
logic is lost.

Absence of the trombone is a crucial rhythmic loss and only
during its brief appearance in *Nobody's Sweetheart* does the
music move. It is carping to observe that this part, full of fast
notes here, makes the music jump, where real tail-gate gives an
easy elasticity to jazz. For even an inferior trombone breathes
new life into the music which the fashionable foghorn, the
saxophone, had murdered.

The riff appears in this music. Now a threadbare device of
swing, then as now, it was wrongly used to replace missing
rhythm and nonexistent melodic invention. The riff replaces the
true variation of jazz polyphony or solo, giving way only to the
spurious, fanciful constructions of the present-day solo. These
records show the exhibitionistic solo alternating with arranged,
harmonized sections. This type of solo often exhibits a technical
facility that obscures its total lack of real creativeness.

The band tone is ruined by the muddy welter of the saxophones. It is a remarkable thing that instruments so unrhyth-
mic, so tonally lethargic, were not removed from jazz long
ago. These Chicago ensembles are so befogged by saxophone
tone that even Spanier's clear lead is often lost.

The attempts at polyphony are ruined by Teschmaker's completely unbridled clarinet playing. As shown on records, this
player's style is wildly rhapsodic and at times completely un-
intelligible. It is, in addition, consistently out of tune. Teschmaker actually has been praised for this with considerable crit-

ical rubbish about dissonance and quarter-tones. Some have supposed his faulty intonation to show "unconscious longing for the quarter-tone." The blues scale, unused by Teschmaker, gives all the opportunity needed for microtonality. His out-of-tune playing led to a sour dissonance in the band, and this, too, has been praised. Dissonance is not just an end, theoretically or actually, in jazz. It occurs functionally and logically in New Orleans through the clashing of polyphonal voices approaching or crossing, and through the blues scale. In this context, dissonance has high aesthetic value as part of an order that, more than any other, combines individual freedom with a disciplined group system.

Teschmaker's playing is often continuous figuration virtually unphrased, anticipating the "modern" saxophone style. He has been praised for a musical creativeness which his extremely hybrid work fails to show, although it exhibits strong personal emotion. His solos are not sound variations on the theme, often not referring to it at all, and thus strongly prefigure the "modern" solo which is esteemed good to the degree in which the theme is lost. His ensemble parts are neither variations nor a heterophonic part which will function properly in the counterpoint. Teschmaker introduced chaotic, disintegrative elements.

Frank Teschmaker died in 1932 in an automobile accident. The reputation that survives him is great but, because it must eventually be based on his recorded work, certain contemporary opinions are important. The great New Orleans drummer, Baby Dodds, often heard Teschmaker when he would come to "sit in" with some of Johnny Dodds's small groups. At such times Teschmaker took Johnny's place, frequently using his clarinet. Baby says that he played very much in Johnny's style on these occasions.

The Chicago pianist, Art Hodes, says on the other hand, "Tesch did not play New Orleans style; he was more for a free-for-all." Hodes heard him, of course, chiefly with Chicago groups in which the saxophones make it a case of every man for himself. These instruments clearly pose a grave problem for the clarinet; the only solution which preserves effective polyphony is to drop the saxophones.

Teschmaker seems to have been unaware of how disastrous the instrumental experiments of his group really were, and frequently played the saxophone himself. His clarinet style is a continuous scramble with the saxophones such as never could happen in a good New Orleans band. He was the most influential and respected of his own group and beyond doubt could have helped to restore proper instrumentation. That such a step might have hurt the feelings of Bud Freeman and other saxophonists is, of course, one thing; the final judgment on Tesch's ability and the merit of his influence is another.

To argue that Chicago style tends to develop from jazz into a new and more modern music is futile; it has not done so. It has been played continuously by substantially the same group from 1923 until today, a period as long as that required by New Orleans jazz to develop through its archaic and into its classic period. Yet it shows no recognizable progress during this period, but rather a degeneration from the increasing emphasis on its own weak elements while its connections with classic jazz become feebler.

The further course of Chicago style can be quickly traced. Through the 1928 Okeh, *Sugar,* the 1930 Vocalion, *Barrel House Stomp,* and the 1933 Brunswick, *Home Cooking,* Chicago style continues to deteriorate although it includes, at times, Dixieland players like the white New Orleans trumpeter "Wingy" Mannone, Negro players like the drummer, Sid Catlett, or a white barrel-house pianist like Frank Melrose. Teschmaker's shoes are filled by "Peewee" Russell who carried his predecessor's rhapsodizing on into musical nonsense set forth in phlegmy, rasping, "spit" and "growl" tones. The trombone returns at times, but its harmonic-rhythmic function is by this time a lost art.

By 1936 with *Tillie's Downtown Now* (English Parlophone and Decca) the style momentarily takes on a sentimental cast set forth in riffs and solos. Nevertheless the hot elements in Chicago style prevailed and led, in 1939–1940, to an event which might have had — may yet have — a far-reaching effect on white playing. Spanier organized his Ragtime Band for the Sherman Hotel, moved it later to play at Nick's in New York. Before financial difficulties broke up this group, it made sixteen sides for Bluebird. Not a ragtime band at all, Muggsy's outfit was an attempt to return, via Dixieland, to Negro jazz itself. The instrumentation is almost, but not quite, that of classic New Orleans; one saxophone mars it. The first four sides, made with the fine barrel-house pianist George Zack, later replaced by the rather effete player Joe Bushkin, are perhaps the best.

Despite faulty tempos, lack of a real rhythmic pulse, and various minor shortcomings, these records nevertheless represent the most mature white attempt to play pure jazz since Dixieland came out of New Orleans. Nearly all musicians and collectors know them. Reformations in Chicago style were indicated here: fine trombone by Brunies, a degree of lucidity in Rod Cless's clarinet which Tesch never achieved; a solider, firmer beat; real polyphony with a better balance of the voicings.

The years 1939 and 1940 marked a stage in the awakening of a serious interest in jazz to which we shall refer later. Muggsy's Ragtime Band records, *Someday Sweetheart, That Da Da Strain, Eccentric, Big Butter and Egg Man,* and the others, are symptomatic of this awakening. So likewise are the records made by Art Hodes' Columbia Quintet, the group including Cless and Brunies that, modeled after the instrumentation of the Original Dixieland Jazz Band, played for a few ill-fated weeks at the 103rd Street Childs' Restaurant to audiences not only unprepared for the impact of jazz but strongly conditioned by two decades of sweet music.

It was shown that, given players like Spanier, Kaminsky, Brunies, Hodes and Zack, progress can be made. These men who make the music know, logically or instinctively, that Chicago style must go farther back than Dixieland — all the way to the Negro jazz of New Orleans. Given any financial opportunity these men may find their way back.

When Spanier's band fell apart, Chicago style reverted to its previous chaotic state, recorded on Commodore records and in various "Chicago Albums" of the large commercial companies which sought for, and got, the worst features of the school. In extreme cases, as in the 1940 Commodore, *Oh, Sister, Ain't That Hot?*, these combine into an atmosphere of wild impulse let loose without restraint.

Chicago gave to the world the wild, public *jam session*. Originally, even in New Orleans, musicians gathered after hours to play as they wished, literally to compare notes, to learn, and to compete. But these sessions were orderly affairs in which the band instrumentation was kept normal, and men alternated with one another in the process known as *sitting in*. The street-corner contests between band wagons in New Orleans were famous, too, but in these each band played to the limit of its abilities. The modern jam session is another thing: it becomes the devil take the hindmost, any combination of instruments banging and blasting away in the hysterical attempt to seize the spotlight, to receive the cheers of the noise- and rhythm-maddened audience. It is improvisation reduced to cacophony. The jam session is the chaotic, nihilistic element of Chicago style in its ultimate form.

Chicago style is a white imitation of Negro jazz, one that is sincere but not profound. Inept in the beginning as was to be expected, its development has been characterized by a progressive loss of control, by a consolidation, in the main, of its weakest features, by the gradual loss of any assumed Negroid elements. It began by committing errors in instrumentation, ensemble, tone, rhythm, and phrasing which have never been permanently rectified. At the same time it contained too few original elements to permit an independent development.

This is all true: it is easy to criticize the playing of the Chicagoans and yet impossible to praise too highly the ardor and the fidelity of their pursuit of jazz. With some of these men it has approached dedication and they have willingly disdained the "big money" to scuffle for a living while they played the music they believe in. They have remained, perpetually and delightfully, boys.

Jazz found, for a time, a friendly home in the Illinois city. It remained there in the wholehearted dedication of its young devotees. That Chicago style should take its defining characteristics from the truth and the error which are both in it, is of a piece with a fair historical judgment.

The Chicagoans beyond doubt feel that they have mastered jazz. Even if they have not, what Chicago style, and all of the jazz playing of younger white players throughout the country, has been for years, is the real "second line" of jazz; white-faced boys following the memory of a music. The dark-faced ones, weaned away by white commercialism and the easy success of their own ruined music, no longer wish to play jazz.

Consciously or unconsciously, white men led most of the Negroes into deserting the music that had come from their hearts. In Chicago, however, the white boys kept the jazz spirit alive until, today, some of the faithful Negroes are getting a fair chance to be heard again. None can deny that there is a poetic justice in this as there will be in the gentle verdict that history one day will pronounce on the Chicago "boys" and the bad, good music they have made.

11.

golden discs

RECORDED classic jazz, beginning with the Oliver band, is the veritable Golden Age of the music which had begun perhaps fifty years earlier with the humble Negro street bands in New Orleans.

Jazz — even archaic — requires a high degree of sympathy and an alert cooperativeness between its players. It demands willingness to limit the individual role, a state of high rapport. All of these qualities, important in the performance of *composed* western music, must, in jazz, be extended into a creative perceptiveness that operates on the rarefied plane of mutual artistic creation. This is by no means the comic medley of the *Quod libet* ("what you please") with which European players once amused themselves, an improvised entertainment of musicians by musicians, part burlesque, part serious. Jazz is, at its gayest, serious.

What happens in jazz? Three, five or seven men begin to create — not re-create — music together. One states a theme; others weave an intricate and arduous polyphony around it; one fills in harmony momentarily; another enters canon-like in imitation, proceeding instantaneously into rhythmic phrases. Meanwhile several play a rhythmic ostinato which is a counterpoint of percussions and, at the same time, an exposition of harmonic progression. The voice instruments evolve their polyphony in purest harmony or mutually move over into dissonance, their several variations on a single melodic theme developing into individual, separate, created melodies. From this, a heterophony results.

Each instrument phrases independently yet with regard for the phrasing of the others; the result is an over-all phrasing through which the polyphony expresses the original theme or melody. This occurs while variation proceeds endlessly.

Meanwhile the momentum of the music is maintained unflaggingly; the exuberant impulse continues without a letdown; the inner tensions mount while the fixed tempo is kept rigorously under control. Each player does the *momentarily* necessary, yet keeps within the character of his own instrument, be it cornet, trombone or clarinet. Throughout a performance, the questions of over-all tone quality, of polyphonal texture, of proper volume and just tempo, are never lost sight of.

Nor is this — as a classical musician would almost inevitably suppose — a free rhapsody, an improvised *fantaisie*. It is a coherent and logical sequence of variations on a theme: variations tonal, rhythmic and melodic; variations *within* variations. It is, at the same time, a counterpoint combining melodic polyphony and polyrhythm into an over-all contrapuntal fabric.

Proceeding freely, and yet systematically, this music phrases fresh, hot utterances: the cliché has no place in it. Individual inspiration feeds on that of the group, expands to unheard-of limits; a state of ecstasy seizes the band wherein collective miracles happen.

We are accustomed to hearing great musical masterpieces performed by symphony orchestra or string quartet, in which a consummated masterpiece is re-created. We tend, therefore, to take for granted the miracle of jazz creation — hot, vitally, and precisely *of the moment* — as we would the re-creation of a *scored* masterpiece. It is not re-creation; it is like the externalization of the inner workings of a composer's mind. Each player, and his instrument, impersonates, like an actor, the composer's idea of that instrument while — secluded and unhurried — he allowed his inspiration to flow out on the interlined and corrected manuscript. No correction can be made in a jazz performance. It is unalterably a composition in performance. Decisions are of the split-second; swift intuitive judg-

ment, sure taste, and hot inspiration are of the essence. Nor
has any serious composer succeeded as yet in writing out a
polyphony of this sort. It is necessary to grasp the import of
what happens *when the group becomes a single individual in
the throes of creation.*

Even the term virtuoso, so designative of individual importance and ability in western music, becomes inadequate here.
When a jazz player says fervently of another player, "He's a
solid, swinging gate," [1] he is trying to express this quality of
individual creative greatness which fits into that of the group
and lifts it to inspirational heights.

From such *virtuosities of the group* the systemic form of
jazz developed and the classic style took form. Not that each
band of the classic period was such a superlative group. Yet in
New Orleans, at least from 1900 to 1918, in relation to the
number of players there were a great many indeed. The bands
that played in Storyville in that period, with the rapidly changing personnel typical of jazz, must have included groups which
were equal to the great Creole Jazz Band of King Oliver. But
these bands were never recorded and the only scores which jazz
can leave behind are the golden discs of its great performances.

Beginning with the Oliver records of 1922, almost the whole
period of recorded classic jazz took place in Chicago in the
brief period of time ending with the year 1928.

The recording companies — which elsewhere have done so
much to feed the cancer of commercial music — performed a
service here to jazz and to all culture. A great existing band
like Oliver's was recorded — inadequately and insufficiently
perhaps — but recorded. The financial position of these companies permitted the assembling of the special recording groups
which musicians call "pick-up bands" that, in certain cases,
reached the summit of classic jazz. Such recording sessions are
comparable to the assembling of virtuosi for the performance
of a masterpiece of European music. In jazz, at least, they do
not always come off; the output may be uneven and may vary

[1] *Gate* means musician.

241

in quality from master record to master record. One must consider the magnitude of that which is attempted. Frequently, too, men are included who have never played together; the surroundings of the studio are at best unsympathetic. Especially lacking is the inspiration of dancing listeners who are an integral part of jazz music. Too, there may be added the positive nuisance of a recording director's ideas as to music or placement of instruments and the occasional, onerous need, because of some unimportant minor defect, to remake a number over and over until inspiration has fled.

Everything considered, the high level of classic jazz is a thing of wonder; the occasional lapses, during a performance, or in a bad record here or there, are no legitimate objects for criticism. The recorded masterpieces of classic jazz number at least two hundred record sides. The number could as well have been ten thousand!

The accuracy of a swing band is no valid criterion for comparison. Such a band, highly rehearsed and playing a mechanized arrangement, should — and often does — produce records free of technical flaws. Not inspiration, but mere accuracy is needed in such a case, if one excepts the improvised solos; even in these, everything is calculated to make the soloist's task an easy one. There is no polyphony, continuing softly, for him to consider; in a large band, he can even stay out of the ensembles for a chorus or two while he makes ready. But a swing band can play only swing. The vast majority of its players are totally unable to invoke the creative inspiration of jazz or to perform its mechanics.

Recorded classic jazz centers around a comparatively few great figures. From King Oliver through the records of Morton's great period, through the Hot Fives, the New Orleans Wanderers, the Chicago Footwarmers, and the others, we find the same key names appearing: Louis Armstrong, King Oliver or George Mitchell; Kid Ory or Honoré Dutrey; Omer Simeon or Johnny Dodds; Andrew Hilaire or Baby Dodds; Johnny St. Cyr, Jelly Roll Morton.

GOLDEN DISCS

By the early 1920's Jelly Roll Morton's piano style was matured and did not change, in any important respect, for the rest of his life. No other player in jazz history has combined so many rich elements into a piano style so orchestral, so varied, so relaxed yet formidable technically, so highly developed in its subtle use of every tonal and rhythmic device. Ragtime's dance-like precision, French melodiousness, barrel-house blues intonation, magnificent variational imagination and the head-long impetus of stomping, are combined into a whole essentially simple in its integration.

Except for an obscure early band record on Paramount, Morton's first records were piano solos made for Gennett in 1923 or 1924 while he was recording with the New Orleans Rhythm Kings. The five solo sides which resulted from this and a subsequent session, are among Morton's most characteristic original melodies. Four were recorded later in band versions. A comparison of piano and band versions reveals how solo anticipates instrumental rendering. Tempos are identical; thematic arrangement is similar; passages which, in the solo record, are heard as purely pianistic in character, are revealed later as equally orchestral.

Morton was a composer in the only sense that the term can exist in jazz. He created nearly one hundred and fifty beautiful melodies adapted to jazz playing, and his thinking was orchestral. More than any other individual, he knew the requirements of jazz: how to employ arrangement to heighten improvisation, the solo to heighten ensemble, dissonance to heighten harmony. There is not a record of Morton's great period which is not as truly modern as the day it was played.[2]

Jelly Roll Morton's greatest recorded period begins with his first Victor session in 1926 and extends into 1928. He never was able to assemble or maintain a permanent band of the high

[2] Morton's recorded work on commercial records totals about 160 sides, with more being discovered. His recording for the Library of Congress amounts to about 116 large sides and, in addition, he made an unknown quantity of player-piano rolls. Three, the first to be rediscovered, turned up recently in Texas.

caliber of his recording *Red Hot Peppers*. Ten of the first eleven sides are his finest. In these performances Morton's real greatness appears, far beyond his pianistic accomplishments, in his grasp of the whole meaning of jazz that he shows when working with and expressing himself through the finest players. An ensuing session, which included Johnny and Baby Dodds, produced six band sides only slightly less fine, and two superlative trio records.[3]

The New York recording which followed shows a falling off in quality that continued progressively, except for a few notable exceptions, into the early 1930's when Morton's connections with the Victor Company ceased. Morton can scarcely be blamed for this deterioration for he did not personally yield to commercialization. At this time Victor, acquired by RCA, began to develop a "sweet" policy which plugged the banal sentimental tunes from motion pictures. The forces of money-music were too strong for Morton to combat singlehanded.

Morton's ten greatest records are of a quality that might have continued to unknown heights. All except the second, third, and eighth titles are Morton tunes.

Recorded September 15, 1926.

CITATION 53. *Black Bottom Stomp*
CITATION 54. *The Chant*
CITATION 55. *Smoke House Blues*
CITATION 56. *Steamboat Stomp*

Recorded September 21, 1926.

CITATION 57. *Sidewalk Blues*
         Dead Man Blues

Recorded December 16, 1926.

         Original Jelly Roll Blues
CITATION 58. *Doctor Jazz Stomp*
         Grandpa's Spells
         Cannon Ball Blues

---

[3] *Mr. Jelly Lord* and *Wolverine Blues*, Jelly Roll Morton, piano; Johnny Dodds, clarinet; Baby Dodds, drums. Original issue, Victor 21064; reissue Bluebird, B–10258.

Personnel for all above records: George Mitchell, cornet; Omer Simeon, clarinet; Kid Ory, trombone; Morton, piano; Johnny St. Cyr, guitar and banjo; John Lindsay, bass; Andrew Hilaire, drums. In *Sidewalk Blues,* Barney Bigard and Darnell Howard, clarinets and unknown cornet (?) added.

The Victor contract was Jelly Roll's first chance to reach a large audience; he faced this opportunity as a mature man of thirty-seven. He could not have been unaware of what the opportunity meant. If, as it turned out, it was not the open doorway to recognition during his lifetime, it will eventually be that to his permanent fame.

Six of these discs might well be collected and played together under the title of *Pictures of New Orleans.* Such a description or implied program would not be as literary as it may seem for the jazz of the New Orleans Negro is remarkably evocative in a partly descriptive, partly allusive way, of its scene and its time. Nor is such a program beyond the subtle imagination of a man like Morton who, outside of music, used language in as free, as personal, and as creative a way as many a modern writer has ever done. On these records Jelly seems to say, "Here's what jazz is, here's where it came from, what it's made of, and here *I* am!"

The first strains of *Black Bottom Stomp* are blackface minstrel music coming from a tent show of Reconstruction days. From these lightly skipping, haunting, melodious measures, the hoarse, laughing, sliding trombone seems to call

1870 !

Dreamlike, the music merges into a country dance on the outskirts of New Orleans. The clarinet, imitating the rural fiddler, seems to sing on a twanging string

1880 !

A short high cornet fanfare intrudes, is repeated, as a street band approaches. Suddenly, the full, golden blare of the marching brass bursts on the ear

1890 !

Everyone rushes in great excitement out of the dance hall to follow the band. Liltingly, the music lures them along down Canal Street over Galvez, past Basin Street, past Rampart Street and Royal! The followers linger, peeping through antique doorways into dim interiors.

1905 !

Through one such doorway, framed with lacy ironwork, a crowded saloon is revealed. In the corner a trio is playing through the noise: clarinet, string-bass and piano, ragging a gay popular song of the day. Next door is a honky-tonk. Through the smoky air the hanging gas lamps paint on the wall the moving shadows of girls who dance. In the corner, at a battered upright piano, sits Mr. Jelly Lord Morton himself, "professor" of the Tenderloin, playing his ragtime as delicate yet strong, as precise, as dainty, as French, as porcelain!

1910 !

Onward the parade moves, past St. Charles Street, past Chartres, across Decatur to stop by the river front. The bystanders begin to dance the *Black Bottom* on the heavy, resounding planks of the quay with the band imitating the gay, grotesque rhythms. Suddenly, from a show boat moored alongside, come the plinking-planking chords of a raggy banjo with a string-bass plucked and slapped.

1914 !

Rested, the band moves on, back through the town, playing at the same bright tempo, with the same fresh, untarnished gaiety, right into Storyville.

1917 !

War! And the beautiful, evil city closes. Undaunted, the band marches on not missing a beat; turns northward leaving behind at the city limits the last few straggling followers.

1922 ! Chicago!

With an even greater sureness, an even greater exuberance, the music swells out, dances on.

1926 !

The first triumphant pealing trumpet fanfares of *The Chant* announce, "Now *this* is jazz!"

Incredible *tour de force* — *The Chant* — incredible master-piece, too! Here is all that New Orleans polyphony means, much of what it can mean, pointed to swiftly by fingers that flash on clarinet and piano keys, on cornet valves! The sheer creative outpouring of communal song, like the chant rising from African plains, from Congo Square or from the sweltering, sunny cotton fields! Communal song of the humble blacks, in its sweet, hoarse tones all of their irrepressible gaiety, flashing humor, half-buried sorrow!

The clarinet, mournful and low, soars to sharp, high cries, "Here is how we sing the blues."

And the chorus answers, "Here is how we drive them down."

As clearly as if Morton introduced them by name, each instrument shows what it can — and should — do in jazz: the bold, clear driving trumpet, the sharply sweet and fervent clarinet, the blues-shouting trombone, the plangent banjo, the swift-striding stringed bass, the light, elastic, but firm piano, the rolling parade drums. Late in the record, Jelly Roll's piano takes its first solo spot. Thus Morton takes his bow as composer and organizing genius while the order of his appearance indicates, as clearly as his band playing always does, that he recognizes the somewhat minor position of the piano itself in the band.

Beautifully harmonized, *Smoke House* shows the full extent to which harmony can be allowed to enter jazz. The third of his great records seem to indicate that Morton is showing where the blues belong, at the very core of jazz.

"These are the slow-drag blues, these are the low-down blues, these are the blues like we no doubt play them in New Orleans."

It is all blues, the blues of the alley den and the barrel-house — from the superb ensemble opening that, like slow-motion movies, shows the polyphony transparent and extended, through Ory's fine trombone solo, to Jelly's sober restrained and thoughtful piano solo, during which he himself calls out, "Oh, Mister Jelly!"

The panorama of *Steamboat Stomp* opens with the Sunday

hubbub on the pier just before the excursion boat departs. A real steamboat whistle blows and a voice calls, " 'Board!" Over the clamor of voices we hear:

"Man, come on, let's catch that boat, we're gonna be late!"
"Aw, we got plenty of time to catch that boat. I gotta get another ham."
"Gettin' back at me — don't even know how to carry a mule without lettin' its legs hang down — you little tadpole!"

Soft banjo chords and the boat's band plays its "come-on" for the last straggling, paying customers. Shortly the deep-toned whistle can be heard through the polyphony and the steamer is off.

The trombone and clarinet in close harmony make a sly, oblique reference to sentimental popular music. A wonderful, free ensemble follows and, after a modulation, the trombone takes over again, shows that it "was only fooling around with sweet tunes — that it knows how to play hot." And hot it is — hot music, a hot day on the river, a hot time for all!

As swiftly as the river banks that glide by, the musical panorama unfolds: a magnificent polyphonic passage never excelled in recorded jazz music, orchestrated whistle blasts symbolic of impending landing, two sustained chords which dam up the music's momentum as the back-paddling wheels slow up the boat, a racing, fugitive passage of piano ragtime — the excitement of band and passengers mounts — the music seems about to fly apart from its own momentum — the whistle chords again and the music speeds on with reckless gaiety to a sudden dramatic end. The boat docks with the closing chord and the low-toned, mournful whistle dies slowly away on the summer air.

After a curtain raiser (and hair-raiser) of automobile horns, whistles and shouted imprecations, *Sidewalk Blues* gets under way with successive breaks by piano, trombone, cornet, and clarinet. Jelly says almost as if in words, "This is Mr. Jelly Lord, composing-arranging genius of jazz, and these are the three voices that sing the polyphony of my music."

There is a section of fine jazz, a transition, and we are immediately in the midst of a sweetly harmonized passage that sounds as if Morton had borrowed from the *Liebestraum* of Liszt. The two extra clarinets, which were idle in the preceding jazz section, now come into play as in the sweet or swing of the big band, filling in the lush, heavy harmony. As if in protest, the automobile horns and the whistling intervene for a few shocking seconds. But the sweet music resumes, apparently victorious.

Then, as if Jelly had said, "That's the way you play it in Chicago and New York — here's the way we play it in New Orleans," the band suddenly plunges into the beautiful, moving, flexible dissonance of jazz. The contrast is breathtaking and utterly convincing.

As if to insure an understanding of his lesson, Morton repeats this episode, and once again the dulcet chords give way to the vital outpouring. Morton, who employed many chordal devices to dam momentarily the flood-water impetus of rhythm, never used one more effective than this, where the harmonic and rhythmic bulwarks symbolize the very fetters of European style and form when they are applied to jazz. Six bars of coda culminate in street noise and Jelly shouts into the microphone, as if to clear the road for the players of real jazz, "Let 'em roll!"

Doctor Jazz is quoted more often than any other single record to demonstrate the New Orleans style. Nearly every device of subtlety and variety which the classic style came to include, is shown here. Many of these were developed by Morton to their greatest degree, some he originated. The break, for example, is a very important device in jazz and certainly no one has ever employed it with more consistency, variety, and originality than he. The sudden solo episode, which is the break, gives the last fine fillip to the Red Hot Peppers' music, like the final pinch of that condiment added by a Creole cook.

No other record can excel this in sheer, infectious gaiety, compelling rhythm, and sustained interest. It is an exhaustive demonstration of the various instrumental combinations obtainable in a seven-piece band, and it carries the break to a degree of development never attained before. Even the short introduction includes two by clarinet. Clarinet breaks, brass fanfare breaks, then a chain of six virtuoso breaks: two bars of high clarinet, two of banjo and piano, two clarinet, two banjo, two of high, muted cornet, and two of vigorous trombone. These twelve measures extend the solo stop-time over into one for successive instruments. Such a feat, that only great players can accomplish, points to the unexplored possibilities of uncommercial jazz in gifted hands.

Contrapuntally, *Doctor Jazz* is remarkably varied in its combinations of instruments that at times employ the rhythm instruments in the voicings. Another remarkable feature is the sustained eight-bar pedal point by clarinet, a single high register note whose tension is released in eight bars of rapid, very rhythmic low-register passage work. Another eight-bar pedal point ensues which moves down a three-note step, again the rapid runs for four measures, and then another high sustained note that leads directly into Jelly's vocal chorus, authentic jazz vocalism, full of contrasting clear and dirty timbres, rhythmic, infectiously lively.

> *Hello Central, give me Doctor Jazz.*
> *He's got what I need, I'll say he has.*
> *When the world goes wrong*
> *And I got those blues:*
> *He's the one that makes me*
> *Get out both my dancing shoes!*
>
> *The more I get, the more I want, it seems;*
> *I page old Doctor Jazz in all my dreams.*
> *When I'm trouble-bound and mixed*
> *He's the guy that gets me fixed —*
> *Hello, Central, give me Doctor Jazz!* ⁴

Jelly sings over rhythm and clarinet and the full band, as in the blues, provides forte answers. As this chorus ends, Morton clips out two crackling vocal breaks.

Doctor Jazz reveals most of the qualities of classic jazz in

⁴ *Doctor Jazz,* by Joseph "King" Oliver, lyrics from the sheet music. Copyright 1927 by Melrose Music Corp., N. Y.

their fullest development. It is difficult to exhaust its variety: wide contrast of timbres; African polyrhythms; held and released momentum; breaks, chain-breaks and solos; "head" arrangement,[5] free polyphony, and Afro-American variation shown by the constant mutations of rhythmic pattern, tone, instrumentation, and melody.

There is a chronological character in this group of records. Some refer to the past, others to the present, still others point to the future, while *Black Bottom Stomp, Sidewalk Blues,* and *Doctor Jazz,* combine within one frame the forms of yesterday, today, and tomorrow. *Sidewalk Blues* may be the most prophetic, for in this record Jelly shows his concept of the large band, one that can combine arranged episodes of sweet swing with episodes of properly instrumented New Orleans hot polyphony. Such a record, taken as a whole, is neither all jazz nor all swing. There are interesting possibilities in the combination of large-band arrangement and small-group improvisation of a real New Orleans character, and it is strange that the swing leaders have not thought of it. Such a combination, not jazz in any pure sense, would certainly be less moribund than present-day swing music.

It is tempting but perilous to predict the jazz of the future. Still, general lines of possible development are clear. Variations of instrumentation are among them but these will have to function polyphonically. Another is to be found in episodes of contrasted mood and tempo. More modulation into contrasted keys might be used but it is clear that this cannot be allowed to bring in an excessive harmonic development. Characteristic Africanisms, like the chain-fourths and fifths would be powerfully fecundating in jazz. So, too, might be an antiphony-polyphony of the present horn section over a rhythm section consisting of a typical African drum battery. In any event it is evident that jazz, in the hands of great, unhampered players, is rich in undeveloped potentialities.

[5] A memorized, not written arrangement, that leaves ample room for improvisation.

St. Cyr, Ory, and Simeon have described the typical recording date of Morton's great period. Assembling his musicians, some of whom had never worked with him, he played over for them one of his intricate, multi-themed compositions, which many or all of them had never heard before. Twenty minutes of playing and direction, in which solos and breaks were assigned and their placing and character explained, the order of episodes determined, and transitional harmonies outlined, was generally sufficient time. One or two run-throughs, a check of playing length to fit the record space, and recording would begin. Two or three masters might be made — as often as not the first would be the best. There were no scores here: with Morton no music stands were necessary. Such was his grasp of form and so communicative was his inspiration, that these men, playing freely in the most flexible of frameworks, could realize almost to a complete degree Morton's idea of jazz, their own ideas, and untold possibilities of the music itself. By such unorthodox means, Morton and the Red Hot Peppers engraved on wax, in three short days, ten of the authentic masterpieces of classic jazz.

In New Orleans, from the unknown players of the archaic street band, through Bolden and Bunk Johnson, Lorenzo Tio, Sr., Keppard, King Oliver, and all the great instrumentalists, the history of jazz is written in biography. As it moved to Chicago and within range of the recording horn and microphone, its story is still that of men of genius who worked together. But there are types of individual genius. One type seems to encompass a particular stage of art development rather than to be its opportunistic product.

Jelly Roll Morton was such a genius. Although thwarted short of his completed life work he — working individually and through others — defined a period of jazz as he found it; marked out for others the path which he was not to be permitted to follow. The organizing type of genius like Jelly Roll almost unfailingly benefits an art whenever he is allowed to function at all. The breadth and coercive power of the creative vision of such men seem almost invariably to preserve their integrity.

Another type of genius is the great instrumentalist, the creative improviser, who outlines the style and the role of his own instrument. The story of what happened to classic jazz from 1928 on, centers around two such figures, Johnny Dodds and Louis Armstrong. It is almost universally agreed that New Orleans clarinet is epitomized in the former, New Orleans trumpet in the latter.

Dodds's style, like Morton's, matured early and thenceforth ripened. Playing with Oliver in 1922, his work is as definitive — if not quite as varied and assured — as it was ever to be. Johnny's playing always centered around, developed out of, the blues. His remarkable virtuosity is no more than a necessary factor in his style. His tonal power in unmatched; his variety of timbre and the roundness of his tone, unrivalled. But it is when we leave technical phases and proceed to his feeling and his ideation, that his genius begins to be made clear. Dodds's nature was introspective but brilliant, moody with true temperament. He kept in balance the contradictory forces of melancholy and bright exuberance, fervent lyricism and deep thoughtfulness. The elements of his personality shaped the technical and emotional outlines of his style and sum up so many qualities within the race which created jazz, that his style is the full flowering of the clarinet and its role in the music.

Dodds plays on some two hundred record sides; these give a clear picture of unflagging inspiration. Few men have recorded with so wide a variety of hot groups. From blues accompaniments to the great classic bands of Oliver and Morton, the series includes solo records, many combinations built around ragtime piano and the percussive washboard, trios with piano and drums or guitar, the small hot five-piece bands, and the southern "jug" band typical of Tennessee and Mississippi. The power and personal quality of Dodds's tone stamps the timbre of every record with his trademark. While listening to his varied but typical phrases one immediately gets the *Dodds sound,* a pervasive fluid quality that colors the sound as sunset tints the clear air.

Some of Johnny Dodds's greatest work is on records of his own groups, the Chicago Footwarmers, his Washboard Band, the New Orleans Wanderers, and the New Orleans Bootblacks. In passing, a number of beautiful discs should be mentioned. The hot "jug" band is not a New Orleans jazz band by any means, but records like the Dixieland Jug Blowers' *Memphis Shake* (Victor 20415) and *House Rent Rag* (Victor 20420) show — when a fine New Orleans clarinet is added — many possibilities for extensions of instrumentation, in the archaic ragtime quality and in the peculiarly beautiful woodwind sound of jug-blowing. The washboard records also suggest instrumentations, with this percussive instrument, tapped and strummed with thimbled fingers, evoking exciting polyrhythms. Trio records for clarinet, piano and washboard like *Little Bits* (Vocalion 1035) and ones for the trio expanded by the cornet as in *I'm Goin' Huntin'* (Vocalion 1099) deserve an important place in the recorded hot repertory.

Four of Dodds's masterpieces can be joined into a longer piece of serious blues variations. Such a piece would have a profound inner unity against which the sonata form, with its separate movements, frequently operates in European music. Unity achieved by a Beethoven working in the sonata form represents, indeed, a triumph of the creative spirit, but one achieved over self-imposed problems, for the essential nature of music is not that of formal unity between separate forms but that of a flowing stream, a continuum that is homogeneous and persistent as time.

Jazz has this *moving unity;* in the blues it has a single theme with a thousand meanings. The four records from which we will fashion our longer piece are from a group of discs made in 1928 by Johnny Dodds's Washboard Band which had the following personnel: Natty Dominique, trumpet; Johnny Dodds, clarinet; Kid Ory, trombone; John Lindsay, string-bass; Baby Dodds, washboard; James Blythe, piano.[6]

CITATION 59.   *Bull Fiddle Blues.*
CITATION 60.   *Bucktown Stomp.*
CITATION 61.   *Weary City Stomp.*
CITATION 62.   *Blue Washboard Stomp.*

In the order in which they stand, these records add to a longer form with the appropriate variations in tempo, brisk, slow, moderate, and fast. There are no elaborate modulations; in fact there are no changes in key. Yet, besides the wide variety of rhythm and of solo and contrapuntal texture, there is that of the many-faceted meanings of the blues, their adaptability to different and complex variations, and, throughout, derived from the communicative nature of the blues, a sequence of moods, light and dark, a stream of unfolding meaning. There is precedent for the longer piece in actual, unrecorded jazz performances that often extend to a quarter of an hour or more of uninterrupted variation growing constantly in interest and intensity. Not the least notable of the features attending such a performance, as in the four discs we have cited, is the thorough and musicianly exploitation of the tonal and expressive possibilities of the various instruments, solo and in combination.

The unity of this piece derives not only from the blues but, as in all jazz, from the basic principle of a continuous variation, always melodic and recognizably derived from the theme. Jelly Roll Morton said, "You've got to keep the melody going somewhere all the time." Negro folk tunes and the blues have never frozen into a set form; their perennial vitality springs from this. The following statement is attributed to the English composer, Constant Lambert, "All that you can do with a folk song, when you've played it once, is to play it again louder." After listening to the thirty-seven blues variations in the four records just cited, it is difficult to agree.

Among the greatest of all the classical jazz records are the four discs made for Columbia in 1927 by a six-piece band called,

6 This personnel, hitherto in part unknown, is furnished by Baby Dodds.

on two of them, the New Orleans Wanderers and, on the other two, the New Orleans Bootblacks. This band was an offshoot of Louis Armstrong's Hot Five which, because of Louis' contract with Okeh, substituted George Mitchell in his place, adding at the same time another instrumentalist. The Wanderers and Bootblacks present four of the immortals of jazz. Besides Johnny Dodds, there were Kid Ory, who combines in his playing all the various great possibilities of the New Orleans tailgate trombone; George Mitchell, the "Little Mitch" of Louisville, Kentucky, who proves here, as he did with Morton, that New Orleans jazz belongs to any American Negro who is willing to play it; St. Cyr, the handsome, dark Orleanian who stands head and shoulders above all other recorded banjoists; and, in addition, frail, light-colored, .oriental-looking Lillian Hardin, who came from a Tennessee classical conservatory to play a sound jazz piano.

These records, like the Hot Five discs, are notable examples of rhythmic horn playing, using horns, of course, in the New Orleans sense of any "blown" instrument. Not even including drums, the rhythm section would be inadequate except that Mitchell (like Armstrong), Ory, and Dodds were formidable rhythmic players, and Lil Hardin and St. Cyr could lay down a beat solid enough for an even larger band. With these players, such a small combination as this, rather than losing strong and complex rhythm, gains mobility.

The added instrumentalist, perhaps "Stomp" Evans, plays saxophone and clarinet. It must be said that his saxophone style, as he plays with Dodds, is the most lucid and intelligible of which that instrument is capable. Tonally, it does not add any beauty to the ensemble tone; nor, on the other hand, does his melodic line conflict too greatly with that of Dodds. When he plays clarinet, the four-voiced polyphony becomes one of great and exciting beauty, complex but crystal clear. On at least one side, according to Ory, Dodds himself plays saxophone.

At least five sides of this group are masterpieces. *Perdido Street Blues* and *Too Tight* both present Johnny Dodds at the peak of his genius where he has never been approached. *Gatemouth* and *Papa Dip* are in march style of the most brilliant élan, with parade or tail-gate trombone by Ory of a sheer inventiveness which even he never matched elsewhere on records. *I Can't Say* is a simple popular tune transformed by jazz into a thing of classically phrased line. Mitchell's cornet playing throughout is of the utmost clarity and compressed, driving simplicity.

Speak of jazz to a group and three out of four people will think of Louis Armstrong. The trumpet, leader of the polyphony, and its player come quite naturally — if not quite justly — to stand for the music. The public, which likes and no doubt needs to personify whole movements and eras of human activity in single figures, naturally finds the triumvirate of New Orleans horns too complex and depersonalized a figure. Yet on this triumvirate — if not, indeed on the whole band — should such a symbolic designation fall. So, from the earliest days of record, New Orleans crowned its trumpeters as Kings; in the fine cooperative days of true jazz such bestowals carried the weight of a dignity and an honor in which the entire band shared.

Louis Armstrong inherited naturally the honors relinquished in turn by Bolden and Keppard, took the scepter from King Oliver's failing hand. Bunk Johnson was in an eclipse that bade fair to be permanent.

Had Armstrong understood his responsibility as clearly as he perceived his own growing artistic power — had his individual genius been deeply integrated with that of the music, and thus ultimately with the destiny, of his race — designated leadership would have been just. Achievement is not without responsibility; progress is not always what it seems; the revolutionary must himself be judged by the fruits of his revolution.

Around Louis clustered growing public cognizance of hot music and those commercial forces, equally strong and more persistent, which utilize the musical communications system of the phonograph record, the then new radio and talking motion picture, and the printed sheets of the Tin Pan Alley tunesmiths. And behind this new symbolic figure was aligned the overwhelming and immemorial need of his own race to find a Moses to lead it out of Egypt.

Perhaps no other artist has been as fully recorded as Armstrong. By 1945 he had played on at least 520 known sides. Beginning in 1922 with the Oliver records on Paramount and Gennett, through 1924 on the King's later labels, followed by the Clarence Williams' Blue Five records of 1924–1925, and into his own Hot Five and Hot Seven records from 1924 to 1929, Louis recorded copiously. Playing with small combinations, his work on these records represents New Orleans jazz which, despite marked unevenness, reaches some very high points of quality. Nevertheless, during the latter part of this period, after he left the great Oliver band, Armstrong was publicly associated with larger bands, several of Erskine Tate's groups and in particular, from 1924 to 1925, with Fletcher Henderson's Orchestra. It is important, too, to note that his own playing changed during this period as may clearly be heard in the records of his own small recording groups.

The change is subtle, hard to define, because his personal style, if analyzed apart from the band, seems to represent progress. The expression becomes more virtuoso, complex, and fantastic, and yet in this period Louis could play whole choruses on a single high note or on one repeated weird glissando. But while he was extending the technical resources of his instrument as all great jazz players have done, Louis, playing with larger bands which tended to the solo, was stressing the solo more and more within his small groups.

One criticizes the results of Louis Armstrong's fine work with the greatest reluctance, indeed sadly, because, more than a man of true personal charm, he is one of personal artistic integrity. His grasp of what jazz means, the sort of group effort which it must represent, unfortunately failed to match his genius. For, ironically, any of Louis' solos, executed as they are in front of a large swing band as before a tinseled backdrop, are a part of pure and authentic jazz that could be translated bodily, note for note, into the context of the small band polyphony. Louis was — and remains — an ineffably hot individual creator. But the trumpet is not jazz; it is only the leading voice of the polyphony and an occasional soloist; the lead, by its nature, can be transferred to harmonized large band swing, where the inner voices of clarinet and trombone cannot.

It is therefore no wonder that the public, dazzled by Armstrong's true brilliance, was fooled; that to this day swing is considered to be that which it is not — a development from, and of, jazz. Swing borrows two qualities from jazz: hot accent and characteristic timbres. The average listener does not go deeply into musical structure; even in listening to pure jazz he is likely to concentrate only on the trumpet as, in watching football, he sees only the man carrying the ball. Even today, with swing deep in the narrowing walls of its blind alley, the public thinks that it is jazz which has reached its senility!

The crucial point is that Louis Armstrong himself was fooled; however misled, his sincerity cannot fairly be brought into question. Armstrong did not invent the large band. As a tendency, it has existed parallel with jazz almost from its beginnings. His seemingly revolutionary act was that he appeared to effect an amalgamation of jazz with the large-band form; this hybrid is what is known as swing. It was not obvious to him — or, for that matter, to scarcely anyone else — that everything vital in jazz was left out in a sterile crossing. Jazz itself is revolutionary: Armstrong's act was that of counter-revolution.

Ellington's later act, the crossing of swing with the music of various European composers, is a further countermove that seems abortive enough now but may, ironically enough, complete the process of de-Africanization so that the large band will lose its last vestiges of hotness and African accent to become a variety of music thoroughly and solely in the western tradition. Such an end development, regardless of its musical value, might help to clear away the clouds of confusion which now obscure the subject. Nevertheless, revolutionary or counter-revolutionary, Armstrong, like Ellington, must be judged in the end by the value of what he has done.

Ferdinand Morton was the rare individual who combined two functions in his work. He completed an entire period of jazz and marked the pathway the future should take. He was personally identified with the whole development of the music to a degree that seldom happens in any art. When Jelly Roll said that all the jazz styles are "Jelly Roll Style," his words are, if obviously not actually true, at least symbolically so. It is a wholly remarkable indication of the scope, insight, and greatness of the man, that Morton, a powerful individualist if there ever was one, could be so thoroughly imbued with the principle of group creation as to direct a great part of his activity into it. We find his greatest qualities as an *individual creative artist* not in his solos but in his work with, and as a part of, the group.

Louis Armstrong, an equally powerful creator, falls, on the contrary, into the category of the individualist. Although in his early phases he joined with the collective group playing improvised polyphony, obviously feeling in those years the stimulus and incomparable satisfaction from so doing,[7] lent to that group new and powerful characteristics and might, in common with Morton, have contributed vastly to its continued logical development, he chose, nevertheless, and chose unfortunately, another course. At a time when the whole development of hot music was at a crisis, he directed his vast creative power toward the growing big-band swing that is opposed to jazz.

Events robbed Morton in his later years of the opportunity to serve the music of his race; Armstrong had the opportunity and threw it away. So, although all of Louis Armstrong's work is impressive, even in relation to all music, that from his mature period is in a field hostile to jazz and, it may be believed, to his own truest expression.

Had Armstrong chosen to develop polyphonic jazz, together with the utmost employment of the solo within, and in just re-

[7] Does not, indeed, the character and quality of his later work derive from these experiences?

lation to the polyphonic framework, this would have necessitated working with the greatest of the other instrumentalists. It would have meant a continued and continuous association with Ory, St. Cyr, and the Dodds brothers; it would have meant working ultimately — as he never did — with Jelly Roll Morton. But this is to speak of what might have been. Armstrong's path led him elsewhere and herein lies not merely a serious blow to art but the tragedy of Louis Armstrong, the artist.

Armstrong's work with small polyphonic groups in the middle 1920's may stand as his greatest achievement. Far short of results he might have achieved in his maturity, that alone of all his work has the perennial freshness, vitality, and value which are to be found in creative work within its tradition. And if jazz is destined, as it seems, to resume its development, it must set about heroically to rid hot music of all its present spurious forms and practices, and begin development again substantially at the point which Armstrong and Morton, separately, had reached in those four golden years, 1924 to 1928.

The Hot Five records of Louis Armstrong will be considered in the next chapter as a development leading into swing. There is a recent change in Louis' personal style which may be significant. This is a return to the simple, driving expressiveness of his jazz style of the middle 1920's. Indicative perhaps of his own dissatisfaction with swing, if it should lead him back to the small polyphonic group, it would be a significant and decisive move by a key figure in the present strong trend back to New Orleans jazz.

12.

manhattan swing

WHERE jazz is the symbol of a struggle and a hope, swing music is that of defeat. The Negro's success in America is not to be measured by the chimera of popular acclaim nor to be counted in the dollars that will not buy equality. Swing music, as a form and as a whole tendency, is an abandonment of the truly Negroid elements of jazz in favor of white elements more intelligible and acceptable to white society. Thus swing, outwardly the symbol of triumph, is inwardly that of the failure of Emancipation.

Why should Emancipation have failed? Because it needed to begin as a spiritual freeing of the whites themselves. Only those who are inwardly, spiritually, free can truly confer freedom. How tragically the Negro trades the liberation of his own music for only another sort of slavery! How tragically unaware he remains of the power of his own art, through the pure, magnetic compulsion of which the white man was being forced to imitate his darker brother!

It was in New York that jazz met its apparent defeat; swing scored its apparent victory. The stage was set early with a false emphasis on white jazz, for here, as in Chicago, Dixieland led the way when the Original Dixieland Jazz Band came in 1916. Soon a school of northern and eastern white players — who had failed to notice the earlier appearance in the metropolis of the Original Creole Band and its fine Negro jazz — began a literal imitation of the Dixieland that was, of course, only a third-rate version of real jazz.

New York Dixieland, as the playing of this imitative school

should be called, centers around a number of groups, each of which recorded under several names with considerable interchange of personnel. An early group, obscurely and inadequately recorded, was the Original Hot Five, first formed in 1923. Of no great importance, it consisted of Bostonians who gravitated around the clarinetist Jim Moynahan and the valve trombonist Brad Gowans. A better known, but not very hot, early small group, The Georgians, began to record in 1923. Centered around the bass saxophonist, Adrian Rollini, who later played vibraphone as well, was the group called variously, California Ramblers, Goofus Five, Little Ramblers, and Birmingham Babies. Perhaps best, from a hot jazz standpoint, of all these early-day New York white groups, was the Original Memphis Five group, also known as The Cotton Pickers, Ladd's Black Aces, and by other recording names. The recording of New York Dixieland begins in 1922 with this group. On many labels and with numerous changes in personnel it made records up to 1932. "The usual personnel features: Phil Napoleon, trumpet; Miff Mole and Vincent Grande, trombones; Jimmy Lytell, alias Sarrapède, clarinet; Frank Signorelli, piano; Jack Roth, drums." [1]

The typical early Memphis Five Record, like *Snake's Hips*, has a few hot moments. About half is arranged, the rest is crude ensemble polyphony with barely adequate trumpet and trombone and inept clarinet. If the Negroes' ebullient relaxation is not achieved, the Chicago mistake of seeking it in chaotic wildness is avoided. Further comparison of the Memphis Five and the Chicago school shows that the occasional hot moments of the former are overbalanced by the more consistent hotness of the latter. Likewise, the Memphis Five played a great number of "pop" tunes in a sweet and sentimental manner; the Chicagoans play more hot tunes and play the sentimental ones more hotly. The Memphis Five style quickly deteriorated into sweet European arrangement and its brief hot revival in the early 1930's came through a temporary amalgamation with Chicago-style

[1] Delaunay, Charles: *Hot Discography*. New York: 1940.

players. This deterioration came about chiefly through lack of basic sympathy with jazz; Chicago, on the other hand, lost control from a lack of understanding of how jazz functions.

Broadly speaking, New York Dixieland represents the intellectual, Chicago the emotional approach. If artists are to work successfully in an art form not their own, their approach must combine clear understanding with deep sympathy. The New Orleans Dixielanders had a fair measure of this combination but their mastery was not sufficiently advanced nor their group numerous enough for their music to stand early transplanting to the north and east. Thus it died early and the New York and Chicago styles are little more than sprouts from the roots below the dead trunk.

New York was an unlikely place for such music as that of the early Memphis Five to endure. It lasted as a quasi-hot music until 1926. Opinions of this white band are mainly at one extreme or the other. The ultrapurists, who seek to limit all jazz not only to the Negroes but to those of New Orleans in a certain period, dismiss the Memphis Five records as "junk-pile stuff." The opposite school, that of white supremacy in jazz or of confused or ill-grounded European criticism, speaks of the great character, of the "hot and savage" style of this band. The band itself falls in the middle for, where hybrid styles exist, confused taste exists. A music like that of the Memphis Five, which is a half-stirred mixture of European and Afro-American, pleases those who like hybridism.

By 1924, records of the Memphis Five show the extent of progressive dilution of the jazz element. Arranged and harmonized ensemble enters in, the voice instruments playing with the concerted line and attack of European music. This movement toward European practice, necessary in the large band, is not so in a small five-piece group like this. It is, however, a tendency natural to these players and the music immediately takes on a sweeter sound. This stage is clearly to be heard in the Cotton Pickers' record, *Just Hot*. The result is just lukewarm.

MANHATTAN SWING

In the meantime, by 1923 or 1924, the *vo-de-o-do* style of Beiderbecke's Wolverines had invaded New York in the recording groups built around Loring "Red" Nichols, a disciple of Bix. A typical record of one of these bands from that period is *Milenberg Joys*, by the Tennessee Tooters. This fine Jelly Roll Morton tune is properly named *Milneberg Joys* after the Lake Pontchartrain resort. Well recorded by Morton in 1924 with the New Orleans Rhythm Kings, a comparison reveals the heavy arrangement and many solos of the Nichols record. Polyphony is absent and the *vo-de-o-do* lead is even more stylized and restrictive when memorized and played by two trumpets. The playing of this nine-piece band with its three saxophones, has definitely gone over into the large-band style now called swing.

The next step in New York Dixieland, its merging with the *vo-de-o-do* through interchange of personnel, is shown by a record dating from about 1928, *Rampart Street Blues*, by the Cotton Pickers. Phil Napoleon, of the original Memphis Five-Cotton Pickers group, plays with Tommy Dorsey, trombone; Jimmy Dorsey, clarinet and saxophone; Arthur Schutt, piano; Stanley King, drums; and an unknown bass. *Rampart Street* is not a blues at all, but almost completely sweet swing.

The merging of the two styles is complete by 1932 with a record like *St. Louis Gal* by the Original Memphis Five. (Personnel: Phil Napoleon, trumpet; Tom Dorsey, trombone; Jimmy Dorsey, clarinet and saxophone; Frank Signorelli, piano; Ted Napoleon, drums.) Here every defining element of jazz has disappeared and the basis of sweet-swing is established. The whole band is firmly on the beat; a certain amount of simple syncopation is present but this is an unimportant element of jazz unless compounded with intricate and unpredictable polyrhythm. The displaced accents, the pulsating stresses within tones, the counterpoint of independent rhythms, and the constant variation of all of these are the complex sources of jazz momentum.

Polyphony has completely disappeared; the melody is played

over a harmonized ground-bass. The rich, voiced texture disappears with polyphony, and with it the vitality of multimelodic variation.

The instrumental tone has lost all elements of hotness. Pure in the European sense, it has gone to an extreme of sweetness. The trumpet's voice has almost assumed the languishing tones of the crooner; the suave, devitalized trombone has learned drawing-room manners; the clarinet, its fine reedy timbre gone, has acquired a cloying quality and its melodic line flows in a drooping, decorative pattern like that of Artie Shaw and much of Benny Goodman's playing. Gone is the flashing, elastic, whiplike quality of Dodds's phrases, his blue and surging tone, his swinging stresses. So this music sings, not in the African tones of jazz, but in bathetic and sentimental accents. It is salon music.

Were it professedly so, no confusion would result. In its own way, a record of this sort has considerable beauty, but none of the beauty of jazz. A clear separation of the values of jazz from those of other music is vitally important in borderline cases like this. If the distinction is made here, that this music is one thoroughly in the European tradition, confusion will not arise when one comes at length to baffling hybrids like the music of Ellington.

Three of the elements of jazz are indispensable: polyphonic variation, polyrhythmic variation, hot and vocal tone quality. Perhaps improvisation can be left out. Until a real attempt has been made to score jazz polyphony accurately and to play it in jazz style from the score, this point must be reserved. It is difficult to believe that the very spirit of jazz does not come from improvisation and from the mutual inspiration of the players like fire feeding fire. Nevertheless, we can assay any music for the other essential qualities and safely say if it does not have all three — even if it may have two — that the particular example is not jazz.

Since the inclination to European style and sweet playing is general, it absorbs a number of streams, black and white. It is the tendency of white men playing hot; it is one, too, with those Negroes who have succumbed to false sophistication or to direct social pressures.

One of these white streams was the Mound City Blue Blowers. This group from St. Louis began as a novelty trio; what it called blue-blowing was "scat" singing through a paper-covered comb, combined with kazoo and banjo. Led by the comb player, Red McKenzie, the trio went to Chicago in 1924, on to New York and to London the same year.

McKenzie was identified as promoter or vocalist with a good deal of the recorded Chicago style in 1927 and 1928. The next two years, his groups began to include New York white players and various Negroes. One of his early records, *The Morning After Blues*, shows the trio style. It is a kind of novelty vaudeville number that combines some of the rhythmic quality of jazz with attempts at hot tone and a great deal of white hill-billy style. It is trivially sentimental rather than hot; McKenzie's most rhythmic phrases end in the slurred downward tones characteristic of the love ballad in vaudeville. The playing of a later Mound City Blue Blowers group of eight pieces is shown on the two sides of a 1930 record.

The first, *Hello Lola,* is the last gasp of the hot jazz spirit in the octopus grip of sweet, romantic harmony. The beat of the rhythm section is fixed and pulseless, and jazz polyrhythms are lacking in the melody section. The monotony of most swing music is here.

McKenzie's comb solo is grotesquely sentimental; "Peewee" Russell's clarinet solo, more lucid and better toned than his later work and with better tone, is nevertheless in the Teschmaker vein of disconnected, rhapsodic rambling.

Coleman Hawkins has two manners: the rapid and the slow. His saxophone playing, a *tour de force* musical decoration, has had an incalculably bad influence not only on saxophone style but on jazz as a whole. The solo on *Hello Lola* is in his fast style, a glib outpouring of unmusical, meaningless scale arpeggios, a series of rising and descending multi-note outbursts interspersed with drawn-out, whinnying tones. This style has invaded and deteriorated that of other instruments. The passage work of pianists like Art Tatum and Teddy Wilson, for example, is clearly allied to the Hawkins fast manner.

Glenn Miller's trombone solo derives from the manner of Jackson Teagarden, a style that came originally from the Negro, Jimmy Harrison. It has no relation to jazz trombone style. Powerless in ensemble, its solos are empty exhortations. Ensemble, in fact, appears only in the concluding eight bars, with McKenzie on his paper-covered comb trying, like a cornetist, to lead the diffuse, chaotic instrumental groping.

The reverse record side, *One Hour,* is precisely like the mood-music prevalent today in the special salon-swing which is mistakenly considered by some writers to be a great and creative advance in modern music. Masquerading, or fatuously considered as jazz, this is an impressionistic montage of solo moods in which the vagaries of an absent-minded, wayward, and willful romantic improvisation replace the hot, logical, imperious collective improvisation of the New Orleans ensemble. Hawkins sets this sort of idiotically romantic mood perfectly, against the sweet, wailing chords of the background.

In McKenzie's slow solo the maundering inflections of his faster work come clearly to the fore; Hawkins' solo is legato with a profusion of quick passages which simulate the sudden outbursts of true temperament; Russell's clarinet passage is a kind of sad and childish piping; the trombone utters sugary mouthings.

This music is infected with the mysterious malady of all swing. It creates an unnatural atmosphere in which dull monotony, listless melancholy, and a hectic, hysterical, exacerbated excitement alternate under an unchanging sky of gray disillusion.

The further vicissitudes of hot music, outside of New Orleans, from 1924 up to today, present a complex picture of which only the main points need to be outlined. The whole state of hot music, white and Negro, has been much like that of unstable chemical combinations, constantly disintegrating and re-forming into new compounds. Yet the playing of jazz in its pure form has gone on without a break in New Orleans and to a lesser extent, and almost underground, elsewhere. In New Orleans, of course, most of the important elements which entered jazz still remain.

So the white Dixieland style of New Orleans died out; the New York Dixieland changed into a sweet, arranged music and then merged with the *vo-de-o-do* style; the Blue Blowers' music blended first with Chicago and then again with the *vo-de-o-do* –New York Dixieland mixture. The shifting pattern continues. Various groups or schools keep combining and recombining until, later, the types of sweet swing and the small salon swing group become firmly established.

The school of jazz or pseudo-jazz violin playing existed in New Orleans among the colored Creoles. Society orchestras were built around a violinist like Armand Piron as much, perhaps, because of French deference for the classic viol as for the reason that a violinist was apt to be a skilled reader. Even in New Orleans, the violin does not seem to have been a hot element or, at all events, could not hold its own against jazz instruments. It dropped out of the real jazz band quite early. Jelly Roll Morton said, "The violin was never known to play illegitimately even in New Orleans."

Violin and piano ragtime teams like that of the Jockers Brothers were recording in New York around 1917; the violin thereafter entered white jazz in small groups headed by players like Joe Venuti, and the violin section was an element in the large pseudo-jazz bands like those of Paul Whiteman and Jean Goldkette. Venuti's style can be heard, typically, on a 1927 record *Black and Blue Bottom*, on which, with the guitarist, Eddie Lang, he plays music in the Tin Pan Alley vein. Venuti's style is violinistic, but his phrases are related to the inflections of Red McKenzie's singing and the *vo-de-o-do* pattern; it has the rhythmic stresses of spirited academic playing with little syncopation and virtually no polyrhythm; the tone is pure, often

269

proceeding in the harmonized form of double-stops; grace notes and harmonics abound.

The Negro violinist, Eddie South, fits into the Venuti pseudo-jazz trend. He went to France about 1928 and was a great influence there. The French took to jazz naturally, at least in the already Europeanized forms in which they always have heard it, since it reached there chiefly after the recording days of classic New Orleans jazz. Yet there are affinities to French classicism in jazz classicism and the pure form might very well receive an intelligent reception in France. The partial change in the viewpoint of the critic, Hugues Panassié, after he had visited America, is evidence of this.

The impression of early hearings of Negro brass like that of Jim Europe's Band during World War I, the great sensation made by Louis Armstrong's swing band in Paris in 1934, combined with the effect of the numerous small groups of Negroes playing there during and after World War I, and other tours of great jazz players like Sidney Bechet, planted an early seed of jazz feeling in France that crystallized in the 1930's in the Hot Club of France and the playing of its string combinations, especially the Quintette of violin, string-bass and three guitars.

This string music has a dark, romantic, and exciting quality while at the same time it is not jazz at all. Strikingly similar in its instrumentation to the early string combinations of New Orleans, it is interesting to speculate that those Louisiana groups conceivably would have sounded a little like this had the French influence been stronger and the Afro-American thinned out to the vanishing point.

Jazz purists condemn the Hot Club music unequivocally. Yet, although not a thing sympathetic to the natural talents of Negro performers, it may very well be a starting point for a minor white development to lead out of jazz. Outstanding in the Quintette was the Hungarian gypsy, Django Reinhardt, not a jazz guitarist but nevertheless a fine improvisatory artist.

MANHATTAN SWING

French experiments with groups based instrumentally on jazz have not been successful. Their playing of brass and wood-wind is conditioned by European methods of attack and tone production. Lack of race prejudice in France has allowed much mixed playing and recording by whites and Negroes. This tendency is a good thing but the results abroad have been rather sad due to the uneven caliber of the Negro musicians involved. A great deal of this mixed recording resulted in swing inferior even to our own.

The violin tradition in jazz continues weakly in America today with Eddie South and with Stuff Smith who once attempted hot rhythmic effects unsuccessfully but has lapsed almost completely into a style of moody sentimentality. South is an incurably sweet player while Smith's work is a hodgepodge of chaotically impulsive ideas.

The trend of the small sweet group, playing the salon version of pseudojazz, continues through groups like those of Rollini, Red Norvo and the Benny Goodman Trio, Quartet and Quintet, and expands into the larger swing groups. This continuity can be traced through recordings.

Riverboat Shuffle (1934) by Adrian Rollini and His Orchestra, an eleven-piece group, presents a devitalized salon swing that, like many a commercial product, is blended until all its elements are alike. One instrument phrases just like another, one sounds like another. The fine individual quality, the personal tone and idiom of each, are lost. Goodman's tone is thin and meager, almost squeaky, his empty phrases are not unlike those of Venuti's violin elsewhere; Teagarden's trombone style is almost a legato saxophone manner, the thrusting, sliding hotness, the punched staccato phrases of hot trombone irretrievably gone. The whole performance on this record is almost nauseatingly sentimental.

Another Rollini record, *Weather Man* (1935), in which the white trumpeter Mannone and others participate in a mixed white and Negro group, makes abortive attempts at improvised

271

ensemble polyphony in the New Orleans manner, but is intelligible only in the solos. The whole is at a rather plodding swing tempo and in a romanticized *tea dansant* vein.

By 1939 the sweet tendency is completely ascendent in records like Jack Teagarden's *Junk Man*, with its inclusion of so-called "swing-harp," and Artie Shaw's *I Used To Be Above Love* which includes a string-quartet playing a chamber music travesty! The ultimate absurdity comes in the attempt to transmute the qualities of hot New Orleans polyphony into the sweet manner in a carefully prepared score, as in the pseudo-jazz records of Alec Wilder's Octet on Columbia records, in the decadent "jazzing" of the classics by the New Friends of Rhythm and the completely insincere and artificial New Orleans style of the Chamber Music Society of Lower Basin Street both recorded by Victor.

Another phase of developed sweet swing is shown in the 1937 record, *I Can't Get Started*, by Bunny Berigan and His Boys, an eight-piece orchestra. The drooling sentimentality of sweet swing is epitomized here, from the sticky vocal through the muddy ensembles in which the clarinet is not even audible; the trombone, once a lion, is now a mouse. If the *Boys* can't get started it is because they are all afraid to let go. The late Bunny Berigan played in a style modeled eclectically on that of Louis Armstrong. His tone was pure and clear, his high notes impeccable, but the accents of the romantic Irish tenor crept in very subtly and Louis' hot, clipped, commanding phrases crept out.

The white sweet style continues today in phases of the playing of large commercial bands like those of Goodman, Tommy Dorsey, and Glenn Miller although all of these have two styles, a hot riff manner and a sweet swing reserved for sentimental popular tunes.

A sweet tendency existed in small Negro groups in Chicago like the Apex Club Orchestra of the New Orleans clarinetist, Jimmy Noone, whose recordings began in 1927. As the Prohibition era continued, the early rough dives in which hot jazz prospered began to be supplemented by luxurious speak-easies, that had a quieter and more elegant atmosphere in which the patrons might drink the standard rough liquor. The surroundings shaped the music, and a band like Noone's, continuing to play in more or less of a New Orleans manner, was forced by the management to dispense with the essential trumpet. The lead devolving on the clarinet changed the style of that instrument into a florid, overdecorative manner to be found in the playing of many present day clarinetists. Later the trumpet was readmitted, as in the polite Café Society band of John Kirby, but it was throttled with mutes and its voice had become a high querulous scolding.

The Negro sweet salon style appears in New York about 1929 with the Chocolate Dandies and later in the organizations of Lionel Hampton, Teddy Wilson, and John Kirby. A record like *Bugle Call Rag* (1931) by the Chocolate Dandies needs only to be compared with the early one of *Bugle Call* by the New Orleans Rhythm Kings (Gennett 4967, date 1921) to see the vast disintegration of jazz which took place in ten years everywhere except in New Orleans. This version is a montage of clichés, wholly arranged except for solo details and it is not nearly as hot as it is sweet. Standardization is already coming about between the various instruments; Benny Carter, for instance, played the clarinet precisely as if it were a saxophone.

Sweet-hot swing, as a Negro music derived from the whites, culminates in the music of these Hampton, Wilson, and Kirby groups. It tends to become a *non sequitur* of solos, a nervously irritating thing of suppressed dynamics, a ceaseless jumping like a bodily twitch or a facial tic, a frenetic, cerebral excitement. At once a musical repression and a palsied movement almost epileptic, its expression is introvert and highly neurotic.

Negro jazz, as contrasted with swing, was preceded in New York prior to 1920 by a pseudo-form exemplified by Wilbur Sweatman's Original Jazz Band. This form attempted to capitalize on the sudden success of the Original Dixieland Jazz Band at Reisenweber's, as did the local white group of Earl Fuller, and, slightly later, the early band of Ted Lewis. Negro jazz in New York begins almost simultaneously with groups which played with the Harlem party-piano players James P. Johnson and the late Thomas "Fats" Waller. Their music is not New Orleans but, like the Kansas City and St. Louis jazz of this period, is an imitation of the original with its own divergences. Johnson was uniformly unfortunate in the groups which played and recorded with him. Waller, however, had rather better luck. Whatever may be said of Waller's band music, it seldom lacked a rocking rhythm. Composer of many catchy tunes as well as organist and pianist of long and varied training, "Fats" frequently secured in his recordings a true musical quality although one that was closer to Harlem or even to Europe than to jazz.

In a 1927 record, *Red Hot Dan* (Victor 21127), Waller plays with the Morris Hot Babies, a small early New York Negro jazz group whose records, without Waller, are markedly inferior. "Fats," however, had a faculty of swinging a band and getting a certain uncontrolled hotness from it. *Red Hot Dan* moves somewhat like swing, in single rhythmic patterns and simple syncopation. There is little jazz polyrhythm mainly because clarinet is lacking and the trombone plays too much on the beat. Charlie Irvis, otherwise, furnishes a fair ensemble trombone with hot and husky vocal tone, and when occasionally he gets off the beat the rocking jazz rhythms appear. Thomas Morris' cornet has hot tone but no sharpness or drive. The guitar solo is markedly inept. Waller's piano work is simple and solid here, but when he changes to the pipe-organ, all jazz feeling is lost.

A 1929 Waller record shows little progress. One side, *Harlem Fuss*, plods on the beat with double-time episodes used, as in Chicago style, in an attempt to secure momentum. On the reverse side, *The Minor Drag*, the five-piece group performs almost entirely in solo. There are only two spots of ensemble and in these the three voice instruments phrase a very quick riff based on the rhythms of banjo strumming.

New York Negro jazz from this point amalgamates at times with Chicago style in mixed bands both on records and in public performance. Often it is indistinguishable from Chicago proper although Negro participation establishes a firmer and more regular beat. This mixed style is to be heard in such records as *Lookin' Good But Feelin' Bad* (1930) combining Waller, Teagarden, Condon, Krupa, and others; and *Yellow Dog Blues* by the Rhythmakers (1932) combining Waller, Henry Allen, trumpet, Pee Wee Russell, clarinet, "Pop" Foster, bass, and others.

Waller made a great number of recordings from 1934 until his death in 1944. The majority of these, by his own five-piece group, called "Fats" Waller and His Rhythm, are uneven in quality and marred by Waller's excessive tendency to "jive," or to clown. None approaches the quality or style of New Orleans jazz, yet nearly all are improvised and have some elements of polyphony. Waller, like the Chicago boys, helped to keep small-group improvisation alive during a period when every force of commercialism and popular response was hostile to it.

New York jazz, even at its best, was inept. New York is not only farther than Chicago from New Orleans in geographical distance, it is infinitely farther in spirit. The center of a popular music commerce that dates back to the 1890's or earlier and that, during this century, has become progressively more mercenary and less inspired, it is also the location of the largest Negro community in the world, Harlem, one that far antedates New Orleans jazz itself.

The Negro community in New Orleans was scattered and more in contact with the white population. More uniformly made up of Negroes from a close group of West African tribes, this was quantitatively increased by the influx of emigrants as a result of the Haitian revolutions from 1792 to 1806. These Haitian Negroes were close to their African origins.

The Manhattan Harlem dates from 1643 to 1647, when

patents for land were given to emancipated slaves of the West India Company, New Netherland. These grants . . . near the Tombs, were west of the Bowery and between Canal Street and Astor Place.[2]

A large community existed by 1790, and by 1827 boasted its own newspaper, *Freedom's Journal.* Not only has the make-up of the population always been varied — runaways and manumitted slaves from the South, many generations of native Harlem born, immigrants from South America, the West Indies, and the Caribbean Islands, and a small number of residents direct from Africa — but Harlem had the isolation of an almost autonomous separation from the rest of New York.

It was sophisticated very early. Never musical in the sense that the New Orleans Negro community was, Harlem, nevertheless, had musical conservatories and legitimate music teachers long before New Orleans. Harlem's trend toward European classical music was strengthened in the early 1900's by its hatred for the "coon" songs of near-by Broadway. Where in New Orleans the "society" and hot bands remained separate, the former were pre-emptive in Harlem. The funeral and the street parade, rich parts of the New Orleans environment, were of small importance in Harlem, nor were there African survivals as pure as those of Congo Square. So we find factors in New York which prevented a music like jazz from originating among its Negroes, militated against its imitation there, and quickly destroyed it after it arrived.

It is not surprising, therefore, to find a large Negro swing band arising in New York as early as the local white and Negro imitations of the Original Dixieland Jazz Band. From 1922 to 1924, Fletcher Henderson's Orchestra was playing at the Alabam Club and making many records. A ten-piece organization which gradually expanded to fourteen, this orchestra was the first and strongest influence in the field of the hot, large band. White swing came to be largely based on Henderson, and

[2] Stokes, I. N. Phelps: *The Iconography of Manhattan Island,* Volume IV. New York: 1915.

his arrangements were the chief foundation of Benny Goodman's swing success in 1935. New York Negro swing centers around three big bands, that of Henderson, Luis Russell and His Orchestra which played at the Saratoga Club in 1929, and Duke Ellington's large group which played at the Kentucky Club in 1926 and at the Cotton Club in 1927.

Henderson tried at first to make the sluggish swing mechanism, with its brass and reed choirs, move and sound like jazz. But this momentum comes only from a free, polyrhythmic polyphony; at length he gave up and established the current trend of riff-swing. But the damage was done. Henderson had made a popular thing out of the impressive-looking, uniformed large group. Not only was the small band committed to set and stilted arrangement but his early efforts, sounding superficially like jazz, had completely confused the issue and were accepted by the public as readily as were the symphonic monstrosities of Paul Whiteman. Most of the critics succumbed to the same error.

Swing, as a name, did not come into existence until the 1930's. Until that time "jazz" was used to designate real jazz, pseudo-jazz, symphonic jazz, and the arranged harmonized music sweet or hot, of the large and small groups. The commercial groups, inflamed by success, contemptuously disavowed the name of jazz until the early 1940's when renewed popularity of the New Orleans style began to alarm the music racketeers and their puppet bands. They now use the fatuous argument that swing and jazz are the same thing but the New Orleans style is "corny" and old fashioned. Let us examine the truth of this.

In 1923 Henderson's orchestra consisted of two trumpets, trombone, clarinets alternating with alto saxophone, alto and tenor saxophones, piano, banjo, tuba, and drums, a group modeled — except for the saxophones — on Oliver's Creole Band and which, in turn, influenced the King to ruin his own instrumentation two years later. The records of this ten-piece Henderson group, as in *Cotton Pickers' Ball* (circa 1923) alternate solos and arranged ensembles with many outright imitations of

Oliver. The concerted brass and reed ensembles are limping and permeated by a hollow, artificial, mediocre sound. Or with a six-piece group, instrumentally suited to jazz, as in his *Midnight Blues* of the same period, we find a completely arranged thing moving in carefully rehearsed concerted lines with no trace of real jazz character.

Louis Armstrong, joining Henderson in 1924, could not change this music. Many Armstrong followers consider *Copenhagen* a great record because of the magnificent Armstrong solo. Actually, except for Louis' few moments, it is inferior and boring. For an instant, his trumpet leaps out like lambent sunlight and then the fog of saxophones rolls in again.

> A big sixteen-piece band cannot play — nor arrangements provide for — rhythms which are anything but simple compared with the complex polyrhythms of five men improvising freely. There are many who doubt this but they are not listening analytically. They are being fooled by full tone, rich harmony, and complex *single* rhythms played concertedly by whole sections. But the most complex single rhythm is simple compared with several different rhythms playing together. No one has been able as yet to write the sort of free counterpoint which small bands improvise nor arrange for even the most gifted section to play it.[3]

Henderson made two versions of Oliver's *Dippermouth Blues* under its later title of *Sugarfoot Stomp*. These shall be compared with the great Oliver records of 1922–1923.

CITATION 63. *Dippermouth Blues* by King Oliver's Creole Jazz Band. (Personnel as previously cited.)

Taken at the proper moderate tempo, this great example of classic New Orleans rocks with the street band's varied momentum. Free weaving ensemble leads into Dodds's liquid stop-time clarinet chorus. There soon follow Oliver's definitive cornet choruses, high and muted. Stamped with the hallmark of genius, his expression is as dual as African speech: an imploring, re-

---

[3] Rudi Blesh: *This Is Jazz,* lectures at the San Francisco Museum of Art, 1943.

strained wildness in a phrase that, repeated, rings with a far away eerie, mocking laughter.

CITATION 64. *Sugar Foot Stomp*, by Fletcher Henderson and His Orchestra, eleven pieces including Armstrong (1925).

The tempo is right but the ensemble plays an arranged rhythmic figure intended to imitate the rock of the crossing polyphonic voices of New Orleans. A trio of clarinets in sugary harmony replaces the inspired single clarinet. Louis' chorus, learned from Oliver, is no more than a wonderful episode. From this solo the music degenerates into the formula of nauseatingly sweet portions interrupted by mechanized riffs.

CITATION 65. *Sugar Foot Stomp*, by Connie's Inn Orchestra, pseudonym for Henderson's orchestra. Thirteen-piece instrumentation featuring Rex Stewart, trumpet (1931).

Sugarfoot is played here at the grossly overfast tempo of jump-swing, that aptly named music which cannot be danced to but must be jumped to in the various hopping gyrations of the jitterbug. "Jazzing the classics," the mere rendering of a piece of European art music with jazz mannerisms, has been greatly censured although it is more often a "swinging" of the great composers as in the fairly recent rage for swing versions of Tschaikowsky and Grieg concertos. This version of *Sugarfoot* is *the swinging of a jazz classic.*

Finally, comparison of the Morton and Henderson versions of *The Chant* should convince anyone of the musical inferiority of swing and its complete lack of connection with jazz. Jelly's *Chant* is vital, creative, white hot with energy; Henderson's is sluggish, sweet, aping Morton's rendering and ruining it in the process.

Jazz cannot be imitated, it can only be played. To hire New Orleans players and then leave them free to play jazz, never occurred to the natty swing "front men," and today none disparages jazz more violently than the swing musician, nearsighted from reading scores, who cannot play it.

In 1936 the Henderson saga ends with swing facing the blank wall of its blind alley in its *reductio ad absurdum* — the simplification of everything to the bare, empty, rhythmic phrase of the riff.

The recorded career of the band leader, Edward "Duke" Ellington, begins in 1926 with the Gennett discs of his Washingtonians. With the third and last of this series, the growl trumpeter, Bubber Miley, joined the group. Ellington has been quoted as saying that with that event his idea of music changed, that from then on he "could play only hot." Certainly the first record with Bubber is no evidence of this. One side of this disc (Gennett 3342), *L'il Farina*, is a "coon" song melody of the utmost arranged sweetness, complete with the coy inclusion of *Mighty Lak' a Rose*. The other side, *I'm Just Wild About Animal Crackers*, is completely in the manner of the average musical comedy pit band of the 1920's.

Ellington's 1927 New York engagement at the Kentucky Club produced a number of records, several of which have achieved considerable renown, like the *East St. Louis Toodle-o* that shows Ellington in the vein which he has since exploited, one of hot solos over a smoothly articulated and rather prolix sweet swing. Here, too, is the growl trumpet, an atmospheric part of the tissue paper jungle in which the band was then ensconced. Beside the true primitive voice of the blues, such atmospheric effects are what, in the theater, is called "ham." Ellington is an eclectic rather than a creator, a fanciful rather than an imaginative, man. Effects for their own sake are the clue to his work. An adroit technician, he produces seemingly complex arrangements. The true work of art is either of a baffling surface simplicity which hides infinite shades of meaning and directions of reference or of a complexity that grows organically from an inner simplicity. Ellington's hodgepodge montages of sound effects have complexity without meaning, are glittering structures without function, form-aggregates without developmental logic.

The search for effects is often dangerously close to the banal as in *Daybreak Express* (1931) with its literal train imitations, not like the sublimated symbolism of boogie-woogie but akin to the bit of theatrical "corn" with which the Ted Lewis band started its stage programs in the 1920's.

Ellington has come to be regarded as a creator of great modern music. About 1936 he began delving into the harmonies of composers like Debussy, Delius and Franck, and commenced to assemble olios derived from these sources that, of course, are far from modern in a European sense today. Played by a highly trained band with magnificent tonal possibilities, these undigested and essentially callow productions are dazzlingly deceptive to many. By 1937 or 1938, the Duke was attempting long compositions like the four-part *Reminiscing in Tempo* that lasts twelve minutes. This composition, and others like *Diminuendo and Crescendo in Blue* and the recent *Black Brown and Beige*, have an impressive sound but contain literally nothing to grapple with in the way of coherent logical content. From an emotional point of view they are vague, diffused, and nostalgic. The beautiful phrases and the shining sounds are only those of an evanescent sensuousness.

Ellington's fame is now such that he gives Carnegie Hall concerts of a swing completely divorced from dance function, a *tea dansant* music trapped out with his borrowed effects from jazz, the Impressionists, and the French Romantics. Some hail him as a foremost genius of modern music, a few lament that "the Duke has forsaken jazz." Both are wrong: the laurels of Hindemith, Stravinsky, and Bartok are safe and, as for jazz, the Duke has never played it.

The Negro swing developing in other cities gravitated to New York as a commercial clearing house. A fair sort of jazz, imitated from the river-boat jazz, was being played in the early 1920's in St. Louis and Kansas City by bands like Charlie Creath's and Bennie Moten's. The dives of these two river cities were, from the earliest days, the scene of fine blues singing and barrel-house and ragtime playing. As late as 1928, in a record called *Get Low-Down Blues* Bennie Moten gives samples of both piano styles. The Moten band expanded, came under the leadership of Count Basie, and the Kansas City style

281

of swing was established. Under Basie's leadership, Moten's band wailed the rugged "Southwest blues" from which barrelhouse piano came. Its riffs — not, like Ellington's, reminiscent of Europe — were those of boogie woogie used antiphonally by brass and reeds, with solo saxophone or trumpet wailing between in broken phrases while the bass underneath "walked" like the boogie woogie left hand. When sustained, the effect was massively hypnotic like the endless thunder of drums. Until his recent addition of a string section, Basie's band was the hottest of the swing organizations, but this hotness was expressed mainly in a savage and primitively simple rhythm. The hot-riff band is called in musicians' parlance a *powerhouse* band. In this category, the band next to that of Basie was for a long time the Jimmy Lunceford outfit; today it is the large, recently organized Lionel Hampton band.

These same swing elements have formed the work of many small groups, like the Kansas City Five made up of members of Basie's band, and are the stylistic nucleus of the small jump bands that are constantly forming and disbanding.

The Chicago stream of swing gathered, around 1924, in such bands as Erskine Tate's Vendome Orchestra and that of Carroll Dickerson. When Armstrong left Oliver's Creole Jazz Band in that year, the King himself was shortly to desert jazz for the different music of the larger band; simultaneously, his star began to wane. Although he subsisted for a few years on the glory of his name, it was the downward arc of a slowly falling star, as misfortune after misfortune beset him. Failing health, bad teeth — fatal to the trumpet player's embouchure — and financial difficulties were increasingly his.

His first large band, the Savannah Syncopators, 1925–1927, was his best of this sort. The nucleus of this same group was to re-form as Luis Russell's large band which in turn was taken over by Armstrong about 1935.

By 1931, the King's luck was played out. His large band broke up in Kansas City and he wired Bunk Johnson in Louisi- attempting to form a new one, but their plans miscarried.

Successful in forming a new group, a projected tour into the South was stranded in Pennsylvania and obscure years in West Virginia followed. A breakdown in the bus which the band used for transportation, the final loss of all his teeth — and Oliver's day was over. After another tour full of mishaps, Joe was in Savannah, Georgia. There Louis Armstrong saw him in 1937. By the spring of 1938 he was dead, just as the swing craze was climbing to its crest; with it was climbing the boy, grown now, whom he and Bunk Johnson had taught to play, the Louis Armstrong whom he had brought to Chicago for his first important opportunity.

The fortunes of jazz, itself, had never been lower nor had its future ever seemed blacker. But, symbolically, Oliver himself and Louis, too, in the main, never ceased to play the simple, hot trumpet of New Orleans jazz. In the King's last recorded solos (made when he was in ill health, with failing powers) or in Armstrong's today, all made with large sprawling swing bands, one can still hear the leading voice of the marching brass band. The year that Oliver died, jazz was stirring in its sleep, its followers were rallying.

Louis Armstrong could conceivably return to jazz tomorrow; he did it once before, from 1925 to 1928, when he left Henderson and returned to Chicago to record. It was during this period that he made the Blue Five records with Clarence Williams, and the series by his own Hot Five and Hot Seven. Toward the end, particularly when the pianist Earl Hines and the saxophonist Don Redman joined the group, the quality deteriorates into a sort of sweetness foreign to Louis' nature, one belonging to sweet-swing. During this period, he was playing publicly with large groups, his own ten-piece Stompers, following a period with Carroll Dickerson, and with Erskine Tate. By 1930 Armstrong was firmly into the swing trend both in public and on records.

But, in the meantime, he had made an important series of New Orleans jazz records. The Hot Five discs achieved a great popularity. Selling in large quantities, they gave the idea of hot jazz a wide distribution throughout the country, but not in time to counteract the gathering commercial forces. They nevertheless influenced musicians more than is commonly recognized and planted in their minds a seed of jazz which remains alive even while the musicians themselves are buried in the sections of the swing orchestras. They left, too, an unforgettable memory with the public. Five years after they were made, the Hot Five records were plentiful in the secondhand stores. Found there by the first collectors, the music that came from the worn-out grooves stirred an awakening to real jazz.

Despite their markedly uneven musical quality, many of the Hot Five records belong among the golden discs of classic jazz. This group played the music of New Orleans, the blues and good jazz tunes, and took the popular music of their day and, in many cases, transformed it into jazz. This is a function of jazz that, while it is operating, encourages the composition of popular music suitable to it.

Among the more than fifty recorded selections by the Hot Five and the Hot Seven which grew out of it are several masterpieces. There is Kid Ory's fine rolling tune, *Muskrat Ramble*,[4] of brazen and beautiful timbres. In it Johnny Dodds discloses in solo the secret, forgotten by swing soloists, of preserving momentum by ragtime syncopation and inner-rhythm. Or there is *Got No Blues* with Ory's soaring trombone chorus and the three-way conversation among his instrument, the cornet, and the clarinet. There is *Cornet Chop Suey* in which Louis demonstrates how trumpet (or cornet) virtuosity can be used to lead the New Orleans ensemble without needing to be isolated into the solo. Thus the full polyphonic meaning is preserved and how much more thrillingly and beautifully the virtuosity is revealed in this, its proper setting! The Seven's *Gully Low Blues* has an inspired clarinet solo, a vocal by Louis, husky, guttural, African in timbre, and a cornet solo of dramatic, repeated descents from a clear, high note.

Vividly evocative of the barrel-house and honky-tonk atmos-

4 Mistakenly labeled and copyrighted as *Muskat Ramble*.

284

phere of New Orleans is *Yes, I'm in the Barrel* which, with its occasional crudities and technical lapses, nevertheless conveys, through an improvised concordance of strange and beautiful sound, the rhythms of speech, the unspoken words of the blues.

Similarly evocative is *Gut Bucket Blues*. The bucket is the one which is placed in the barrel-houses under the leaky spigots to catch the "gutterings" or drippings of the cheap wine. In *Gut Bucket Blues*, each member of the Five is introduced during his solo.

Louis speaks:

Aw, play that thing, Mr. St. Cyr, lawd, you know you can do it!
Aw, whip that thing, Miss Lil, whip it, kid! Aw pick that piano, gal!
Aw, blow it, Kid Ory, blow it Kid!
Blow that thing, Mr. Johnny Dodds, aw do that clarinet, boy!

And Kid Ory speaks:

Aw, do that thing, Papa Dip!

Then there was the best-seller, *Heebie Jeebies*. For nearly the whole year of 1926 it was on everyone's lips. *Heebie Jeebies* opens with Lil Armstrong's broken chords and then Ory's long swelling, upward glissando leads into an ensemble which is an object lesson in New Orleans polyphony, every instrument filling its role perfectly. Dodds's solo is no mere "noodling" around the tune, nor the fantastic ramblings of today's swing players, but a remarkable and musical variation on the theme. Louis sings above St. Cyr's banjo, his first chorus with words, his second a rhythmic, guttural scat, the epitome of the voice becoming an instrument in jazz. Ory's trombone solo, in tantalizing delayed stresses, proceeds in the New Orleans way, in polyphony, joining here with Dodds's subdued clarinet.

Kid Ory's fine tune, *Savoy Blues*, has overtones of melancholy, its sliding brass chords and undulant trombone phrases derived from the nostalgic sound of a faraway locomotive whistle. St. Cyr plays the blues on the banjo and then Louis' cornet enters, singing with gentle, caressing, sad tone in high phrases. Ory declaims gruffly and abruptly, then sounds long, upward thrusts of sonorous tone upon which the other instruments dance.

Louis' second solo chorus in *Potato Head Blues* reaches heights of invention and subtle eloquence few cornetists or trumpeters have ever reached. Dodds plays in the stomp style which other clarinetists seem unable to achieve. Louis re-enters almost immediately in a stop-time chorus which is almost definitive of the meaning of this term, his tone more reminiscent of that of Bunk Johnson than it is of Oliver, his phrasing full of elements of Bunk's style and yet thoroughly assimilated into Armstrong's own. The Hot Seven's [5] ride-out ensemble sounds like a free-blowing parade band.

At this point Louis was already working away from jazz ensemble. Ory, Johnny Dodds, Lil Armstrong, and St. Cyr drop out to be replaced by Fred Robinson, Jimmy Strong, Earl Hines, and Mancy Cara. Zutie Singleton is added on drums and a little later the saxophonist, Don Redman, enters. The recording then moves steadily over to arranged swing, hot or sweet.

West End Blues is immediately indicative of the change. Oliver's tune is named after the resort on Lake Ponchartrain where so much fine jazz was once played. The record is of mixed character: Louis plays real blues over an inappropriate harmonized background; his scat vocal with clarinet obbligato is beautiful and mournful, but Hines's solo which follows is built on harmonies that do not belong to the blues; at the end the long high notes of the trumpet, resolving into complex and inspired figures, should close the record — but are followed by the anticlimax of Hines's sentimental coda.

Departing from the jazz concept, *West End Blues* is, nevertheless, a record of great beauty although it narrowly misses banality. In the same vein is a record made shortly afterward,

[5] The Hot Five plus Baby Dodds, drums, Ed Garland or Pete Biggs, bass.

Basin Street Blues. The tendency of *West End* is extended in this undeniably beautiful disc into a sort of sad *morbidezza* broken only by Armstrong's intensely dramatic trumpet solo which spends itself descending into soft, low register. The prevailing mood is one of a dark romanticism foreign to jazz.

A few months after recording *Basin Street*, Armstrong began to make swing discs which, except for four sides for the rather abortive Decca New Orleans Album of 1940, have since comprised his recorded work. An idea of the loss to music which has resulted from Louis' public and recording devotion to swing, can be had by listening to any of these recent records.

The musical phase known as *symphonic jazz* is a part neither of jazz nor swing development. Originator of this amorphous music, neither jazz nor symphony, was Paul Whiteman. Lest his concoction not be considered jazz, Whiteman so advertised it while he gracefully accepted from his own hands the crown of King of Jazz. Whiteman never played jazz, not even when his band employed men like Beiderbecke and Teagarden. Beginning in the early 1920's he has played inferior music which "dates" immediately. He merely added to the confusion of the various decadent, inferior imitations of the Negro music. Much critical writing on jazz of the 1920's and 1930's refers not to jazz at all but to the Whiteman sort of product.

One of the most significant developments of the last decade was the white Dixieland swing style introduced by Bob Crosby and His Orchestra. An attempt to score for large band the ensemble and solo work of the original Dixieland school in particular and of New Orleans jazz in general, it really represented a tentative or incipient movement back to jazz.

The impetus of the Crosby attempt derived indirectly from the success of another large white band, the Casa Loma Orchestra, which from 1930 until 1935 achieved considerable success with a type of hot swing embodying a degree of jazz feeling. The Dixieland swing style cannot be called a successful attempt to score jazz, since twelve instruments cannot do the work of seven in a clear polyphony. Even Crosby's smaller unit of eight pieces, called the Bobcats, drawn from his orchestra personnel, played an arranged, stylized pseudo-jazz.

Judged as jazz, Crosby's music is scarcely closer to the model than early Henderson. The significant thing was its popular reception. Its rhythms, nearer to the free-moving ones of jazz, and its approximation of brass-band tone, were quickly accepted. Public taste, not too perceptive of musical form, was clearly responding to virtues which are pre-eminently to be found in hot jazz. Beyond any doubt the pseudo-jazz, Dixieland swing of Bob Crosby was another of the factors which, in the 1930's, contributed to the revival of jazz.

Bitter opposition to New Orleans jazz centers today in the commercial music magazines, in hanger-on in the music racket, and in a number of swing musicians themselves. On its face, the commercial front is formidable in its control of the radio, movie music, large scale record production, the juke box, sheet music and publication, and even the booking agencies for bands. At times the collusion against jazz approaches the conspiratorial. Nevertheless the commercial hold has shown clear signs, in recent years, of weakening enough to allow jazz to penetrate to the general public. The racket is by no means a united front; varied self-interests intrude. From small café owner to large recording company, one and all eye the main chance. Reissues of rare old records continue and will be accelerated; current pure jazz is being increasingly recorded; public concerts, like those of Eddie Condon at Carnegie Hall, augur better ones to follow. The people may have the final referendum on their own music.

Bitterest fighters, at the last ditch, are many swing musicians from the most corrupt to the veritable tyro. Their motivation is apparent: commercial self-interest, inability to play the highly difficult, creative parts of jazz, the illusion of progress in swing itself, the blinding glare of acclaim whipped up by high-powered publicity salesmanship. Varying from an ill-concealed mercenary attitude to a sincere belief that jazz is old-fashioned and swing is modern, the musicians' front, too, is by no means a solid one; among them there is a considerable body of opinion and ability, more or less submerged, favorable to pure jazz. In the swing bands are many young musicians whose potential abilities and sympathies are with jazz. A number of older players from the New Orleans tradition earn their living, in the precarious musical field, by swing playing. Omer Simeon, for example, after years with Earl Hines's swing band could join with Kid Ory and others in 1944 and 1945 recording sessions playing classic jazz of a very high quality. Louis Armstrong, for another example, could participate in the hopelessly commercial broadcast sponsored by the ubiquitous and ill-informed Esquire Magazine early in 1945 and put program and sponsors to shame by teaming with Bunk Johnson and Sidney Bechet in an episode of fine hot jazz. Such things are not lost on the public as a whole. If a man has once played or heard jazz, he seldom forgets it.

The vast misconception regarding swing is adroitly fostered by the commercial interests. It is supposed to be modern and this modernity is alleged to be a remarkable development from the "crude, early stages of New Orleans jazz." Swing musicians, like Goodman, Tatum, and many others are esteemed to possess fabulous instrumental techniques which make the old New Orleans players by comparison, "fumbling, inept, and uncertain."

This remarkable viewpoint is completely unsupported by facts. Swing is a reactionary music which sacrifices the truly modern tendencies of polyphonic jazz. And the swing techniques are largely mythical. Dexterity is less than a complete technique. It utilizes the obviously impressive while avoiding the unspectacular, truly difficult things, especially those requiring a genuine melodic and rhythmic creativeness. The present-day solo is esteemed modern and full of ideas in direct proportion to the more unrecognizable it makes the melody. Such "getting off" conceals lack of true invention or the ability to produce logical variation.

Swing has been no more modern than styles in women's clothing are modern. Its ceaseless search for novelty, rather than the truly original, has kept it faddishly changing, hectically striving to avoid being out-of-date. It has had from this an euphoric illusion of progress. As a result however — while jazz remains modern and in advance of the times — swing has steadily deteriorated and is now reaching a nauseous state of disintegration more and more apparent to the public. Its champions are being slowly discredited. It has degenerated during the last five years into the extreme forms of its two categories, sweet and hot. The former has become a completely devitalized, sentimental, hodgepodge of Tin Pan Alley ditty, and the Romantic and Impressionistic types of European music. In theatrical terms it is a tear-jerker. Large string sections are added by bands like that of Tommy Dorsey or even by a once quasi-hot group like that of Basie.

Hot swing during the last fifteen years, and particularly in the last five, has been simplified to a half-dozen screaming brass and bleating reed riffs. It is easy to prove that any swing is completely anti-jazz, completely anti-New Orleans, opposed to the real musical values which jazz represents. Of still greater importance and significance, is the fact that riff-swing is anti-music. There is scarcely a canon of art or common good taste which it does not violate. Establishing no new art form, developing no older one, it is nihilistic, cynically destructive, reactionary.

Hot swing, with its riffs, is a highly organized form of instrumental noise devoted to the superinducement of a wholly unnatural excitement. This music and the response of audiences to it constitute, indeed, a social phenomenon deserving of psychological and psychiatric study. The listeners come to a swing concert obviously prepared and eager for the release of excitement which is touched off by the first notes or drum blows. No music seems to be needed. The psychological reaction is instantaneous, coming with the sounding of a handful of threadbare rhythmic tricks. The mass autohypnosis thereupon vents itself in anarchic, orgiastic, and dangerous excitement.

MANHATTAN SWING

Where jazz is a communal and participative activity resulting in a normal and healthy release of tensions, swing is a form
of rabble rousing that elicits for itself and its exponents the
same blind idolatry the demagogue or the dictator receives from
the mob.

13.

hot piano

IN *the wild and drunken disorder of the barrel-house the blues player sits oblivious in a dark corner like an African seated at his drum. While the dusty old rosewood box, with its broken music rack and its swinging candle brackets bearing smoking, kerosene lamps, vibrates to the fierce rhythms of a dozen drums and sings the blues in a cracked and grieving treble, he sits in the world he builds for himself. A world it is of sound, remote, dark as night with flashes of lightning and glow of fires. It is sound threaded by locomotive whistle and tramp-boat horn; of slave work-song and West African chant; of wild dancing and of prayer and song as wild; the wide liquid tone of great rivers, the Niger and the Congo, the Mississippi; of grass crackling in long drought, then sudden thunder and long, sweet rain. Amid riotous sin the player dwells in a dream, in its bright-dark meanings of memory and of hope. He is a lonely man and yet he is a thousand men. Men without even the dignity of a name except the casual ones of the roads and the dens: Little Brother, Speckled Red, Stormy Weather. Names go with homes — homes do not go with wandering — but home is in the dusty road trod by shoeless feet, dignity is in the people, even in their desperate sin; power and glory shine in their dream.*

Hot piano playing began when the American Negro first approached the instrument. A frank and realistic approach, the Negro's, one deeply formed and motivated by a native musicality in which intuition serves him better than academic learning, this approach leads him to explore each instrument as if he himself had just invented it. His exploration extends technical possibilities by disregard or ignorance of supposed limitations, directs those possibilities into new channels through which the characteristic African creativeness can flow, abstract but vivid, personal as only a true racial distillation within the individual can be.

The first style to appear was the early blues one. This was followed by ragtime. The ragtime piano, not yet combined with the band, was used perhaps as early as the 1880's for indoor entertainment, including dancing. No doubt it combined on occasion with the usual string trio, and in any event it absorbed the multi-themed dance and march melodies, the Creole and popular songs, of the trio, and developed its own repertory, which late in the 1890's became known as ragtime. Piano ragtime and classic jazz — originally called ragtime too — had decisively formative interrelations and influences at the time that the street bands began to play for summer lawn parties. They played in town and open air picnics in Gretna, on the Lake Pontchartrain shore, at popular resorts, like West End and Milneburg, and the later portion around the old Spanish Fort that was especially frequented by Negroes. On the Lake, and at some lawn parties in town, were roofed pavilions so that dancing might continue through the sudden summer rains. The influx of white music was being constantly balanced by authentic Negro content and transformed by Negro technique.

Morton told of the great barrel-house blues players of his youth, 1895–1900. Wonderful names, theirs, "Trigger Sam," "Skinny Head Pete," "Old Florida Sam," "Game Kid," and "Brocky Johnny." One of Brocky Johnny's tunes, Jelly related, was

All you gals better get out and walk
'Cause he's gonna start his dirty talk.

proving that the custom of walking home was well established in the days of the "Merry Oldsmobile" and, for all we know, was a commonplace even earlier, when walking got the insulted female home just as quickly as the horse and carriage might have done.

In his youth, Morton barnstormed throughout the South and he mentions many fine barrel-house and rag players. This confirms — if confirmation were needed — that the characteristic Negro piano styles were of rather general origin throughout the region.

The more trained and sophisticated players of the New Orleans of this period, men like Alfred Wilson, Albert Carroll, and Sammy Davis, were distinguished by their more dignified names and by their brilliant ragtime playing. Morton, never one to give undeserved praise, said, in his rich personal idiom, of Davis, "He was one of the greatest manipulators of the keys I have ever seen in the history of the world on a piano." But these men were Negroes, and not one but could play the blues or whose playing — when the going got rough in Hillma Burt's or whatever brothel they were working in — would fail to take on a little of the fine, hot barrel-house quality which is the piano counterpart of unadulterated jazz. Many of these players could, like Tony Jackson and Jelly Roll Morton, sing the blues too, and invent as well the pretty, catchy tunes which are still standard jazz numbers. Unforgotten even today is Tony Jackson's *Pretty Baby.*

Hot piano music is often called jazz and it is true that its development parallels that of Negro instrumental music in time, in sequence, and in character. Nevertheless, the two need to be separated into categories as, in European music, symphony is separated from piano music even when both set forth pieces of sonata-style development. The piano is not essential to instrumental jazz. On the other hand, the hot quality of Afro-American improvisation and variation forms both; each is nourished by the blues. Either can develop independently. If any piano style deserves the name of jazz it is that of Morton, with its full orchestral implications. Still, the terms of ragtime, jazz, and swing cause less confusion if applied as adjectives to the music of Negro pianists and those white players who follow the various trends.

HOT PIANO

Hot piano, black and white, falls into the following main categories:

> Blues or barrel-house piano.
> Ragtime piano.
> Jazz band piano.
> Swing or "modern" piano.

The blues-singer, wandering through the countryside like a medieval minstrel, with his guitar and his store of blues and ballads, sang on street corners in the cities and in the saloons, barrel-houses and honky-tonks. Restless, in a few weeks he might wander on, but during his brief stay indoors in the low, rough, roaring dives he was drawn by an inescapable fascination to the battered, disreputable piano, square or upright, sometimes found there. He learned to play it as he had learned to play his guitar, directly and experimentally. He transposed his chord and rhythmic patterns from the fretted fingerboard to the keyboard treating the piano not as a singing instrument but as the percussive one which it essentially is; in his hands it became a speaking drum.

The barrel-house style contains all the primitive or archaic piano playing of the Negroes. It is almost entirely of the blues but includes a primitive ragtime, some stomped tunes and various topical songs. Boogie-woogie is a special phase or development of blues piano. The whole barrel-house style is often connected with singing and with the spoken monologue, like the speaking blues. It is frequently interwoven with various small and casual instrumental combinations — duos, trios, and quartets — employing instruments like guitar, banjo, mandolin, string-bass, drums, washboard, the paper-covered suitcase used as a drum, kazoo, harmonica, comb, jug, musical saw, and accordion. Battered cornets and trombones, broken clarinets tied or taped together join, too, with this rich and earthy piano playing, called by extreme jazz purists with an ear for the picturesquely accurate, "whore-house piano."

In all of these combinations, barrel-house piano is entering jazz through the swinging doors of the saloon, dragging its sometimes ill-assorted but musically creative fellows along with it. And it is an integral part of jazz at its constantly existing archaic, formative level. The street band of New Orleans lent to the first sounds of jazz a clear, brassy, clarion tone, accents articulate and superb. The underworld of Storyville, of St. Louis, Memphis, Atlanta, Birmingham, Kansas City, Houston, and scores of lesser cities, brought in its own discordant, blaring din, clarifying it by the miraculous chemistry of folk art.

The upright piano of the saloon, is a distinct instrument, different in character from the concert grand. Loose in action, it settles into a certain permanent degree of "out-of-tuneness" related approximately to jazz dissonance, to the blues scale, to African handling of pitch. It often has a device known as the mandolin attachment that gives a plucked and twanging percussive quality not unlike a harpsichord. Veteran players in their "horror of clean sound" [1] secure a rasping, dirty tone by inserting old newspaper or heavy manila in the strings; their foot-tapping and drumming or knuckle-rapping on the wooden front panel are percussive-rhythmic parts of the music. This type of piano is the proper instrument for the music; experienced players can choose from a dozen apparently hopeless instruments and select one as carefully and wisely as a violinist inspects a group of Stradivarii. The playing of barrel-house blues on the concert grand is, in itself, a Europeanization of this profoundly Afro-American music.

Blues piano has been variously and rather extensively recorded, especially on the race lists which are a fortunate aid to authenticity. Race-list recording, particularly that done early, is unsophisticated. Recording directors, fortunately, did not take it seriously nor think it worth "improving." Thus, in the piano solos, blues accompaniments, and small instrumental combinations, we can find many which convey accurately and colorfully the atmosphere of the "guzzle shop." One such is *Shreveport Farewell* (Bluebird B–10953), piano solo by Little

[1] Gide, André: *Travels in the Congo.* New York: 1929.

HOT PIANO

Brother, as Eurreal Montgomery has always been known in his native New Orleans and in Chicago where he settled about 1927.

Shreveport Farewell has close-knit musical values in its ordered thematic development, its variety, and its scope of variation. Not a precise blues, it can only be called a barrel-house number with typical elements of ragtime, of player piano imitation and boogie-woogie and much of the real blues feeling.

Montgomery's archaic style is solid but not heavy; it moves lightly enough over its percussive bass. Like all barrel-house music, gaiety when present is never unshadowed. Little Brother's music is haunted; sorrow sleeps uneasily in its tones; its revelry is preoccupied. There are many passages of great beauty such as treble tremolandi over a ground bass like the plucked string-bass or single-string playing of the guitar. *Shreveport Farewell* ends beautifully through a final dark, descending bass.

The blues could be played authentically and still have regional characteristics apparent to musicians and, still further, allow the development of markedly personal styles. Records show these individualities clearly.

Barrel House Woman (Paramount 12753, reissue Signature 910) by the Midwestern pianist Will Ezell is a case in point. This record is a slow blues, grave and somber. It sings with a sad brusqueness; train bell figures, with a melancholy sound, are used over the "walking" bass of ascending and descending spread octaves with the movement of a locomotive; there is a stomped section with delayed beats; single notes are drummed ominously. The line of *Barrel House Woman* is starkly simple and is as classic in its own way as that of a Bach invention.

Or there is the playing of the St. Louis man, Henry Brown, in his *Henry Brown Blues* (Paramount 12825, reissue Signature 909). This has its own flavor, solid and rich, moving percussively but elastically through dark harmonies. There is a chanted songlike quality in measures which are of a shadowy and unfathomable beauty; stresses which suspend impalpably like movement suddenly frozen, alternate with an elegaic, inexorable forward motion. Broken treble chords and tremolandi sound over walking octaves which descend to the deepest bass and resolve into solid, repeated chords.

The wine parlors had their humor, too, a humor gustily Rabelaisian and often grim. Barrel-house players were primarily entertainers; their sung and "talkin' " blues were an important part of their repertory; their "show-pieces" of boogie-woogie train imitation blues soothed and cajoled their listeners with a promised escape from sordid reality more alluring than that of the poisonous liquor served.

An eccentric and highly temperamental Chicago player, "Cripple" Clarence Lofton, has a wide barrel-house repertory. Besides boogie-woogie, his blues are authentically archaic; others, like *Brown Skin Gals*, are of a rich, veiled bawdiness and a rowdy humor. A masterpiece of this genre is his

CITATION 66. *Strut That Thing*, sung by Lofton to his own solid blues piano chords, that roll forward in rhythmic blocks of four, and traps played percussively in washboard style.

> *Woke up this mornin' feelin' bad*
> *Thinkin' 'bout times I've had:*
> *You went out and stayed all night.*
> *Do you think that's treatin' me right?*
>
> *Aw, you shouldn' not do it at all*
> *Shouldn't do it at all*
> *Shouldn't do it at all.*
>
> *I'm tellin' you lover*
> *How do you strut that thing*
> *Night and day?*
>
> *Gettin' sick and tired of the way you do*
> *Gawd, Mama, gonna pizen you,*
> *Sprinkle goofer dust* [2] *'roun yo' bed*
> *Wake up s'mornin', find yo' own self dead.*

[2] Dust from a grave, Goofer Dust, like Mad Water, 6th and 7th Book of Moses, Five Century Grass, Anger Powder, etc., are Voodoo charms.

HOT PIANO

Another barrel-house entertainer, and one of the roughest and most exciting of pianists, is Speckled Red (Rufus Perryman). Playing in a simple, forceful style and singing in a high-pitched, often strident, voice, he has recorded honky-tonk favorites like *The Dirty Dozens, You Got to Fix It, Do the Georgia,* and blues like *Welfare Blues* that, with its ironic description of the politics-ridden, local relief of Depression days, shows the blues being created out of daily life.

CITATION 67. *St. Louis Stomp,* by the Speckled Red Trio, is played by one of the casual combinations of the drinking dives, piano, guitar, and mandolin. The violent percussion, jangling and twangy, evokes almost pictorially the wild, rowdy, boisterous scene in the early morning hours. Through the musical din, Speckled Red's falsetto humming can be heard; in the midst of rhythms that tumble headlong he plays on the highest treble keys, trilled ostinati that crackle with a whirring, high sibilance over string arpeggios.

Very few white players play an authentic barrel-house style. George Zack is as successful at this underworld pianism as any. Zack's solo records are unfortunately still unissued [3] but his work can be heard in the Muggsy Spanier Ragtime Band records. One of the best of the remaining white players in this style was Frank Melrose, known as Kansas City Frank. He made pitifully few records before his early and tragic death near Hammond, Indiana. Although white, he lived the underpaid, scuffling life of the wandering Negro honky-tonk pianist. His work assumed marked ragtime qualities through his friendship with Jelly Roll Morton in Chicago. *Pass the Jug,* taken at an easy but firm tempo, is full of Morton's manner grafted on a stomped, barrel-house style. *Jelly Roll Stomp* is a direct tribute to Morton. Both selections, played with trap drums, achieve a relaxed, Negroid beat found but rarely in the work of white piano players. (Brunswick 7062, reissue Brunswick 80031.)

[3] Commodore released two solos by Zack in 1946: *Lazy River* and *Snowball,* which, unfortunately, stress the romantic side of this player more than the hot. They are nevertheless easily rhythmic and rather beautiful sides.

Among the most Negroid of all living white pianists is Art Hodes. His style is a very personal form of barrel-house firmly based on the blues. Hodes, in particular, shows in the degree of his achievement, the result of a serious, intellectual white approach to pure Afro-American music. *Ross Tavern Boogie* and *South Side Shuffle* (both on Solo Art 12007) show his sincerely felt and communicative style, although recently his work has tended to fall into his own clichès.

Among younger white pianists of this category the west coast player Johnny Witwer is one of the leaders. His style, combining barrel-house and some of Morton's stomping, is forceful and developed rhythmically. He plays the blues well and revives many fine tunes from the period 1915–1925.

The most phenomenal white pianist to appear in at least a decade is the young Baltimore player Don Ewell. Appearing at Town Hall in New York, January 1, 1946, in a trio with Albert Nicholas, clarinet, and Baby Dodds, drums, he proved a sensation. He revealed a style based on that of Jelly Roll Morton but so completely assimilated that he is able to create individually within it. Rhythmically he is accurate and Negroid; technically he is accomplished.

Immediately after the Town Hall appearance he recorded for Circle with the trio (J–1001 A: *Wolverine Blues* and J–1002 A: *Albert's Blues*, and *Buddy Bolden's Blues*, unissued at this date), and solo in a fine original stomp-ragtime composition of his own (J–1002 B: *Manhattan Stomp*). The trio record of *Wolverine Blues* makes an interesting comparison with that made nearly twenty years before by Morton with Johnny and Baby Dodds.

At the present time (May 1946), Ewell is playing at New York's Stuyvesant Casino with Bunk Johnson's Band, a supremely difficult assignment for a white pianist and one in which Ewell acquits himself well while deriving the invaluable experience of playing with one of the great Negro bands of history.

Blues or barrel-house piano is essentially percussive; its effect is based upon impact or attack. The development of piano

HOT PIANO

construction through sounding board and sustaining pedal has extended its tone into a singing legato. Its original character, nevertheless, is to be heard at the moment the hammers strike the strings, its dry and clipped quality when played staccato with no pedal. The Negro, penetrating to the meaning of the noble instrument, thus developed his style. He uses the pedal only to tap on for beat or rhythmic counterpoint; it is seldom pressed down to prolong the tone. Fingers remain on the keys only as long as the volume remains relatively full, then are raised, clipping it off short like a blues singer's tones. By utilizing the piano mechanics, the player thus produces the dynamic quality of hot tone.

From this basis barrel-house piano became a distinct Afro-American style, clipped, percussive, polyrhythmic. It may be dry and pungent, or rich with a dark and bitter sweetness. Each hand builds rhythms as on a drum; each is filled with inner-rhythmic patterns; the two combine into the polyrhythms of the African large and small drum, the *hun* and the *hunpi*.

Melodically the piano, under Negro hands, sings either in clipped staccato phrases or its tones are prolonged percussively by trill, tremolando or drummed notes. The rhythmic quality of each of these devices is at least as important as the tone-sustaining function. In addition to drum simulation, the treble impersonates the leader and chorus of Africa over the bass ostinato which is like drums.

The scale is implicit, but harmony is merely latent, in the piano keyboard. So the Negro, just as he chose the simplest harmonies from the early hymns for his spirituals, blues and jazz, draws from the keyboard the same tonic-dominant sequences which undergo no elaborate development but revolve cyclically as a basis for the superimposition of free melodic variation.

Barrel-house is a qualitative category which includes a number of formal elements: primitive ragtime and ballad, the blues, and the special form of piano-blues called boogie-woogie which may in turn be mixed with the others but, by itself, is a distinct formal and technical development.

The basis of boogie-woogie is that of treble variations, percussive, melodic, or both, over a rhythmic ostinato in the bass that often consists of rising and descending figures in intervals much more chromatic than in any other form of blues. This combination derives musically from the African chorus singing over the drums. The melodic-harmonic theme is that of the blues, in the eight-, sixteen-, and especially the twelve-bar form. The right hand improvises ceaseless blues variations while the left supplies rhythmic patterns in ascending and descending chords, single notes in a punctured organ point, or the walking bass of octaves moving up and down in scales or arpeggios. The treble may digress momentarily from melody into rhythmic chords and set up exciting and subtle, or harsh, cross-rhythms with the bass through which the basic harmonic progression moves in repeated cycles.

Boogie-woogie is an arduous, serious music with an ascetic, disciplined classicism of its own. The definitive piano version of the blues, it inherits, within the limits of the piano, the same vast possibilities of development. It is sober and unsentimental. Somber, it does not tear tragedy to tatters; however gay, it laughs with wise and restrained laughter. Without words, it is the blues in their most abstract and concentrated form. As the blues are properly sung so it is played, fast or slow, its fastest tempo still moderate. It is a form of precise power, of incredibly rocking momentum, of cumulative stress and tension and, on its highest level, it makes severe demands upon the performer's technique and endurance. This technique is rhythmic more than digital requiring rhythmic abandon with control, rhythmic poise and presence of mind, and a sense of momentum almost vertiginous. On this level, it is a noble if somewhat limited art.

The origins of boogie-woogie, like that of the parent blues, are obscure as to date, but there is no doubt that it developed from banjo and guitar playing, its original regional differences disappearing to a degree through the nomadic character of its players. Like the blues, it does not seem to have originated in

New Orleans. The earlier New Orleans barrel-house piano style has bass elements of boogie-woogie but they were not maintained in the long ostinati which form one of the defining elements of the strict style.

Boogie-woogie reached its highest and, perhaps, its first definitive development in the Middle West, in Kansas City, St. Louis, and Chicago, having arisen spontaneously, with strong regional differences, in Texas, Mississippi, Louisiana, Alabama, Arkansas, Tennessee — everywhere, in fact, in the South. I myself heard it in Oklahoma City at least as early as 1913 or 1914, never solo but combined with instruments like string-bass, guitar and mandolin, and kazoo. It was not called boogie-woogie there, but passed for ragtime, casually considered a crude imitation of this style with which it has so little actual connection. Like jazz, it was christened late and did not get its name until 1928, when Clarence Smith's record, *Pine Top's Boogie-Woogie*, was issued.

From 1910 to about 1933, Chicago, at the confluence of rivers and railroads to the south, became the center of a great northward industrial migration of the Negroes and thereby a meeting place for barrel-house and boogie-woogie players. The great South Side institution of "rent party" (locally known as "skiffle," "shake," or "percolator") run by the landlady, paid the rent by the proceeds from the sale of home-cooked food and nefarious, bootleg liquor, and was the scene of gambling, dancing, brawls, and "good time." These social affairs of a submerged, underprivileged, and partly expatriate dark population were the haven of these piano blues players who, making the rounds of the innumerable "skiffles," subsisted on the free food and drink and the large tips from those who emerged as winners in the crap game.

At their height in the 1920's, these parties kept together the bodies and souls of several hundred players. Native Chicagoans like Jimmy and Alonzo Yancey, Hersal Thomas, Jimmy Blythe, Dan Burley, "Cripple" Clarence Lofton, Meade Lux Lewis, and Albert Ammons, rubbed elbows with players from other sections, some of whom are well known and recorded, like Pine Top Smith and Montana Taylor, while others, like "The Toothpick," "Tippling Tom," "Detroit Red," and the 375-pound James Hemingway, have disappeared, surviving only as legends.

During the hectic, pre-depression decade, Chicago became the melting pot of Afro-American blues piano. A dozen regional styles met there and their characteristics of bass and treble, of rhythm, and of harmony, became amalgamated in the work of a few gifted players. Montana Taylor, for example, playing numbers like *The Fives* and *The Four O'Clocks*, remembers the now-forgotten players, men like Phil and Tom Harding, "Funky Five," Harold Farmer, and "Slick" Collins, from whom he originally learned them, later to make them peculiarly his own. Many of these he recently recorded for Circle (1946) after I had discovered him in Cleveland, Ohio, living obscurely and withdrawn altogether from professional music.

The Chicagoan, Dan Burley, now business editor of the *Amsterdam News* of Harlem, is master of more than two dozen different basses and recalls the geographical origin of these as well as the complete sectional styles of which they were distinctive parts. He likewise can reproduce with fidelity the personal idioms of individual players of his day, just as Jelly Roll Morton did with the New Orleans players of his, as shown on Library of Congress records. Burley's playing of regional and individual styles, as well as his own, has been thoroughly documented on Circle records.

The depression seriously curtailed the "skiffle" institution, to which, previously, Prohibition raids had been, more or less, only a perpetual annoyance. (Dan Burley says, "Real playing — the ' arm-breakers' — began about midnight when the crap game broke up, and went on until five or six, whenever the 'wagon' came.") The legalizing of liquor effected what the depression and the Prohibition raid could not, the end of the "skiffle." The hundreds of fine players scattered and went into other forms of employment, and a wonderful folk art all but disappeared. Recorded to a degree on the race lists of the 1920's,

Paramount, Champion, Vocalion, and Okeh, it seemed to be a lost art. But ten years later, by 1937 or 1938, the serious new interest in jazz and its allied forms began to result in the rediscovery of some of the forgotten players.

An early player of boogie-woogie is Jimmy Yancey and he remains one of the greatest in technique, in profundity, and in powers of invention. Prior to his piano playing, which he rarely performs publicly, he was a minstrel tap dancer. In this role he is said to have performed in London for George V and the Royal Family. Discovered in Chicago in the late 1930's, he was recorded after many other exponents of this style, some of whom he had instructed. Two dozen sides comprise his issued output up to the present.

CITATION 68. *Midnight Stomp,* piano solo by Jimmy Yancey. This twelve-inch disc dates from 1943. *The Fives,* or *Five O'Clock Blues* is the original name of this number, one of the earliest of all known boogie-woogie numbers. Yancey has played it in Chicago since 1913. Its name came from the fact that it was played at rent parties in the early morning to arouse all guests who were merely asleep and not dead drunk. Nearly every Chicago barrel-house player had his own tune which went by the same name. Yancey's first record, made about 1939, for Solo Art, is of *The Fives* and shortly thereafter he played it for Victor under the title of *Yancey Stomp.* The Solo Art disc is perhaps the best recorded; *Midnight Stomp,* which is on the Session label, perhaps the least; both of these versions excel the Victor record in performance.

Midnight Stomp develops through eighteen complete twelve-bar choruses. It is a fast blues and the tempo is the fastest at which boogie-woogie should be played.

The lashing Yancey bass, derived from locomotive rhythms and one of the most phenomenal in all boogie-woogie, begins to move immediately. The basic rhythmic device of this bass can be seen in Ex. 18, back of book. It is an accelerating sequence of dotted-eighth, eighth, and sixteenth notes. This geometrical ratio, 3–2–1, snaps like the childhood game called

305

"cracking the whip." Above this bass, which continues with gathering momentum practically without a break throughout, the treble chimes in broken chords, enters in trilled rhythmic figures, and shifts to swiftly repeated chords. There is a downward section, repeated, a bugle call or hunting horn motive executed by concerted bass and treble in broken rhythms. Clusters of chords for the right hand create disquieting cross-rhythms with the heaving bass, against which, in the next to the last chorus, the treble builds a fantastic overrhythm.

CITATION 69. *Yancey's Bugle Call*, piano solo by Jimmy Yancey.

"Show-piece" numbers of this sort were in the repertory of every player, for the competition among these performers was keen and their contests, in which the audiences delighted, were known — as they also are in jazz — as "cutting contests."

Yancey can be somber and tragic, moody, introspective and profound. His *Bugle Call* makes the piano sound with the trumpetings of victory.

The bugle call is a break occupying the first four measures of each twelve-bar chorus. The call and chorus appear in a fresh variation each time. Yancey often plays this number in unrecorded performance for fifteen minutes; the swift-paced choruses roll out fresh and varied as if his ideas and his inspiration would never dissipate. The call motive offers a series of mutations like those of African solo drumming and Bessie Smith's *Careless Love* phrases. These seemingly slight changes have an importance in music equal to that in language where the shifting of emphasis from word to word, delay of one, et cetera, can alter the whole meaning of a sentence. (A number of Yancey's variations are shown in Ex. 38, back of book.)

These phrases are good examples of the hot quality in melodic line that is no more definable than are the subtleties of European phrasing. Demonstrable by example, identifiable by continued listening, it is that ultimately inexplicable thing which in any art is called style, at once the most intangible and the most essential. These bugle calls are of the very essence of tonal and rhythmic hotness. The minor third, not a part of the major arpeggio of the bugle call, converts the scale in effect to that of the blues and inescapably conveys the idea of the blues' third. Rhythmic hotness is found in the variation in stress displacement, particularly in the inversion of the four measures marked A, with the entry of leading notes delayed in each measure. The element of surprise is of great importance in hotness. A record played over and over may lose its elements of the unexpected; true hot improvisational performances never do.

In the fifth chorus occurs a polyrhythmic exposition of the theme that is of the highest creative order. Compared with the variety and complexity of this rhythmic development the syncopations of Schumann, the dual meters of Brahms, or even the rhythmic experiments of the modern composers seem almost elementary. The jazz and hot piano of the American Negro may not pursue harmonic or formal melodic development to any but a simple degree, but his polyrhythmic, melodic variation is the utmost modernity.

A comparison that shows the wide divergence of personal styles in barrel-house piano is to be found by playing Montana Taylor's *Low Down Bugle* (Circle: J–1009). Preserving the bugle call, it is profoundly different in spirit. Played at a slower tempo, it is forceful rather than jubilant and full of strong hot tensions. Taylor's playing on the Circle label of other numbers, like his *'Fo' Day Blues* and *Rag Alley Drag,* shows a somber moodiness and a deep poetic vein, expressed in unusual minor harmonies and subdued dynamics, that represent a real personal contribution to the barrel-house style.

As we have noted, Pine Top Smith made the first record of boogie-woogie style to reach general notice. Even among barrel-house players Pine Top was a notably eccentric character. His brief recording career was cut short by a stray bullet in a dance-hall brawl. He was a gifted exponent of boogie-woogie, and his records made the art known beyond its own immediate circle. His style has momentum but stresses delicate imagination rather than sheer power, and his essential genius lies in his ability to make much of the simplest material. His musical pieces, *Pine Top's Boogie Woogie, Pine Top's Blues, Big Boy They Can't Do That, I'm Sober Now, Jump Steady Blues, Now I Ain't Got Nothin' at All,* and the others, are varied and beautiful, with the flavor of real popular folk music, or are firmly based on the blues expressed in rhythmic and chromatic train imitation.

The two masters of *Pine Top's Boogie Woogie* have appeared on the original label and in separate reissues. The nature of improvisation on a theme is shown by these two records. The arrangement of piano choruses and the speaking, with its description of the boogie-woogie dance, are different on the two discs.

Meade Lux Lewis made a number of records for Paramount in 1927. Eight of these were accompaniments. One solo, *Honky Tonk Train Blues,* was not issued until 1929. Lewis lapsed almost immediately into complete obscurity. In 1936 he was rediscovered in Chicago washing automobiles and immediately recorded *Honky Tonk* as well as other numbers for English Parlophone, and Victor. Lewis also appears on Solo Art, Blue Note, and other records.

Meade's first appearances in New York, in 1936 and 1937, were rather unsuccessful. Teaming in 1938 with his fellow Chicagoan, Albert Ammons, and Pete Johnson of Kansas City, Meade scored a sensational success at Carnegie Hall and the three went on to Café Society and national fame.

Boogie-woogie has been, perhaps, overrated by some critics or at least its superb qualities have not led to an appreciation of the greater New Orleans jazz. This will no doubt follow, because ears accustomed to the hot qualities of barrel-house piano are ready for authentic jazz. Boogie-woogie has become almost a cult and its many followers have accepted a large number of spurious imitations, the pseudo-boogie on piano or harpsichord of smart lady performers or symphony conductors, all of the socially correct dilutions and corruptions which society — looking for the easily understood and the merely palatable — fosters and encourages. Inferior but flashy players, like Maurice

Rocco, are too readily accepted, and authentic exponents are misled into debasing their style by devoting themselves to the sensational *tour de force*. Even Meade Lux Lewis, greatest of the three, has gone, as Louis Armstrong did, into a period of sensationalism.

The locomotive or train theme in boogie-woogie proceeds from literal imitation through ascending degrees of poetic symbolism to the attenuated melancholy of escape or the fugitive hope of deliverance as sublimated as the faraway train in Chirico's painting, *Les Joies et Les Enigmes d'Une Heure Étrange.*

The direct and explicit symbol, enforced and clarified by spoken commentary, is to be heard in the guitar blues which precede barrel-house piano. Such an early form is to be heard in Blind Sammie's *Traveling Blues* (Columbia 14484–D).

A masterpiece of the piano genre is *Honky Tonk Train Blues* of Meade Lux Lewis. Of the four recorded versions, the 1927 Paramount is the best musically, the worst from the standpoint of reproduction. The tempo is easy and it is the most melodic of all, although Lewis is customarily more rhythmic than melodic and employs such full chords in both hands that the fullness of harmony, plus the marvelous cross-rhythms for which he is famous, give the impression of two pianos. The chromatic harmonies of *Honky Tonk* are unique. They convey a feeling of almost overwhelming melancholy and evoke a tonal landscape that is lonely, almost desolate.

Each version presents new variations and there is definable change. The Parlophone and Victor records are slightly faster than the early Paramount and offer beautifully registered recording. In these, Lewis begins to omit the melodic development and devote his right hand to riffs. The Blue Note record is not only badly recorded, seeking brilliance in an overemphasis on the high sound frequencies, but it shows a marked musical deterioration. Although still a masterpiece, the twelve-inch *Honky Tonk* is taken at a tempo far too fast. The music in consequence jumps rather than rocks; melodic content has disappeared and has been replaced completely by right hand riffs.

Surrounded in New York by the riff-playing jump swing bands Meade shows the effect of his environment.

Among the many boogie-woogie train pieces a number are outstanding. Davenport's *Cow Cow Blues* has a large detachment, the calm slow power of the Cannon Ball express loafing along ahead of schedule. The *No. 29* of the St. Louis player, Wesley Wallace, is a fine, easy rolling, descriptive number with commentary comparable to the *Traveling Blues* of Blind Sammie. Wallace's imitations are beautifully conceived and musical to a high degree. *Streamline Train* by "Cripple" Clarence Lofton is rollicking and light-hearted, more like a Sunday excursion train than a streamlined express.

Lofton is capable, nevertheless, of profound music. The slow *Had A Dream*, permeated with moody thoughtfulness, shows the other side of a creative nature. "Cripple" Clarence is sometimes somber, even tragic, although his chromatic blues have a prevailing major modality. He is extremely melodic; his right hand sings in lightly moving treble figures, occasionally gathering its forces in chords or tremolandi which sound like sudden outcries in the midst of song. *In de Mornin'* is at a faster tempo, its feeling that of a sober detachment. In *South End Boogie*, recorded in 1944, we find Lofton's masterpiece to date. It is slow paced, darkly introspective, and thoughtful. Gloom and foreboding are lightened by gentle episodes of sad melody beneath which walks the deepest bass.

Meade Lux Lewis has been a ceaselessly inventive artist and numbers like *Bear Cat Crawl, Six Wheel Chaser,*[4] *Deep Fives,* and *Whistling Blues* are all of great beauty and individuality. *Celeste Blues* resulted from Meade's first meeting with the small, bell-toned, keyboard instrument. His grasp of its potentialities is revelatory; his full employment of its mellow, dissonantal sustained sonorities produces a unique masterpiece. His four-part improvisation, *Variations On a Theme*, played on harpsichord, is less successful. Its sonorities are complex and tangled.

The work of Albert Ammons is characterized by an overpow-

---

4 The coal car attached to the locomotive.

ering dynamism; it is sheer force and exultant power set forth by ample technique. *Shout for Joy, Bass Goin' Crazy, Mecca Flat Blues*, and *Boogie Woogie* are superb records, completely extravert, almost without metaphysical overtones.

Pete Johnson of Kansas City is a slightly less dynamic player. *Buss Robinson Blues, How-Long-How-Long, Kaycee on My Mind* show his style. In barrel-house vein are his records *Goin' Away Blues* and *Roll 'Em Pete*, with vocals by Joe Turner, then an unspoiled shouter.

Johnson and Ammons join in a two-piano version of boogie-woogie, *Foot Pedal Boogie*. In this number, Johnson's beautiful and characteristic chorded treble passage work accords well with Ammons's solid bass. A stirring climax, unusual in boogie-woogie, is achieved.

Other great barrel-house records can only be mentioned: Jabbo Williams' fantastic and exciting *Jab Blues;* Romeo Nelson's unrestrained *Head Rag Hop;* Montana Taylor's *Detroit Rocks* and *Indiana Avenue Stomp* (both recorded in 1928 for Vocalion and in 1946 for Circle), very individual in rhythm and harmony; Hersal Thomas' fine *Suitcase Blues;* and the grim and ominous *Hastings Street* by Charlie Spand with the guitarist Blind Blake.

Chief element in barrel-house piano is the hot African element of the spiritual and the blues. In ragtime piano, on the other hand, the European melodic element is predominant, with subsequent Afro-American transformation. The melodic nucleus of ragtime is the march tune, and the minstrel song and dance first evolved by white men as Negro imitations. Converted by Negro playing, these never underwent the degree of Africanization of the earlier music. The most melodic elements — in our sense — in Negro piano playing came from the minstrel shows and the marches, and in jazz from the marches which were thematic compositions of the same type as the quadrille and the long cake-walk tunes. A hotter and more African element entered jazz with the blues.

Ragtime piano would seem to antedate the barrel-house style.

This is merely because it appeared in printed score as early as 1897 and on phonograph records by about 1912, while barrelhouse awaited recording until the 1920's and has hardly even touched paper. Ragtime piano does not include the blues, and the blues can scarcely even be played in a "raggy" manner. Its repertory is the multi-themed tunes of *a-b-c-d* form with trio, often in two keys. It is a very rhythmic duple-timed style almost always gay, sometimes pensive, never somber. The left hand plays in octaves, single notes, or chords which generally divide the common 4/4 time into 2/4. The accent of the bass may shift to the weak beats setting up simple syncopation. The bass part constitutes an accompaniment and corresponds to one of the banjos in a minstrel duo and to the tuba in the brass band.

The right hand carries the melody and is very free, formally and rhythmically. The melody can be expressed in single notes or consecutive open chords, thirds, fifths, and octaves, in runs and figurations, and in the fuller triads and four-note chords. The rhythmic contribution of the treble is in syncopations and the inner-rhythms of displaced accents, patterns which are often rather complex and extend over several measures. Many devices are used; anticipation and retarded entry add to the variety. The treble and bass together form a constantly varied polyrhythmic continuum. Melodic variation is less characteristic of ragtime than rhythmic variation. Repeated themes, which in jazz are subjected to exhaustive melodic variation, in ragtime are often repeated verbatim or else varied by slight changes in figuration. This is not true of the work of a man like Jelly Roll Morton who was much more than a ragtime player.

The great ragtime composers were Scott Joplin, James Scott, and Thomas Million Turpin. Joplin's first published rag was *Original Rags;* by common consent his *Maple Leaf Rag* is the classic of all ragtime compositions as well as the best known. Joplin, who died in 1917, has around fifty fine rags to his credit as well as two unperformed ragtime operas. One is *Treemonisha,* published; the other, *A Guest of Honor,* unpublished and lost.

HOT PIANO

James Scott composed, among others, *Climax Rag*, *Grace and Beauty*, and *Frog Legs Rag*, each an outstanding composition. Turpin, a very heavy man, was called the "human metronome" so powerful and accurate was his beat. A busy player, his published output including *Buffalo Rag* and *St. Louis Rag*, is small in quantity, high in quality.

The city of St. Louis was the capital of ragtime activity, which extends mainly from 1896 to 1917. It reached an early high point in the ragtime contest at the St. Louis Exposition of 1904 which Morton refused to enter because he had heard that the great New Orleans player, Tony Jackson, was entered. Jelly, who felt he was not yet ready at fifteen for such competition, was much disgruntled when he found out that Jackson had not appeared in the contest.

Ragtime seized the popular fancy almost immediately. A national rage, at its height the moralists inveighed against it almost as loudly as they did later against jazz. It was spread far and wide by itinerant players and by the rolls of the newly invented player piano. White players imitated it; every high school pianist, looking for popularity, essayed it; it was the musical accompaniment of the silent motion picture; every nickelodeon echoed with its tinkly strains or its "fast western" bass played by neighborhood pianist or the mechanical piano; it accompanied tap-dancing and the vaudeville act and was played — at least after a fashion — by the respectable military bands.

Ragtime was already on the wane when it reached the New York commercial tune-smiths and the imitation rags turned out by Irving Berlin and others did nothing to give it new life. Yet ragtime persists. It is still, with the blues, at the core of jazz; it is still one of the formative elements in all jazz piano. It even entered barrel-house piano early and many entertainers play ragtime numbers of a distinct character and flavor which derive from the basic qualities of blues piano. The most authentic ragtime will suddenly be heard in a talking motion picture, as in the fairly recent *Random Harvest*. It may have reached the film sound track from a player roll, the hands of a veteran player, or those of a young disciple.

Ragtime is charming, graceful, and piquant, a music of tantalizing beauty and one, besides, that requires execution as virtuoso as any European music. The ragtime left hand, moving at rapid speed, is beyond the ability of the classically trained executant, let alone its combination polyrhythmically with the right.

Not even excepting the records of Jelly Roll Morton, which are a highly personal development out of ragtime, one must go to very recent records to hear this music played by an authentic master. Such a master is Lucky Roberts, who today, in his middle fifties, retains the incredible dynamism, verve, and technical accomplishment of his youth. Hearing him, one can understand why Scott Joplin forty-odd years ago could praise ragtime as a music to be seriously considered and could heap fiery denunciation on its "long-hair" detractors.

Coming to New York's Harlem very early in this century, Lucky, instead of joining the Midwestern school of ragtime pianists and composers, founded the later Harlem party-piano school. His early rags, like *Junk Man* — widely enough known to be played in New Orleans bands — were the foundation for the Harlem display pieces known as "shouts." In the Circle album, *Ragtime King,* are to be heard a number of his famous rags and shouts, *Junk Man;* the almost incredibly dexterous and rocking *Railroad Train Blues;* the melodic *Shy and Sly;* and *Ripples of the Nile,* a fast piece with right-hand figuration of the highest technical difficulty. Since none of Roberts' pupils, including the since-famous James P. Johnson, could perfect this piece, Lucky eventually issued it, scored as a slow number, under the title of *Moonlight Cocktail.*

Late in 1944, Session Records secured Alonzo Yancey, older brother of Jimmy, for a recording date from which three sides of barrel-house ragtime and one of barrel-house resulted. The date was timely because Alonzo died a few months later. J. H. Shayne, who had appeared on Paramount about 1925, recorded his own *Mr. Freddy's Rag* in 1946 for Circle (J–1011). The tune is as authentically, delightfully, barrel-house as if played in 1920.

Will Ezell furnished a good recorded example of barrel-house ragtime in *Mixed Up Rag* (Paramount 12688, reissue Signature 911) which has the fine, plangent sound of the upright piano. The themes are varied, fresh, and attractive. The playing lacks a little of the crispness of the great rag players; it has a little solidity held over from the barrel-house and the walking bass enters in.

The quality of white ragtime to be heard from professional players during the music's height, is demonstrated by a 1923 Gennett record, *Mah Jong*, by Sid Reinherz, a player prominent in Boston in the 1920's and still living there. *Mah Jong*, not a particularly original composition, is played with crispness and a certain charm although the rhythmic snap and freedom of really fine Negro playing is lacking.

Thoroughly decadent ragtime is shown by *Panther Rag*, a record from the late 1920's played by the Negro pianist, Earl "Father" Hines. This selection is played much too fast; it is not pure ragtime but a hybrid with jazz band piano and it is full of the merely sensation-seeking rhythmic devices of this pianist. Most noticeable of all are the glaring aberrations in tempo; no good rag player would have been guilty of these.

The current strong revival of interest in jazz is leading to one in ragtime. Young players are striving to learn the difficult style. It is fortunate that classical training does not act as a barrier to learning ragtime as it does to jazz and blues piano.

A regional style allied, as we have seen, to ragtime is the sophisticated New York Harlem style. The colorful pseudonyms of early Negro music designated the "dispensers" of party piano, the roster abounding in titles like Jack the Bear, Kid Lippy, and the Beetle. A leader of the Harlem school was, and is, James P. Johnson, who, without a nickname, nevertheless managed to play the style in a definitive form. Harlem piano was, more than any other style, akin to the player piano, no doubt because many Harlem pianists made early player rolls. Certain devices like the tremolandi and flashy, two-handed descending breaks, common on the rolls, appear with great frequence in the New York style. The party piano has a ragtime trunk upon which grow the player piano characteristics; to these are grafted European display figurations and elements of the midwestern barrel-house which men like Johnson heard and brought back from their extensive tours. The true blues, however, are not a part of Harlem piano as we know it, although pseudo-blues are played.

From 1915 to the early 1920's, James P. Johnson was a best-selling favorite on the rolls. His phonograph recording career began in 1922 or 1923 with two acoustic discs made for Okeh. Ragtime characteristics are uppermost in one of these, *Keep Off The Grass* (Okeh 4495), a version of one of James P.'s party display pieces used to "carve" his rivals. It is a tantalizingly beautiful number, with its chiming treble in a kind of stomp pattern which speeds up and then slows down over a steady, unvarying bass, and harplike treble arpeggios interrupted by measures of lightly moving rhythm. *Keep Off* has a typical ragtime structure of four separate themes in two keys.

Another, *Carolina Shout*, is probably the best-known display number of James P. In it the *blues clusters*, (the minor and major thirds or sevenths struck together) are played rhythmically over a walking bass. The music moves in a fine, easy, relaxed, and remarkably even tempo. Johnson is a human metronome like Turpin was, and his left hand work is very solid with much syncopation between the two hands. The ending is in typical player piano style, the treble and bass approaching in contrary motion just before the final chords.

Johnson's subsequent work has slowly deteriorated, becoming more sophisticated and decorative, and strongly hybridized with European classical music, although even today in his playing there are moments when, in a particular mood, he recalls his greater early accomplishments.

316

HOT PIANO

Most famous and accomplished of James P. Johnson's pupils was the late Thomas "Fats" Waller. His style was very solid and with great momentum, but without quite the rhythmic variety or the subtle nuance of Johnson at his best. Waller was also one of the best of jazz band pianists and the ragtime element remained very strong in his work. His early and thorough classical training likewise colored his playing. The result was a homogeneous but not completely hot style. Waller's playing, like Johnson's, is hot mainly in rhythm; it does not have the indefinable but pervasive hot texture derived from the peculiar harmonics and timbres, the archaic simplicity of the blues pianists. His rhythms too, which sound complex, are often much simpler in basis, arising from accented scale work and figuration, rather than from the involved cross-rhythms between the simple chords of boogie-woogie.

Waller's first solo record, made for Okeh, dates from about 1924. The two sides, *Muscle Shoal Blues* and *Birmingham Blues*, show an early style far from barrel-house but much simpler than his later manner. Organ solos of slight importance follow, recorded by Victor in 1926 and 1927. Piano solos of 1928 include several of Fats's own popular ballads, *Ain't Mis behavin'* and *I've Got A Feeling I'm Falling*, among others. In the same session he recorded two of his party "show-pieces." *Numb Fumbling* is in a slow tempo with the blues harmony converted into the sophisticated Harlem pseudo-blues. Pianistically, it has passages of great beauty but it is not completely Negroid. The other side, *Smashing Thirds,* is a fast piece built around a motive of fugitive scale work in treble thirds, irregularly spaced. A piece of extreme technical difficulty in certain passages, it is a far cry from barrel-house blues although musically very beautiful.

A 1935 group includes *Alligator Crawl*, which uses the barrel-house walking bass decoratively in contrast with more sophisticated elements, and *Clothes Line Ballet,* which deliberately contrasts slow sentimental sections with brisk ragtime episodes in a pastiche of musical comedy music. Fats, with his

317

prodigious technique and his combination of classical and hot training, was well equipped to make and vastly enjoy such a satire.

Fats Waller lived and played expansively; his zest for life and music was vast. He will long be remembered for his gay and infectious humor, his many melodic compositions, and for his devotion, so far as he understood it, to hot music. He found his own answer to commercialism in satire and concealed irony. In his own way he met and mastered the Pharisaic enemy. He drank — not as Beiderbecke did — for escape from defeat, but as a part of his lusty living; and under the sweet right hand chords of the sentimental trash he had to play, the solid left rolled on like heat thunder on a summer day.

The ideal band pianists were Fats Waller, at his best, and Jelly Roll Morton. Different in individual styles, both had the same concept of the piano in the band. They kept it subordinate in the ensemble; in their hands it became a sort of liaison agent between the rhythm section and the polyphonic melody section. They both produced a steady, firm, and continuous beat but did not indiscriminately add treble melodies to confuse the polyphony and to be lost in it. In this respect they were adroit and highly imaginative, placing their melodic comments on, and in addition to, the polyphony, much as the clarinet does in the caesuras of the progressing counterpoint. At other times, by a wise selection of register and melodic line, they would fit a melody into a complete band polyphony. The piano would emerge in solo, as Fats and Jelly Roll played it, not in a fatuous exhibition unrelated to the context but in real variation on the basic theme that carried the musical development onward. Such is the ensemble and solo work of Morton as we find it in *The Chant,* for example, and of Waller in *You're Not the Only Oyster in the Stew.* In the jazz period of 1925–1928, the much lauded Earl Hines provided no such intelligent piano part in the band. Rhythmically he tended to be a disrupting influence and in solo he said the little he had to say in a sensational, exhibitionistic manner.

HOT PIANO

We have already analyzed the chief elements of Jelly Roll Morton's solo piano style and scored significant excerpts. His playing is the definitive jazz piano and represents the highest development of and from ragtime in which the set form of the score is subjected to ceaseless and significant variation. He broadened the expressive power of ragtime, infusing it with the hot elements of jazz and the blues, making ragtime piano tone hotter and bluer, choosing judiciously elements of harmony, rhythm, and figuration from barrel-house. He introduced true stomping into the rag.

Morton's numerous solos appeared on many labels and were recorded from 1922 or 1923 through 1939. A number are supposedly available currently. On the Jazzman label: *Honky-Tonk Music, Winin' Boy Blues, Creepy Feeling, Finger Buster.* On the S–D label (reissues): *Frogimore Rag, 35th Street Blues, Mamamita.* In the General album (called New Orleans Memories): *Mister Joe,*[5] *The Crave, Original Rags* (Joplin), *The Naked Dance, King Porter Stomp.*[6] On the Bluebird label: *Fat Frances, Pep.* On the Victor label. *Freakish,* and *Seattle Hunch.* On the Brunswick label (reissued from Vocalion): *The Pearls, King Porter Stomp, Sweetheart O' Mine (Frogimore Rag),* and *Fat Meat and Greens.*

More reissues are in prospect and at least one recent discovery, a twelve-inch version of the beautiful *Pearls,* is planned for early issue. The recent *Freakish* is a different master than the original Victor, and Jelly's reputation for never playing a number in the same way twice is borne out by these variant discs. The striking composition is quite differently articulated on each master with differences that are subtle but important.

Among other Negro pianists with strong elements of ragtime, the late Alex Hill should be mentioned. *Stompin' 'Em Down,* played with traps, is his own composition, a tune of great melodic charm. Hill's playing was raggy with an exciting and

[5] A tribute to King Oliver. In band version this tune is called *Buffalo Blues.*
[6] Named for a fine early pianist, Porter King, greatly admired by Morton.

319

very Negroid rhythmicality. A stomped bass section has considerable barrel-house feeling.

The Kansas City player, Mary Lou Williams, has a style based on ragtime and very akin to Harlem piano. The playing of her best period, as shown on *Night Life*, recorded about 1931 for Brunswick, is scarcely comparable to that of James P. Johnson. Of late an entertainer at Café Society, Mary Lou has become sophisticated and her style has lost much of its original vitality. Her recent essays in boogie-woogie are unconvincing.

The white Chicagoan, Joe Sullivan, plays a hybrid style with barrel-house elements compounded with Fats Waller and Earl Hines influences. The assimilation of the varied elements is not complete, nor does he play a real blues; he misses in harmony and in phrasing. His best record is perhaps *Little Rock Getaway*, his own composition, in which Harlem piano and Hines's trumpet style (which was based on Louis Armstrong's trumpet phrasing) are fairly well integrated. This record, although hybrid, has an exciting quality.

Among many other white pianists, Jess Stacy played originally in a style modeled after that of Earl Hines. His most recent work is in the vein called "modern" piano.

Modern piano is a highly decadent form. One phase is an overornamented, decorative style; another is a pastiche of the Romantics and Impressionists, particularly Delius and Debussy, even interlarded at times with pseudo-boogie-woogie or ragtime.

Art Tatum and Teddy Wilson are the leading exponents of the decorative style. Their work, like Ellington's band music, is a string of effects, a thoroughly shallow piece of showmanship. There is no logical continuity in this musical hash. It resembles the contemporary orchestral radio arrangement in which no instrument or group of instruments is permitted to carry any development through, but must give way to the next effect which enters even in the midst of a melody. The playing of Tatum, Wilson, and their followers is a musical sampler cross-stitched with runs and filigrees, grace notes and trills.

HOT PIANO

Tatum's technique, which is regarded with awe, is largely a myth. His technique is show technique, his most dazzling effects "lie under the hands" as pianists say. Until he plays one of Morton's truly difficult compositions, in a manner worthy of its composer, his technical prowess will still remain to be demonstrated.

Best-known exponent of matinee piano and the "famous composers pastiche" is Duke Ellington. A record like that of his own *Solitude* on Victor is a thoroughly languishing opus, stemming completely from European sources, without a shred of hot rhythm or tone. Objectively judged, this is a completely derivative European romantic salon piece.

The myth that swing and this kind of piano playing are modern music is one that needs to be exploded. They are either decadent or they are reactionary, harking back to European compositional schools which can no longer be called modern. Hot piano and hot New Orleans jazz are modern in the truest sense because they introduce new ideas and lines of development into music. Their pathway leads to tomorrow.

14.

trumpets
for tomorrow

As New Orleans jazz stands today it is in a favorable position. Even though it is played but little compared with earlier days, skilled players are alive to play it, and young players abound who might learn it before the tradition is broken. Although, to a degree, it still carries the unfavorable connotations of its name, jazz has never before had the ethical and social sanctions it is beginning to receive today. And while its revolutionary quality as an art form still eludes the understanding of some and conflicts with the various self-interests of others, liberal, intellectual, artistic, and social forces are beginning, nevertheless, to align themselves behind it. Its wide popular acceptance dissipated fifteen or twenty years ago, but critical understanding of the artistic meaning and the social and cultural import of jazz, is beginning to develop. In the long run this will be of permanent value to jazz activity.

Today's growing understanding and activity in the jazz field are one stage in a process of gradual awakening that began in the early 1930's. The impetus for this came partly from abroad, particularly in France where a small group viewed Afro-American music with a perspective that has been difficult for us in America to achieve. Hugues Panassié assumed leadership of this group with the publication of his book *Le Jazz Hot* in 1934. This work was of great influence. We now know that its content is confused because of the failure to base its values on the or-

322

iginal jazz of the New Orleans Negroes,[1] but the great enthusiasm displayed for the music and the total absence of racial prejudice gave a favorable bent to the serious interest beginning to arise here.

From France, too, came the first serious work in record analysis so important in jazz. The *Hot Discography* of Charles Delaunay is a cataloguing of records with dates and personnel, and is still the most comprehensive work of its sort. Only today is this activity beginning to be correlated and carried forward in America.

Before 1935 a small number of Americans, turning their backs on the hybrid and rapidly degenerating hot music then current, had begun a cultivated study of the great polyphonic, improvised jazz still being played not only in New Orleans but also (unrecognized and almost underground) in many other cities.

The small magazines, characteristic of an *avant-garde* artistic movement, began shortly to appear. The first of these, *The Ray*, first published in 1938 was, during its comparatively short life, the organ of the Hot Record Society. This group, like another membership organization also nonexistent today, the United Hot Clubs of America, served to channelize the activity of jazz lovers in this country. The magazine was the first to begin the assembling of discographical information and biographical material in America.

This upsurge of serious interest resulted in the publication, in 1939, of the book *Jazzmen* [2] which proved a strong force in stimulating the jazz awakening. This book was the first to attempt an authentic description of the New Orleans background, accurate and appreciative biographies of the then almost unknown early players of jazz, and indications of the origin of the music. Against this positive accomplishment must be set its

---

[1] A fault rectified to a degree in Panassié's later book, *The Real Jazz*. New York: 1942. The first book was written before the author had any considerable access to the authentic music.

[2] By Frederic Ramsay, Jr., Charles Edward Smith, William Russell, and others.

attempt — arising from its collaborative authorship — to reconcile the irreconcilable natures of jazz and swing.

Other magazines appeared, discontinued publication and still others began. This process, indicative of healthy and growing interest, continues today. Clubs and societies have formed and disbanded, each in its way contributing to the cultural cause which jazz represents. Club and museum lectures, high school and college study courses are being given and these, too, help to spread the truth.

White musicians, especially young ones, began to show an interest in pure New Orleans jazz. This was due partly to an instinctive revulsion to over-commercial swing, partly to the tendency among musicians to collect and study old records. Bands were formed that attempted, with more or less success, to play real, polyphonic jazz. Best and most successful of these groups was the Lu Watters' Yerba Buena Jazz Band. This group, with the King Oliver Creole Band instrumentation, was formed in 1939 and disbanded in 1942, not, however, without having made some records for the Jazzman label. The band's appearances at the Dawn Club off lower Market Street in San Francisco (near to the spot where Oliver had played almost twenty years before), welded together a strong jazz following on the Pacific Coast. The records, during this period, exerted a considerable influence throughout the country, rather especially, perhaps, because the band was white. Watters' group did not survive long enough to work itself free of its arrangements based on Oliver and Morton records. These, nevertheless, are interesting as the most successful attempt up to now to cast jazz polyphony in a permanent form. Watters is a more than capable cornetist, although his tone is white. More Negroid and more inspirational is the playing of Turk Murphy and Ellis Horne, trombonist and clarinetist, respectively, with the Yerba Buena group.

The Watters Band re-formed in 1946 and, at this date, is playing again in San Francisco. During the Watters disbandment, New Orleans jazz itself began strongly to revive.

TRUMPETS FOR TOMORROW

All of this, of course, has aroused the hostility of the commercial music interests. Sensing a serious challenge to their monopolistic vending of the mediocre, but financially profitable slick packaged musical trash, they have consolidated their forces and are fighting back. Their program is twofold: to discredit real jazz — which means the New Orleans, Dixieland and, from their point of view, Chicago styles; and to effect a virtual censorship of the listening public by using their almost complete control of the outlets of distribution to keep jazz from being heard.

This clarifying of the issues is a good thing. Commercialism will not, of course, be able to interdict jazz. It will be — is being — heard. But the result of the present campaign will be that very shortly swing will not be able to masquerade blandly under the name of jazz.

Besides the commercial, two kinds of hostility remain. The one, moralistic, is diminishing and will disappear more or less completely with time. The other, opposition of the musical classicist, familiarly dubbed "long-hair," is one which will be at least partly cleared up by a real understanding of what jazz is and what it means, in itself and in relation to other music.

As a musical force, the influence of jazz on the serious composer in the European style has been very strong, particularly in the last twenty-five years. But its intrinsic value is not to be measured by this. In European terms it is a profoundly revolutionary music and if, seventy years ago, it anticipated many of the trends of modern music, it represented as a whole a direction which Western music cannot take without losing its own identity. Its composition in performance by the improvising group, horizontal variational-development with an eschewal of architectural form, different concepts of timbre, pitch, and tone production, the principle of perpetual polyrhythms and rhythmic counterpoint — all of these are antithetic in whole or part to European practices.

The step in understanding which remains to be taken is to perceive that disparity need not imply a mutual hostility. The cause of classical music, like that of jazz, is best served by making the basic distinction and setting up for hot music the separate system of critical standards which it requires. This task, which is nearing completion, has been long and difficult because of:

a. Hostility of the classicist and the moralist.
b. Refusal, on many grounds, to take jazz seriously.
c. Complications due to the race situation.
d. Difficulty in hearing jazz freshly with an unconditioned mind.
e. Confusion with many forms of hybrid or pseudo-jazz.
f. The resulting difficulty in separating those elements common to the various kinds of music from those peculiar to the one or the other.

Regardless of hostility, hot music goes on strongly in one or another of its forms and the principle of hot playing is very strong. It is in at least as healthy a condition as the classical. Recognition that it has arrived to stay will do much, not only to clarify the situation vis-à-vis the composed Western music, but the situation within the field of hot music itself. Jazz will emerge not only as an important music in the general scene of culture but as incomparably the most serious and valuable manifestation in its own field.

Jazz can and should be — once its artistic quality is generally recognized — an important factor in alleviating the racial tensions between Negro and white in America. To proceed from acceptance of the Negro as a creator or executant in the white musical arts, to his acceptance as creator of his own, is only a single step, if a long one. In this way jazz, already a complex and powerfully beneficial social force, can become one of great importance in the problems of our democracy. The concept of two great musical arts existing side by side is one of practical as well as symbolic salutariness. Apart from prejudice, the simplicity of this concept is all that stands today in the way of its acceptance. For jazz, indeed, although primarily the music of a race, as a cultural and social force is not thus limited.

326

Although there is little point, today, in rehashing the bitter controversy and critical confusion which greeted jazz in the 1920's, it is of value, perhaps, to highlight the salient points in comparison with the chief contemporary points of view.

It is most important to recognize that, while most of the critical pronunciamentos on jazz originated, in that period, in New York and Paris, real New Orleans jazz was not then being heard in the former city at all, and only to a slight degree in the latter. Judgments were based on the spurious white and Negro forms of so-called symphonic jazz and swing. In view of this fact, adverse critical comments are less surprising than the occasional favorable and discerning ones. Most of these older articles — like many written today — must be read with the understanding that what is being written about is not jazz at all.

The extreme venom of some of the approaches of that day would be more surprising if it did not persist, covertly and better disguised, today. The very titles of some early articles give a clear idea of the bitterness which jazz, for one reason or another, evoked. The Ladies' Home Journal in 1921 published an article entitled, *Unspeakable Jazz Must Go.* Another article of the same period appeared under the heading, *To War on Jazz with Better Songs.* The magazine Etude asked uneasily in 1924, *What's the Matter with Jazz?,* a question which was more generally being asked — particularly outside the music profession — about serious composed music itself. A little later in this year the same magazine held a symposium, *Where is Jazz Leading America?,* to which an extraordinary variety of writers contributed. A few of the opinions, learned or otherwise, follow.

George Ade, humorist: "Good syncopation is legitimate and probably enjoyed to the limit by many people . . . slow to admit the fact. It has been evolved naturally from Negro songs and dance tunes and is the characteristic American music if we have such a thing." Ade then proceeds to praise Paul Whiteman!

Mrs. H. A. Beach: "vulgar . . . debasing."

327

Felix Borowski: "not pernicious." "Disapproval . . . result of dancing . . . rather than of the music itself."

Charles Wakefield Cadman: "Jazz is not spiritual."

John Alden Carpenter: "I am convinced that our American popular music (please note that I avoid labeling it jazz) is by far the most spontaneous, the most personal, the most characteristic, and, by virtue of these qualities, the most important musical expression that America has achieved." Carpenter, deploring moralistic judgments, avoids the word jazz apparently for this reason.

Dr. Frank Damrosch: "Jazz is . . . caricature . . . its effects are made by exaggeration, distortion and vulgarisms." "Self-expression of a primitive race."

John Philip Sousa: "There is no reason, with its exhilarating rhythm, its melodic ingenuities, why it should not become one of the accepted forms."

Henry T. Finck quoted from the New York Sun an interesting observation on the origin of the name jazz. "The word jazz is African in origin. It is common on the Gold Coast. In his studies of the creole patois and idioms, Lafcadio Hearn reported that the word jazz, meaning to speed things up, to make excitement was common among the blacks of the South, and had been adopted by the creoles as a term to be applied to music of a rudimentary, syncopated type. In the old plantation days when the slaves were having one of their holidays and the fun languished, some West Coast African would cry out, 'Jazz 'er up!' and this would be the cue for fast and furious fun. . . . Not necessarily speed, for an exceedingly popular jazz is the slow drag." [3]

Dr. Stephen T. Wise: "I am not sure jazz is leading America. . . . If America did not think jazz, feel jazz, and dream jazz, jazz would not have taken a dominant place in the music of America. . . . When America regains its soul, jazz will go, not before — that is to say, it will be relegated to the dark and scarlet haunts whence it came and whither unwept it will return, after America's soul is reborn."

Robert M. Stults, listed as composer of *The Sweetest Story Ever Told:* "It is hard to talk about this mongrel music and keep calm . . . but I am optimistic! There is every indication that the ballad of the past, with its strong heart appeal, is

[3] *Jazz-Lowbrow and highbrow.* Finck, H. T.: *Etude.* August, 1924.

again coming into favor. This is strongly indicated by the number of love songs that have recently sprung into popularity. I may be pardoned if I mention *The Sweetest Story Ever Told,* a song [with] sales now approaching the three million mark. . . . Jazz has created a 'malarious' atmosphere in the musical world. It is abnormal. The air needs clarifying!"

Leopold Stokowski: "Jazz has come to stay. It is an expression . . . of the breathless, superactive times in which we are living, and it is useless to fight against it. Already its vigor, its new vitality, is beginning to manifest itself."

Many important composers have seen valuable elements in jazz even when they have not uniformly perceived its complete nature. Maurice Ravel has been quoted as considering jazz the only original contribution America has so far made to music. A posthumously published magazine article by Sergei Rachmaninoff stated, "The seed of the future music of America lies in Negro music."

The modern French composer, Darius Milhaud, has furnished me with a special translation of an article which he wrote in 1923. It was published in the German magazine, Der Querschnitt, and appeared in this country in 1924 in Living Age. In this article, entitled *The Jazz Band and Negro Music,* Milhaud analyzes the large swing band, Negro and white, from a compositional and orchestral standpoint, perceiving the distinctive tonal, instrumental, and rhythmic features of this sort of group. This was to him — as to everyone in the confusion of the times and in lieu of the real thing — the jazz band. Nevertheless he did his own research in Harlem and heard — if not jazz — at least the blues and puts his finger on the important elements of Negroid quality and hot improvisation. His words are worth quoting in part. They are historic writing on jazz.

Side by side with this music, which is as mechanized and as precise as a machine thanks to its clear style of writing and the unique instrumental combinations obtained by American jazz orchestras, we find another kind of music which, although it came from the same source as the other, has developed in a completely different manner among the Negroes of North America. We must obviously trace the origin of jazz music back to the Negroes. The primitive African instincts have remained deeply rooted among the black race of the United States, and it is there that we must look for the source of this terrific rhythmic power as well as the source of the very expressive melodies full of the lyricism which only an oppressed race can ever produce. . . . Here we find the same tenderness, the same sadness, the same faith that was expressed by the slaves, who in their songs compared their fate to that of the captive Jew in Egypt, and appealed with all their soul to a Moses who would save them. (Go down, Moses!)

With the Negroes, the racial elements have remained more intact. While in the jazz of the Americans everything is carefully studied, among the Negroes improvisation plays a larger part; however, one must have tremendous musical resources and power of imagination to do this successfully. From the technical point of view they seem to have greater ease; each instrument follows its own melodic line and improvises in accordance with the harmony of the piece. We are constantly presented with a play of lines often disconcertingly complex, and the use of simultaneous major and minor chords, and quarter-tones obtained by mixing the glissando and vibrato techniques (lengthening the slide of the trombone, strong vibration of the trumpet valve, and the imperceptible misplacing of the finger on the violin string).

The quarter-tone has a uniquely expressive character and belongs to diatonic harmony, in the same way as chromatics which are considered as passing notes in the course of a diatonic scale. This has no connection, however, with the quarter-tone system which is at present being studied in central Europe, and which is based on the multiplication by two of twelve notes and belongs to the atonal scale.

With Negro music, moreover, we get away from that purely mundane character which is too much a part of American jazz music. The Negro dance music still has a savage and African character; the intense and insistent rhythms and the melodies in which there is something desperate and tragic. In a little night club, like the Capitol, at the upper end of Lenox Avenue toward 140th Street, it is not unusual to hear a Negress singing the same melody for over an hour, an often poignant melody with a pattern as pure as any classic recitative, and supported by jazz which forms a background of incessantly varied melodies. Such variations seem to give the fullness of a symphony. This is a far cry from the elegant Broadway dance music one hears here at the Claridge Hotel in Paris. Among the Negroes we find the source itself of this music — its profoundly human side, which can be as completely moving as any universally recognized musical masterpiece.

Perceptively sympathetic to jazz is another noted composer, the American, Virgil Thomson. In 1936 he wrote of Louis Armstrong:

His style of improvisation would seem to have combined the highest reaches of instrumental virtuosity with the most tensely disciplined melodic structure and the most spontaneous emotional expression, all of which in one man you must admit to be pretty rare.[4]

And in 1943 he wrote of Bunk Johnson:

He is celebrated in the histories of hot music not only for his integrity as an artist but for his mastery of that imperious trumpet tone chiefly familiar to laymen nowadays through the work of his pupil Louis Armstrong. . . . "Bunk" Johnson himself is an artist of delicate imagination, meditative in style rather than flashy, and master of the darkest trumpet tone I have ever heard. He is also the greatest master of "blues," or off-pitch notes it has been my pleasure to encounter. The degrees of his deviation from normal pitch are infinite, and the taste with which he exploits this variety merits no less a word than impeccable. His timbres, his intonations, and his melodic invention are at all times expressive, at all times reasonable, and at all times completely interesting. His work takes on, in consequence, and so does that of those working with him, depth, ease, and lucidity. Nothing could be less sentimental or speak more sincerely from the heart, less jittery or move around more freely. Certainly no music was ever less confused.

This quotation and that following are from Thomson's book, *The Musical Scene.*[5]

---

[4] In the *Modern Music Quarterly*, May–June, 1936.
[5] Thomson, Virgil: *The Musical Scene.* New York: 1945.

Hearing the New Orleans style — or at least an approximation of it — in the band which was playing with Bunk, Thomson wrote of the music itself:

> The basic rhythm of his band is so solid and so plain that its
> effect on players and public alike is the opposite of that nervous
> exasperation that is frequently a result of jazz [6] performance.
> It stills, rather, the nerves and allows the mind free play in
> that purely auditory perception of feeling that is the alpha and
> the omega of music. . . . This sort of music is as cultural an
> activity as any and more so than most. Certainly it is more
> rarely to be encountered at a high degree of purity than
> the symphonic stuff. Both kinds of music, of course, are de-
> plorably commercialized these days. Its purity, nevertheless,
> a noncommercial quality, is wherein any music's cultural value
> lies.

In a recent interview with Frederic Ramsey, Jr., the Bra-
zilian composer, Hector Villa-Lobos, made a number of interesting comments on jazz which are indicative of the growing
contemporary viewpoint. At one point he remarks, apropos of
improvisation and technique:

> You see, when the jazz musicians play, it is an expression of
> themselves as musicians. It takes great originality and spirit to
> improvise. And when a composer writes down, he is working
> with the intellect, consciously, with the intention that others
> should follow his instructions, and in so doing, re-create his
> music. In this, the composer is the individual, in the romantic
> tradition of European concert music. That is why, also, the
> classical musician cannot approach the jazz musician — he
> simply cannot do the things a jazz musician can do with his
> instrument, any instrument!

At another he shows an awareness of the separate and distinct characters of jazz and Western music, remarking, "Of
course, there are great resources in jazz. And I'm sure every
modern composer is studying them — but many are doing it
secretly," he added with a smile. "But as for transposing the
great jazz improvisations into concert music, that is ridiculous,

---

[6] Thomson undoubtedly refers here to swing.

it is silly. I do not use jazz in my music. . . . But you know that business about writing down jazz and using it in composed music — *c'est du pur chichi, du chichi de musiciens!*"

When a serious composer praises jazz music or even swing, it is unbiased praise, for jazz is the music without formal, written scores, composed by the players in the playing, while swing is the field in which the arranger is of much greater importance than the composer. So, naturally enough, many composers are opposed to pure jazz, some because they do not understand it — or perhaps have never heard it — others because they do not like it, others still because they have tried and failed to use it in their earlier music. What is needed, of course, is the understanding that the two musics are separate fields and need not conflict.

The prevailing line among composers who, inimical to jazz, nevertheless recognize the power and position of hot music today, is the familiar technique of "damning with faint praise." Others are more outspoken like the European Ernst Křenek, who writes, "Many composers who worried over the salvation or re-establishment of tonality have resorted to jazz as a method of regeneration. For a time I was one of them." [7]

Křenek's attack on jazz is based on the narrow viewpoint of atonality (dispensing with fixed musical keys) which he considers essential to modern music. His critique is along the following main lines:

a. Jazz is anti-music: it explodes the tonal order in the European sense.

The old idea that jazz is not a music in its own right but a movement to destroy the European. [8]

b. In its character of anti-music "jazz generally takes an unscrupulous attitude toward the traditional choice of musical elements, and of harmonic elements in particular, since the latter are the most direct characteristics of the sound language."

Jazz, of course, has its own traditions in line with the true

[7] This and succeeding quotations from Křenek are from his book, *Music Here and Now*. New York: 1939.

[8] My commentary in italics after each point.

nature of music. Melody and rhythm are the most direct and natural characteristics of the sound language while harmony is an artificial development.

c. Excitement and rhythmic disturbance. "The excitement is not due to harmonic boldness alone, but rather — and here we find the mainspring of the jazz extravaganzas — to apparently unrestrained disturbances of the meter, the so-called syncopations. Accents within the two breaks which ensure the regular period are quite freely distributed, without regard to the constant meter underlying the composition as a whole."

This is a partial and incorrect view. Jazz presents a rhythmic counterpoint of cross-rhythms and inner-rhythms of which the fixed beat is a part. Křenek refers to "fictitious" supensions. In the counterpoint one voice may actually suspend the beat while another sounds it or, in Morton's silent breaks, the beat is completely suspended for a period of time.

d. "The machine-like frame is America's contribution to later tonality."

This criticism would be valid applied to swing but not, as Křenek applies it, to jazz. For jazz is the freest and most un-machine-like of musics although one of the most systematic. Ceaseless melodic and rhythmic variations are substituted for changes in meter, tempo, and key, that is all.

e. Jazz does not invent, it copies the progress of serious music. "However, in the elementary simplicity of the basic metrical conditions established by jazz, entertainment music found a last chance to participate, if only partially, in the progress being made in the new material."

Why, then, did some of the revolutionary qualities of modern music, from 1910 onward, appear in jazz by 1875? Why then did Křenek try early to copy jazz? And by what subtle definition is a symphony concert not entertainment, or a Strauss or Chopin waltz not dance music, however sublimated?

f. Jazz is ultimately conservative. "Jazz is progressive as to material, but conservative so far as its ultimate attitude and effect are concerned . . . jazz represents the last grandiose attempt of tonality to hide its disintegration."

This is wide of the mark. Material in jazz is unimportant; treatment is important and revolutionary. Jazz cannot be tied to any European modernisms, like atonality, because it has its own concepts, processes, and aims. Even that it anticipated, and now coincides with certain modern European trends, is coinci-

*dental and unimportant because jazz is modern and growing
in its own right.*

g. The deprecation of improvisation.

*With the last, the real bone of contention appears. Neithei
Křenek nor any other composer opposed to jazz has dared to
put the controversy on its actual basis. This is its real challenge
of the composer on his own ground. The first move in self-defense
was to try to take over, to use it, to assimilate it, to go it one
better. This attempt failed because of the intractibility of the
flowing jazz movement to formal construction and notation, and,
in somewhat lesser degree, because of the marked inability of
the legitimate performer to speak the language or to master the
formidable technical difficulties which the jazz player surmounts
with ease. Jazz is made in spontaneous group improvision; this
is a threat to the composer unless, of course, he is willing to
remain in his own field and leave the jazz player to his. This
he is not always content to do. Jazz, therefore, must be deprecated, belittled, and discredited by every subtle and unfair means
at his disposal. This is the age-old pattern of prejudiced self-
interest. It is not surprising to find some of these men allying
themselves with the arch enemy of jazz, the commercial interests
and the big swing band. Swing, a mediocre hybrid, is no real
competition to the symphony-smith and he knows it. The nar-
rowness of this viewpoint can only be deprecated as one not made
necessary by jazz itself. There is room enough for both jazz and
Western music. The greatest enemy of both is the commercial,
the opportunistic, the plagiaristic, and the trivial.*

A common way to attack jazz is to point at its alleged nar-
rowness of emotional, expressive scope, or of technical means.
For example, the composer Aaron Copland writes:

> From the composer's viewpoint, jazz had only two expressions:
> either it was the well-known "blues" mood, or the wild, aban-
> doned, almost hysterical and grotesque mood so dear to the
> youth of all ages. These two moods encompass the whole gamut
> of jazz emotion.[9]

The only reply necessary to such an observation is that one
should know whereof he speaks. Let the authors of such dicta
take the trouble to hear jazz, *real* jazz, and enough of it.

9 Copland, Aaron: *Our New Music.* New York: 1941.

A subtler technique is that of making an ostensible study of jazz as a background for the invidiously comparative, debunking process. This sets up the straw man, then knocks him down. A typical maneuver of this sort is the book *Jazz, Hot and Hybrid*, by Winthrop Sargeant.[10] The book is not a study of jazz at all but the notably vulnerable music of Tin Pan Alley which the author chooses to call jazz. The compositions of Zez Confrey, Irving Berlin, and Gershwin are given great space. The only band music approaching the hot that is examined is the swing of Fletcher Henderson, Benny Goodman, and others.

With the blues and Bessie Smith, Sargeant comes close to the New Orleans jazz of which he is quite evidently ignorant. Of Bessie, in fact, he is constrained to say, "But almost any unbiased and musically sensitive person will admit, on hearing them, that Bessie Smith's recordings . . . are musical experiences of a high and poetic order."

After a deal of apparently erudite musical analysis, Sargeant proceeds to his final chapter, *Jazz in Its Proper Place*. Here he attacks jazz for its lack of architectural form and proportion, and finally, from the moralistic point of view which has been outdated since Ruskin and the reign of Queen Victoria. "Jazz," he writes, "is an art without positive moral values, an art that evades those attitudes of restraint and intellectual poise upon which complex civilizations are built." [11]

In his obsession with introspective meanings and the architectural complexities of European music, Sargeant is deaf to the extraverted, living meanings, the *moving* complexities of jazz. The blues captivate him momentarily, for these give an inkling of the profound — but not subjective — emotional depths and drama of which jazz, like the blues, is capable.

It needs to be pointed out that attacks on jazz do not ultimately affect the music or, to a decisive extent, its dedicated players. Of all musics none has remained purer than the proper Negro jazz of New Orleans. It is still played and as long as it

10 Sargeant, Winthrop: *Jazz, Hot and Hybrid*. New York: 1938.
11 Ibid. p. 217.

is played it is the best possible rebuttal of inaccurate or false statements. A music whose essential message strikes directly to the heart even if the mind is slow to grasp its complexities, its place, whether or not it shall resume development, is secure both in musical and in general social history.

Some of the greatest and purest jazz has been recorded, in fact, in 1944 to 1946. Kid Ory reappeared triumphantly with the trumpeter, Mutt Carey, in eight sides which picked jazz up where the New Orleans Wanderers left it in 1927.[12]

A number of current twelve-inch discs on the American Music label present classic New Orleans jazz with strong street-band characteristics. Bunk Johnson plays on most of these sides with a great band which included George Lewis, perhaps the finest jazz clarinetist since Johnny Dodds, and Jim Robinson, a very strong tail-gate trombone player.

In 1946 Harriet Janis and Eugene Grossman undertook recording activity with me. We had several objectives in mind. One of the most important of these, in our estimation, was to combine writing and recording to get pure jazz and other Afro-American music not merely to collectors but to the large public of today that has seldom, if ever, heard it. Another was to hunt out the great talents of twenty or more years ago that have lapsed into obscurity and give them new opportunity and hope. Supplementing this was the desire to discover and encourage young players of promise.

To date the project has borne fruit in a series of recordings on the Circle label that cover many phases of hot music. Older talent brought out of obscurity includes the great blues singer "Chippie" Hill; the New Orleans clarinetist Albert Nicholas, and trumpeters Peter Bocage and Lee Collins; the fine barrel-house piano players Montana Taylor, J. H. Shayne, and Dan Burley; a number of gifted Harlem pianists in the "party-

[12] Crescent Records: No. 1. *South* and *Creole Song,* (cited in Chapter IX.) No. 2. *Blues for Jimmy* and *Get Out of Here.* (Personnel: Kid Ory; Mutt Carey; Omer Simeon, clarinet; Ed Garland, string-bass; Bud Scott, guitar; Buster Wilson, piano; Alton Redd, drums.) No. 3. *My Maryland* and *Didn't He Ramble.* No. 4. *Down Home Rag* and *1919 March.* (Same personnel, except Darnell Howard in place of Simeon, Ram Hall in place of Redd.)

piano" tradition; and several fine spiritual singers, one of whom, Berenice Phillips, is an authentic older singer of the Jubilee hymns, and Harold Lewis, her eighteen-year-old nephew, who is possessor of a baritone voice that ranks him as a major artistic discovery.

The success so far attained would seem to justify hope in an ultimate objective of Circle Records, to document fully the cultural continuity from African music to jazz.

Significantly, too, 1945 saw the two great bands of the Crescent and American Music records accorded the opportunity of bringing New Orleans jazz in actual performance to the public for dancing. As this book is written, Ory and his group have played for five consecutive months at the Jade Room in Hollywood, and Bunk Johnson's Band, with a leader of superb, unimpaired power, has been appearing for nearly two months at the Stuyvesant Casino in New York.

In Hollywood, the general public responded immediately; Ory has scored a popular success and seems fairly launched upon a new career. New York, however, which has heard no real jazz except on records since 1916, is a notoriously hard nut to crack and has been slower to respond. Nevertheless, despite unbusiness-like handling and a pronounced lack of advertisement, the nucleus of jazz lovers in the metropolis were able to maintain Bunk's run until publicity had accrued and the music was brought to public attention. Given any considerable success at both ends of the continent, the younger generation of Negro players and the youth cannot fail to become interested, and the folk-academy may begin to function again.

So New Orleans jazz, if diminished in quantity, is unimpaired in quality. Some of the older men seem to improve with age. Chicago jazz, to judge by the latest recordings, shows an improvement, at least temporary. Eight sides, on Blue Note, bring together a white combination built around the pianist Art Hodes. The blues they play come nearer to the authentic style; there is more coherence as a whole in these records as well as a beat — emanating largely from Hodes — much closer to the in-

definable Negro musical pulse. The clarinet of the late Rod Cless
is still in the rhapsodic Teschmaker vein and fits somewhat im-
properly into the ensembles. Max Kaminsky plays a simple and
sober trumpet.

Understanding of the structure and meaning of jazz is growing. Without ethical or social sanctions in the past, it nevertheless commanded through crucial times the utmost purity and
dedication of purpose from its players. As a social force it has
been the opposite of that which was commonly assumed. It is
a liberating, not a libertinizing, force. It has freed the bodily,
mental, and spiritual rhythms, has furnished a catharsis of the
emotions. It does not sing *about* sorrow or frustration: in the
African manner it casts out these devils — acts them *out.*

Jazz has been, and is, a strong social force without becoming
on the one hand propaganda, or on the other the increasingly
self-conscious and sacerdotal message of "serious" music. It
brought dancing back to music where it belongs, and music back
to those who make it and who dance to it. It is more than merely
popular, it is profoundly of, by, and for the people. It is beautifully functional and functionally beautiful rather than pre-
tentiously inutile, gravely pompous. The myth of "fine art" has
needed exploding. Jazz is helping to explode it.

Without the superb and significant dissonances, the vital polyphony and varied timbres of jazz to prepare the way, the
modern composer might have no audience even today. Jazz has
helped restore the open mind to culture. Free melody is once
more comprehensible to those who have learned its symbols and
its movements from jazz. Beautiful and classic music like Bali-
nese and Chinese — which once sounded harsh, enigmatic, and
primitive to our ears — are as open books. And jazz can lead, as
well, to a deeper understanding of some of the really vital things
in great European music. Many a person has pretended to like
the polyphonic intricacies of Bach as he would subscribe to a
respectable religion while understanding not a whit of it. To
the ear trained in New Orleans jazz, the polyphonic streams of
modern music and equally of the great Baroque masters, are

revealed lucid and articulate. With all of this, jazz is *the* one of our musical expressions most universally liked by every race throughout the world.

This is because it is incalculably of our time. It is one of the truly modern arts, allied to the adventurous, philosophic, and scientific speculations of our times, that have restored free movement to us. Modern painting tore down perspective, the third dimension as it had been faked on the lying canvas; tore it down because it had become a limiting force, a path to pursue outward only to retrace inward again. This spurious depth was a trap; it imprisoned rather than freed; it seemed to offer a landscape for the spirit from which it was barred by the wall of a false reality, of a thing pretending to be that which it was not. Painting then set up a new relation of abstract forms keeping this relation mobile, flexible, and free. These forms are not imprisoned. They move as one watches; they advance and recede before the eyes; they overlap and interpenetrate. Not representing anything external they are, nevertheless, representational because they project psychic states and forces.

Jazz music relates equally to the concepts, the discoveries, the motivations of our time. For one thing, its ceaseless movement and its free melodies in combined variation are analogous to pure movement in time and space. Like natural process, jazz has no real beginning, no real end.

Our modern "serious" music is not contemporary in any such sense. Even in its most radical form it is conditioned by earlier and outmoded concepts of form and energy, of time and space. Looked at objectively, it has no direction to take, implicit in its own past development, which will make it contemporary with the vast speculation, the uneasy, ceaseless, and portentous movements of our time. To achieve meaning it must place a forever incipient rhythmic and melodic movement into the pathway of polyphony. This movement is improvisation; with it, Western music as we know it disappears and its composer, too.

Jazz is not musical architecture — namely, form rooted to a foundation — it is flight. It is new to our Western world as a use of rhythmic momentum in an imaginative and daring flight of tone into time. It is the ultimate utilization, indeed, of the intrinsically intuitional and abstract qualities of music and the final rejection of all formal elements which stem or impede movement.

Jazz, whether played by black man or by white man, is a music which has moved out of the long night. Its shining trumpets, held high, seem to beckon. It moves — and its very movement is a message. Rich and moody, infinitely wise and wisely gay, it is a summons to life. Nothing more need be said. For this message, in the largest sense and as involved in the deepest relations of an art to human life, is the real creative meaning of American jazz.

postcript

I HAVE been granted that author's boon, the chance to add a postscript to a book long in print. In the twelve years since its initial publication there have been many developments in jazz. On the one hand there have been events: the deaths of jazzmen, the emergence of new styles and the re-emergence of older ones, changes in the general attitude toward jazz, and technological innovations that will influence the music. On the other hand there has been the simple passage of time, over a decade, to reveal trends and make critical perspective more accurate.

Deaths were frequent among the survivors of the earlier generations. For example, from September 1948 to September 1949, New Orleans jazz lost four trumpeters, Mutt Carey, Shots Madison, Kid Rena, and Bunk Johnson, as well as the clarinetist Louis de Lisle Nelson, while paralysis was stilling the historic drums of Baby Dodds. In the same period New Orleans Dixieland lost trumpeter Paul Mares and clarinetist Irving Fazola, and then, in 1953, came the death of Larry Shields, one of the five of the Original Dixieland Jazz Band, which carried "jass" to Chicago in 1915, New York in 1916, and London in 1919.

The 1950's have seen the Harlem piano veteran James P. Johnson pass from the scene, as well as that big-band pioneer Fletcher Henderson, while the hot blues trumpet of Oran "Lips" Page — long associated with Kansas City jazz — was being silenced. In 1953 a speeding taxi felled a short plain woman in a Manhattan street. Thus was stilled the great blues voice of Chippie Hill, who, like Bunk Johnson, had enjoyed a revival and a later career that eclipsed her earlier one. Even one of the newer styles, bop, lost one of its founders, the Kansas City alto saxophonist Charles "Yardbird" Parker, who died in 1955 at the early age of thirty-five. "Wooden Joe" Nicholas, seventy-four and direct link with Buddy Bolden's trumpet style, died in November 1957, followed shortly by Walter Page, "Big Four," whose bass swung the Basie band.

The vitality of jazz, as well as of its earlier sources, the spiritual and the blues, was as evident as ever in this period when the long grip of the big-band concept was at last loosened.

The New Orleans revival had, in a sense, begun in 1936 after Bing Crosby's twenty-two-year-old brother Bob took over elements of the Ben Pollack Orchestra to give a commercial band what he called "a Dixieland kick." The young generation immediately responded to the brassy march rhythms. However, the revival of the New Orleans idea of a small contrapuntal band — though Crosby as early as 1937 was featuring the eight-piece Bobcats as "a band within a band" — actually began in 1939 at three widely separated points. In Chicago, Muggsy Spanier formed his eight-piece Ragtime Band (see pages 236, 237); in New York, Bud Freeman fronted the new eight-piece Summa Cum Laude Orchestra; and in San Francisco, Lu Watters's experiments would lead the following year to the Dawn Club *première* of the nine-piece Yerba Buena Jazz Band (see page 324); re-forming in 1946 after break-up caused by the war, the band lasted into 1950. Three variations on a New Orleans theme these: Freeman's band revived the Chicago derivants from King Oliver and the New Orleans Rhythm Kings — with Beiderbecke overtones; Spanier's horn, incurably "Joe Oliver," stamped his Ragtimers with the old-time sound; and Watters, Turk Murphy, and the rest indicated the beginnings of the intellectual-historical approach by going directly to the source, modeling instrumentation, style, and repertory [1] on Oliver's Creole Band of 1923–4.

[1] Watters and Turk Murphy wrote many original numbers for the band, in the cakewalk-minstrel, ragtime, and New Orleans stomp styles, as well as that of the blues.

It is interesting to note that my hope — expressed suppositionally in 1946 (see page 261) — that Louis Armstrong might return to the small polyphonic group actually came true in less than one year. Although economic reasons may have been directly responsible, the move attracted universal attention and was an acknowledgment of the New Orleans revival. With the usual changes of personnel, Louis's six-piece group has endured ever since, although it has not projected jazz to equal the best of the classic period. With the small group, Louis's own playing — always New Orleans — has matured into an expressive simplicity that is truly monumental.

By 1948 the revival had spread abroad, with bands forming in England, France, Italy, Switzerland, Germany, and Scandinavia — even down under in Australia. Some rather remarkable band names — the "Roman New Orleans Jazz Band," the "Hep Cats Creole Jazz Band" of Sweden, and others — underlined the youthful enthusiasm and sincerity of the movement. In the main, young white people were involved; for the rest, a few New Orleans Negro veterans, chiefly Kid Ory, Bunk Johnson, George Lewis and, of course, Louis. No younger Negroes joined the movement. They had moved on to new matters like bop.

The net result was that New Orleans jazz was given a second hearing and re-established in the public mind, but no more — although even this was a considerable achievement in view of the many factors involved in the situation. New Orleans jazz had not advanced beyond the point it had reached about 1926, when its development had been cut short. Ory and Johnson aroused merited enthusiasm. Although it was wonderful to hear the gutty, deeply felt old jazz again, still — since it did not move forward — it became an anachronism.

Armstrong, even at this late date, might have carried the whole band along to the terse clarity his own playing reached. Only through such a band development can the New Orleans style itself develop: this, after all, is the logical meaning of the style. But this was not in the nature of Louis's genius, which,

like that of Bechet, is individualistic. There have been un-
merited criticisms of the Armstrong band. Sidemen, however,
are chosen by the leader, and then — if he is a great leader —
are inspired to play to the top level of their capacity. The
Creole Band was no accident, nor was the first group of the
Red Hot Peppers, particularly the latter: certainly Simeon
and Mitchell never again played so well, and Ory never played
better.

The white players concentrated on copying the past, with
Morton and Oliver as their chief models. Some even sought the
cramped, distorted sound of the Oliver acoustical records, with
their imbalance of horns and suppression of rhythm, which
had resulted from the inability of early recording to capture
the low frequencies. Seeking a sound rather than the challenge
of a creative way, they imitated surface aspects.

At this they stopped, content — thus betraying (this was an
intellectual enterprise) the categorical thinking and timidity
of their time. They had sincerity and vast enthusiasm — but
little imagination. In this they were in step with their genera
tion, graduating from war into an alienated world of fear and
tension. Thinking was for them a safe exercise within severely
limited categories. The rules were more important than the
game. The symbol of safety was an almost ritualistic avoidance
of change.

This was one half of the generation. The other half em-
braced whatever was new: swing, bop, and then what they called
Progressive Jazz, a commercialization of bop. They demonstrated their daring by insisting upon perpetual change or,
more accurately, perpetual novelty. This too was a rigid category rationalized as synonymous with progress, equated with
the rejection of all tradition, and — appearances to the contrary — even less daring than the return to New Orleans. It
was in fact the ultra-safe attitude in a society dedicated to the
annual new model on the easy-payment plan. But it was one
generation nevertheless. Perpetual sameness, perpetual change
— the roots without the tree or the tree without the roots. The

typical representative, regardless of affiliation, might be called the Non-creative Intellectual, because creativeness demands imagination and the taking of genuine risks.

The controversy was intense, each side totally rejecting the other. The Revivalists became more and more static lest the slightest change be interpreted as "modernism," while the Progressives searched ever more frantically for the new at any cost. There was no middle ground between the dusty orgy of antiquarianism and the chrome-plated worship of the new. I tried to point out that the New Orleans style was fresh creation or nothing, a statement not yet finished, a "parent style or school wide enough to embrace numberless variants," a seminal idea "above time and beyond geography." But it was not a time for listening. Feelings ran high, as they always have run high whenever this tyrannical yet liberating music of the Negro is again penetrating the protective walls of our society. Nevertheless, and even in the conflict, forces were at work which today are re-unifying jazz and at the same time broadening and making more secure its place in our culture.

I am still occasionally referred to as the man who wanted to take jazz back to 1928. The date is not early enough: I wanted to take it back to 1926, when it had reached its highest point and then stopped. There, I figured, was the place to start again, utilizing the horizontal counterpoint, the microtonality of the Afro-American blues scale, the complexity of the polyrhythm, and the clashing dissonance of heterophonic improvisation. It was modern then — when it captivated yet thwarted a Milhaud and a Stravinsky; it is modern still. It is a matter not of dates, but of ideas.

Anyway, the New Orleans tradition got its revival in the 1940's and was heard again, and it remains apart from history and apart from New Orleans as a city, a workable base for fresh creation. It will certainly re-enter jazz as a vitalizing force. The name "New Orleans" may never be mentioned — this is the difference between a revival and a revitalizing. The fiery vigor and excitement of the weaving and answering voices — voices that are themselves drums — need no vignetting in a period frame. The possibilities of the hot solo have been exploited for a long time, and a lot of genius has gone into this development: Armstrong, Lester Young, Charlie Parker, Dizzy Gillespie, and a generation, today, which is pushing the solo to the most extreme limits of the single linear musical development. Now, at last, it begins to call for the depth and complexity — and the meaning — of a reconciliation with the simultaneous creation of the group. It will come: logic becomes a force when it coincides with necessity.

The chief feeling in the whole jazz world of the 1940's was one of dissatisfaction. The commercial bent of the preceding decade had left a feeling of emptiness. Some primitive, exciting goodness had gone out of jazz. All felt it, from those who were trying to revive New Orleans jazz and ragtime, all the way to the strange, new, goateed breed staging a revolt within the very ranks of commercial swing, a revolt predating the actual break-up of swing. Although the one element produced a faded carbon copy of Joe Oliver and the other produced bop, they had — without knowing it — a common cause.

In 1940 certain Negro swing sidemen began the development of bop. Notable among these were altoist Charlie Parker (who had been with Jay McShann, Earl Hines, and Andy Kirk), trumpeter Dizzy Gillespie (with Teddy Hill, Cab Calloway), pianists Thelonius Monk (with Lucky Millender) and Bud Powell, guitarist Charley Christian (with Benny Goodman), and drummers Kenny Clarke (with Claude Hopkins, Teddy Hill) and Max Roach. Bop was a small-band form, not polyphonic, but an attempt to break up the rigid arrangements of commercial swing and to introduce more varied and complex harmonies into jazz.

Bop reached its height about 1947, having long since moved out from its semi-private beginnings in Harlem to Fifty-second Street and an amplitude of phonograph-record documentation. Bop, as we shall see, was a new development of basic importance in the history of jazz. At that moment, however, it

347

seemed to spend itself by flowing into two different streams. One, a commercial adaptation to large white bands like that of Stan Kenton, was immediately hailed as "Progressive Jazz." The other was "Cool Jazz." With its cerebral emphasis and its fetish of emotional non-involvement of player and listener alike, "cool" fitted well the temper of that time, a middle-of-the-road psychology that swept America.

Nevertheless, "cool," which came in in 1949, by no means characterizes the period. Both before and after its advent, there was a most remarkable ferment going on, all of which could be characterized as unqualifiedly hot. It was, in fact and in its various aspects, a most determined search for hot elements new to this generation, but in actuality ancient. Besides the Revival and bop, there were two strong resurgences of the Negro spirit from what might be called the American grass roots, and in addition a direct infusion of African rhythms from the Caribbean, where they had survived almost pure for centuries. In each case new rapprochements were made between musicians and large segments of the public.

First, the spiritual, as rocking as ever, but now colored by jazz and the blues, came to general attention through a number of Negro singers, mainly women. First and foremost of these was New Orleans-born Mahalia Jackson, who, as a child, had heard Ma Rainey and Bessie Smith. Great, big-voiced, dynamic Mahalia might have stepped from an ante-bellum plantation directly into the present, so powerfully does her singing seem to be not at any latter end, but at the very source of Afro-American music. The distinctions among the blues, jazz, and the spiritual seem to disappear in the creative synthesis of her art — original statement and summing-up all in one. Like African music, it is primitive in its power, complex and subtle in its artistry. Like a Gabon mask, it is both fine art and folk art.

Mahalia's deep contralto, with its indescribable turns and convolutions around a primitively scaled melody, seemed to echo all over America from the very first record she made in

1945 for the Apollo company. *Move On Up a Little Higher*, passing the million mark in sales, was the first recorded spiritual to reach an appreciable white market.[2] Through Mahalia the spiritual once again penetrated into our culture as it had right after the Civil War. But with a profound difference. In the earlier, more religious time, we treated it with reverence, while rapidly denaturing and altering it — with ample Negro help — into a pallid accession to the white concert repertory. This time we were franker and less reverent: white popular singers like Kay Starr and Johnnie Ray were soon trying to sing in that seemingly primitive, but inordinately difficult way and were recording "spirituals" for the juke boxes.

The spiritual, first important musical creation of the American Negro, has never lost its prevalence and power in Negro society. The blues, born out of the spiritual and the field holler, likewise have persisted. Both forms can still reassert themselves with the full force of original principle.

So, the spiritual having once again forced its way into the general consciousness, it is not surprising to find the blues today, as a teenage craze known as Rock and Roll, spreading from America to Europe. Rock and Roll to begin with was nothing more nor less than the rural blues with their "jook band" accompaniment of guitar and harmonica, other instruments like saxophone and drums being added from time to time. These blues vary a great deal in authenticity: some are real Negro blues, others — like those of Elvis Presley — are the blues as they filtered over the years into white hillbilly and country music of Mississippi, northeast Texas, and the Arkansas Ozarks. But as its name says, the music rocks, and it is astonishing at mid-century to see a new generation suddenly discovering a primitive Negro music that was scarcely new in the 1890's. These youngsters, anyway, have left the introversions

---

[2] *Silent Night,* also on Apollo, became the all-time best-selling record ever issued in Denmark and led to a tour by Mahalia of Europe and England in 1952. This was the first hearing of Negro spirituals abroad since the appearances of the Hampton Singers and the Fisk Jubilee Singers there more than seventy-five years earlier.

of "cool" to the teenagers immediately preceding them. Now they dance to rhythms made for dancing, a most healthy sign for the future.

Even these many developments were by no means all. Amid the ferment of the late 1940's there was room for a revival of ragtime piano. It came about with a new generation of players, all of them white. To name only a few, Wally Rose in California, Armand Hug in New Orleans, and Missouri-born Ralph Sutton in New York, suddenly were heard playing the beautiful old rags of Scott Joplin, James Scott, and Joseph Lamb, while from Baltimore came Don Ewell, recreating the ragtime-jazz piano of Jelly Roll Morton. And playing the rags, neither with the rigidity of the mechanical piano nor with the stilted rhythms of the sheet music (which, after all, was only a scored approximation), but with the oldtime fire and improvisatory freedom.

A Tennessee player, John Maddox, even put ragtime on the juke boxes and the Hit Parade lists, so that ragtime's rhythmic melodiousness was heard everywhere. At that time, in fact, ragtime seemed to be flowing back from the past into the present. Everyone was humming and whistling the musical theme of the motion picture *The Third Man* as played on the zither by an old Viennese café entertainer. The tune was generally thought to be a relic of a vanished Danubian gaiety. Actually it was the main theme of *Rags to Burn*, written by a ragtimer long dead, Frank X. McFadden, and published in 1899 in Kansas City, Missouri.

Then the mambo craze began and bands were imported from the Caribbean. The new rhythms became and have remained the basis of social dancing today. The music itself was another matter: again the knowledgeable ear heard one ragtime melody after another played against the mambo and conga rhythms. Again, in a sense, it was history repeating itself. Before 1890, the Eastern ragtimer Jess Pickett had scored a hit with the ragtime melodies of his *The Dream*, played in the tango rhythm, to be followed by Luckey Roberts and his

Spanish Venus and, in New Orleans, Jelly Roll Morton and his many rags composed with what he called "the Spanish tinge." And of course, as we now know, all the so-called Spanish-American rhythms are of African origin.

Now today, the great majority of the "jingles" of "singing commercials" on television and radio are nothing more nor less than sung ragtime. It is as though ragtime's seeds had been lying in the soil — in Vienna, in Havana and Antigua, in New York and San Francisco — for a full fifty years before sprouting into a new crop. It does not even matter that ragtime is now used to sell toothpaste and razor blades and beer — it is as gay and graceful and lilting as ever, a melodic breath of fresh air.

An amazing spectacle of the 1940's was the swiftness with which swing broke up and disappeared. It has been explained on economic grounds: the cost of transporting large bands, the excessive rates that had come about through our acceptance of the Big Name idea, and the new cabaret tax, 20% when there was dancing. These explanations are not satisfying, particularly when we recall that the big band gained its ascendancy during the depression of the 1930's.

The simple fact is that swing progressively deteriorated into a set of clichés of almost moronic simplicity, finally becoming so bad that no one wanted it. If we examine the downfall of swing, we will find at the bottom the same disastrous process of commercialization to which we have more than once referred. How swiftly art can deteriorate when it becomes primarily a trade commodity! For there was something valid at the core of swing.

The same process has been going on in Rock and Roll, which is being converted right under our eyes from a rebirth of the barrel-house blues into still another Tin Pan Alley concoction. About six years ago, a seventeen-year-old boy from Tupelo, Mississippi, made a record at his own expense for a minor record company in Tennessee. The boy was Elvis Presley, and he sang a rocking hill-country blues called *That's All Right*

Now, Mama. Overnight he was a success. RCA Victor bought him. His next records were blues of the same primitive quality, eight-bar blues as archaic in form as Ma Rainey's *Shave 'Em Dry* (see pages 126 and Ex. 21), things like *Heartbreak Hotel* and *Money Honey.*

Presley was controversial from the start. Parents took one look at his hip-swaying antics and immediately condemned this new craze of their sons and daughters. Now, this hip-swaying only made visual the sexual dynamism that has always been part of the real blues. This summary disapproval of a young folk singer who learned, directly or indirectly from the Negroes, was a revelation of the real dual basis of anti-jazz prejudice. As far as the parents were concerned, to the perennial disapproval of the earthy frankness and vitality of jazz and the blues was added the shock of seeing a "nice-looking *white* boy" doing these things.

In any event, that is being rapidly taken care of. Elvis today, barely past minimum voting age, is a millionaire and a valuable property. He is singing mainly Tin Pan Alley trash, and his pre-eminence is being threatened by sophisticated "folk" singers, the breed that infests the cities today with their guitars and their crooning. Exactly thus, in 1926, was New Orleans jazz replaced. It is the old shell game.

However, to return to swing: beginning about 1924–6, there ensued a period of more than twenty years of the most determined effort to evolve the large orchestra — with brass, reed, and rhythm sections — out of the small jazz band. So all-out was the effort that from 1930 to 1940 the small group ceased to exist in any significant way as a part of jazz developmen except in the "backwoods" of Kansas City. The music world was full of big swing bands that did everything except really swing.

It is altogether extraordinary that no one looked at the simple arithmetic of the matter: the six-piece New Orleans band was fifty percent rhythm instruments; the sixteen-piece swing band was only twenty-five percent, an underpowered car if there ever was one. To be sure, the New Orleans horns punched harder, and their weaving counterpoint created a vast horizontal surge. But more rhythm instruments in the swing band would at least have helped. Instead, the maestros were busy adding string sections. To be sure, too, the New Orleans marching bands literally soar with eight horns over *two* drums, but the Northern swingmen can be forgiven for not knowing that.

Anyway, suddenly the whole glittering edifice collapsed, a building on an inadequate foundation. But by then the situation had been irrevocably altered. Twenty years are a long time. They have left their imprint: traditions have been diluted or broken; there are new sounds, new concepts, new rhythms, to be assimilated. Not least important, jazz has at least temporarily lost its primary and honorable function as dance music. Now it is concert music — at least it is listened to, not danced to. The effect is basic; it already shows in tempos and dynamics, in the whole character and bent of invention.

It is impossible to conceive of cool jazz originating in a dance hall. Such a pianissimo and almost pulseless music would have assured the musicians prompt unemployment. If they had compounded their inadequacies by playing with their backs disdainfully turned to the audience (as some cool players actually did), it is conceivable that they might have suffered physical harm at the hands of those itching to dance.

But the cool players were saved by the fact that their music was produced for listening rather than for anything so vulgarly unintellectual as dancing. Listening, in the classical tradition, is a neat trick of disassociation by each listener from those around him. It is as non-participative as it is possible to get. Incurably hot players of the Wild Bill Davison type call it the "audience disease." When music must be only understood, not felt, the easy next step is, "Nobody understands it but me."

Finally, to complete this brief survey of the developments from 1946 to the present, there were three technological innovations. The first of these is the long-playing microgroove phonograph record. Coupled with it is the second: the development of high fidelity sound reproduction. The third is television.

The phonograph record has always been of vital importance in jazz as the sole existing documentation of historical periods and the only means of accurately preserving improvisation. Within jazz itself, the record has been a strong influence through players listening to the work of others. With the LP, its importance has increased in each of these respects. Heretofore only short segments — three to five minutes — of playing could be put on records without a break; now the longest improvisations can be preserved. More, the LP has vastly extended the listening audience, while at the same time its compendious limits allow capturing uncurtailed jazz improvisation and have also encouraged the issuing of jazz histories in record sets.

High fidelity techniques are to some extent tied in with the development of electronic, or magnetic, tape. The influence of high fidelity technology is felt in two main ways: capturing the dynamic range and brilliance of contemporary jazz and the addition of brilliance and lifelikeness to earlier — even acoustically recorded — discs.

Television so far has had small time for jazz — the visual aspects of jazz-band playing minus the dancing are not very sensational after they have been seen a few times. In its early days television showed the Eddie Condon band for some months and then, after all possible camera angles seemed to have been exploited, dropped the matter. "They lost a camera in the piano," Condon said.

Earlier, radio (when once it had been persuaded to broadcast live jazz) was — at least in one instance — more hospitable, both because radio is much less costly and because it has no need to exploit the visual. The radio program to which I refer was my own, called *This Is Jazz*, which ran on WOR–Mutual, the Canadian Broadcasting Commission, and the State Department's short-wave for the better part of 1947.

For the ten months of its existence, *This Is Jazz* was a sustaining program, which means that it had no commercial sponsor. Its popularity, evidenced by mail from all over the world, kept it on the air. Soon it was attracting guest stars of the caliber of Sidney Bechet and Louis Armstrong, who were happy to appear at scale pay. Sponsors kept nibbling at it. The block seemed to be the advertising agencies.

I recall one important potential sponsor who was on the verge of signing a contract. High executives of the interested corporation, together with the agency men, sat in the control room through one of the broadcasts, obviously enjoying everything.

This Is Jazz was a very informal program, with script at minimum and music at maximum. It never turned out on the air as it had in rehearsal. Numbers were "kicked off" slower or faster; players got hot and added choruses, so that near program's end we invariably were either long or short on time. Producer Don Frederick was very calm about this, giving hand signals to add or subtract choruses or even to cut them in half. For my part, I was constantly prepared to ad lib my closing lines, abridging them or adding lines until the magic moment when the studio clock hands would coincide at the hour. *This Is Jazz* always ended on time — something of a feat, everything considered. It was also a lot of fun, a kind of game that detracted not at all from the atmosphere conducive to jazz.

This particular program ended with the customary flurry — "will they make it or will they miss, this time?" Players and all, we had been watching the big people in the control room. As the last note of the theme, *Way Down Yonder in New Orleans*, coincided with the gong, we saw them cheering and slapping each other's backs — just as our live audience was doing. Then they went into the decisive conference.

The advertising men rendered the verdict: "This improvised music is just what we want. However, for sake of accurately timing the program to fit with the commercials, it is necessary that the players read the music from carefully prepared scores." I paid off my bets. One and all, the players, concurring in the belief that "Advertising men don't like jazz," had bet that it would be no sale. The Negro players — I had a mixed band — had gone even farther, offering to resign for the sake of the program. "You can't sell Negroes on radio," they said.

Madison Avenue always denies charges of racial discrimination. Yet shortly before *This Is Jazz* went on the air, Virgil Thomson had observed, "Radio today is almost completely without jazz. . . . One is tempted to put down this persecution, for it is no less, to the standardizing tendencies of a monopolistic industry; and certainly there is some truth in the diagnosis. But there are other reasons, more sinister ones, that make the repressive operation possible. These have to do, I am sure, with a deep-seated jealousy of white musicians and consumers toward their Negro fellow-citizens, who alone can practice the style with integrity and understand it as a language. In any case, a whole complex of circumstances operates toward substituting a debased . . . industrialized product for one of the most vigorous, varied, and original art forms that the creative spirit of man has evolved in recent centuries." Thomson then voiced the serious charge of "conspiracy." [3]

I knew this of course. No one listening critically to radio could be unaware of it. I deliberately chose the course least likely to succeed, in order to deny both Jim Crow and Jim Crow in reverse. It lasted longer than anyone dare to hope, going out over most of Mutual's "world's largest network" of 500 stations — including the South — into Canada, too, and over world wide shortwave.

Television perpetually presents plays about jazzmen, but seldom presents jazz. Trombonist Conrad Janis, who is also

[3] Virgil Thomson: "Jazz Defined," in the New York *Herald Tribune*, November 3, 1946.

an actor, estimates that he has appeared in at least thirty such plays. "Always," he complains, "I am cast as a dope addict or a juvenile delinquent with a horn." Thus are perpetuated yesterday's vicious stereotypes.

Jazz stars like Armstrong are frequently part of the "celebrity mobs" of the expensive "spectaculars." In some, scarcely a note of the Armstrong horn is heard. His mere presence, however, raises the question: why does Louis's band have no regular program? The answer is plain: there is no place in sponsored television for the Negro — if we except the disgraceful "Uncle Tom" show, *Amos and Andy*. Columnist Barry Gray pinpointed it in the *New York Post*: "I accuse the television industry of the most blatant kind of Jim Crow — a kind of racial shutout which is as obvious as the grey-flannel uniforms the team wears."

On the technical-production-directorial side, no Negroes are employed — although a "token" appointment may be made at any moment. In front of the cameras — fairly frequent appearances, *but always as guests of the dominant whites.* In 1957 the entire gifted company that had presented *Porgy and Bess* with such spectacular success abroad — particularly in Moscow — was at liberty at home or else engaged in menial labor. Singer-pianist Nat "King" Cole, a top-selling record artist, bade fair to become the first Negro with a nationally sponsored show of his own. But late in 1957 he disbanded his program in protest against the advertising agencies. The NBC network, Cole reported, had backed him to the limit, even absorbing many costs customarily paid by the sponsor. White television and Broadway stars had appeared for him for "scale" pay instead of their usual high fees.

The ad men could have sold his program if they had wanted to — "They sell much worse," Cole said — but they felt sponsorship would hurt the client's sales in the South.

"You can't always put the blame on the South for these things," Cole declared. "We're always using the South as a whipping boy. But the only difference between the South and certain areas of the North is that Southerners are outspoken. In the North, they smile at you once and then knife you in the back." [4]

No matter what the outcome of the "King" Cole incident, television is fighting a losing battle. Not even ad men are immune to the changes of social history.

The break in the commercial wall of prejudice is in recording — a bit of poetic justice, because the phonograph record, earliest of the technological entertainment inventions, is the page upon which jazz improvisation is indelibly written. Poetic justice, further, is the fact that recording, which began in the late nineteenth-century era of truly free enterprise, is today the only remaining major industry in which small operators can survive.

The phonograph industry has been "killed" three times in the last thirty years: first radio all but wiped it out, then the sound motion picture, and finally, television. Each blow actually strengthened it. Today it is a vast industry; records are selling in almost astronomical quantities; jazz forms a larger part of the total than ever before.

The record still remains the key to the jazz situation. There is employment for more players; pay is better; the field is beckoning to youth. There is no color line in the recording studio. Even in New Orleans, mixed groups are now recording. Records build audiences for live jazz; as a result there is today more jazz in public than at any time since the 1920's. Audiences take jazz more seriously than in the past. The result of all these things is a vast creative ferment; the mood is one of experiment, of pushing at frontiers; jazz is quite evidently entering a period of wide new development. Before considering this further, however, let us complete our survey of the last decade.

Far and away, the most momentous development is this: living jazz is being brought to the whole world. Not merely by

[4] Nat Cole interviewed by Bob Williams, *New York Post*, November 21, 1957.

phonograph record, one remove from reality, nor merely to an intellectual few — but to the people. Our jazzmen now tour the globe as they once did "one-nighters" in America. In West Africa for example, 100,000 natives stood in the hot sun to hear the trumpet of Louis Armstrong.[5] Such crowds are the rule: in England, all over the Continent, in South America and Australia, in the Near and Far East. Altogether impressive, almost awe-inspiring, is the outpouring of human beings everywhere to hear the two trumpets, so widely different, of Louis Armstrong and Dizzy Gillespie and the great voice of Mahalia Jackson. Booked for one concert in Copenhagen, she was held over for five. "I could be singing there yet," Mahalia says. "Seems like they were hungry for the Word."

These are not just audiences; they are a tidal flood. Even where distrust or dislike of America is strongest, they break down the gates and riot in the streets just to hear a music. What manner of music is this? What canons of art can explain it? Quite evidently it is a universal language, its phrases of freedom leaping the barriers of time and the polyglot tongues to address the heart. From Mahalia's throaty richness to Louis's and Dizzy's shining trumpets, it is a "freedom song" just as truly as those first spirituals of two centuries ago when the Negro first celebrated that which was not even his to celebrate.

Mahalia, Louis, and Dizzy now roam the world, our best "ambassadors," sponsored by a State Department that only yesterday shunned jazz and all Negro music like the plague. To everyone except Americans, jazz and the spirituals are *the* American music because they express what America stands for or, at least, once stood for. Esthetic theories, categories of folk or fine art, or talk of musical form are trivial: here is the universal language of freedom and hope. The finest art of all: communication direct and unequivocal.

Only here in its own country does jazz still lack this total

[5] Edward R. Murrow observes (in his documentary film of an Armstrong World tour) that this audience, barring proof to the contrary, forms the largest group of people ever to gather to hear music.

audience. Taking freedom for granted, mesmerized by the making and consuming of material goods, like spoiled children we stand apart from the great movements that are shaking the world, trying to fight the Communist slave state with the glittering trash of our own materialistic enslavement. America was an idea — not a store full of chrome-plated gadgets — but we have forgotten that. The idea and the dream have passed to darker, poorer, humbler races. While they awaken and stir, we toy with the engines of destruction.

"Jazz," as Dizzy Gillespie has said, "is too good for America."

Still, Americans at last are beginning to listen to jazz. It may be the long way around to bring us back to our own country — America the idea. But it will be worth it. There is a lesson for us in the way the rest of the world accepts jazz — any and all jazz, from New Orleans to "progressive." It becomes evident that the points of style over which we have endlessly argued are not comparably important elsewhere. What is important to people everywhere is the mere fact that a music like jazz can exist. Degrees or differences in art are important, of course. But in any event, the art itself is more important.

The jazz minority in America split in the 1940's into bitter factions. It was frequently difficult to distinguish various elements of the music in the general noise, particularly in the fierce controversy over swing versus (New Orleans) jazz. It was even more difficult to differentiate between the statements of those sincerely interested in the esthetic experiment of big-band jazz and the ballyhoo of those with a commercial interest in the Name Bands. It was doubly confusing because both of these elements had the same slogan: "New Orleans jazz is primitive and crude. Swing is modern and progressive." Many were forced — as in a civil war — to take sides, however unwillingly.

That is long since over, and it is possible to see the elements of lasting value in swing. Once again, a great Negro artist, following his people's tradition, made the contribution. It was not Fletcher Henderson or Duke Ellington: the motivation in Harlem has always been toward the white tradition.

Bill "Count" Basie, ragtimer from Red Bank, New Jersey, was the man who, more than any other, made the swing band really swing. Settling in Kansas City, he was the catalyst that united musical impulses that had been operating for a long time in the Southwest.

Kansas City had been one of the ragtime capitals in piano syncopation's Missouri heyday, 1895–1920. Even then — though on a lower social level — the blues were there. Around 1900, brass band marches, Congo Square rhythms, ragtime, and the blues were fused into classic New Orleans jazz through the genius of Buddy Bolden. In Kansas City a fusion of ragtime and the blues did not occur, even by 1920, when ragtime was dying out. By 1923 Kansas City bands were trying to play jazz as a result of the direct influence of New Orleans bands on the riverboats and the secondary influence of the Original Dixieland Jazz Band and King Oliver records.[6] But jazz in a New Orleans sense did not take root in Kansas City.

Throughout the whole Southwest — Missouri, Kansas, Oklahoma, Arkansas, Mississippi, and Texas — Negroes were thinking in terms of big bands that played the blues, not with the lilt of polyphony, but with a harsh four-beat of almost brutal force. In Kansas City, focus of a southwest circuit around which these bands traveled, Bennie Moten's band and others were more aware of the Eastern developments of Henderson and Ellington. These Kansas City groups were smoother and more sophisticated, stomped and wailed less than more typical groups like Walter Page's Blue Devils and Jap Allen's band, both from Oklahoma, and the Terrence Holder and Troy Floyd groups from Texas.

In Kansas City, as in Chicago, the gangsters waxed rich in the Depression. Then, right after the mid-nineteen-thirties, up

6 Example: *Elephant's Wobble/Crawdad Blues*, Bennie Moten's Kansas City Orchestra (Lamar Wright, cornet; Thamon Hayes, trombone; Woodie Walder, clarinet; Bennie Moten, piano; Sam Tall, banjo; Willie Hall, drums), OK 8100, recorded in St. Louis, October 1923.

from the deep South came a Negro labor migration, and with it, a fresh flood of the dark, archaic blues and the rocking, shouting spirituals. The blues were no longer on the wrong side of the tracks. In wide-open Kansas City anyone's money was good.

Basie had been playing with the Moten band, alternating at piano with Bennie. Both were ragtimers, though of different schools, but the Count took to the blues as Bennie never did. Then, in 1935, Moten died. Basie formed his own band, at first a small one — trumpet, tenor saxophone, piano, bass, and drums; then, soon, nine pieces — five horns over four rhythm. The accent was on rhythmic foundation. Walter Page's powerful, striding bass earned him the name Big Four, and Jo Jones's drums, rock-strong, were also subtle and full of surprises. This band expressed Basie's personal aim, which was the feel of Eastern piano ragtime with its free improvisation and its combination of rhythmic force and delicacy.

Basie made a new role for the piano in the band. He left behind the two-handed ragtime fullness, concentrated on the right hand, artfully placing right hand chords and runs to "ride" the band, while Page's walking bass replaced the missing left-hand part. More, Basie's whole band — even the later fifteen pieces — became a personification of the piano, not in the Bolden way of horizontal horn polyphony, but in counter riffs of brass and reeds and in solos over, or fragmented between, the riffs.

The Basie and the Morton approaches were diametrically opposite. Jelly Roll thought in New Orleans orchestral terms even in his solo work. Had the opportunity been his, it seems likely he would eventually have developed polyphonic playing by the sections of the large band. Basie thought of the big band largely in terms of the piano. Impossible as it may seem, he not only made it work, but the effect came out wholly orchestral. Somehow or other he made ragtime the delicate mold into which to pour the blues and the rocking antiphony that he heard both in boogie woogie piano and in the church singing.

POSTSCRIPT

It was unquestionably a deep and partly unreasoned creative instinct that drove Basie. And yet he was at least partly conscious of its significance. "I wanted my fifteen-piece band," he has said, "to work together just like those nine pieces did. I wanted fifteen men to think and play the same way . . . just as tasty and subtle as if it were the three brass I used to use." [7]

As a direct result of the Count's early conditioning in ragtime's forceful delicacy, his band not only wailed and stomped with the southwest sound, but also really swung. Real swing, like the rolling momentum of the New Orleans band, is a thing both delicate and rugged, incompatible as the two may seem. But then, so is African drumming, with its imperious force expressed in the most complexly delicate rhythms and cross rhythms. Any Eastern ragtimer might conceivably have made this large orchestral synthesis of ragtime with the blues. Only Basie did.

So now, after all the factional strife, we perceive that at the core of all the crassly commercial swing was a new concept of the big band, not derived from any European idea, but from the basic impulse that came originally from Africa. Basie showed us how the big band could exist in jazz without using the New Orleans formula. His brass and reed choirs moving in antiphonal masses were more strongly African than even New Orleans jazz.

Basie's band was greatest from 1937 to about 1940. During these years, certain key sidemen enabled him to express his formula definitively. Notable among these players were trumpeter Buck Clayton, tenor saxophonists Lester Young and Hershal Evans,[8] and the original rhythm men: Page, Jones, and guitarist, Freddy Green.

It was a short period, one of relatively heavy recording [9] and

[7] Nat Shapiro and Nat Hentoff, editors: *Hear Me Talkin' to Ya*, New York, 1955.

[8] Evans died in 1939 and was replaced by Buddy Tate.

[9] Basie issued about 100 sides, while in the same period Goodman released over 150, Tommy Dorsey over 250, and Ellington about the same number as Basie.

of uneven quality. The masterpieces, though few, prove Basie's point. The wide variation in quality resulted from several factors. One was the pressure to "sell" pop tunes. Another was the wearing routine of one-nighters. Not the least was the leaving of Kansas City, a hotbed of musical creation, and the sudden immersion of a new and still growing art development into the unfriendly waters of commercialism. Kansas City, from 1929 to at least 1945, was not unlike the earlier New Orleans, where the traditional repertory sufficed and the rivalries were the fair ones of creative and performing art.

Swing disappeared in the 1940's because the white bands gradually transformed the whole thing into a clichéd blatancy so standardized, finally, that all bands sounded alike. But Basie, nevertheless, had shown the way. The road is still there. In fact, the anatomy of Afro-American instrumental music is now potentially as complete as that of European music: the chamber group, the soloist, and the large orchestra. All may be combined some day in bands that can move through the improvisations of solo and interweaving heterophony and on into great clashes of monumental sound.

Lester Young was the most significant of the Basie soloists. He was born in 1909 in Woodville, Mississippi, about eight miles from the Louisiana state line. He was brought up from infancy in New Orleans, a little over one hundred miles southeast of Woodville, and lived in New Orleans until 1919.

"I liked to hear the music," he told Nat Hentoff. "I remember there were trucks advertising dances and I'd follow them all around." [10]

Thus "Press" Young, who developed a tenor style independent of the Coleman Hawkins mold, who was the bop prototype and forerunner of cool jazz, was originally one of the second line in the heyday of New Orleans jazz. He "lined it" after Oliver, Perez, Keppard, and Bunk Johnson.

Lester started on the drums at the age of ten. Five years later he took up saxophone. He played with a number of bands

[10] Nat Hentoff: "Pres," in *Down Beat* magazine, March 7, 1956.

including, he said, King Oliver,[11] before finally landing with Count Basie in Kansas City.

Lester Young's style was formed before he went with Oliver. He had come under an influence that could scarcely seem more remote from New Orleans, the saxophone playing of Frankie Trumbauer, friend and follower of Bix Beiderbecke. Lester mentioned one record in particular as having had great influence on him: *Singing the Blues*.[12] Lester put "Bix on top," with Trumbauer, and also singled out the tenor saxophone work of Bud Freeman. He emphasized that the light reedy tone, which for a long time caused him to be unfavorably compared with Hawkins, was one that he had to achieve: "[Trumbauer] played the C melody saxophone. I tried to get the sound of a C melody on a tenor. That's why I don't sound like other people."

This light, dry, lyric, almost breathy tone of Lester Young is, of course, the acknowledged basis of the "cool" tone of white players like Stan Getz, who have been the rage of the 1950's. And here, with Lester's own testimony, we saw it traced back to Beiderbecke by way of Trumbauer.[13]

The cool side of Lester Young is only half the equipment of any great jazz soloist; Lester often played very hot. The old term, sweet, is no more applicable than cool; actually, lyric is somewhat closer to the mark. In that sense, Fats Waller often played choruses as cool as cool: Bunk Johnson blew them in pale *bel canto* tones; and Louis Armstrong, warming up in his dressing room, blows breathy wisps of vibrato-less tone startlingly like Lester's.

[11] "He was old then . . . but his tone was full. . . . He could play some nice blues. He was a very nice fellow, a gay old fellow." Hentoff, *ibid.*

[12] Original issue: Okeh 40772, recorded February 4, 1927. Personnel: Trumbauer, Beiderbecke, cornet; Miff Mole, trombone; Doc Ryker, alto saxophone; Jimmy Dorsey, clarinet; Itzy Riskin, piano; Eddie Lang, guitar; Chauncey Morehouse, drums.

[13] The few recordings by the white Chicagoans had a greater influence on Negro players than we had thought. Even the Kansas City band of Bennie Moten reflected this influence. See *Band Box Shuffle*, Victor 23007, recorded in Chicago in October 1929. The trumpet solo is an out-and-out imitation of Bix, and the clarinetist follows Teschmaker's sour intonation and chaotic, tumbling phrases.

The term "cool" satisfied me no more than did the tracing of Lester Young's style — and, by inference, cool jazz — back to Beiderbecke as the fountainhead. Bix's first records, though much in the manner of the Original Dixieland Jazz Band, show Bix already playing in the style associated with his name. (Citation 52.) Where did he get this style? No Northern white player in 1924 was getting a jazz style out of thin air.

I reinvestigated the origins of Bix. Once again I discarded Oliver, Armstrong, and Bessie Smith, influences he himself claimed — he shows no stylistic evidences of them. The influence of the white New Orleans cornetist Emmett Hardy has long since been generally discounted as both vague and unprovable. In one legend, Bix heard him on a riverboat at Davenport, Iowa; in another, he heard him in Chicago. Hardy died young; he never recorded; no one really remembers how he played; there is even doubt that a white New Orleans band ever got as far north on the river as Davenport.[14]

To whom could Bix have been listening in Chicago from 1921 to 1923? Freddie Keppard came to mind. Rough, hard-drinking King Keppard who — first to take jazz out of New Orleans — refused in 1916 to be the first to record it. Keppard was playing in Chicago's South Side from 1918 on.

We had judged Keppard mainly by two abominably recorded Paramount records of 1926.[15] His playing here — of a hard-hitting gutbucket simplicity—bears no conceivable relation to Beiderbecke.

Suddenly I recalled a story that Keppard's clarinetist Big Eye Louis Nelson once told me. The Original Creole Band was playing at Coney Island in 1915 or 1916. Keppard was losing his café crowds every Sunday when an Italian cornet virtuoso played outside with his brass band. This triple-tonguing virtuoso held everyone spellbound by blowing opera airs in the florid style of a coloratura soprano.

"Keppard was King — New Orleans, anywhere," Nelson

[14] Edward J. Nichols, "Bix Beiderbecke," in *Jazzmen*, New York, 1939.
[15] *Stockyard Strut/Salty Dog*, Para 12399; *Messin' Around/Adam's Apple*, Para 12376.

366

said. "He didn't like this. So one day he stood at the edge of the crowd and waited for him to finish. Then put his cornet up and played every note the guy had played, clearer, and sweeter, and twice as loud. I'll never forget the tune: it was *Carnival of Venice*."

This was the Keppard, not on the Paramount discs, but the King called unbeatable by Jelly Roll — "his reach was so exceptional, both high and low, with all degrees of power, great imagination, and more tone than anybody," the King whose style, another musician had said, was different from and more lyrical than that of Armstrong. We had enough descriptions. In Chicago in 1919, said Buster Bailey, "Freddie could play as soft and as loud, as sweet and as rough, as you would want. He loved to play *Pagliacci*, too." [16] And Mutt Carey: "Freddie was a trumpet player any way you'd grab him. He could play sweet and then he could play hot. He'd play sweet sometimes and then turn around and knock the socks off you . . ." [17]

This Keppard *was* on records ignored for years because the band was so very bad that it is painful to listen to. I found this forty-year-old Keppard, with Cook's Dreamland Orchestra, on 1923 Gennetts and, much better recorded, on Columbias of 1926. Or rather, the two Keppards: the hot, punching lead in *Here Comes the Hot Tamale Man* (Columbia 727D), and the silver-toned, delicately phrasing prototype of Bix Beiderbecke on *I Got Worry* (Columbia 1430D).

Bix took that sweeter style and cannily — as artists often do — never mentioned Keppard. To make the story complete, Bix tried for the hot Keppard, too. It can be heard on at least one record, made a year before he died.[18] So much for the genealogy of cool.

Cool, anyway — though it needed Lester Young as a link — was most of all a reaction to bop. Bop was hard to swallow,

[16] Shapiro-Hentoff, editors: *Hear Me Talkin' to Ya*, New York, 1955.
[17] *Ibid.*
[18] *Barnacle Bill, The Sailor*, Hoagy Carmichael and His Orchestra: Beiderbecke, cornet; Benny Goodman, clarinet; Bud Freeman, tenor saxophone; Gene Krupa, drums, and others. May 21, 1930, Victor V38139; reissues: Victor 25371 and LP, LEJ-2.

bitter to the core, a movement of revolt. The men who developed it at Minton's Playhouse and other after-hours spots in Harlem were nonconformists right down the line. They rebelled against the restrictions of arranged swing. They despised New Orleans jazz as "corny Uncle Tom music." Raging at the anonymity of the Negro in America and his restriction to the role of entertainer, they developed flamboyantly defiant behavior, growing goatees, taking the beret as their trademark, and evolving a strange, secret language. Then they did something about their names. Or at least some of them did, rejecting Christianity and embracing Mohammedanism, complete to Turkish names and the red fez, which then replaced the beret. Amid a growing social conformity, they were outrageously, deliberately eccentric.

It was naïve. It was laughable.

Life magazine made the most of it, branding Dizzy Gillespie and his fellows clowns. Bop became a funny word for millions who had never heard the music.

It was tragic.

This was the fight, not to be a Negro *and* an American, but a human being and *not* a Negro. It was the bopsters' deliberate attempt to disavow their own heritage, without sensing that, however bitter and frustrating life still was, this heritage had conserved in them the very capacity to rebel.

It was wonderful too, not only in its very forlornness, but also in its final result. And here we must separate bop from its camp followers, the "intellectuals" who are forever worrying jazz as though it were a bone. They all but smothered bop with their embraces; nearly drowned it out with their cries: "Now at last jazz is modern! Hear the chords — just like Stravinsky!" Always the snobbish emphasis on Europe, the concealed disbelief in America.

These white newcomers, knowing nothing of jazz history and caring less, made a cause of bop. The result: its mechanized adaptation by white bands like that of Stan Kenton with his "progressive" jazz. Kenton seriously tried to conform to Stravinsky, hiring arrangers to write "modern" harmony. It was empty, painfully pretentious, and as sterile as every other cross-breeding — past and present — of jazz and "serious" music.

Apart from all this, the bopsters themselves obsessively went through their lonely, violent parturition. They were flaming anarchists all, but when it came right down to the act of creation, anarchy was not an attitude that a Parker or a Gillespie could finally bring to bear. In the strange power of Charlie Parker's alto were unforgettable intensity and naked communication. In the brittle rhythms and crackling wit of Dizzy Gillespie's trumpet was a bitter irony far different from the broad Rabelaisian humor and the muted trumpet mockery of New Orleans jazz. Brilliant though the wit was, it was the protective mask of an artist. One hears the real Gillespie at those unequivocal moments when he plays the blues and an age-old truth speaks once again.

At the last in their music — though the "intellectuals" do not know it — it was not Debussy or Stravinsky or Schönberg who won, but the hotness of jazz and the blues. Through their tones speak both the new Negro and the old Negro — and America, too.

Many of us sensed that, for better or worse, bop was decisive: jazz would never be quite the same again. I found it impossible to roost with those who were touting bop as the "music of the future" while, at the same time, they saw no difference between the latest Tin Pan Alley ballad and the genuine jazz tune, or even between the commercial and the creative. Nevertheless, in 1948 I joined a *Metronome* magazine editor in presenting bop and New Orleans jazz over the government-sponsored radio network program "Bands for Bonds." Then, in March 1949, I presented the two kinds of music factually and impartially at the *Herald Tribune* Forum for High Schools at the Waldorf Astoria in New York. This forum annually brings together high school representatives from many nations for a round table on world problems. I let them hear a bop band led by Parker and a New Orleans band led by Sidney Bechet.

It is important to observe what bop actually accomplished by the introduction of chords new to jazz, extended chords like the thirteenth and unusual ones like the flatted fifth. First, it is clear that the effect might have been deeper and more basic had they been introduced into a multilinear polyphony like that of New Orleans. There they would have changed the whole texture, widened the compass of part-playing, and led to the most startling dissonance. Most important, they would have broken the mold that substantially limits the parts to the traditional three: trumpet, trombone, and clarinet. The New Orleans polyphony is theoretically limited to the tonic triad of a given key (major or minor) — if C major, for example, C, E, and G. It got its freedom, actually, from liberties not allowed in European music, mainly use of the glissando and undulation, and the microtonal blues flatting, plus of course a freedom in the crossing of voices extremely rare in European music.

Observe now what the chord of the thirteenth would mean in such a polyphony. The thirteenth contains two major triads: if in the key of C, these are, the tonic triad of C and, an octave higher, the tonic triad of D, and between the two, the diminished seventh of C major.[19] The acute dissonances of this chord, expressed if the triads are combined in the same octave — C–D–E, F–G, A–B — are diluted by the playing an octave apart. This spread, however, creates new contrapuntal areas for new instruments: the clarinet and alto and soprano saxophones can move into the upper octave; the trombone, tenor and baritone saxophones can work in the lower octave; and finally, the trumpet can retain the traditional lead or, at option, exploit its wide, mobile compass in a free-wheeling part as the clarinet once did.

It cannot be denied that here is a basis for a complex counterpoint just as workable as that of the original three-voice

[19] The C thirteenth: C, E, G, B♭, D, F♯, A.

New Orleans jazz. Nor can we refrain from observing that, while six voices represent the highest accomplishment of baroque music, here is the blueprint for a *seven-voice* fugato, improvised, not written. It is obvious that this would have suddenly opened up the development of polyphonic jazz, challenging to the fullest all the creative resources of younger players. It is inevitable that this step will be taken.

However, a part of bop was its emotional rejection of New Orleans jazz and all that it was supposed to stand for. Bop pre-empted the new chords. But bop is primarily a music of single-line solo improvisation on instruments that play one note at a time, *e.g.*, trumpet, saxophone, and trombone. Furthermore, the piano and guitar, capable of playing chords, usually played scalar runs. Therefore in bop these rich chords *affected only the melody*. The melodic line was altered by the permissible new notes and by unprecedented melodic jumps or intervals prompted by the new chords and, of course — though this has nothing to do with new harmonies — by new rhythmic changes in phrasing. The exotic chords expressed in solo melody — in other words, spread out horizontally and not sounded together [20] — led to a profusion of notes that seemed — and were — dissonant or, more accurately, out of key, in relation to the tonic. This was one element of the unmistakable "new" sound of bop. The other elements were the differently rhythmed and intervaled melody and the omnipresent sound of the saxophone. Although the saxophone was invented in 1840, it really — as the brilliant modern-jazz saxophonist Sonny Rollins says — "is a new instrument." It never found a permanent place either in symphonic repertory or in New Orleans jazz. The difficulty lay in the fact that, as Virgil Thomson observed, it did not have a frank tone, being both brass and reed. Finally, it found its place, in mass and in solo, in swing. Now, it is altogether the key voice of new jazz, and it has had a thorough and searching development. At last it is a real

[20] Chord: a combination of three or more tones in harmonic relation, sounded simultaneously.

voice in the jazz sense, not even remotely connected with the saccharine "sobbing saxophones" of Scott Fitzgerald's day.

Finally, it is interesting to note that bop, in its formal opening and closing ensembles, did not utilize the "fat" chords: the horns played in strict unison. The effect is homophonically bare, most effectively denying the chords where in European practice they would be most fully stated. It is difficult to doubt that these bop unisons relate directly to the West African choral practices. It is extraordinary how the bop players, intellectually embracing the European idea, could instinctively and obsessively obliterate it so completely. Once again, the Negro's revolt was in the direction of his own tradition. A tradition, let it be noted, earlier even than New Orleans. Whether or no, he downgraded harmony, stressed rhythm and the singing melody. Intuition carried Negro music from the primitive holler into the spiritual and blues and on into archaic march music and the polyphonic improvisation we call classic New Orleans. It can carry it on wherever it needs to go and can do so more effectively without the guidance of the "intellectuals."

Yet these people, who do not think creatively and at the same time lack the intuition that determines taste, must forever analyze, weigh, find fault with, and try to improve. Ever since Paul Whiteman's Symphonic Jazz we have heard the perpetual outcry: "More harmony, more instruments, more technique" — an essentially negative approach, an emphasis on what jazz is not rather than on what it is and is becoming. The outcry has muddled jazz values, has confused or shamed the intuitive player, has elevated the merely adroit or clever player far higher than he deserves, has militated against the final simplicity that is the true aim of art's complexities.

Accomplished technique, quickness of reading, purely per se, are needed in European music, which must necessarily re-create what has been written, one, ten, or one hundred years ago. Are they indispensible or even always an asset in jazz, which is created on the spot? The concert player obviously needs enough technique to traverse the most difficult passages in Chopin,

Bach, or Beethoven. But the real jazz-player is expressing —
or should be expressing — only his own ideas. If he is an Armstrong or a Gillespie, he needs the technique of an Armstrong
or a Gillespie. If he is a Joe Doakes — even a Joe Doakes with
a Ph.D. — he needs a Doakes technique. What is more, that is
all he needs, or he becomes a menace.

The concept of *too much technique* is, I grant, a very difficult one to accept, running counter as it does to our present
modes of thinking. Yet in jazz it is only too clearly valid. The
large vocabulary for the man with little to say is an artistic
disaster. Into how much empty display, how many long-winded
discourses, it has led! It is no accident that the great jazzmen
have always managed to write their messages clearly. The
Armstrongs, the Doddses, the Parkers, and the Gillespies have
never been dumb. Their techniques evolve naturally, are not
culled from a *Gradus ad Parnassum* to pass an examination,
but hand-in-hand with the creative evolution of their ideas.
Sometimes however, it is hard to hear these men because of the
storms of scale-work, syncopated fugues, and twelve-tone
"jazz" which blow out of the conservatories.

As to harmony, I still do not feel that it is one of the corner-
stones of jazz. I do not think it ever can be that in a music
that aims at being a horizontal rather than a vertical, a moving
rather than a static, music. The "intellectual" should recall
the stark harmonies to which Stravinsky turned when seeking
in his neo-classicism for a weaving, horizontal music. He should
recall Bartók's deliberate choice of folk harmonies. I have
never heard any of the great composers criticize jazz for its
lack of sophisticated harmony. They have listened to jazz for
what it is.

Then there is the whole ridiculous search for the "long
form," where the thought is of jazz concertos and symphonies,
all the architectural forms which, though the glory of western
music, are anathema to jazz. Duke Ellington strings moods or
blues fragments into long necklaces called "suites," and presto,
we have the long form in jazz.

Let us look at jazz: endless creative variations, rhythmic, melodic, and rhythmic-melodic. Let us look at the endless singing and playing of the blues. Let us look at the long hours of men creating together, excitement compounding excitement, form growing out of shared inspiration. *Jazz in itself is a long form.*

Nevertheless, the "intellectuals" are with us. They brought us cool jazz, which may have been cool simply because it could not be hot or was afraid to be. It was difficult for me to grasp how listeners could be so enthusiastic about a thing that ruled out enthusiasm in itself. Cool jazz undeniably fitted a generation without daring, with so little of revolution in itself that it feared revolution in art. And by revolution I mean evolution, which always, in its moment, is radical.

I do not mean to be flippant about cool jazz. The cool jazz of Waller and Armstrong (at moments), of the one side of Keppard or Lester Young, is cool only in comparison with their hotter work. They were never personally uninvolved in what they did; they did not take the man out of art in order to insert an idea.

The adjectives — supposedly of praise — used to describe cool jazz are on the order of "light, dainty, airy," and we are constantly being reminded that it must be "listened to with care and understanding" because "its appeal is to the head as well as to the heart." From this we might conclude that hot jazz evolved brainlessly and contains nothing to challenge the understanding. But we try: we listen to the long, pale, polite monotone, soft and soothing and muted, with the earth-shaking elements of borrowed chords and borrowed styles. This unpossessed music which never shouts, never wails, never soars is the great achievement of the "intellectuals." It is the fire going out, not even in a whimper, but in a whisper. Like a television sales talk, it is calculated to offend no one, and so is outrageously offensive.

The Gerry Mulligans, the Dave Brubecks, and the Jimmy

Giuffres are adroit, even brilliant, and technically assured. But they play in a deep-freeze. And yet one must credit pianist Brubeck for one astonishing achievement. By a bit of showmanship he makes his audiences aware that improvisation is happening. He trades measures antiphonally with saxophonist Paul Desmond; the one imitates and amplifies the phrases of the other; their smiles of surprise and gratification telegraph it to the audience: They are improvising! They are making it up right now! And then come the storms of applause.

Improvisation — some of it by genuine masters — has been going on in jazz for eighty years, and still in 1958 it must be demonstrated by means of the "sales pitch" to the sophomores. It *has* to be packaged. It is not too difficult to conceive of a time when people will not recognize the fruit hanging on a tree, unless it has first been removed, devitaminized, cellophaned, sealed, labeled "apples," and then wired back on the twig.

The whole approach is the essence of academicism, and an academicism not originally of jazz, but imposed upon it. It fears and opposes the vitality of jazz. But, equally important, the vitality opposes the academicism. The notable fact is that at every stage it is the Negro himself who preserves the vitality of his music and advances it as an art. In the creative sense, jazz is still the Negro's music. And this is so in spite of the fact that the elements of the jazz language are universally intelligible to all not afraid to listen, while its vocabulary is becoming increasingly accessible to all.

When jazz begins to languish under too much Europeanization, a Basie or a Parker goes back to the drum rhythms of the stomping spiritual, to the counter-cries of leader and chorus, to the wailing demi-tones of the hollers and the blues. This ineradicable ounce of intuition cancels a ton of erudition. It is notable that jazz is a fine art that sprang from a people. It is extraordinary that it will not cease being a folk art in the best and most fruitful sense. Its people will not give it up.

Extraordinary above all is the blindness of those who pretend to such delicate and precise knowledge. The "intellectuals" (both white and Negro) who ceaselessly complain that the blues are an "Uncle Tom stereotype, simple, crude and impossible of development" are voicing complaints that fly in the face of the facts.

Was Leadbelly an Uncle Tom? Is Big Bill Broonzy an Uncle Tom? Was a freedom song ever transformed into comment more fearlessly open, revolt more unafraid? Or, to look at it from the other way, is a syncopated fugue based on Bach a revolt against white supremacy?

How about the crudeness and limitation of the blues? What shall we say of the continuous and exhaustive development to which they have already lent themselves? How is it that in 1946 a Charlie Parker could blow them as if he had just invented them? What did the "intellectuals" say when he was doing it? Here, they said, is the new jazz born of the twelve-tone scale.

They have nothing to say, no observations to make, about the profound effect of the blues tonality — the wavering microtonal thirds, fifths, and sevenths — when used in the playing of music not in the blues' own structural eight-, twelve-, or sixteen-measure form. How much more basic a change, one wonders, can there be than a new scale? The tempered scale was the base for western music; the twelve-tone row is the *summum bonum* of modern "serious" music. The blues scale could veritably transform the "Moonlight" Sonata into something darker and more African, as though the Germanic moon were moving behind a cloud. Had the blues scale been evolved in a conservatory, it would be discussed with awe. Instead it evolved from the lonely holler of a slave in the field.

The blues scale is actually only partly complete even today. Its wavering tonalities, with their new concepts of pitch, can be applied to most of the notes of our diatonic scale. The bop players thought that they had invented the flatted fifth. Yet Russell Procope played the blues fifth on *Deep Creek Blues* [21]

[21] Jelly Roll Morton and his Red Hot Peppers: *Deep Creek Blues*, Victor 38055, December 6, 1928.

in 1928, and I have no notion that Procope claimed to be the first to have done so.

A new "blued" interval appears in Basie's *Rock-a-Bye-Basie* of 1939 (Vocalian 4747). This tune is a riff theme that is actually an eight-bar blues: three successive statements of two bars each followed by an answer. The answer is a long, downward slur over two full measures from the *blue second* to the tonic.

Basie's men showed, too, how blues tonality can transform a popular tune when they worked over the thirty-two measures of Gershwin's *Lady Be Good* (Vocalian 3459). The first four notes of Basie's piano introduction set the blue feeling by flatting the fifth; then, in long solos, Lester Young and trumpeter Carl Smith play the show tune as a blues.[22]

The blues by themselves can give the lie to the "modernists" who can find no seriousness or profundity in any early jazz. The typical spokesman for this point of view, Barry Ulanov, even wrote: "until the later Ellington . . . there was little in jazz that could be called really profound." [23] Charles Edward Smith commented in *Record Changer* magazine that Ulanov "by his very use of it puts intellectual limits upon the word, thus narrowing considerably its possible application." Ulanov used the word, Smith wrote, as a "grandiose, crunchy, vitamin-free tid-bit."

Around 1904, painting in Europe was all but suffocated underneath the dead weight of academicism. It was then that Matisse, Picasso, and Braque discovered in the African mask the dynamic impulse that was needed. Out of that almost chance discovery of Negro sculpture has come a half century of plastic art which has revolutionized our seeing and our thinking. It has wiped out our glorification of mere technique, has opened our eyes and minds to the whole wonderful world of the primitive.

Yet, sublimely unaware of this, or at least of its implications as related to music, the academy that would like to saddle it-

22 The New Orleans street bands on the contrary convert *Lady Be Good* into a march.
23 Barry Ulanov, *A History of Jazz in America*, New York, 1952.

self on jazz keeps trying to intimidate those most superb of primitive artists, the players of jazz, with an endless harping on technique. Primitivism saved western painting and has given it a fruitful and exciting half century, a new lease on life.

Primitivism at each crucial point saves jazz. Dizzy Gillespie was reaching for it when he brought the Cuban drummer Chano Pozo into his band. Basie was reaching for it when he cast back to the dark incantations of the rocking spiritual and the holler.

The painters of the French school had to reach out to another continent and another race for that transfusion of life blood which could regenerate a moribund art. Jazz need go no farther than itself. It has its own primitive sources — which have always been the real elements of its modernness. Its Gabon masks are built in.

The blues are such a mask, as though the plastic planes of ancient carved wood were transmuted into sound. They are not the mask of deception or concealment, but one that, like the tragic mask of Greek drama, is the face of reality. The true likeness of the race, for the individual to wear.

The long cycle is swinging around, back to the truth with which it all began. So now, the strongest and newest movement of all is that called "funky," which is the return to barrel-house and the archaic blues and, farther back still, to the African chorus and drums. The vanguard of Negro modernists is leading this return as the result of their "search for the roots." Jazz seminars and round tables, as well as the histories that have not rejected the parent past, have all helped to rouse the interest of jazz-players in their own tradition. Most of all however, it is the artist's instinct to supply what is missing, the same instinct that, by leading the New Orleans horns to "fill all the holes" and "keep the melody going somewhere all the time," developed a superb polyphony that never had been heard before.

The "funky boys" are not playing it safe. They want to play hot with deep, unabashed feeling; they want to rock and wail.

They are bringing more real wisdom to bear than all the "light, dainty, airy" theorists.

A twenty-five-year-old pianist and singer has helped to make funky possible. Ray Charles, born in Georgia, brought up in Florida, and blind from the age of six, is one of the most remarkable figures in jazz history, a true connecting link. Self-taught, he plays and sings the deep woods blues he heard in Florida. He tours a ceaseless round of one-nighters over the circuit that Ma Rainey and Bessie Smith traveled, his blues drawing the same vast crowds, just as if a quarter of a century with its radio, talking picture, and television, had never happened.

And yet this same Ray Charles and his band play modern jazz, too. It was this which first aroused the admiration of the modernists. But it was the blues that run through all of his music that captured and held them — blues suddenly made respectable and valid by this handsome, dapper young man who is an authentic voice in both the old and new. Ray Charles bridged the gulf of the years.[24]

To single out a few names from the spreading funky movement: pianists like Horace Silver and Hampton Hawes are chording the blues; the tenor saxophonist, Sonny Rollins — although appalling everyone by a tone that Whitney Balliett described as "goat-like" — is silencing all criticism by his force and freshness, his slashing wit and irresistible swing.

Two modern drummers, Max Roach and Art Blakey, went back to original sources: Roach to the cult houses of Haiti, Blakey to Africa. These researches — or these pilgrimages — have already borne fruit in a series of Blakey recordings of drums and various instruments which presents a kind of Congo Square synthesis of Africa and jazz. The drums — from five to nine or more — include jazz drums and those of African type, from the Caribbean bongos and congas to the hollow tree log — and even the classic tympani. Telescoping the centuries,

---

[24] Ray Charles's blues: Atlantic 12-inch LP, 8006; his modern jazz: Atlantic 12-inch LP, 1259.

the piano, bass, and even the cello join in. Included are flutes all the way from the European sort to a wide variety of native African ones.

The Blakey drum records are both improvised and arranged, impossible as this may seem. The arrangement is schematic and sketchy, Blakey retaining direction and control by signaling what he wants by the use of his cymbal. The cymbal is more than the conductor's baton: it is the composer's pen. The drums begin thundering, a flute pipes up as in the equatorial forest, the voices rise in an African chant, and then — the piano begins "stacking" the eight-bar blues. And it all fits together. And why not? From African drums to spiritual, blues, jazz, even modern, it is all a part of the same thing.[25]

The Blakey records have an overwhelming emotional impact upon all listeners: rolling jazz, African thunder, they are concentrated statements of vital force. They re-define percussion in terms of the speaking voices that drums really are, voices of infinite tone and pitch, weaving in the sort of polyphony that the New Orleans horns (which sought to be drums) first created in this country.

Soon, the next step will seem obvious: to put the seven brasses and five reeds of the large band together with such a nine-piece percussion section, and thus restore the lost balance between horns and rhythm. When this happens, in Jelly Roll's words on *Sidewalk Blues*: "Let 'em roll!"

When Dizzy Gillespie made his bitter statement, "Jazz is too good for America," we were already beginning to prove him wrong. A "jazz boom" — as one newspaper writer puts it — was already beginning. Today it is evident that America as a whole is becoming more conscious of jazz than at any previous time, even during the fabled "Jazz Age" of the 1920's. Half of Scott Fitzgerald's jazz, the "sobbing saxophones," was not jazz at all, but like bootleg liquor, was only fuel for a national joyride. Today it is no longer one of the toys of hysteria. Hard

[25] Art Blakey: *Orgy in Rhythm,* Blue Note 12-inch LP's, 1554 and 1555; and *Drum Suite,* Columbia 12-inch LP, Cl 1002.

and searching, uncompromisingly pure and difficult, defiantly non-commercial, it is the focus of a time-harried, desperate search. A different music, a different people, hunting — like funky — for our roots.

Jazz — "pure jazz," as the same newspaper writer [26] said — is everywhere, "emanating from nightclubs, concert halls, workshops, college auditoriums, festival tents and open-air studios, to say nothing of uncountable millions of LP records . . . all types of jazz from the restrained, introspective music of the Modern Jazz Quartet to the brash, recidivist music of the Turk Murphy band."

All of this is a slight measure of the time — a mere twelve years by the calendar, but what earth-shaking years — since I wrote the first edition of this book, barely daring to hope then that jazz might come into its own.

But here it is, up from slavery through the underworlds of segregation, from field-holler all the way to funky, a long single cry of hope and the will to be free, heralding more, even, than racial integration. The central symbol indeed, of the recapture of our own integrity.

Over the centuries one long creative act, one undiminished human sound, one affirmation — one thundering "Yes!"

[26] Charles Gruenberg, *New York Post*, September 8, 1957.

APPENDIX A

THE QUESTION of the melodic basis of Afro-American music calls for a broader point of view than it has received. The real point at issue is the survival of African cultural traits and not one of specific melodic material.

The researches of Doctor George Pullen Jackson and Professor George Herzog show a considerable part of the melody in Afro-American music to be of Scotch-Irish-English origin. There is a traditional scientific point of view, exemplified by men like E. F. Frazier, E. B. Reuter, Charles S. Johnson, and others, which argues against the survival of Africanisms among Western hemisphere Negroes. The contrary view, with its rich and accumulating evidence, of a general survival of cultural Africanisms, finds its strongest champion in Professor M. J. Herskovits (who originally held the counterview) and has strong advocates in men like M. Kolinski and Richard A. Waterman.

The crux of the matter lies in the fact that the Negro in the United States has consistently tended to adopt white melodies and harmony that are amenable to the peculiar scalar, tonal, antiphonal or polyphonal, and rhythmic treatment of African music. The *selectivity* involved, plus the undisputed *transformation* of the borrowed material, are an ample basis upon which to establish both the cultural survival and the new musical type, Afro-American.

The quality of this music is predominantly African but its elements are mixed. Thus, one can find in it either European or African elements depending upon which are being sought. Where Jackson finds English hymns, Kolinski compares *notated* Negro spirituals with individual West African songs, finding a conclusively large number of correspondences in tonal structure and other characteristics. It is significant that Kolinski's study was carried out in Europe by comparing scored spirituals of recorded African music, for those clearly African qualities of Afro-American music, which are contained in its performance, have proven almost impossible to convey adequately in our present kind of musical score.

Kolinski found a very large number of spirituals to be related structurally to West African songs, Dahomey, Ashanti, and others. It is important to emphasize that his findings are in no wise opposed to those of Jackson and Herzog. The latter establish melodic origin, the former indicates selection and transformation. One school concentrates on the matter, the other on the manner. Clearly, in any music, the latter is the more important, even in European, where a symphonic movement is more important than its (even exotic) folk music thematic sources.

The long view perceives that the findings of a Kolinski not only supplement those of a Jackson, but, it is clear, point as well to the proper interpretation of all the seemingly conflicting data.

APPENDIX B

BESIDES simple syncopation, stressing the weak beats of the measure, the rhythmic peculiarities of African music are of two kinds. The first, the inner-rhythm, sets up a new metrical count or a new rhythmic pattern within the measure, and this device may extend over several measures. One way in which this is accomplished is by shifting accents to beats on which they would not normally fall, often in combination with normally accented ones. (Ex. 39, back of book, is as typical of Afro-American music as it is of the African. It is shown as it appears diagrammatically in Ex. 40. This indicates how it could be played by two drums as an overrhythm.)

The next example, obeying the African tendency to shift accents, is common in Afro-American banjo and guitar playing and in ragtime and in jazz. A familiar tune employing this rhythm is *Twelfth Street Rag.* (See Ex. 41.)

The second way in which the inner-rhythm is produced is by the employment of tacit beats, through which a pattern is formed. This method, also common in Afro-American music, is shown in the following Dahomean rhythm series.[1] (See Ex. 42. This shows a type of five-beat pattern within a twelve-beat measure that is encountered in boogie-woogie piano music.)

The second type of rhythmic peculiarity, technically known as a polymetric, is the cross-rhythm or overrhythm. This rhythmic counterpoint consists of two or more distinct rhythmic patterns played together. As it appears in European music the time duration of the different metered measures is identical and this principle holds largely true in Africa. Ex. 43 is a four-part rhythmic counterpoint from the Babira of the Belgian Congo. Freedom of improvisational variation is generally limited in African drumming to the solo drummer just as it is to the leader in the antiphonal singing. In this example, a number of measures of the soloist's mutations are shown, and it should

[1] From Kolinski: *Die Musik Westafrikas.*

be understood that these are combined with a steady repetition of the three accompanying parts.

Ex. 44 shows the continuation of rhythmic counterpoint by Negroes in the New World outside the United States. This example is notated from a phonograph record secured by Herskovits in Bahia, Brazil, in 1941. This disc, in the Northwestern University anthropological archives, contains the Congo drumming used to call the Yoruban deity *Omolu*, god of the earth (master No. 24–B/4).

The overrhythms in this case are for two drums, beaten by the hands, the *rum* (African = *hun*) and the smaller *rumpi* African = *hunpi*), and an iron gong hit by a nail. The three-part rhythmic counterpoint that results is shown in Example 44.

APPENDIX C

Ketu for Shango (Master No. 29a), by leader and chorus with
two drums and gong.

This disc is one of an Afro-Brazilian collection recorded in
Bahia, Brazil. The leader in this Yoruban cult song is Ilari,
singing with Vidal's group, and the percussion is by one large
and one small drum, and iron gong. Ketu signifies *Yoruba*,
while *Shango* is the Yoruban god of thunder. It should be noted
that Catholic regions have proven good localities for the survival of African religious forms because the Roman ritual provides a large hierarchy of saints with whom the African deities
can be covertly identified. In certain regions the pure African
cults are set up beside the Catholic church as in Bahia where
the manumited slaves immediately established their own cult-
houses, many of the members of which simultaneously profess
the Catholic faith. Similarly, African customs persisted in New
Orleans until late in the last century, in the music and dancing
of Congo Square and in the practice of voodoo.

The Ketu furnishes a clear example of choral singing over
percussion ostinato precisely as it is practiced in West Africa.
The leader establishes the tempo with the first phrase where-
upon the drums enter. In the same way the jazz cornetist, leader
of the band, *kicks off*, that is to say, taps two or four beats of
the tempo with his foot, and the band comes in.

The singing is antiphonal, the leader improvising freely and
the women's chorus responding in phrases which are rather set
in pattern. In this record the separate antiphonal parts, the
calls-and-responses, tend to overlap producing a true horizontal
polyphony. This is polyphony developing from antiphony precisely as it did in Africa. An identical case in Afro-American
music can be found in the singing of the ballad, *Grey Goose*,
by Lead Belly (Chapter V).

(A score from *Ketu for Shango*, showing the percussive ostinato together with the choral superimposition, and covering a short antiphonal portion developing into polyphony, is given in Ex. 45, back of book.)

Jesus Lover of My Soul (Master No. 58b), sung by the congregation of the Spiritual Baptist Church of the Village of Toco, northern Trinidad. This number, also, was recorded by Herskovits.

The Spiritual Baptists resulted from a schism in the Regular Baptist church. The orthodox church people, who control local politics, make a great deal of trouble for this shouting offshoot from the parent church. The spiritual Baptist meetings wax very hot and arrests by the constabulary on charges of disturbing the peace are so frequent and fines so heavy that the *Carnal Baptists*, as the Regulars call them, are perpetually "going to jail for their Jesus."

No more unlikely place to search for Africanisms could seemingly be found than in this traditional Sankey-Moody hymn. The first two sixteen-bar choruses do little to dispel this idea. They are slow and of an exaggerated mournfulness and there is not enough rhythm to shake a small prayer book.

With the third chorus, however, the shouters commence to come to life; the melody begins to be punctured into rhythmic repeated notes. In the middle of the chorus the tempo accelerates, the meter changes from 2/2 to 4/4; vigorous hand-clapping starts and continues to the end. Acceleration likewise continues and polyphonal devices begin to appear around the melody which proceeds in partly harmonized thirds. One of these devices is the extraordinary deep-voiced sound, the grunted and guttural exhalation which, in West Africa, is the characteristic "voice of possession." It is markedly rhythmic in much the same way as the New Orleans jazz trombone. The other device, which enters just a little later, is a falsetto upper voice, obbligato in effect but actually an element of polyphony. Concurrently the melody continues to be sung and the rendition becomes progressively hotter and more rhythmic.

387

Jesus Lover of My Soul is an invaluable document of the New World Negro transforming a selected melody, through African technique, into something so peculiarly his own that the borrowing itself, becomes of slight musical significance.

APPENDIX D

To postulate differences between Negro psychology and white is to arouse scientific opposition. Yet to ascribe such differences, as present theory does, solely to learned behavior (the conditioning, that is to say, of children in infancy) puts a heavy burden of proof on such a theory if the length of time the Negro has been subjected to our cultural influence be realistically balanced against the continuity of his own traditions up to the present time. Cultural continuity balanced against degree of actual isolation may prove a fair test. The Amish way of life, for example, is unchanged but this persistent integrity has gone with the most extreme self-imposed isolation. Such a community voluntarily embraces segregation as a conscious measure to protect the purity and values of its culture.

With the Negro we find demonstrable strength and character of cultural tradition persisting despite ready imitativeness and an extreme gregariousness. The Negro welcomes new ideas, new artistic and social forms, and imitates them even in segregation. For a long period he did not shun intermarriage as he does today. Yet his process has been to convert our music into African, our social customs (as in the unmarried polygamy of Brazil) into the spirit of those of Africa.

Afro-American music, improvisational, created, and set forth to such large degree from the unconscious, is a phenomenon which cannot be understood without the most extensive reference to psychological factors.

Motor behavior may very well be derived in great measure from the early conditioning of childhood. But the *character* of physical movements, some of which are determined by differences in bodily formation as between racial types, can and does enter into the arts, especially those with a physical and rhythmic foundation like music and dancing. Some of the current scientific tendency — to level palpable differences in racial behavior, and to ascribe those which cannot be argued away exclusively to conditioning — may very well be a rationalization. The almost incredible scope of the problems, and the recentness of most data in fields where centuries of accurate documentation are needed to draw valid conclusions, could conceivably prompt such a rationalization. Most important of all, perhaps, is the specialization of our life sciences, each of which attacks a small segment of that which in reality is a continuum. If specialization by necessity must be the method, then a well-balanced field trip should include psychologists, ethnologists, physiologists, and specialists in all the branches of culture together with anthropologists.

Such conditions as these do not, of course, affect the *fact* of African survivals in America. Nor, on the other hand, does the mere fact of survival explain the difference, wide as the world, between African art and ours; childhood conditioning in the home and the community explain why, *in the beginning*, such different arts, such different cultures, ever began. Such terms as instinctive behavior, racial memory, and others may be outmoded and scientifically *déclassé*, but the facts which they were invented to describe still remain and are not destroyed by ruling out the terms. Wider anthropological and psychological data must be accumulated and correlated before the question of racial memory or similar questions be regarded as settled. While observation covers only one or a few generations, conclusions should be limited to such a period or else proposed in a frankly tentative way.

APPENDIX E

Long John (Library of Congress, No. AAFS 13), sung by "Lightning" and group at Darrington State Prison Farm, Sandy Point, Texas, (1934).

1.

Leader: *It's a long John,*
He's a long gone,
Like a turkey through the corn
Through the long corn.

2.

Well, my John said,
In the ten chap ten,
"If a man die,
He will live again."
Well, they crucified Jesus
And they nailed him to the Cross;
Sister Mary cried,
"My child is lost!"

Chorus: *Well, long John*
He's long gone
He's long gone
Mister John, John,
Old Big-eye John,
Oh, John, John
It's a long John.

"The axes flash up in unison, bite into the log in unison as the leader sings: 'It's a *long* John.' . . .

"Negro axmen singing in the hot woods of the South . . . could endure long hours of hard-driving work in the sun, could sing as they worked, pouring a new language and new ideas into the old African leader-chorus form. The wildness and savage joy of this work song come from the leader. . . . The song is the sketch of a . . . legendary character named Long John who outran the police, the sheriff, the deputies with all their bloodhounds and got away from jail to freedom. The song is a picture of the chase . . . full of double meanings and asides." [1]

Long John is very similar to certain children's songs which follow the leader and chorus form. The instant repetition by the group of short phrases by the leader and the periodic joining of all in a refrain compares for example with *Little Girl, Little Girl* (Chapter V).

The following additional examples of work-songs recorded in prison are recommended for hearing and study.

> *Library of Congress AAFS–14* (10-inch).
> A — 1: *Rosie.*
>   2: *I'm Going to Leland.*
> B — 1: *Jumpin' Judy,* (solo) (1933).
>   2: *Look Down that Long, Lonesome Road.*

---

[1] Alan Lomax in descriptive folder accompanying this record. "Ten chap ten," a Biblical reference, means tenth chapter, tenth verse.

APPENDIX F

The Street Cries of Charleston, by various callers. (Society for the Preservation of the Spirituals. No Record number; master numbers 13 and 14.)

A. 1: Blackberry, Strawberries (Male Voice)
    2: Flowers (Woman)
    3: Blackberries, Watermelon, Cantaloupe, Cucumber, Red Pepper, et cetera (Male)
B: Various fish calls (Male Voice)

These cries are of great beauty and variety. A–1, a berry call, is sung by a man with a voice of mellow and hornlike quality.

The strawberry refrain will be recognized as the source of the song *Strawberries* in the first act of Gershwin's opera, *Porgy and Bess*. (See Ex. 46, back of book.)

A–2, a flower call, by a woman's voice, is slightly self-conscious, but the melody, nevertheless, is beautiful and imaginative; the words have a poetic meaning and carry the double allusion of Negro speech:

> *O, come and buy now*
> *For I'm here today*
> *And tomorrow I'll be gone*
>   .   .   .   .   .
> *Flowers are going by.*

Flowers passing by in the vendor's basket today, the same white lilies heaped on a coffin on this same street, tomorrow!

A–3, the male voice calls:

> *Black berries*
> *Black-a-black berries*
> *Black beans*
> *Pretty black beans*
> *Oh, watermelon now*
> *Watermelon now*

393

The voice is wavering and fugitive as a flute or a reed pipe and with the same tone, hollow and wine-sweet. The singer repeats the word "black," enunciates it lovingly and significantly, feeling kinship with the berries and beans that share the dark stain of his skin.

B. A male voice, wonderfully like a flute or the ancient triple-recorder full of flageolet tones, calls the fish. The vocal line is very free and imaginative, sung and declaimed with great varieties of pitch, with sudden changes of rhythm, a smooth legato, and continuous upward and downward portamenti, interrupted by repeated staccato phrases. The voice slides upward in flute tones that disappear like echoes; it glides through the whole compass swiftly upward and as swiftly downward in long, smooth lines of melody. (See Ex. 47.)

APPENDIX G

I'm Runnin' for My Life (on Library of Congress Record, AAFS 49), sung by the Congregation of the Church of God in Christ at Clarksdale, Mississippi (1942).

This hymn, sung chorally with stomping and hand-clapping, shows a characteristic use of antiphonal response (as it develops into polyphony) which produces an overlapping of the verses, sometimes delayed enough so that the response gives the effect of an echo of the preceding line. This effect of pulsing periodicity is in turn overlapped with one of another kind in which the phrases of the male leading voice are capped (in some cases interrupted) by one or another male voice shouting a loud exclamation like "Ho-ay." Even the percussion pattern periodically changes in alternate measures.

The choral background, with a periodicity characteristic of this entire record, enters in certain measures only and is of male and female voices together. Taking the form of a polyphony it moves up and down with the effect of a continuous tone, a glide or extreme portamento, somewhat akin to glissando double-stopping on the violin, and at times the polyphonic weaving produces perfect triads. Compare this record with *Manbetu Songs* (in General Record Co. Album G 10), another Belgian Congo record. These strange, beautiful songs show, definitely formulated, what the Negroes in the little Clarksdale church were unconsciously striving for. Here the solo voice enunciates a commanding recitative with the chorus responding in continuous gliding consecutive fourths. No doubt what is really represented in the Clarksdale record is the combination of two tendencies: one, backward toward the rigidly defined and separated antiphony of this phase of African music, and the other forward into the complex polyphony, rhythmic as well as melodic, which is a prime characteristic of jazz.

Such a dual reference is evident in *I've Got a Hidin' Place* (on Library of Congress Record, AAFS 45), sung by the Congregation of the Church of God and Christ at Moorhead Plantation, near Lulu, Mississippi (1941).

Here, where leader's pronouncement and choral response are kept definitely separate in the main African tradition, we find side by side with this a tendency, during the recitative, toward jazz polyphony. Below the high-pitched lead voice, a lower voice enters in an off-beat counterpoint. The two voices function precisely like the jazz trumpet and trombone in New Orleans. Completing the analogy, the guitar, stomping, and hand-clapping furnish not only the African polyrhythmic drum ostinato but also prefigure the steady rhythmic, pulsing base of the rhythm section of the New Orleans street and dance jazz bands.

In *I Am a Soldier in the Army of My Lord* (on Library of Congress Record AAFS 49), sung with trombone and guitar by the Congregation of Silent Grove Baptist Church at Clarksdale, Mississippi (1942), the *soldiers* make Silent Grove resound with a martial sixteen-bar hymn performed at quick-step tempo. The singing is orchestral, in the jazz sense of a freely improvised polyphony, syncopated and polyrhythmic, that pays little attention to harmony.

The trombone fills in underneath with strong propulsiveness, entering on the strong beats with decisive upward portamenti or slides that end with great emphasis on the normally weak beats. In a wonderful middle section the trombone plays solo with pulsating fluctuations in pitch against the percussive rhythm, and the voices enter sparsely and sporadically. Sudden, electrifying, and possessed, a high tenor voice leaps out in magnificent downward wails, "Oh, Jesus!" and "Jesus," in a wild and fleeting counterpoint to the trombone. (Ex. 48, back of book, is an attempt to score this passage that confronts and startles the listener with its creative form emerging white hot, spontaneously evolved in the midst of strong communal feeling.)

APPENDIX H

Lonesome Day Blues (Decca 7213), sung by Jesse James, with piano and guitar. Nothing seems to be known of Jesse James who, as though he were the ghost of the outlaw whose name he bears, emerged from obscurity one single June day of 1936, to record four record sides in Chicago.

The style and the words of this performance are highly archaic. The Nation (the old Cherokee Nation) and the Territo' (Indian Territory) existed up to 1907 when the Oklahoma and Indian Territories were combined and admitted to statehood; mention of them may even refer to a period before 1889, when some of these lands were first opened to white settlers.

The fine rhythmic barrel-house piano accompaniment is strongly suggestive of the Chicago player, "Cripple" Clarence Lofton. The guitar is inaudible. James's voice is a husky baritone with the gravelly, rough texture, expressive and agreeable, of many Negro voices and of the brass tone often heard in jazz. In the held or the clipped syllables, and in the spontaneous extension of tonal possibilities, we find speech transcending prose and the prosaic, proceeding upward through ascending planes of poetry to that of music.

> *Now this day's been a long-lonesome day.*
> *You hear me talkin' to you, do you hear what I say.*
> *Lawd this day has been a-long old lonesome day.*
> *And now my life, Lawd, will be the same old way.*
>
> *I've been all through the Nation — roun' the Territo'*
> *You hear me talkin' to you, gotta reap what you sow.*
> *I've been all through the Nation — roun' the Territo'*
> *But I foun' no heaven on earth, Lawd, nowhere I go.*
>
> *I'm going to the big house and I don't even care.*
> *Don't you hear me talkin' to you, scoldin' 'em out dere*
> *I'm goin' down and I don't even care*
> *I might get fo', five years, Lawd, and I might get the chair.*

. . . . .

Some got six months, some got a solid year.
You hear me talkin' to you, Buddy, what made you stop by here?
Some of 'em got six months, pardner, and some got a solid year
But I believe my pardner, Lawd, got lifetime here.

Southern Casey Jones, by the same singer, is a remarkable transformation of the well-known ballad into a sixteen-bar blues.

Jimmy Yancey's *Death Letter Blues* (Bluebird record, B–8630), which he plays and sings is an archaic record of great beauty and importance.

1.

I received one letter, little girl's all dressed in red
I received one letter, little girl's all dressed in red
Then it said down the bottom, Jim yo' baby's dead.

2.

Well I wrote back one letter, 'ddressed in white and black
Well I wrote back one letter, 'ddressed in white and black
You just set and cryin' girl, cryin' won't bring me back.

3.

And I went to her coffin, peeped down in her face
Cryin' I went to her coffin, peeped down in her face
Cryin', I'm sorry, girlie, but nobody can take yo' place.

4.

I went to the graveyard; fell down on my knees
Cryin' I went to the graveyard; fell down on my knees
Cryin' I asked de good Lawd to give my babe some peace.

Yancey's voice, mellow and mournful as a French horn, encompasses in plainest accents the farthest, dark reaches of sorrow and vain regret. The piano, played in the deepest bass, is veiled and shadowy, rocking slowly as a mourner may rock, hands clenched around the shoulders. With the last line Yancey's right hand soars to the treble in glorious, triumphant chords above the bass.

APPENDIX I

SONGS about the Negro, composed and sung by white performers, date back as early as 1799. In this year a German, Johann Graupner, sang in a Boston theatrical performance a number entitled *The Gay Negro Boy*. A complete part, that of a West Indian slave, Mungo, occurs in a comic opera, *The Padlock*, presented at Drury Lane, London, in 1768. A surprising (for the period) compassion for the Negro is to be found in those lines of Mungo's which run:

> *What a terrible life I am led!*
> *A dog has a better, that's sheltered and fed.*
> *Night and day 'tis the same;*
> *My pain is deir game:*
> *Me wish to de Lord me was dead!*
> *Whate'ers to be done,*
> *Poor black must run,*
> *Mungo here, Mungo dere,*
> *Mungo everywhere;*
> *Above and below,*
> *Sirrah, come; Sirrah, go;*
> *Do so and do so.*
> *Oh! Oh!*
> *Me wish to de Lord me was dead!*

From these early beginnings came an American institution, the blackface minstrel show, which began as an organized complete stage entertainment in 1843, when the "Virginia Minstrels," a company of four which included Dan Emmett, later composer of *Dixie*, gave a performance at the Chatham Theater in New York. Emmett wrote later that they were then all of them "end men, and all interlocutors. They sang songs, played their instruments (fiddle, banjo, bones, and tambourine), danced jigs, singly and doubly, and did the *Lucy Long Walk Around*."

The idea caught on; by 1850 there were many large troupes touring the United States and England. This was white entertainment; nearly all — and in the early stages, all — of the music was white melody to which were fitted lyrics in a Negro dialect no more accurate than that of Jupiter in Poe's *Gold Bug*. The Negro suffered far more as the butt than he gained as the inspiration and subject of this comic entertainment. The black-face minstrel did yeoman service in spreading and perpetuating the false stereotype of the Negro. He is pictured by the minstrels as an amiable, docile, indolent, foolish, yet very musical figure who sings the music of his white masters while, off the stage, he was in actuality tearing at the yoke of slavery, rebelling, dying or escaping to live in Florida swamps or wherever he could subsist; and all the while he was really creating a serious, rich, and noble music which puts the minstrel jingles to shame.

Negro melody in time was borrowed to enrich the thin and anemic stream of minstrel melody. Such unacknowledged borrowings were subjected to the destructive sentimentalization and grotesque parody of the white performer. Nor could the real Negro break into such select company. One of the early white performers, Andy Leavitt, recalled "the time when the fine sensibilities of the audiences would not tolerate the presence of a genuine Negro on the stage." He was once, he relates, with a company which hired a Negro singer and dancer, called Juba, "a real sensation, who could sing and dance more grotesquely than any actor he had ever seen." To avoid detection, Juba's face was to be blacked with burned cork, but the secret leaked out. Public indignation in the *Northern* town where this took place resulted in threats that if the "Nigger" appeared the theater would be burned down. Juba, before his first appearance, was jobless.

With Emancipation, the Negro was to have his chance to enter minstrelsy and he did so immediately. That he acquitted himself with great success is a tribute to his art; that, blackening his own dark face with the traditional burned cork, he turned the one-time travesty on the Negro into a caricature of the original caricaturists, is a tribute to his patient humor, the

keen and subtle edge of his wit, and his penchant for double
and inner meanings.

Brander Matthews writes [1] of a minstrel show given about
1880–81 by the Negro waiters at one of the large summer hotels
in Saratoga. "When the curtains were drawn aside, discovering
a row of sable performers, it was perceived, to the great and
abiding joy of the spectators, that the musicians were all of
a uniform darkness of hue, and that they, genuine Negroes as
they were, had 'blackened up,' the more closely to resemble the
professional Negro minstrel." We may judge that the art of
the performance was lost on an audience that perceived compli-
ment rather than irony in this situation.

[1] In an article, *Negro Minstrelsy,* in the *Saturday Review,* London, 1884.

LIST OF RECORDS
CITED IN THE TEXT

KEY TO RECORD–LABEL ABBREVIATIONS

AS = Asch
BB = Bluebird
BC = Belgian Congo (General)
BER = Berliner
CI = Circle
CLAX = Claxtonola
CO = Columbia
COM = Commodore
CRE = Crescent
FO = Folkways
GE = Gennett
GEN = General
GTJ = Good Time Jazz
HRS = Hot Record Society
JM = Jazz Man
JP = Jazz Panorama
JR = Jolly Roger

JT = Jazztone Society
LC = Library of Congress
ME = Melotone
OK = Okeh
PARA = Paramount
PAX = Pax
PE = Perfect
PUR = Puritan
RI = Riverside
SD = SD (Steiner-Davis)
SE = Session
SIG = Signature
ST = Stinson
UHCA = United Hot Clubs of
      America
VI = Victor
VO = Vocalion

NOTES

Record sizes are ten-inch unless otherwise indicated. The first number or numbers shown are those of the original issue. Reissues, if any, follow, preceded by the symbol: (RE). Long-play (33⅓ microgroove) reissues, if any, follow *in italics.*

CITATIONS

1. *Drum Improvisation No. 1* Baby Dodds   CI J–1001
2. *Jumpin' Judy* Kelly Pace and group   LC AAFS–13
                                      (12″)
                                      LC L3
                                      (12″)
3. *Long Hot Summer Days* Clyde Hill   LC AAFS–13
                                        (12″)
                                      LC L3
                                      (12″)

RECORDS CITED

4. *Ol' Riley* Leadbelly
                                 AS 102
                                 ST SLP–17

5. *Heaving the Leadline* Sam Hazel   LC AAFS–36
                                     (12″)

6. *The Gambling Man* Rev. W. M. Mosely   CO 14186–D
7. *I'm Gonna Lift Up a Standard For My King* Church of God and Christ, Lulu, Miss.   LC AAFS–4775
                                     (12″)

8. *Bahutu Songs and Dances*   BC GEN–10
                                   COM DL–30,005
                                     (12″)

9. *Babira Circumcision Ritual*   BC GEN–12
                                     COM DL–30,005
                                     (12″)

10. *Run Old Jeremiah* Joe Washington Brown and Austin Coleman   LC AAFS–12
                                     (12″)
                                   LC L3
                                     (12″)

11. *Jesus Goin' To Make Up My Dying Bed* Mitchell's Christian Singers   OK 04357
12. *Jesus Goin' To Make Up My Dying Bed* Blind Willie Johnson   CO 14276–D
Note: Certain Blind Willie sides are reissued on Folkways 12″ LP's FG–3585 and FG–55
13. *Stewball* ⎫
14. *Grey Goose* ⎬ Leadbelly and Golden Gate Quartet   VI 27267
15. *Negro Lullabies, Ring Games and Children's Games*   LC AAFS–20
                                     (12″)
                                   LC L4
                                     (12″)

16. *Cat Man Blues* Blind Lemon Jefferson   PARA 12921
17. *Raidin' Squad Blues*   VO 1528
18. *Pallet On the Floor* Jimmy and Mama Yancey   SE 12–003
                                     (12″)

19. *Down In Boogie Alley* Bessie Jackson (Lucille Bogan)   ME 13116

20. *I Can't Sleep* Montana Taylor

    CI J–1009
    RI Limited Edition No. 2

21. *Dyin' Rider Blues* Romeo Nelson   VO 1494
22. *Hell Hound On My Trail* Robert Johnson   PE 7–09–56
23. *Shave 'Em Dry* Ma Rainey   PARA 12222
24. *Jelly Bean Blues* Ma Rainey   PARA 12238

    (RE) UHCA 84
    RI RLP–1001
    RI RLP–12–101
    (12″)

25. *Countin' the Blues* Ma Rainey   PARA 12238

    (RE) UHCA 83
    RI RLP–1001
    RI RLP–12–101
    (12″)

26. *See See Rider* Ma Rainey   PARA 12252

    (RE) UHCA 85
    RI RLP–1001

27. *Careless Love* Bessie Smith   CO 14083–D

    (RE) CO 3172–D
    CO GL–503
    (12″)
    CO ML–4807
    (12″)

28. *Put It Right Here* Bessie Smith   CO 14324–D
29. *Winin' Boy Blues* Jelly Roll Morton
    GEN 4001   *COM*
30. *Mamie's Blues* Jelly Roll Morton   *DL–30,000*
    GEN 4004   (12″)
31. *Gambler's Dream* Hociel Thomas   OK 8289
32. (a) *Trouble In Mind* (1926) Chippie
    Hill   OK 8312
    ME 61270

    (b) *Trouble In Mind* (1946) Chippie
    Hill   CI J–1003
    RI RLP–1032

33. *Trouble Everywhere I Roam* Sippie
    Wallace   OK 8212
34. *Skeet and Garrett* Roosevelt Sykes   OK 8749
35. *When You Feel Low Down* Lonnie
    Johnson   BB B–9006

RECORDS CITED

36. *Milk Cow Blues* Pinewood Tom (Josh
White) PE 0316
37. *Fine and Mellow* ⎱ Billie Holiday ⎧ COM 526
38. *Strange Fruit* ⎰ ⎨ COM
  ⎩   *DL–20,006*
39. *That's a Serious Thing* Eddie's Hot Shots VI V–38046
(RE) BB B–10168
  VI LX–3005

40. *If I Ever Cease To Love* Original Zenith
Brass Band CI J–1005
  RI RLP–1058
41. *Cotton Blossoms* Orchestra BER 1482
  (7″)

42. *Oh Didn't He Ramble* Jelly Roll Morton's New Orleans Jazzmen BB B–10429
43. *Creole Song* Kid Ory's Creole Jazz Band CRE 1
  GTJ L–10
  GTJ
   L–12022
  (12″)

44. *Panama* Bunk Johnson's Original Superior Band JM 8
45. *Bogalousa Strut* Sam Morgan's Jazz
Band CO 14351–D
  FO FP–75
  (12″)

46. *Tiger Rag* Jelly Roll Morton CI JM–1/2
  (12″)
  CI L–14001
  (12″)
  RI RLP–9001
  (12″)

Note: Circle issued the Morton Library of
Congress documentary on forty-five 12″
records (78 rpm) in a subscription set,
The Saga of Mr. Jelly Lord (JM 1
through JM 90). Subsequent reissues on
12″ LP: Circle, *L–14001* through
L–14012; Riverside, *RLP–9001* through
RLP–9012.

47. *Dixie Jass Band One Step* Original Dixieland Jass Band   VI 18255
VI LX–3007

48. *Original Dixieland One Step* Original
Dixieland Five   VI 25502

49. *Panama* Friars Society Orchestra   GE 4968
RI RLP–1024

50. *Mabel's Dream* King Oliver's Creole Jazz
Band   PARA 20292
CLAX 40292
PUR 11292
(RE)   SD 100
(RE)   SIG 905
RI RLP–1005
RI RLP–12–122
(12″)

51. *Canal Street Blues* King Oliver's Creole
Jazz Band   GE 5133
(RE)   UHCA 67
RI RLP–1029
RI RLP–12–122
(12″)

52. *Jazz Me Blues* The Wolverines   GE 5408
(RE)   HRS 25
FO FP–65
(12″)
RI RLP–1023
RI RLP–12–123
(12″)

53. *Black Bottom Stomp* Morton's Red Hot
Peppers   VI 20221
(RE)   BB B–10253
JP 1818
JR 5001
VI LX–3008
VI LPT–23
FO FP–63
(12″)

54. *The Chant* Morton's Red Hot Peppers   VI 20221
VI LPT–23
(RE)   BB B–10253

JP 1818
JR 5001
VI LX–3008

55. *Smokehouse Blues* Morton's Red Hot
Peppers   VI 20296
(RE)   BB B–8372
JP 1818
JR 5001
VI LX–3008
JT J–1249
(12")

56. *Steamboat Stomp* Morton's Red Hot
Peppers   VI 20296
(RE)   BB B–8372
JR 5001
VI LX–3008

57. *Sidewalk Blues* Morton's Red Hot
Peppers   VI 20252
(RE)   VI 40–0118
JR 5001
VI LX–3008

58. *Doctor Jazz Stomp* Morton's Red Hot
Peppers   VI 20415
(RE)   BB B–10255
JP 1818
JR 5001
VI LPT–23

59. *Bull Fiddle Blues* Johnny Dodds Wash-
board Band   VI 21552
(RE)   BB B–10239
VI LX–3006

60. *Bucktown Stomp* Johnny Dodds Wash-
board Band   VI V 38004
(RE)   BB B–8549
VI LX–3006

61. *Weary City Stomp* Johnny Dodds Wash-
board Band   VI V–38004
(RE)   BB B–10239
VI LX–3006

62. *Blue Washboard Stomp* Johnny Dodds
Washboard Band   VI 21552

(RE)	BB B–8549
	VI LX–3006
63. *Dippermouth Blues* King Oliver's Creole Jazz Band	GE 5132
	GE 3076
	RI RLP–1029
	RI RLP–12–122
	(12″)
Dippermouth Blues (variant)	OK 4918
(RE)	HRS 4
64. *Sugar Foot Stomp* Fletcher Henderson and His Orchestra	CO 395–D
65. *Sugar Foot Stomp* Connie's Inn Orchestra	VI 22721
	VI LVA–3013
66. *Strut That Thing* Cripple Clarence Lofton	VO 02951
67. *St. Louis Stomp* Speckled Red Trio	BB B–7985
68. *Midnight Stomp* Jimmy Yancey	SE 12–002
	(12″)
	PAX 6011
69. *Yancey's Bugle Call* Jimmy Yancey	VI 27238
	VI LX–3000

MUSICAL EXAMPLES

REFERRED TO IN THE TEXT

The musical scores on the pages which follow are referred to at various places in the book. For convenience of cross-reference the following index shows the text pages where each reference to a score is made.

Ex. 1

VARIANT

Ex. 2

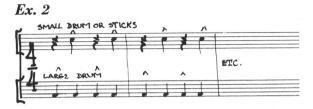

SMALL DRUM OR STICKS

LARGE DRUM

ETC.

Ex. 3

HANDCLAPPING

FOOT STOMPING

ETC.

Ex. 4

CYMBAL

BASS DRUM

Ex. 5

FAST

SPEECH

CHORUS, SINGING

SINGING

SOLO

SLOW

SINGING

FLAT

AXE BLOWS

SHOUTING

Ex. 6

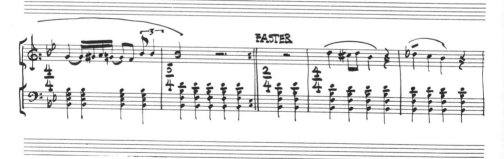

Ex. 6 (continued)

Ex. 7

Ex. 8 a

Ex. 3 b

VARIANT

Ex. 9

Ex. 9 (continued)

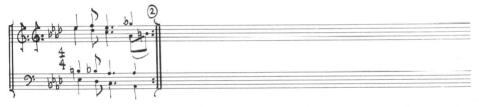

Ex. 10

YOU BET ON STEW-BALL, AN YOU MIGHT WIN, WIN, WIN BET ON STEW-BALL

AN YOU MIGHT WIN

Ex. 11

Ex. 12

Ex. 13 a

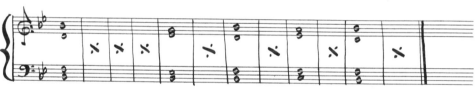

Ex. 13 b

Ex. 13 c

Ex. 13 d

Ex. 13 e

Ex. 14 a

Ex. 14 b

Ex. 14 c

Ex. 15

Ex. 16

Ex. 16 (continued)

Ex. 17

Ex. 18

Ex. 18 (continued)

Ex. 19

Ex. 20 a

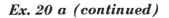

Ex. 20 a *(continued)*

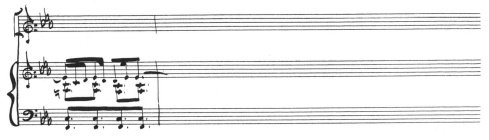

Ex. 20 b

Ex. 21

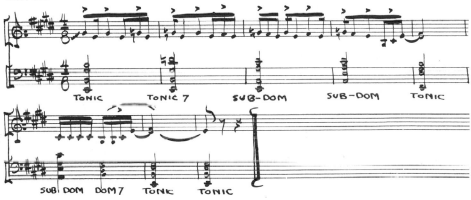

TONIC TONIC 7 SUB-DOM SUB-DOM TONIC

SUB DOM DOM 7 TONIC TONIC

Ex. 22

Ex. 23

Ex. 24

Ex. 24 (continued)

Ex. 25

Ex. 26

Ex. 27

Ex. 28

Ex. 29

Ex. 29 (continued)

Ex. 30

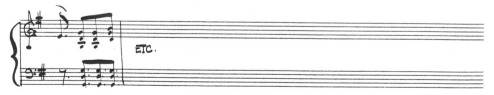

Ex. 31

Ex. 31 (continued)

Ex. 32

Ex. 33

Ex. 34

Ex. 35

Ex. 36

Ex. 37

Ex. 38

Ex. 39

Ex. 40

Ex. 41

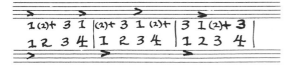

Ex. 42

Ex. 43

Ex. 44

Ex. 45

Ex. 46

Ex. 47

Ex. 48

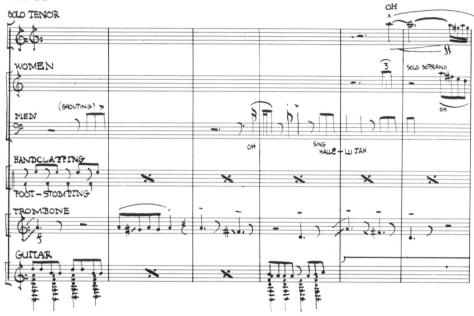

INDEX

(See also special Index of Music, page xiv)

i

INDEX

INDEX OF MUSIC

xiv